SOCIETY FOR NEW TESTAMENT STUDIES
MONOGRAPH SERIES
General Editor: G. N. Stanton

51

WOMEN IN THE MINISTRY OF JESUS

Women in the Ministry of Jesus

A Study of Jesus' Attitudes to Women and their Roles
as Reflected in His Earthly Life

BEN WITHERINGTON III

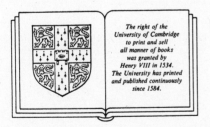

The right of the
University of Cambridge
to print and sell
all manner of books
was granted by
Henry VIII in 1534.
The University has printed
and published continuously
since 1584.

CAMBRIDGE UNIVERSITY PRESS

CAMBRIDGE
NEW YORK · NEW ROCHELLE
MELBOURNE · SYDNEY

Published by the Press Syndicate of the University of Cambridge
The Pitt Building, Trumpington Street, Cambridge CB2 1RP
32 East 57th Street, New York, NY 10022, USA
10 Stamford Road, Oakleigh, Melbourne 3166, Australia

First published 1984
Reprinted 1985
First paperback edition 1987
Reprinted 1988

Printed in Great Britain by
Redwood Burn Limited, Trowbridge, Wiltshire

Library of Congress catalogue card number: 83-18957

British Library Cataloguing in Publication Data
Witherington, Ben
Women in the ministry of Jesus: a study of Jesus'
attitudes to women and their roles as reflected in
His earthly life – (Monograph series/Society for
New Testament studies; 51)
1. Women in the Bible   2. Women – Social
conditions
I. Title   II. Series
220.8'30542   BS680.W7

ISBN 0 521 25658 5 hard covers
ISBN 0 521 34781 5 paperback

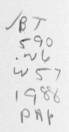

CONTENTS

PREFACE

An earlier draft of this work was a doctoral dissertation accepted by the University of Durham, England in 1981. I am greatly indebted to Professor C.K. Barrett for his efforts at every stage in the writing of this study. His lucid and erudite comments and suggestions were invaluable to me. I should also like to thank my examiners, Dr John McHugh and Professor A.T. Hanson, as well as the editors of this series, Professor R. McL. Wilson and Dr M.E. Thrall, whose suggestions made the revision of this work a great deal easier than it might have been. For the financial support which made these years of study possible I wish to thank A Fund for Theological Education, based in Marshall, Texas, under the leadership of Dr Edmund Robb. Finally, I should like to dedicate this work to my wife, Ann, who typed each draft and helped in more ways than can be enumerated to produce this manuscript in good time and order.

Christmas, 1981

ABBREVIATIONS

Reference Works

APOT	R.H. Charles, ed., *The Apocrypha and Pseudepigrapha of the Old Testament in English* (2 vols.; Oxford, 1913).
A–S	G. Abbott-Smith, *A Manual Greek Lexicon of the New Testament*, 3rd ed. (Edinburgh, 1937).
BAG	W. Bauer, W. Arndt and F.W. Gingrich, *A Greek–English Lexicon of the New Testament*, 4th ed. (Chicago, 1952).
BDF	F. Blass and A. Debrunner, *A Greek Grammar of the New Testament* (trans. R.W. Funk; Chicago, 1961).
CII	J.-B. Frey, ed., *Corpus Inscriptionum Iudaicarum* (2 vols.; Rome, 1936).
Danby	Herbert Danby, trans., *The Mishnah* (London, 1933).
Gaster, *DSS*	T. Gaster, trans., *The Dead Sea Scriptures* (Garden City, 1964).
LCL	The Loeb Classical Library, ed. G.P. Goold (London/ Cambridge, Mass.).
LSJ	H.G. Liddell and R. Scott, *A Greek–English Lexicon*, 9th ed.; rev. H.S. Jones and R. McKenzie with supplement by E.A. Barber [1968] (Oxford, 1940).
Metzger, *TC*	Bruce M. Metzger, *A Textual Commentary on the Greek New Testament* (London, 1971).
MHT	J.H. Moulton, W.F. Howard and N. Turner, *A Grammar of New Testament Greek* (4 vols.; Edinburgh, 1908–76).
ML, *Anthology*	C.G. Montefiore and H. Loewe, *A Rabbinic Anthology* (New York, 1974).
MM	James Hope Moulton and George Milligan, *The Vocabulary of the Greek Testament* (Grand Rapids, 1930).
Moule, *I-B*	C.F.D. Moule, *An Idiom-Book of New Testament Greek*, 2nd ed. (Cambridge, 1959).
NIDNTT	Colin Brown, ed., *The New International Dictionary of New Testament Theology* (3 vols.; Grand Rapids, 1975–8).
NTAp	Edgar Hennecke, *New Testament Apocrypha* (2 vols.; ed. W. Schneemelcher; trans. R. McL. Wilson; Philadelphia, 1963–5).
NTGNA	E. Nestle and K. Aland, eds., *Novum Testamentum Graece*, 25th ed. (London, 1971).

Robertson	A.T. Robertson, *A Grammar of the Greek New Testament in the Light of Historical Research* (Nashville, 1934).
Str-B	Hermann L. Strack and Paul Billerbeck, *Kommentar zum Neuen Testament aus Talmud und Midrasch* (6 vols.; Munich, 1974–5 repr.).
Synopsis	Kurt Aland, ed., *Synopsis Quattuor Evangeliorum*, 8th ed. (Stuttgart, 1973).
TDNT	Gerhard Kittel and G. Friedrich, eds., *Theological Dictionary of the New Testament* (10 vols.; trans. G. Bromiley; Grand Rapids, 1964–76).
UBSGNT	Kurt Aland, *et al.*, eds., *The Greek New Testament*, 3rd ed. (London, 1975).
Vermes, *DSS*	G. Vermes, trans., *The Dead Sea Scrolls in English* (Harmondsworth, 1965).
Zerwick	Maximilian Zerwick, *Biblical Greek* (trans. J. Smith; Rome, 1963).

Journals and Series

AER	*American Ecclesiastical Review*
AJP	*American Journal of Philology*
ARW	*Archiv für Religionswissenschaft*
ATR	*Anglican Theological Review*
AusBR	*Australian Biblical Review*
BETS	*Bulletin of the Evangelical Theological Society*
Bib	*Biblica*
BJRL	*Bulletin of the John Rylands University Library of Manchester*
BSac	*Bibliotheca Sacra*
BT	*The Bible Translator*
BTB	*Biblical Theology Bulletin*
BZ	*Biblische Zeitschrift*
CBQ	*Catholic Biblical Quarterly*
CGTC	Cambridge Greek Testament Commentary
EstBib	*Estudios Biblicos*
ET	*Expository Times*
ETR	*Études Théologiques et Religieuses*
EvQ	*Evangelical Quarterly*
Exp	*Expositor*
FBBS	Facet
Greg	*Gregorianum*
HeyJ	*Heythrop Journal*
HR	*History of Religions*
HTKzNT	Herders Theologischer Kommentar zum Neuen Testament
HTR	*Harvard Theological Review*
HzNT	*Handbuch zum Neuen Testament*
ICC	International Critical Commentary
IEJ	*Israel Exploration Journal*
Imm	*Immanuel*

Int	*Interpretation*
JAC	*Jahrbuch für Antike und Christentum*
JBL	*Journal of Biblical Literature*
JETS	*Journal of Evangelical Theological Society*
JJS	*Journal of Jewish Studies*
JNES	*Journal of Near Eastern Studies*
JQR	*Jewish Quarterly Review*
JR	*Juridical Review*
JSS	*Journal of Semitic Studies*
JTS	*Journal of Theological Studies*
LTJ	*Lutheran Theological Journal*
MNTC	Moffatt New Testament Commentary
MS	*Marian Studies*
NICNT	New International Commentary on the New Testament
NIGTC	New International Greek Testament Commentary
NovT	*Novum Testamentum*
NRT	*Nouvelle Revue Théologique*
NTS	*New Testament Studies*
PAAJR	*Proceedings of the American Academy of Jewish Research*
PNTC	Pelican New Testament Commentary
RB	*Revue Biblique*
RevExp	*Review and Expositor*
RHPR	*Revue d'Histoire et de Philosophie Religieuses*
RSR	*Recherches de Science Religieuse*
RTP	*Revue de Théologie et de Philosophie*
Scr	*Scripture*
SJT	*Scottish Journal of Theology*
SNTS	Society for New Testament Studies
SS	*Sein und Sendung*
TQ	*Theologische Quartalschrift*
TS	*Theological Studies*
TT	*Theology Today*
TZ	*Theologische Zeitschrift*
WayS	*Way Supplement*
ZAW	*Zeitschrift für die alttestamentliche Wissenschaft*
ZNW	*Zeitschrift für die neutestamentliche Wissenschaft*
ZTK	*Zeitschrift für Theologie und Kirche*

WOMEN AND THEIR ROLES IN PALESTINE

Jesus' view of women has become in the last two decades a subject of increased discussion both inside and outside the Church community. The better part of this discussion has been purely on a non-technical level, and there still seems to be a need for a detailed exegetical treatment of the relevant Gospel material. This monograph attempts to meet that need.

It should be said at the outset that my discussion will be limited to the material dealing with Jesus' words and deeds during His earthly ministry. Thus, the material in the Birth and Resurrection narratives will not be treated. There will be sóme attempt, however, to deal with the Evangelists' perspectives on women as a secondary area of interest as it is reflected in the pericopes that will be examined.

Since our main focus is on Jesus' view of women, our discussion of the relevant background material will be limited to an examination of women and their roles in Palestine. Background material on other areas in the Mediterranean will be referred to in passing where it seems to bear on the Gospel material under examination (e.g., Mk 10). Finally, our investigation of background material must also be limited in scope to certain major issues or areas that shed light on the portion of NT material under discussion — (1) women and their roles in marriage and the family; (2) women and their roles in religion; and (3) women and their roles as witnesses, teachers and leaders. It will be assumed that general attitudes toward women and their roles in Palestine during the NT era have been sufficiently indicated by others.[1]

In attempting to discuss first-century Palestinian Jewish women, the problem of dating the possibly relevant material immediately confronts us. A considerable amount of material in the rabbinic literature is of an unknown date, since it is not identified with a particular rabbi or school. Thus, this essay relies primarily on Mishnaic information which was certainly in existence before the Mishnah's codification around A.D. 200. Materials from the Talmuds and Midrashes are used when they seem to summarize attitudes that prevailed throughout the era of rabbinic Judaism.[2]

The Mishnaic material must be handled with care, of course, but since in many instances it presents actual situations and issues (not merely hypothetical ones), and since even in the purely 'academic' debates it often reflects actual attitudes with which we are vitally concerned, it is not inappropriate to use such material. In any case, the material presented here has been selected as 'typical' of the way of thinking among Jewish leaders and rabbis from before Jesus' day through the Amoraic period. Thus, without glossing over crucial differences, we may expect our material, even if it originates from a period somewhat after the NT era, to give us a reasonably clear glimpse of attitudes about women in Jesus' day among His countrymen. That this is not an unreasonable expectation is shown time and again when the attitudes found in such texts as Lk. 24.11 and Jn 4.9, 27 are also found in Josephus, Philo and material from the Mishnah and Talmuds of various dates.[3]

A. Women and their Roles in Marriage and the Family

There can be little doubt that the family was almost the exclusive sphere of influence for Jewish women in the first century A.D. A glance at the titles of the subdivisions in the Mishnah under the heading Nashim (Yebamoth, Ketuboth, Nedarim, Nazir, Sotah, Gittin, Kiddushin) indicates that women were only of importance legally to the rabbis in the areas of marriage and divorce, inheritance and heredity, and the extremes of holiness (vows) and unholiness (Sotah). A woman's sphere of influence or importance in the legal sense was confined to her connection to her family, her faithfulness to her husband, and her domestic responsibilities.[4] This limiting of a woman's sphere of influence is partly attributable to Jewish marital customs of that day. One must bear in mind the extraordinary *patria potestas* a father had over his daughter and a husband over his wife. The laws of inheritance, betrothal and divorce were heavily biased in the male's favour with only a few checks and balances (such as the wife's *ketubah* and a daughter's right of maintenance). A woman was passed from a father to her husband's sphere of authority usually without being consulted. Since a woman changed families when she married, she could not be expected to preserve the family name or keep property in the same family. For this reason, the laws stated that she was entitled to maintenance rather than inheritance in most cases.[5] That R. Ishmael can bemoan the poverty of Israel's women is perhaps an indication of how hard and rare it was for a woman to inherit property.[6]

While a girl was under-age she had no right to her own possessions, and the fruit of her labour or anything she found belonged to her father.[7] If she was violated, compensation money for the indignity was paid to the father.[8] An under-age daughter could not refuse a marriage arrangement made by her father, though she could express her wish to stay in the home until puberty.[9] She could, however, refuse any arrangement made by her mother or brothers after her father's death and before she was 12½.[10] Once she was of age she could not be betrothed against her will.[11] A wife, like a Gentile slave, could be obtained by intercourse, money or writ.[12] Considering the early age of betrothals and marriages, it would be rare indeed for a woman to have acquired an inheritance prior to marriage or to have refused a marital arrangement made by her family.

Though a woman usually had to be paid her *ketubah* even if the husband went into debt,[13] this requirement was not as strict as it might have been since a woman could be put away without her *ketubah* on certain grounds.[14] Further, we are told that a woman's *ketubah* is to be paid out of the poorest land one had.[15] A woman's security in her husband's family was attenuated further by the fact that the husband could divorce her if she caused an 'impediment' to the marriage. This privilege was not extended to the wife.[16] Unlike the case with a man,[17] a woman could be divorced without her consent for reasons ranging from unchastity only (School of Shammai), to burning a meal (School of Hillel), to finding another fairer than one's own wife (R. Akiba).[18]

A wife's security was threatened in some cases by the fact that polygamy was permitted in Tannaitic times as it was in the OT.[19] S. Lowy draws the following conclusions after an extensive survey:

(1) some sources presuppose a polygamist state of affairs, but this may be purely academic legislation as was common in the Mishnah;[20] (2) the Targum to Ruth 4.6 based on a Midrash says explicity, 'I am not permitted to marry another', but this may reflect a minority opinion and may be late Amoraic material; (3) the polygamy of the royal families, such as Herod's, is not to be taken as typical; (4) Tosephta Yebamoth I.10, 13, says that the high priests in Jerusalem had rival wives, but this is probably an instance of Levirate marriage (which is a form of polygamy, though due to a relative's childlessness); (5) the brother of R. Gamaliel took a second wife because the first was barren; (6) The Babylonian Talmud reveals no significant source pointing to widespread polygamy and in fact much of the terminology used for marriage ('pairing', 'she of the house') intimates that monogamy was the normal practice; (7) possibly rabbis insisted on the legal rights of having more than one wife because various related religious groups (Christians and possibly Qumranites) insisted that monogamy was the only legitimate biblical practice; (8) thus, it is likely that

monogamy for economic and moral reasons was the ruling practice, but
that polygamy did exist in both Tannaitic and Amoraic times as more than
a technical possibility.[21] In fact, the Mishnah records cases of and rules for
a man betrothed to two women, and there is no dispute over the issue.[22]
Thus, the threat of lost security because of polygamy did exist for some
Jewish women in rabbinic Judaism, however seldom it may have been
realized. There were always some rabbis who for theological and moral
reasons objected to polygamy.[23]

In spite of these limitations, it would be wrong to assume that a Jewish
woman had no respect or rights in Jesus' era. The rabbinic literature re-
iterates in various places the OT maxim that the mother is to be honoured
equally with the father.[24] The command to honour father and mother was
the epitome of filial piety, and since in Exod. 20.12 the father is mentioned first, while in Lev. 19.3 the mother comes first, it was deduced that
they were to be revered equally, indeed revered as God is revered.[25] The
Talmud instructs a man to love his wife as himself and to respect her more
than himself.[26] While normally it was the man or the man's family who
initiated the betrothal process, a woman is said to be able to betroth a man
on her own initiative in some circumstances.[27]

In the family, the wife's duties involved grinding flour, baking bread,
washing clothes, breast-feeding the children for eighteen to twenty-four
months, making the bed, working in wool,[28] preparing her husband's cup,
and washing his face, hands and feet.[29] The extent of a wife's household
duties depended on how many servants she brought with her. If she
brought four bondwomen she could sit all day in her chair, though R.
Eliezer said that no matter how many servants she brought she still had to
work in wool.[30] R. Johanan b. Baroka said that the commandment to be
fruitful and multiply was incumbent on the woman as well as the man,
though this undoubtedly was not the majority opinion. Usually we read
that this commandment was required of the man alone.[31]

The husband's duties were equally extensive. A man had an obligation
to provide for his wife, whereas he had a choice as to whether or not he
would provide for his slaves.[32] Thus, a wife was not treated as property.
The marriage contract bound the husband to provide food, clothing and
material needs for his wife,[33] and a woman could demand these things
before a court. A husband's responsibilities also included fulfilling his
connubial duty, redeeming his wife from captivity, and providing shelter.[34]
Unlike a man, a woman was said to have a *right* to sexual pleasure.[35] The
School of Hillel said that a man had not fulfilled Gen. 1.28 until he had
both a son and daughter — the School of Shammai said that two sons

would fulfill one's duty.[36] It was rare for a father to prefer his daughters considering the importance of a son to a Jew who wished to preserve and pass on his name and heritage. Thus, it is significant that R. Hisda once said, 'Daughters are dearer to me than sons.'[37]

With rare exceptions, a woman could not divorce her husband,[38] while a husband could divorce his wife practically at will so long as he could afford to pay the *ketubah*. There were, however, situations and ways in which she could precipitate a divorce. If a husband refused to consummate the marriage, was impotent, had an unpleasant occupation, had leprosy, was unable to provide support, or if he was to be separated from her for a long time, then she could sue for divorce in the courts.[39] A woman could leave her husband and return to her parents' home, thus precipitating a divorce in most cases.[40] Though a woman normally could not pronounce the formula of divorce which finalized the act, she was able to write her own bill of divorce and its validity depended on her.[41] Thus, while technically only a husband could initiate a divorce, and a bill was only valid if written specifically for the woman,[42] a woman had means of legally precipitating the dissolution of a marriage. It should be added that divorce was frowned upon by many, if not most, rabbis. R. Johanan interpreted Mal. 2.16 to mean that the man who divorces his wife is hateful to God. R. Eliezer said that the altar sheds tears over one who divorces his first wife.[43] M. Nedarim 9.9 makes clear that for a man to divorce was to dishonour his wife and children, and to disgrace his own character.[44] There were legal impediments that prevented a husband from extricating himself from certain difficult situations. A man whose wife had lost her mental capacity after they had been married was not allowed to divorce her, for it was feared she could not ward off illicit advances.[45] A woman who could not guard her *Get* could not be divorced.[46] Finally, in Jewish law, unlike early Greek and Roman law, a husband was never allowed to take the life of his wife if she was an adulteress.[47]

In regard to property rights, an Israelite woman was allowed to hold property in her own right, as discoveries at the Dead Sea have shown.[48] She was allowed to inherit property, though male heirs had precedence over her. Further, a married woman of age who lost her husband either through divorce or death (but not her misconduct) was allowed to keep her *ketubah*.[49] If she remarries then her property remains her own, though her husband has a right to the usufruct of it. This was especially true of a wife's slaves.[50] Both the Schools of Shammai and Hillel agreed that a woman may sell or give away any of her inherited property prior to her betrothal. Shammai adds that she could sell it after betrothal as well.[51] R. Gamaliel says he is at a loss to see why a husband should gain any right to property a woman inherits either prior to or after her marriage. In addition to rights of inheritance, a woman also had a right to 'maintenance' from her father's or husband's resources. Indeed, if a man died leaving only a little property, his daughters had a right to maintenance before his sons could inherit, even if this meant that the sons had to go without.[52] This was also true of widows who remained with their former husband's household.[53]

A certain spiritual significance was assigned to a woman's presence or role in the home. For instance, R. Jacob says, 'One who has no wife remains without good, and without a helper, and without joy, and without blessing, and without atonement.'[54] Even more dramatic is the comment by R. Phineas b. Hannah that a woman has an atoning force not inferior to the altar if as a wife she remains within the domestic seclusion of her family.[55] Of a similar nature is the saying attributed to R. Joseph when he heard his mother's footsteps coming: 'Let me arise before the approach of the Shekinah (Divine presence).'[56] The spiritual influence of the mother in the home is perhaps indicated by the fact that a child was considered a Jew by the rabbis only if his mother was a Jewess and regardless of his father's religious predilections.[57] Another indication of the rabbis' appreciation of a woman's potential spiritual influence is indicated by a midrash which points out that if a pious man married a wicked woman he will become wicked, but if a wicked man marries a pious woman, she will make him pious. 'This proves that all depends on the woman.'[58]

B. Women and their Roles in Religion

The training which equipped Jews for participation in the synagogue or Temple services and, in the case of men, for religious leadership whether as a scribe, rabbi or priest, began in the home. It was debated whether and how much a woman should teach or be taught Torah even in the home.

Although R. Eliezer says that teaching one's daughter Torah is teaching her lechery (or extravagance), his opinion is said to be a minority one by Jewish scholars.[59] Support for this verdict can be found in several places. R. b. Azzai says, 'A man ought to give his daughter a knowledge of the Law.'[60] So too, M. Nedarim 4.3 reads, 'he may teach Scripture to his sons and daughters'.[61] On the other hand, negative remarks about wives cannot be ignored. In one place we are told that a wife is not to teach her children.[62] This is perhaps a result of the fact that women were exempt from studying Torah.[63] Nevertheless, women are said to be expected to know the holy language.[64] It was inferred from Exod. 19.3 that women accepted Torah before men.[65] There are even cases of women being taught the oral law and being consulted on its fine points. R. Meir's wife, Beruriah, is especially well-known in this regard.[66] Possibly the maid servants of R. Judah the Prince received similar training, for there are instances where they gave some scholars enlightenment on rare Hebrew words in the *Tanak*.[67] Imma-Shalom, sister of R. Gamaliel II and the wife of R. Eliezer, was prominent enough to have some of her sayings recorded in Talmudic literature.[68] Finally, R. Nahman's wife was said to vex him continually because of her expertise in Halakic matters.[69] Though these examples are exceptional, they do show that even when Judaism was beset with the problems of foreign occupation and influences, and there was a tendency to protect and confine Jewish women and children to preserve important traditions, some women were able to become learned in both oral and written law and tradition.

According to various texts in the Mishnah, a woman may not be deprived of her right to eat the Heave offering even if her husband is a seducer, uncircumcised, or unclean.[70] Thus, she is not treated as a subheading under her husband as far as this cultic practice is concerned. Women took Naziritic vows in Tannaitic times, as the example of Queen Helena shows.[71] We are informed that women could and did bring sacrifices; Miriam of Palmyra is mentioned as an example.[72] Even a suspected adulteress' offering is not refused.[73] M. Zebahim 3.1 says that women could legally slaughter the animals used for sacrifice, even those animals used for the 'Most Holy Things'.[74] There are cases recorded where women were allowed to lay hands on their sacrifice, despite the fact that M. Menahoth 9.8 says they cannot.[75] Even more significant is that some women were able, with the priest's aid, to wave their own meal offering.[76] A woman of priestly stock had certain priestly rights and privileges in regard to the offerings.[77] Women were obligated to light the candles at the Feast of Dedication because they too benefited from the ending of the Seleucid persecution.[78] Though women were limited to their own court in the Jerusalem Temple, it is not certain when the practice of having special galleries for women in the synagogues began, though apparently they existed in Trajan's time.[79] We know that such popular feasts as the Feast of Tabernacles took place in the women's court.[80]

B.T. Megillah 23*a* tells us that women were qualified to be among the seven who read Torah in the synagogue, though it appears that by Amoraic times and perhaps before that they were expected to refuse.[81] Further, there are no known examples of women reading in the synagogues during Jesus' time.[82] In the domestic observance of the Sabbath, women were responsible for preparing the dough offering and lighting the Sabbath lamp.[83] Women were required to say the *Tefillah*, the eighteen benedictions, the table blessings, and to maintain the *Mezuzah* on the doors of the houses.[84]

From the above evidence we may conclude that at least in theory a woman's position and privileges in regard to the Jewish cult during the Tannaitic and Amoraic periods differed little from their status and rights in OT times with two important exceptions — a separation of women and men in the Temple and synagogue was introduced after OT times, and perhaps women were not allowed to read Torah in the assembly by Tannaitic times. The OT's high regard for women's religious rights seems to have been preserved legally in the rabbinic literature with notable exceptions.[85]

In order to understand why a woman was restricted in regard to place and function in the Temple one must bear in mind the restrictions of Leviticus 15. Whatever one may think of the precepts found in Leviticus 15, it should be clear that a woman could not be a priestess in the cult because of the ordinance about her uncleanness during her monthly menstrual period, and not because of rabbinic prejudices. A priest must be clean and holy at all times in order to offer the sacrifice (Lev. 21, 22). Further, it is because of the ordinances about a woman's uncleanness during her period that women were excused from those positive ordinances of the Law which were periodic in nature (certain feasts, daily appearance in the synagogue to make a quorum, periodic prayer). A woman could not be depended upon to be ritually clean on every occasion when these ordinances were to be observed, and thus she could not be depended upon to fulfill them. This is probably why we read in M. Kiddushin 1.7, 'The observance of all the positive ordinances that depend on the time of year is incumbent on men but not on women, and the observance of all positive ordinances that do not depend on the time of year is incumbent both on men and women.'[86] Thus, one should not argue or imply that it was due to rabbinic prejudices that women were not allowed to be among those who made up the quorum, recited the daily *Shema*, or made pilgrimages to Jerusalem at the feasts of Passover, Pentecost and Tabernacles.[87]

The evidence concerning Jewish women's roles in religion indicates that by and large the religious privileges and functions they had were those they could participate in in the home. The biblical injunctions in Leviticus 15 and its rabbinic interpretations restricted their participation in the Temple cults, and certain views about propriety appear to have taken away a woman's theoretical right to read the Scriptures in the synagogue even in Jesus' day.

C. Women and their Roles as Witnesses, Teachers and Leaders

In regard to a woman's word of witness, her vows, or oaths, there was no unified opinion among the rabbis.[88] For instance, a woman may be paid her *ketubah* after swearing to her claim on oath, even if she has 'impaired' her *ketubah* or if a witness testifies she already has received it.[89] Thus her oath carries more weight in this legal matter than the testimony of the witness, presumably even if the witness is a man. A woman's testimony about a death or her virginity normally is to be believed.[90] A woman's vow is binding on her husband's brother in regard to the duty of the *Levir*.[91] M. Nedarim 11.10 gives nine cases where a woman's vow is valid and binding.[92] This tells us that women's vows were as valid as men's if the women were not under the control of father or husband, or if the father or husband did not revoke or controvert such an oath. M. Nazir 9.1 reveals that women are not in the same category as Gentiles or slaves in regard to Naziritic vows (a Gentile cannot make this vow; a slave's vow cannot be revoked; a wife cannot be compelled to break the vow).[93] If a woman is independent (over 12½ and unmarried), neither her father nor her future husband can revoke her vow.[94] A woman's witness is counted equal to a man's witness in a number of cases, and though sometimes she is differentiated from a set group called 'witnesses', she nonetheless can give valid testimony.[95] Cases where a woman's uncorroborated testimony about herself is said to be unacceptable do not militate against a woman's right to bear witness, since it is true of both men and women that usually a second party is required to verify a statement.[96] In view of the above evidence, and admitting that some rabbis did not accept women as valid witnesses,[97] it is going beyond the evidence to say that most rabbis considered women to be liars by nature. The evidence suggests that a woman's vow or oath generally was accepted, and that her word carried more weight than that of Gentiles or slaves in some cases. Thus, J. Jeremias is probably wrong in saying that a woman's word was accepted only in rare cases.[98] In practice her word was accepted even in some doubtful cases.[99]

Apart from the role of the woman in the home in giving her children some basic religious instruction (and even this was disputed), a woman had no educational functions except in very rare cases (for instance, Beruriah). There was an OT precedent for women to be prophetesses (Jdg. 4.4, 2 Kgs 22.14, 2 Chron. 34.22) and such roles may have been assumed by a very few Jewish women in Jesus' day (cf. Lk. 2.36–8), but the actual examples that can be produced are too few to lead us to assume that this role was a realistic possibility for the majority.

There were no 'official' leadership roles that Jewish women could assume, though on occasion women had roles that gave them *de facto* positions of authority. M. Ketuboth 9.4 reveals that women were entrusted with maintaining their husband's shops or being guardians, or even creditors.[100] The practice which became common among the rabbis was for their wives to maintain the family and business while the husband and possibly the older son studied the Law. R. Akiba credited his wife for his wisdom because she supported him for years while he studied.[101] This was long seen as an ideal of Jewish social practice.[102]

In conclusion, it is fair to say that a low view of women was common, perhaps even predominant before, during and after Jesus' era.[103] Since many of the positive statements about women to which we have referred come from later Tannaitic and early Amoraic times, it is conceivable that a woman's lot in Judaism improved in some ways after the destruction of the Temple made impossible full observance of various precepts of the Law. On the whole, we cannot agree with R. Loewe's overly favourable assessment of rabbinic Judaism's views of women. G.F. Moore's evaluation that women's legal status in Judaism compares favourably with other contemporary civilizations is also questionable, as we shall see.[104] On the other hand, the numerous positive statements made about women by the rabbis reveal that many Jews had a higher view of women than Jeremias and J. Bonsirven seem to indicate in their books.[105] We will close this section by pointing out that there was no monolithic entity, rabbinic Judaism, in Tannaitic times and that various opinions were held about women and their roles, though it appears that by the first century of the Christian era a negative assessment was predominant among the rabbis. It is into this environment that Jesus came and, as we shall see, he not only countered the negative evaluations of women, but also endorsed and extended women's rights beyond the positive evaluations we have mentioned.

WOMEN IN THE TEACHING OF JESUS

Our first task will be to examine the attitude of Jesus toward women as reflected in His teaching.[1] This will entail a discussion of His views on parenthood, childhood and the single state, and on marriage, divorce and adultery. Through this investigation we should be able to begin to evaluate the way Jesus thought the new demands of the Kingdom would affect women in their roles as mothers, daughters, wives, widows, harlots and believers. The second half of this chapter will be devoted to an investigation of women in the parables and judgment sayings of Jesus.

A. The Physical Family

1. Parents, Children and Widows

At various times and for various reasons there has been a feeling of uneasiness on the part of many people about Jesus' view of the family. Some have been willing to say that for Jesus the claims of the family of faith necessarily supplant any claims of the physical family on Him and His followers. Yet there are clear indications in the Gospels that Jesus not only accepted but also strengthened the physical family's bond in some respects.

The Gospels reveal two separate instances where Jesus reaffirmed Exod. 20.12, Lev. 19.3, and Deut. 5.16, thus indicating that honouring one's parents was an important part of His teaching. The first instance comes in Mk 10.19 and parallels where Jesus indicates that the keeping of certain of the Ten Commandments is crucial if one wishes to inherit eternal life.[2] The command to honour parents is counted as part of the cost of discipleship which is necessary in order to obtain a place in the Kingdom.[3] Thus, Mk 10.19 and parallels is an indication that there was a place for the physical family and the promotion of filial piety within the teaching of Jesus. It is significant that Mark, followed by Matthew, places this affirmation of Mosaic teaching after two other pericopes in which the physical family is reaffirmed in different ways.[4] In the placing and presentation of this pericope, Mark, Matthew and, to a lesser degree, Luke, make their own affirmation of these values.

Passing on to Mk 7.9–13 and parallels, we find a saying that because of its conflict with Jewish attitudes of Jesus' day concerning the oral law, and because of the improbability that the Christian community would create a saying involving the matter of corban, has high claims to authenticity. In fact, Vincent Taylor says, 'There can be no reasonable doubt that the words were spoken by Jesus and illustrate His attitude to the oral law.'[5] Possibly, Mark has added this saying to the section in 7.1–8 (because of the connection between verses 8 and 9) and Dibelius argues that 7.14–19, 20–3 are secondary Christian additions.[6] In this passage we find Jesus affirming the same Mosaic commandment in the midst of a pronounce-ment concerning the traditions of men and the commandments of God. Jesus, with more than a little anger and irony, charges His audience[7] with 'setting aside the commandments of God in order to keep your own traditions'.[8] In this instance, Jesus is attacking the misuse of the practice of making something corban to someone. First, Jesus reminds His listeners that Moses said one was to revere both father and mother. This is signifi-cant since some rabbis taught that one should honour father more than mother.[9] In addition, Jesus also reasserts the negative enjoinder of Moses: ὁ κακολογῶν πατέρα ἢ μητέρα θανάτῳ τελευτάτω.[10] It is hard to imagine a more strongly worded way of enforcing the obligations of children to parents and, especially in this case, to dependent parents.

In Jesus' day it was possible to declare in a vow using the term κορβᾶν or κονάμ that one's parents were forbidden to benefit from one's property because that property was dedicated to other purposes (perhaps to the Temple). What originally had been intended as a means of setting aside property or even oneself for the purposes of God became a means of preventing others from having a claim on one's person or property.[11] Contemporary inscriptions and Mishnaic parallels suggest that such a practice was well-known in the era in which Jesus lived.[12] Such a vow might be taken in a moment of anger and thus might involve some hint of an imprecation.[13] If this is the case in Mk 7.11, then this may explain why Jesus makes reference to the commandment against cursing or speak-ing evil of one's parents. Some rabbis taught that by means of a legal fiction or because of the honour due to one's parents, such a vow could be circumvented or annulled in some cases if the vower wished to do so.[14] On the other hand, there is evidence from Jesus' time that in some in-stances a person could not repent of his oath even if it was taken in haste or anger because some rabbis believed that his life would be forfeit and he would stand in danger of the judgment of God against oath-breakers.[15]

Apparently, it was against this last opinion that Jesus was inveighing (cf. verse 12 – οὐκέτι ἀφίετε αὐτὸν οὐδὲν ποιῆσαι τῷ πατρὶ ἢ τῇ μητρί).[16] Jesus' point seems to be that any vow that makes void the word of God *must* be annulled.[17] Because of their traditions, the rabbis had allowed one's duty to fulfill any vow to take precedence over (and in effect nullify) the duty to honour one's parents.[18]

Thus, in Mk 7.9–13, we have a strong affirmation of the traditional family structure with special emphasis on the obligation for a child to provide for his aging or indigent parents. This obligation is not to be overriden by any vows or oaths. Jesus, far from taking a less stringent view of filial duties than His Jewish contemporaries, actually intensified the demands placed on a Jewish son or daughter by disallowing any interfering vows. In this He makes clear His desire that both mother and father be honoured in word and deed.

Some indirect evidence about Jesus' attitude toward women in their roles of child-bearer and mother may perhaps be derived from an examination of the two separate Synoptic incidents in which a very positive attitude toward children is in evidence – Mk 9.33–7 and parallels, and Mk 10.13–16 and parallels.[19] Considering the Gospel writers' selectivity, the very existence in the Synoptics of two separate incidents of a positive nature about children may intimate that the attitudes expressed in these pericopes were seen by the Gospel writers as characteristic of Jesus and His ministry,[20] and noteworthy because they stood in contrast to common attitudes of that era.

Even in the first century A.D. exposure of infants (especially girls) was known in Roman and Greek contexts. As A. Oepke points out though, there was a gradually improving attitude toward children in the Graeco-Roman world from the early period of the Republic to the latter days of the Empire: 'The promotion of the diminished rising generation only reached its climax from the 2nd cent. A.D.'[21] It is true that children were valued more highly in Judaism than in first-century pagan cultures; nonetheless, generally sons were valued more highly than daughters even among Jews.[22] There is no evidence that children, either male or female, were considered as religious models by the rabbis, for in rabbinic Judaism it was the wise and learned rabbi, not the child, who was set up as an example to disciples who wished to be great in the Kingdom.[23] Further, no rabbi is known to have so closely identified himself and his teaching about the Kingdom with children as the Evangelists portray Jesus doing.

The history of the tradition(s) found in Mk 9.33–7 appears to be complex. It is possible that these verses comprise a brief pronouncement story placed at the outset of a collection of sayings related to each other on the basis of catch-words or phrases (ἐπὶ τῷ ὀνόματί μου, cf. verses 37, 38, 39, 41).[24] The mention of Capernaum and the house in verse 33 may point to Petrine reminiscence,[25] and both the wrangling of the disciples and Jesus' response (verse 35) are historically credible.[26] Verses 36 and 37, however, may belong to a different circle of ideas altogether (cf. Mk 10.40, 42). Verse 37 (τοιούτων παιδίων) seems to presuppose some such incident as we have in verse 36, and thus they probably belong together. In any case, the original and present form of this tradition is about children, not unimportant community members (contrast verse 42), which speaks for its earliness.[27] Matthew, perhaps in an attempt to spare the disciples, omits Jesus' question about the disciples' dispute and Mark's comment about their response to this query, and includes at 18.3–4 sayings which do not derive from this section of Mark. E. Schweizer suggests that the saying in 18.3 in some form may go back to Jesus Himself as it bears a strong resemblance to other sayings having to do with a child or being child-like in the Gospel tradition (Mk 10.15, cf. Jn 3.3, 5). These examples begin, 'Truly, I say to you, if (or who) does not', and end, 'enter into the Kingdom of God (or, of heaven)'.[28] Verse 4 is possibly Matthew's rephrasing of verse 3 (cf. στραφῆτε καὶ γένησθε ὡς τὰ παιδία...; ταπεινώσει ἑαυτὸν ὡς τὸ παιδίον), or perhaps his adapting of Mk 9.35a, b, which he presents in reverse order (18.4b οὗτός ἐστιν ὁ μείζων, corresponding to εἴ τις θέλει πρῶτος in Mk 9.35a; humbling self as a child corresponding to being last of all and servant of all). To sum up, there seems no significant objection to taking Mk 9.33–5, and perhaps separately verses 36–7, as authentic Jesus material. Concerning Mt. 18.3, there may be some doubt and possibly 18.4 is purely redactional. Nonetheless, the ideas conveyed in Mt. 18.3–4 may perhaps be said to be 'typical' of Jesus' attitudes (especially if Mk 10.15 is authentic) even if they were not actually spoken by Him.[29]

Mk 9.33–7 is set in the context of the disciples' dispute about who would be greatest in the Kingdom.[30] At verse 36, which may begin a different saying, Jesus calls a παιδίον (a term usually used to denote those between the stages of infancy and young adulthood)[31] and puts him in their midst. Mark and Luke make the child an object lesson with only a concluding summary (Mk 9.37, Lk. 9.48), which involves the rather remarkable assertion that whoever receives one of this sort of children in Jesus' name, welcomes Him.[32] The verb translated 'receive' here often is used to refer to hospitality, the welcoming of a guest.[33] ἐπὶ τῷ ὀνόματι μου probably means 'for my sake'.[34] It is not likely that Jesus is suggesting that the child is His representative (but cf. verse 37b), though that is grammatically possible. Rather, Jesus is saying to the disciples who are His representatives, 'receive a child such as this for My sake'. He is identifying Himself with the helpless so that they may be helped by those who wish to serve Jesus. His disciples are to serve even children and in so doing they serve Jesus Himself.[35] If Jesus had held certain of the negative opinions about children that existed in the Roman empire, or if He had a low view of the family and its offspring, then it is not likely that He would so closely identify Himself with children.[36]

Few scholars would doubt the authenticity of the material found in Mk 10.13–16 and parallels.[37] Dibelius includes this narrative in the category of paradigm (or example-narrative) in a state of noteworthy purity.[38] There is some question, however, whether or not verse 15 originally belonged to this pericope. Bultmann is right that verse 15 cannot be seen as an editorial expansion of verse 14 because the two verses make different points.[39] Possibly then verse 15 was originally an independent logion and Matthew has presented his version at 18.3 rather than in this context. In Mark and Matthew we have a series of incidents intended to give Jesus' teaching on marriage, divorce, children and possessions (Mk 10.1–12, 13–16, 17–31).[40]

The narrative begins with parents, and perhaps older children,[41] bringing younger children to Jesus so that He might touch them. Perhaps reflecting the typical attitude that children were less mature and thus less important than adults, the disciples rebuked those who were bringing children forward (all three Synoptics).[42] Jesus reacts to the disciples' action with anger: 'Allow the children to come to Me and do not hinder them for τῶν ... τοιούτων ἐστὶν ἡ βασιλεία τοῦ θεοῦ.' Though Plummer and others insist that τοιούτων refers not 'to these children, not all children, but those who are childlike in character',[43] it seems more likely that it refers to those children who come or are brought to Jesus as well as those adults who are 'of this sort'.[44] G.R. Beasley-Murray is right in remarking, 'many normal occasions of the use of τοιοῦτος are intended to denote a class, of which the one mentioned in the context is an example ... it is impossible to make the primary reference of τοιοῦτοι a comparison with other individuals'.[45] Thus, the term cannot refer only to adults who are or become like children.

After this saying there follows in Mark and Luke (cf. Mt. 18.31) a word of Jesus: 'Truly I say to you, unless you receive the Kingdom ὡς παιδίον you shall not enter it.' ὡς παιδίον may mean 'as a child' receives the Kingdom, or 'as a child (in childhood)', or finally 'as a child (as though the Kingdom were a child)'.[46] The second possibility can be rejected outright since Jesus calls adults to follow Him and enter the Kingdom. The third possibility, while conceivable, is unlikely since Mk 10.13–14, 16 and parallels concern how Jesus received children and the place children have in the Kingdom, and Mk 10.15 and parallels appear to concern how disciples should receive the Kingdom. The point of this material seems to be that the Kingdom of God involves or is made up of children and those like them, not that the Kingdom of God is like a child.[47] In the context of Mk 10, the contrast between the ease with which children enter the Kingdom and the difficulty with which the rich enter is notable. In Mark (10.16), this pericope closes with an action of Jesus which indicates as clear an acceptance and affirmation of children and of the intentions of the parents who brought them as one could want. If children are received openly by Jesus and if they have a place in the Kingdom, this may imply that giving birth to children and being a parent are seen as good things.[48]

Far from setting up the family of faith as an alternative to the physical family, Jesus uses the smallest member of the physical family as a model for members of the family of faith and gives children a place in the Kingdom. The evidence of Jesus' positive attitude toward children, their place in the Kingdom, and how they might serve as models for disciples and be served by disciples seems to imply a positive estimation of a woman's role as child-bearer and mother (as well as a positive estimation of the father's role). While it might be objected that this material tells us only about Jesus' attitudes toward the helpless who are already born rather than about the bearing of children *per se* (and thus about women's roles), at the very least it would seem that Jesus would have refrained from such remarks about (and actions for) children if He had not wished implicitly to endorse the continuance of the physical family with its parental and filial roles. These roles seem to have been affirmed by Jesus without reservation so long as they did not conflict with the priorities of the Kingdom of God.

At this point we must give attention to two passages (Mk 12.40 and parallels, Mk 12.41–4 and parallels) that may reveal something about Jesus' attitude toward widows. In regard to Mk 12.40 (cf. Lk. 20.47), there are no significant critical problems or reasons to doubt that this saying goes back to Jesus' actual conflicts with and denunciations of the scribes. It is possible, however, that this saying is not in its original setting but has been placed here together with a collection of similar sayings. Taylor conjectures that the degree of opposition reflected in 12.37*b*–40 intimates that this passage derives from 'an advanced point in the ministry best associated with Jerusalem'.[49]

Scribes were the scholarly lawyers of Jesus' day and their chief function was to give expert advice and interpretation concerning matters of the Law.

It was forbidden that they be paid for their teaching and it appears that in the main they lived on subsidies and were poor save for the few scribes employed by the Temple priests.[50] This (and the Temple setting, if it is authentic), makes it likely that Jesus is referring to the Temple scribes who had the status to wear fine robes and attend large and expensive banquets.

In this context we may understand Jesus' warning to His disciples to beware the scribes — οἱ κατεσθίοντες τὰς οἰκίας τῶν χηρῶν[51] καὶ προφάσει μακρὰ προσευχόμενοι. Most likely, this phrase connotes a sort of abuse of a widow's property. 'To devour a house' is a technical phrase in extra-biblical Greek sources for bilking someone of their funds or property.[52] How were the scribes doing this? The most common suggestion is that the scribes were taking advantage of the kindness and hospitality of well-to-do widows beyond all reasonable bounds.[53] This view sees no necessary connection between Mk 12.40a and 40b. A more likely view, advanced by J.D.M. Derrett, holds that these scribes, as a trade, were legal managers of well-to-do widows' estates, and were taking more than their fair share of expenses for the task.[54]

This saying presents us with a picture of widows of some means being taken advantage of by unscrupulous scribes who were their legal estate managers. The widows' trusting nature is contrasted to the scribes' deceitful and avaricious practices. G. Stählin remarks, 'Perhaps the μακρὰ προσεύχεσθαι may also be interpreted as a highly charged plea for the cause of the widow.'[55] Jesus is stepping forward as a strong advocate of oppressed or abused widows.

The second passage of interest, Mk 12.41–4 (Lk. 21.1–4), follows immediately after the verse just discussed in the Marcan outline probably because of its similar content. Luke follows Mark at this point and we have here a clear example of how Luke 'can considerably alter the wording of a Marcan narrative while preserving the element of discourse almost un-altered'.[56] Bultmann, because of Jesus' supernatural knowledge that the woman gave all, and because of certain Buddhist, Greek and Semitic parallels to this narrative, regards this pericope as an ideal construction, while Dibelius conjectures that this narrative perhaps went back to a saying or parable of Jesus.[57] The argument from the parallels is questionable both because of problems of content and of dating. As Taylor remarks, 'The story is not so distinctive that similar incidents, with differences, could not happen in the case of other teachers ... Further, the story is in harmony with His teaching elsewhere (cf. ix.41, Lk. xii.15) and the use of ἀμὴν λέγω ὑμῖν is characteristic.'[58] The possibility raised by Dibelius that a story by Jesus has become a story about Jesus cannot be ruled out. Jesus may well have used His own variation of a familiar parable to make His point about giving here. For our purposes it is irrelevant whether this is a story once told by Jesus and now transformed, or an actual incident in His life. In either case, it will reveal to us something of His attitude about widows.

In the Marcan narrative Jesus is in a place in the Temple where He could see the crowds streaming in to pay their private offerings to the Temple treasury.[59] Particularly noticeable by their apparel and perhaps by the length of time they spent putting in their money, were the πολλοί πλούσιοι who ἔβαλλον πολλά.[60] Also noticeable by apparel was one poor widow wanting to make an offering to God out of devotion.[61] Her offering was two λεπτά, copper coins of the smallest denomination.[62] In Mark's account, Jesus, by calling His disciples to Himself (12.43), is portrayed as wishing to use this woman as a model for His disciples. It is not the amount given, but the attitude of self-sacrifice on which the narrative focuses. In a startling statement, Jesus says, 'Truly I tell you,[63] this poor woman put more into the treasury than all the others combined.'[64] She gave ὅλον τὸν βίον αὐτῆς (Mark).[65] Even more significantly, the reason why Jesus says she gave more than all was that she gave out of her deficit, while the others gave out of their abundance. Her devotion and her self-sacrifice were complete. This is a clear model of devotion.

In these two sayings we may note certain obvious contrasts. In Mk 12.40 (Lk. 20.47) there is the contrast between rich widows who trust their managers and the deceitful male scribes. In Mk 12.41–4 (Lk. 21.1–4), a poor widow is set over against the rich men.[66] In addition, the devotion and self-sacrifice of the poor widow stand out against the dark background of the self-indulgence and false piety of the scribes and the easy and ostentatious giving of the rich. In the former case, Jesus defends a group of women; in the latter, one woman is His model of self-sacrificial giving. Jesus' special concern and admiration for women is perhaps nowhere more strikingly juxtaposed with His disgust over certain groups of privileged and supposedly pious men than here. The theme of reversal (the last being first, the humble being exalted, the exalted being humbled) comes to the fore. Jesus' choice of the widow as a model reflects His view of how the advent of the Kingdom means just recognition of the truly godly, and just judgment of those who oppress the poor and disenfranchised (the widow being a prime example).[67]

2. Marriage, Adultery and Divorce

The matters discussed in Mt. 5.27–32, Lk. 16.18, Mt. 19.3–9 and Mk 10.1–12 are of great importance for our understanding of Jesus' view of marriage, family and women's roles. The sayings on marriage and divorce fall into two categories: isolated sayings (Mt. 5.31–2, Lk. 16.18) and the controversy dialogues (Mt. 19.3–9, Mk 10.1–12).[68] We will deal with each group in turn.[69]

The saying on marriage and divorce in Mt. 5.31–2 is located in a larger section of the Sermon on the Mount (5.27–32) that deals with μοιχεία (cf. verses 27, 28, 32), and is presented in the familiar antithesis form: 'You have heard that it was said ... but I say to you.' The saying which precedes the divorce discussion deals with the related matter of sexual sin; therefore, we must see how it sets the stage and relates to the content of what follows. First, however, a word on the critical problems raised by 5.27–30.

Verses 27–8 present few problems. Applying the criterion of dissimilarity, the antithetical parallelism and the first person address speak strongly in favour of its authenticity.[70] This is so not only because of the uniqueness of the form ('You have heard it said ... but I say') in a Jewish context where rabbis were careful to build on past traditions (biblical and otherwise), but also because, 'The evidence shows that the large number of cases of antithetic parallelism in the sayings of Jesus cannot be attributed to the process of redaction, and only in isolated examples is it to be seen as the work of the tradition.'[71] This passage is not an exception to this rule, and Bultmann indicates that verses 27–8 are from the older stock of tradition.[72] In regard to verses 29–30, there are more difficulties. Here we appear to have a case where Matthew had two different sources for virtually the same saying: 5.29–30 from M;[73] 18.8–9 from Mk 9.43–7. As Taylor indicates, Mk 9.43–7 is not in its original context but has been placed with a compilation of other sayings,[74] and clearly these verses are an insertion in Matthew, for 18.10 would follow naturally on 18.7.[75] It is possible then that Matthew found 5.29–30 connected with 5.27–8 in his source, and if Derrett is correct about the meaning of verses 29–30, the connection would belong to the earliest stage of the formation of this tradition and be traceable ultimately to Jesus Himself. As we shall see, 5.29–30 could refer to punishments known in Jesus' day for sexual sins.[76] If the M version of this saying is the more authentic, then it follows that at some point the Marcan version was expanded to include a reference to the foot (9.45) at a stage in the tradition when the original sexual context and implications had been forgotten.[77]

Mt. 5.27 opens with, 'You have heard that it was said, "οὐ μοιχεύσεις", but I say to you πᾶς ὁ βλέπων γυναῖκα πρὸς τὸ ἐπιθυμῆσαι αὐτὴν ἤδη ἐμοίχευσεν αὐτὴν ἐν τῇ καρδίᾳ αὐτοῦ.' Two important questions need to be asked: (1) What is the meaning of μοιχεύω? and (2) How should γυναῖκα πρὸς τὸ ἐπιθυμῆσαι αὐτὴν be translated? μοιχεύω and its cognates are used most commonly in the specific sense of extra-marital intercourse by a married man or woman with someone betrothed or married who is not his or her legal spouse. This word group can be used in a wider sense of various sorts of sexual misbehaviour — feelings, thoughts, or acts that involve sexual sin. It appears that the term is used in its narrower sexual sense of adultery in 5.27, 32, and in a somewhat wider sense in 5.28.[78]

Traditionally, Mt. 5.28 has been translated, 'Anyone looking on a woman lustfully has already committed adultery with her in his heart.'[79] K. Haacker rightly challenged this translation. First, it is questionable whether πρὸς το ἐπιθυμῆσαι αὐτὴν should be translated adverbially so as to link the seeing and desiring as part of one act. Πρὸς with the accusative, as in 2 Cor. 5.10, may yield the sense 'in accord with' which would lead to a translation 'looks in accord with his lust for her'. This translation, however, does not take proper account of the infinitive and its relation to αὐτὴν. There is a further point to be considered — what shall we make of ἐμοίχευσεν αὐτὴν? Usually, this phrase is rendered 'commits adultery with her', or else the αὐτὴν is neglected entirely. Haacker suggests we translate 'has led her astray to adultery', since in rabbinic Judaism it was almost always the woman who was associated with the act of and term adultery.[80] Αὐτὴν can logically be the subject of ἐπιθυμῆσαι. Possibly we should translate 'Anyone who so looks on a woman that she shall become desirous has in his heart already committed adultery with her.' If this is correct, then it is not the same idea that we find in rabbinic sources, where men are warned against looking at women (or women looking at them) lest they, the men, be led astray.[81] Here we have the antithesis to such an idea, for what is being treated in our passage is not male instability in the face of a temptress, but male aggression which leads a woman into sin. Thus, the responsibility for such sin is placed on the male, and consideration is given to the woman, often the weaker and more suspected party in a male-oriented society. This saying is at one and the same time a reaffirmation of a man's leadership and responsibility for the community welfare, and an attempt to liberate women from a social stereotype.[82]

Consistent with this stress on restraint of male aggression is the radical remedy Jesus proposes for those unable to control themselves: 'If your right eye causes you to sin, gouge it out and throw it away. It is better for you to lose one part of your body, than for your whole body to go into hell. And if your right hand causes you to sin, cut it off' (Mt. 5.29–30). While it is often assumed that this is Jesus' hyperbolic way of saying that we must sever ourselves from whatever causes us to sin,[83] in this context it is possible that sexual sins are being alluded to in verses 29–30. This becomes more likely when we realize that loss of eyes was a well-known punishment for sexual misbehaviour, and loss of hand was a punishment for stealing another's property, even his wife.[84] 'Thus, the whole passage ... is speaking in terms of punishments actually known in Palestinian practice in order to throw light on the great difficulty of remaining effectively loyal to ... the Kingdom of heaven.'[85] Jesus' words would have sounded more like a threat than a dramatic hyperbole to the male listeners he addressed.[86] All of the above is like Jn 7.53—8.11 where men's motives are questioned in a similar way, and their failure to live up to their responsibilities in such a situation is pointed to. Perhaps then a brief digression into this Johannine material is in order at this point.

The story of the woman caught in adultery, while probably not a part of the earliest and best text of the NT, is still included in most modern translations, albeit often in the margins.[87] How are we to assess the historical value of this material in light of its textual history and problems of positioning? There are several factors which point to the earliness of this narrative. Daube points out that the reference to stoning indicates that this story originated in the first century, since strangling was substituted as a punishment soon thereafter.[88] Further, as Cadbury points out, 'its internal character, agreeing as it does with the Synoptic stories, bespeaks its genuineness as a tradition'.[89] The external evidence seems also to demand an early date for this story.[90] It is difficult to explain how this narrative ever forced its way into any of the canonical Gospels unless there were strong reasons for assuming that it was authentic Jesus material.[91] It is plausible that because the story recorded ideas found elsewhere in the Gospel tradition and because it may have called into question the early Church's strict disciplinary measures when sexual sin was committed, it was not originally included in any Gospel.[92] This last factor also argues against the view that this material is simply a Church creation. That the story 'represents the character and methods of Jesus as they are revealed elsewhere',[93] favours the view that the portrayal here is an accurate description of Jesus' 'typical' attitude in such cases even if it is not a description of one particular historical incident. Thus, it seems reasonable to expect that by examining this material as a literary unit we can deduce something about what was characteristic of Jesus from Jn 7.53—8.11 though we shall not contend that this text records a particular historical occurrence.

The setting for this encounter is the women's court in the Temple,[94] where Jesus is teaching the people. Suddenly, into this court come the scribes and Pharisees with a woman caught in the very act of adultery.[95] There is no reason to doubt that a married woman is meant, as Daube and Blinzler have shown independently.[96] In order to have the proof required by the rabbis for this crime, the woman must be caught *in coitu*. Thus, the Evangelist depicts a highly suspicious situation: Where is her partner in crime? Did the husband hire spies to trap his wife? Did he wish to set aside his wife without giving her the *ketubah*, or did he want certain proof of her infidelity?[97] Why had not the husband utilized the usual practice of the 'ordeal of the bitter waters' if he had reason to suspect his wife of unfaithfulness?[98] Finally, why had not the witnesses warned the woman if she was seen in the very act?[99]

The scribes and Pharisees confront Jesus by saying that Moses prescribed stoning for such a woman, and by asking, 'σὺ οὖν τί λέγεις?'[100] Thus, Jesus is invited to set Himself against Moses, and perhaps openly against the Roman law.[101] At this point Jesus appears to avoid the issue, for He stoops down and draws with His finger on the earth. There are many possible interpretations of this act, but since the Gospel writer does not think it important enough to tell us what Jesus wrote, it is likely that the gesture, not the words, are important.[102] The gesture implies that Jesus does not wish to be associated with the wickedness of this business, or that He is as ashamed of their actions as of the woman's sin. If it is true that only Mosaic law opposed adultery, but only the Roman law could pass the death sentence, then it seems that Jesus is caught in a trap. If He fails to pronounce judgment, then He will appear to reject Moses; if He pronounces judgment, then He will appear to usurp the Roman *jus gladii*.[103] Jesus does not refrain from judgment; rather, by implication He pronounces this woman guilty by saying, 'If anyone of you is without sin, let him be the first to cast a stone at her.' Here, ἀναμάρτητος probably means 'without serious sin' in the matter at hand.[104] Jesus has good cause to suspect the motives of these men (cf. the editorial note in verse 6), but He does not render invalid their judgment on the gravity of this woman's sin.[105] He applies the principle, 'He who reproves others, must himself be above reproach in the case at issue.' It is the motives of the witnesses and their own culpability, not the woman's lack of sin, which decides the matter here. The witnesses who must cast the first stone (Deut. 17.7), though technically qualified, are not morally qualified. Neither are the scribes or Pharisees qualified, for they are guilty of trying to use God's law to trap the one man in this crowd who *is* morally qualified to pass judgment. Jesus effectively springs the trap that hovers over Himself and the woman by passing judgment in such a way that its execution is impossible.

The Jewish leaders, who were supposed to be moral examples to the people, knew what Jesus was implying about them, and thus one by one beginning with the elders, they silently slipped away.[106] The hunters have lost not only their game, but also their bait. When the woman tells Jesus that no one has condemned her, Jesus says emphatically, οὐδὲ ἐγώ σε κατακρίνω. Perhaps He rejects implicitly the whole procedure that the scribes and Pharisees were following as inherently discriminatory against women in such a sin-tainted setting.[107] Jesus does not approve of a system wherein a man's lust is not taken as seriously as a woman's seduction. Jesus, by saying, 'From now on do not sin',[108] does not pronounce this woman's sin forgiven since she has not repented; rather, He shows her the balance of mercy and justice calculated to lead one away from a sinful life to repentance and salvation.[109] As in Mt. 5, we see a critique of men who fail to live up to their responsibility of being examples of virtue for the community, and we see a rejection of certain stereotypes in which women are treated as scapegoats responsible for social ills.[110] This comports with the emphasis we find in some of the Synoptic material (notably Mt. 5.32, 19.9) to which we must now turn.

The Synoptic divorce material is by no means easily handled for there is no broad consensus among scholars about any of the following questions: (1) Which of the isolated sayings (Mt. 5.31–2, Lk. 16.18) is the more primitive? (2) Which of the controversy dialogues (Mt. 19, Mk 10) is the more primitive? (3) Do the sayings and dialogues go back to one primitive saying or dialogue? (4) How are the exceptive clauses in Matthew to be understood? Only on the last question is there a fairly general agreement that the exceptive clauses are serious qualifications of Jesus' teaching and are not original (though even this has been recently challenged). Even if they are later additions, whether these additions break the general rule prohibiting divorce, or simply make it applicable to a particular problem is open to debate, since the meaning of πορνεία here is uncertain and the context in neither Mt. 5 nor 19 favours an actual exception being introduced.[111] In Mt. 5 the broadening of the meaning of adultery in 5.28 and the antithesis form used in 5.27, 29, 30 naturally lead one to expect an intensification of OT and rabbinic teaching in Mt. 5.31–2. Verse 32 continues the unique stress on a man's responsibility (cf. verses 27–8) by saying that it is the male who causes the woman to commit adultery if he divorces her and she remarries.[112] Further, the second husband commits adultery if he marries the divorced woman.[113] In Mt. 19 we also run into difficulties if we take 19.9 to involve a genuine exception because then 19.10, in terms of the logic the Evangelist is trying to convey in placing 19.1–9 and 10–12 together, makes no sense. Thus, simply talking in terms of Matthean logic, we meet problems if we too quickly assume that the exceptive clauses are serious qualifications of an absolute prohibition of divorce. It should also be noted that the view that the exceptive clauses are later additions is partially based on the assumption that Matthew is following Mark here – an assumption that even the 'apostle' of Marcan priority, B.H. Streeter, had considerable doubts about. He posited that the First Evangelist was following in some detail a parallel version to Mark's divorce dialogue found in his own special source and that 'Matthew's account appears to be in some ways more original than Mark's.'[114]

In terms of historical probabilities, there is much to be said for the suggestion that the First Evangelist here has more primitive material than the Second. For one thing it is much more probable that the Pharisees would ask Jesus about the grounds of divorce than about the rectitude of divorce *per se*.[115] Again, it is *a priori* more probable that the discussion would have proceeded as we find it in Mt. 19.3–9 than in Mk 10.2–12 since it seems likely that Jesus would have spoken of a Mosaic *permission* to divorce (Mt. 19.8) rather than a Mosaic *command* (Mk 10.3).[116] In the Marcan form of this debate Jesus is placed in the unlikely position of putting Himself between a rock and a hard place by speaking of a Mosaic command which He then shows is in opposition to God's creation plan as expressed in the first book of Moses! By contrast the Matthean form of the debate makes perfect sense. It is the Pharisees who speak of Moses' command while Jesus counters that it was only a permission and quite logically He is able to appeal to a higher and prior principle found in God's creation plan (verses 4–6, 8*b*). Further, the 'in house' motif in Mk 10.10 is characteristic (cf. Mk 4.34), and it is more natural that Jesus goes on to make the pronouncement in Mt. 19.9 (Mk 10.11) in public,[117] and that the disciples reacted as we find them doing in Mt. 19.10. In the Marcan narrative the public discussion ends rather abruptly at 10.9 with no clear statement of what exactly the OT principle means for the practice of divorce. It seems somewhat ironic that many scholars will argue at some length that Mk 10.12 is Mark's expansion for a Hellenistic audience and yet not consider the possibility that he had recast the entire narrative for that audience. What the Gentiles (who lived in an atmosphere of much more widespread divorce than did the Palestinian Jew) needed to hear was not that there were legitimate grounds for divorce but rather that divorce was completely against God's intentions. Thus, in almost every regard the debate as we find it in Mt. 19 looks to be more primitive and genuine than Mark's debate.[118]

In regard to the more primitive form of the isolated logion (Mt. 5.31–2, cf. Lk. 16.18) there are several difficulties. The differences between Mt. 5.32 and Mt. 19.9 suggest that the First Evangelist has not simply modified the saying in 19.9 and placed it in 5.32. It will be noted that Lk. 16.18*a* is close to Mt. 19.9 while Lk. 16.18*b* is like Mt. 5.32*b*. Mt. 5.32*a* is unique.

Thus, it may be that we should not too quickly equate Mt. 5.32 and Lk. 16.18 in their entirety as two forms of the same saying. This leads to the conclusion that the antithesis formula in Mt. 5.31–2a may not be secondary.[119] The contrast between the statement from Deut. 24.1 and Mt. 5.32a tells in favour of the authenticity of this antithesis for it is unlikely that an Evangelist, who includes such sayings as we find in Mt. 5.17–19, would create such an antithesis. Further, if Mt. 19.7–9 is authentic tradition, then it appears we have evidence that Jesus made such a contrast between Deut. 24.1 and His own teaching. Finally, perhaps the rather surprising 'causes her to commit adultery' speaks for the authenticity of at least 5.32a. We have already seen in Mt. 5.27–30 how Jesus placed responsibility on the male for allowing a woman to go astray into sin. Mt. 5.31a comports well with such teaching. Some tentative conclusions should be stated at this point:

(1) In regard to the controversy dialogues, the Matthean form appears to be the more primitive and more authentic form with the possible exception of the exceptive clauses. This is not to be taken as an argument *against* general Marcan priority but *for* the use by the First Evangelist of a parallel version which he probably derived from his special material. (2) The Marcan discussion and particularly 10.12 appears to be a modification of Jesus' original teaching for a Hellenistic audience. (3) The antithesis formula found in Mt. 5.31–2a may be original or at least modelled on the authentic contrast in Mt. 19.7–9. (4) The saying found in Mt. 5.32b and Lk. 16.18b appears to be an isolated logion possibly found in the Q material and probably quite primitive.[120] (5) Lk. 16.18a is probably a saying found in Q and possibly more original than the form found in Mk. 10.11.[121] We are now in a position to discuss the controversy dialogues and the isolated logion.

In the pronouncement story presented in two different versions (Mt. 19.3–9, Mk 10.2–12) Jesus is confronted by a group of rabbis who wish to ask Him a question about divorce in the hopes of trapping Him in His own words.[122] Daube has isolated a specific familiar form of debate in the Marcan version of this pericope: a question by an opponent (10.2), public retort sufficient to silence listener but stating only part of the truth (10.5–9), private elucidation demanded by followers (10.10), and private explanation given in a full and clear way.[123]

In Matthew the discussion begins with the Pharisees' question, 'Is it lawful for a man to divorce his wife κατὰ πᾶσαν αἰτίαν?'[124] As the verb ἀπολύω indicates, the Pharisees are asking about divorce, not separation (the latter did not exist as a legal reality in first-century Judaism).[125]

Matthew and Mark differ as to how Jesus began to reply. The Matthean form (in which the Pharisees ask Him, 'Why then did Moses command to give a bill of divorce and to divorce?') is probably the more original response to Jesus' first remarks on divorce. Jesus answers their question with, 'Moses permitted you to divorce your wife πρὸς τὴν σκληροκαρδίαν' (Mt. 19.7–8).[126] The Mosaic permission referred to, Deut. 24.1–4, required a bill of divorce be given to make clear that the woman was no longer married, in order to protect her from further charges or abuse.[127] Jesus intimates that Moses' provision was meant to limit a practice widespread at that time, but it was not meant to license divorce for any cause as some rabbis had deduced.[128]

In the Matthean account, Jesus quotes two different texts in response to the Pharisees' initial question. The phrase ὁ κτίσας 'απ' ἀρχῆς (cf. 19.8)[129] prefaces the first text: 'He made them male and female.' (Gen. 1.27, cf. 5.2). Then the text, citing Gen. 2.24, reads, 'Because of this (fact)[130] "a man shall leave his mother and be joined to his wife,[131] and the two shall become one flesh".'[132] The implication is that the one flesh union becomes more constitutive of a man and a woman's being than their uniqueness. Only two can become one, and when they do they are no longer two. From these texts Jesus deduces that a man and a woman are no longer two, but σὰρξ μιά.[133] What then God συνέζευξεν, man must not χωρίζειν.[134] Jesus argues that because of the nature of mankind's creation in two distinct but complementary genders (a divine act) and the nature of marriage created by God between male and female (a divine act), no third human party is allowed into this relationship. Anyone[135] who seeks to divide those who share such a marriage and a one flesh union attacks not only the marriage and the two people united in marriage, but also the unifier, God.[136] Jesus has appealed to the intended creation order and the Creator, both of which undergird, not undermine, Mosaic law and its true intention even if it may seem to contradict a certain concession to sinfulness. Mosaic law was meant to be used as a tool to limit, not license, an existing evil.[137]

In the Matthean account of this discussion, Jesus goes on to say to the Pharisees that even though Moses permitted divorce, this was not God's original plan.[138] Thus, despite what Moses had allowed: 'λέγω δὲ ὑμῖν,[139] whoever divorces his wife μὴ ἐπὶ πορνείᾳ, and marries another, commits adultery.' As in Mt. 5.31–2, the words of Jesus have built up to a point where one naturally expects Jesus to contrast His teaching with that of other rabbis, or even Moses. Certainly the λέγω δὲ ὑμῖν points in this direction. It thus appears unlikely that even the First Evangelist intended the exceptive clauses to be seen as real qualifications of Jesus' absolute prohibition of divorce in cases of legitimate marriages. If an incestuous or zenût relationship is in view in these clauses the Evangelist may have introduced an exception that merely interprets Jesus' absolute prohibition for an exceptional situation or problem.

Before we conclude this section a few words about Mk 10.11–12 are necessary. There is a unique feature about Mk 10.11 that deserves attention. Normally μοιχᾶται ἐπ' αὐτήν is taken to mean commits adultery against her (the first wife). While this is grammatically possible, the Jews never spoke in terms of a man committing adultery against his own wife. This does not mean that Mark would not do so. N. Turner, followed by B. Schaller, has suggested that ἐπ' αὐτήν be translated 'with her' (with the second woman). This makes sense of the text because adultery by definition is committed by a married person with a third party. Further, this translation still means that the husband is labelled an adulterer, contrary to the common use of the word. It also implies there has been a crime against one's wife, but reveals that the crime itself was *with* a third party.[140] As we stated previously, the ἐπ' αὐτήν appears to be Mark's addition intended to clarify the meaning of the basic teaching of Jesus which probably took the form we find in Lk. 16.18a.

Mk 10.12 is said to be Mark's adaptation of Jesus' teaching on divorce to a Graeco-Roman setting.[141] It is a saying not included by Matthew. Despite its textual difficulties,[142] there is no doubt that it is referring to the act of a woman. The woman either 'separates from' or 'divorces' her husband (probably the latter). Most scholars argue that this is a Marcan formulation and not a word of Jesus since it is assumed that Jewish women could not divorce men in first-century Palestine. Even though this is true in most cases, it is conceivable that Jesus could make such a remark either as a Semitic parallelism, meant to complete and balance the saying in Mk 10.11, or as a pronouncement to place women on equal terms with men even in hypothetical legal matters. The statement need not have been hypothetical. E. Bammel has shown that there is some evidence that even Jewish women in first-century Palestine could not only write out their own divorce bill, but also pronounce the divorce formula. Some Jewish women of high rank, such as Herodias, and later Salome, were able to divorce their husbands (though in Herodias' case it may have been a matter of abandonment rather than divorce).[143] Without doubt most scholars will continue to see Mk 10.12 as Mark's own formulation meant to convey Jesus' basic teaching to a Hellenistic audience — and they may well be right. However, considering the remarks Jesus appears to have made elsewhere about Herodias (Lk. 13.31–2), and His commendation of John the Baptist, the possibility that Jesus Himself made an allusion to Herod's wicked wife by way of a general statement on women divorcing men is far from inconceivable and should be given more serious consideration than it has received in the past.[144]

In conclusion, in Mt. 5.27–30 Jesus places the burden of responsibility for a woman being led into sexual sin on the man, thus rejecting certain common stereotypes (cf. Jn 7.53–8.11). Lk. 16.18 is an absolute prohibition against divorce and remarriage. The onus for divorce and its consequences is placed on the man in both Mt. 5 and Lk. 16. While the First Evangelist speaks of the first man making his divorced wife an adulteress, and the second man who marries a divorced woman becoming an adulterer, Luke speaks of both the first husband as an adulterer (if he remarries), and the second man as the same if he marries the divorced woman. What is new in this teaching, besides making the man primarily responsible for sexual sin or divorce and its consequences, is the idea of a man committing adultery against his former wife by remarriage, or making his wife an adulteress by divorce.[145] In all probability this new thrust, because of its originality, goes back to Jesus,[146] who believed that the first one flesh union, as the basis of marriage, was indissoluble.[147] Jesus opposed with vehemence both male aggression that led a woman astray (5.27–30), and the adultery that resulted from it. The net effect of such views is that various stereotypes of women as temptresses are countered, and at the same time a woman is given greater security in marriage by making the man responsible for its continued maintenance and by prohibiting the man from using his power to cause its dissolution. Jesus thus reaffirms and also reforms the traditional family structure. This resulted in giving women a more stable foundation on which to operate in their traditional roles.

3. Eunuchs for the Kingdom – Mt. 19.10–12

The pericope on eunuchs in Mt. 19.10–12 is uniquely Matthean and is perhaps to be traced to the First Evangelist's special source. The radical nature of the teaching expressed in verse 12 as well as the fact that, 'The saying is undoubtedly off the rabbinic line'[148] probably supports the view that verse 12 is to be traced back to Jesus Himself.[149] The phrase, 'for the sake of the Kingdom', also relates this saying to other teachings in the Gospels generally accepted to be from a *Sitz im Leben Jesu* (cf. Mk 10.28–30).[150] Also in suport of this is the fact that the first two categories of eunuchs mentioned reflect the common Jewish division between natural and man-made eunuchs.[151] The question remains, however, whether or not verse 10 is a redactional connection to the marriage and divorce teaching fashioned by the Evangelist himself. Lending weight to this view is the fact that Mark has none of the material found in verses 10–12. Against this contention, however, is the fact that the First Evangelist frequently edits Mark in a way that spares the disciples (and verse 10 could hardly be said to present the disciples in a favourable light). As Davies says, 'they virtually make the attractiveness of marriage contingent upon the possibility of divorce, and that on easy terms. Such an attitude as they express is historically possible, if not probable'.[152] Thus, it is perhaps more likely than not that we have here both a genuine teaching by Jesus on eunuchs and the actual reaction of Jesus' disciples to His divorce teaching — a reaction which reveals that they had typically male Jewish attitudes about these matters. It is still likely that 19.10–12 relates part of a separate (authentic) discussion to that found in 19.1–9 and the juxtaposition is the Evangelist's. This is so because the dramatic pronouncement in Mt. 19.9 nicely concludes the controversy dialogue and silences the opponents, and because the disciples were not mentioned at the introduction of this dialogue and play no part in the discussion.

The First Evangelist records that the disciples' reaction to Jesus' marriage teaching is both amazement and dismay — 'If this is the case of husband and wife, then it is not profitable to marry!'[153] This may be called a typical reaction from a group of Jewish men used to having the freedom of both polygamy and divorce. That the First Evangelist places this reaction here is another indication that he did not intend the exceptive clause to mean that Jesus was siding with the School of Shammai in the rabbinic debate. The verb συμφέρω perhaps indicates the common Jewish view of marriage as essentially a property transaction between the groom (including his father) and the bride's father in which both hoped to profit financially and otherwise (through the birth of children).[154] On the other hand, it may mean that the disciples were saying it is better not to marry in such a case because of the difficulties of remaining faithful to or keeping the loyalty of one's spouse.

The response, 'Not all can accept (understand) this word but only those to whom it is given' follows. Does the phrase 'this word' refer to Jesus' teaching on marriage and divorce in 19.3–9, or the disciples' reaction to that teaching in 19.10? On the whole it seems likely that the Evangelist intends 'this word' to refer to Jesus' previous teaching and is implying that it is given only to some to follow His strict teaching on marriage and divorce.[155] The question then immediately arises — what of those to whom this word is not given? What other option is there to lifelong marital fidelity?

Jesus answers, 'Some are born εὐνοῦχοι from their mother's womb, and some are made εὐνοῦχοι by other men, and some make themselves εὐνοῦχοι for the sake of the Kingdom.' The eunuch was well-known in various oriental cults and often served in royal houses as a guardian of a king's concubines.[156] Jesus' disciples would be familiar with such men through contacts with people from Syria, Asia Minor or Northern Africa. But it is more likely that they would have met or heard of the celibates of the Qumran community.[157] The attitudes toward sexuality and celibacy reflected in such cults and communities were not compatible with the mainstream of rabbinic thinking since most rabbis found castrated men abhorrent and viewed non-castrated celibates as violators of God's commandment to procreate.[158] It is likely that Jesus' teaching on eunuchs was as shocking to the disciples as His instructions on marriage and divorce.

There are some difficulties in regard to the meaning of εὐνοῦχος. The word ἄγαμος usually is used of someone who simply lives a celibate life. The selection of the word εὐνοῦχος is remarkable because for the Jewish, as well as the Greek, listener it has a very negative connotation. The man who is simply an unmarried single is never called εὐνοῦχος in classical literature; this appears first in Christian literature.[159] Normally, a person known as a eunuch was one incapable or unfit for marriage through castration, deformity, etc. Clearly, this is the subject in 19.12*a* and 12*b*. The Evangelist's audience would probably have understood the term literally in verse 19*c* as well.[160] It is not likely, however, that Jesus or the Evangelist was advocating literal self-mutilation, though Origen at first thought so.[161] The following arguments may be adduced against such a deduction: (1) In view of His Jewish background, it is likely that Jesus would have found literal castration abhorrent; (2) There is no evidence that Jesus had any sympathy with asceticism for its own sake; (3) The use of the term εὐνοῦχος in early Christian literature (Clement of Alexandria) of 'spiritual eunuchs', a sense unknown in classical or Hellenistic Greek, requires an adequate explanation.[162] It is doubtful that it is adequate to suggest that the usage simply derived from the three verses in Matthew 19 under present scrutiny since it appears in Clement's discussion about castrated household servants and their lust, not about abstinence for the kingdom's sake. (4) In regard to the Evangelist's view, it appears that his inclusion of the (probably authentic) phrase 'for the Kingdom's sake' clarifies matters. It has also been suggested that the First Evangelist distinguished between the first two types of eunuchs and the last by the use of a paratactic καί before the third class. It may be that the phrase, 'the one who can accept this should accept it' in 19.12 implies in itself that we are talking about a spiritual gift from God, and thus not a physical act undertaken by man on his own. Only those to whom it is given can accept such a calling.[163]

The structure of this saying on eunuchs from a Jewish perspective proceeds from least objectionable (eunuchs by nature) to more objectionable (man-made eunuchs whether by crime or as punishment for a crime), to most objectionable (self-made eunuchs). The saying builds to a climax, and the third group of eunuchs is marked out in a special way from the other two groups. When Jesus says, 'The one who is able to accept this', He implies that His words are addressed to those who have an option, unlike the eunuchs of verses 12*a* and 12*b*. Blinzler suggests we should translate 19.12, 'There are those who are born unfit for marriage from their mother's womb, there are those who are made unfit for marriage by men, and there are those who have made themselves unfit for marriage for the sake of the kingdom of heaven.'[164] The key to understanding 19.12 is in the phrase 'for the sake of the Kingdom'. 'The motivation for accepting the celibate life ... was eschatological.'[165] Jesus' views of this subject and those of the Qumran community are similar in this respect. But the reason for renouncing marriage or family in Jesus' teaching has nothing to do with ritual purity or the idea that sexual relations made one impure (as the Qumranites taught).[166] As Jeremias points out, the phrase εὐνούχισαν ἑαυτοὺς διὰ τὴν βασιλείαν τῶν οὐρανῶν has no parallels in the language of Jesus' contemporaries, though it has some similarities to other parts of Jesus' teaching.[167] While there is a close connection between Mk 10.28–30 and the eunuch teaching, they are probably not the same in meaning. The word εὐνούχισαι is never used to refer to a disciple's past, once-for-all decision to give up everything to follow Jesus. Rather, in our text it refers specifically either to the giving up of the right to marry for the sake of the Kingdom, or less probably to the giving up of one's family for the sake of the Kingdom. In short, it is the decision to follow Jesus that precipitates the renunciation of marriage or family, but the two decisions are not synonymous.[168]

Jesus thus provides two alternatives for His disciples: some are given the gift to be joined by God as husband and wife and to live in exclusive monogamy to the glory of God; others are able to make themselves eunuchs for the sake of the Kingdom because God has enabled them to do so. In neither option is obeying God's word or following Jesus absent. Schweizer says, 'Er kann ebenso vom Geheimnis der unauflöslichen Ehe wie vom Geheimnis der Ehelosigkeit reden und beide Worte können echte Jesusworte sein.'[169] Jesus thus rejected the rabbinic teaching that marriage and propagation were a divine imperative enjoined on all normal men (and all women, according to some rabbis). Possibly, it was Jesus' teaching on eunuchs for the Kingdom that allowed women to be present among the travelling company of disciples (Lk. 8.1–3), and to remain single and serve the community of faith (Ac. 21.9). In any event, it is clear that Jesus' reasons for giving such teaching were because of His view of the radical claims of the Kingdom, not ascetical tendencies in His thoughts. That Jesus offers two equally valid callings, either to life-long marriage or to being a eunuch for the Kingdom, is in itself evidence that Jesus did not have negative views about human sexuality or sexual relations in marriage. Nor did He accept the connection of holiness with abstention from sexual relations. There is no hint here that being a eunuch for the Kingdom was a higher or more holy calling than life-long marriage (unless one sees this teaching as a reply to the disciples' remark in 19.10).[170]

Jesus' teaching on marriage and the single life strikes an intriguing balance between old and new. His views remain patriarchal, but male headship for Jesus entails extra responsibility, not extra liberty (cf. Mt. 5.27–32). It is a vision where the creation order and also the new demands of the Kingdom are appealed to in order to reform common misunderstandings in regard to God's will on divorce and marriage, children and the family. It is a vision that Paul seems to have imbibed and implemented further some twenty years after the ministry of Jesus (cf. 1 Cor. 11.2–9). In light of the broad-based feeling in the Mediterranean during the days of the Roman Empire and even earlier about the duty of procreation, one must adequately explain why, in the community of Jesus' followers, singleness was seen as a viable option. It appears that the acceptance of the authenticity of Jesus' teaching on eunuchs, combined with His teaching on the primacy of the call to discipleship and to join His community, provides the best explanation of the origin of the attitude of the primitive Church.[171]

4. Wives in the Resurrection – Mk 12.18–27, Mt. 22.23–33, Lk. 20.27–40

It has been said by NT scholars that Mk 12.18–27 and parallels tells us that Jesus expected an existence without sexual differences, without marriage, and without reproduction in the life to come.[172] Ladd's remarks illustrate this approach: 'Here is a truly inconceivable order of existence. There are no human analogies to describe existence without the physiological and sociological bonds of sex and family.'[173] It may be questioned whether this is either the clear meaning or the implication of this text.

The possibility that this passage is a post-Easter community formulation seems remote despite the claims of Bultmann and others that it is.[174] Consider the following reasons: (1) 'In sekundärer Traditionsbildung werden nie (ausser in der Bearbeitung von Tradition bei Mt) die Sadduzäer als Gesprächspartner Jesus eingefuhrt';[175] (2) in the discussions in the early Church about Resurrection, the focus was not on the angels' state but on the resurrected Lord (Rom. 8.29, 1 Cor. 15.49, Phil. 3.21); (3) the 'fact' of resurrection was grounded not in Exod. 3.6 but in Jesus' Resurrection (1 Cor. 15.12ff) in the early community;[176] (4) it seems most unlikely that a Church-formulated debate on resurrection would have used as its starting and focal point a discussion of Levirate marriage which even in Jesus' day was falling into disuse;[177] (5) the question raised by the Sadducees probably falls into the category of a *boruth*,[178] a puzzling or mocking question often posed by Jews of Jesus' day to ridicule or expose a belief of a rabbi or an erroneous popular belief;[179] (6) the mention of angels probably reflects special knowledge of Sadducean beliefs on Jesus' part for they rejected the existence of such beings.[180] Both in form and in content this pericope is thoroughly Jewish, as is the way Jesus uses Scripture in this debate, and thus it may safely be assigned to a *Sitz im Leben Jesu*.[181] Luke, however, has made some additions to his Marcan source at Lk. 20.34–6 (and 38b–39). The Semitic style of verses 34–6 might point to the use of another source at this point, or oral tradition, but it is usually thought more likely that this material is an example of Lucan expansion for the sake of explanation.[182] These verses then will only be treated as reflecting the thinking of the Third Evangelist.

The Synoptic accounts of this story are divided into three sections: (1) the Sadducees' question (Mk 12.18–23 and parallels); (2) Jesus' response about the nature of the resurrection state (Mk 12.24–5 and parallels); and (3) Jesus' response about the reality of the resurrection (Mk 12.26–7 and parallels). Only the first two sections concern us here. The question the Sadducees pose seems to be purely hypothetical.[183] The fact that Levirate marriage was in general disuse in Jesus' day, and the use by the Sadducees of the number seven (which may be a way of saying *ad infinitum* in this case),[184] seem to point in this direction. Usually, the sole purpose of Levirate marriage was to preserve a family name by propagation — a deceased man's brother would 'raise up a seed' for him.[185] After performing this obligation, he was not required to treat his brother's wife in the same way he would treat his own.[186] In the case put forward by the Sadducees, six brothers had tried and failed to sire a child for their dead brother and, furthermore, the widow was single at death having outlived all her mates. The Sadducees' question is predicated on the assumption that in the life to come there would be a continuity with this life in regard to the existence of marriage.[187] With their logic, if this continuity existed, then resurrection was ruled out, since no doctrine can be believed which leads to such an impossible situation as one woman having to choose between seven partners.[188]

Jesus responds, 'You know neither the Scriptures nor the power of God.'[189] Luke omits this sentence and alone adds, οἱ υἱοὶ τοῦ αἰῶνος τούτου γαμοῦσιν καὶ γαμίσκονται, οἱ δὲ καταξιωθέντες τοῦ αἰῶνος ἐκείνου τυχεῖν.[190] All three Gospels go on to say that in the resurrection people will neither marry nor be given in marriage. This is important on several accounts. The use of the terms γαμοῦσιν and γαμίζονται reveals that at least the Synoptists and probably, in their view, Jesus, accepted the distinctive roles men and women assumed in their society in pursuing a marital union. The men, being the initiators, marry (γαμοῦσιν), while the women are given in marriage (γαμίζονται).[191] These terms also reveal that the act of marrying, not necessarily the state of marriage, is under discussion. Thus, the text is saying, no more marriages will be made,[192] but this is not the same as saying that all existing marriages will disappear in the eschatological state. As noted, Jesus grounded marriages in an indissoluble union and in the creation order plan.[193] The difficulty here is to have the proper understanding of both the continuity and the discontinuity between this age and the next. If Jesus is answering the Sadducees' question in a specific way, then He is arguing against a certain view of continuity between this age and the next.

The Sadducees are arguing about a case of marriage for the sake of propagation and the preservation of a family name. If we may take a hint from Luke's redactional expansion and explanation in verse 36 (οὐδὲ γὰρ ἀποθανεῖν ἔτι δύνανται) of Jesus' statement,[194] the point of Jesus' remark about marrying is that in the resurrection state believers, like the angels, will not be able to die. Where there is no death, there is no need or purpose either to begin or to continue a Levirate marriage. The question the Sadducees raise is inapplicable to conditions in the new age. On this interpretation Jesus is answering specifically the case in point without necessarily saying anything about marriage apart from Levirate marriage.[195] Perhaps, like many of the rabbis, Jesus distinguished between marriage contracted purely for propagation and name preservation, and the normal form of marriage. Since the first marriage of this woman was not a Levirate marriage, then perhaps it is not dealt with in this discussion. Elsewhere Jesus recognized that non-Levirate marriage had a more substantial origin, purpose and nature than merely the desire to propagate and maintain a family name.

Jesus does say there will be no more marrying in the next age (probably of any sort for any reason). In this cessation of marrying we are ὡς ἄγγελοι (Matthew, Mark).[196] The meaning of this comparison is not elaborated upon except in Lk. 20.36 (a redactional addition). Nowhere in the Synoptic accounts of this debate are we told that we become sexless, without gender distinctions like the angels, or that all marital bonds created in this age are dissolved in the next.[197] The concept of the *bodily* resurrection indicates that there is some continuity between this age and the next which leaves the door open for continuity in the existence of marriage.

J. Denney seems correct when he asserts that Jesus is concerned to deny 'that there will be any natural relation out of which the difficulty of the Sadducees could arise'.[198] It is even conceivable that Jesus does not answer the Sadducees' question at all, but simply shows that because of the discontinuity of this age with the next, their question is meaningless and built on false presuppositions.[199]

In conclusion, our text argues that the act of marrying will cease in the life to come. It does not follow that Jesus or the Gospel writers envisioned the dissolution of all marriages in the resurrection, or that mankind will live a sexless, genderless existence in that age. Such ideas are imported into the text on the basis of the statement that we will be like the angels which, if Luke's addition is a correct interpretation, refers to the righteous attaining a deathless, not sexless, state. That Jesus is arguing for resurrection shows that He sees at least one point of continuity between the two ages — a body in some sense. Possibly, Jesus believed that death dissolved all marital bonds, as later Christian tradition argued, but this text does not say so explicitly. Jesus' handling of the Sadducees' question probably indicates a negative evaluation of Levirate marriage. This would further support His attempts to give a woman greater security and dignity in a normal marriage, and give her the freedom to feel that raising up a seed through Levirate marriage was not a necessity. More certainly, the Gospel writers and possibly Jesus had no objections to the patriarchal marital procedure in which the man initiates a marriage and the woman is given in marriage.

B. Women in the Parables of Jesus

1. The Obstinate Widow and the Obdurate Judge — Lk. 18.1–8

Perhaps no form of Jesus' teaching has received closer scrutiny or more diverse treatment than His parables. The lack of uniformity, either in the means or in the results of parable interpretation, has not deterred scholars from trying to make sense of these vignettes which make up about one-third of Jesus' reported teaching.[200] If, as A.M. Hunter suggests, the parables were 'Jesus' justification of his mission to the last, the least, and the lost', then it is not at all surprising that women figure prominently in some of them.[201] Lk. 18.1–8, a parable unique to the Third Gospel, lends credibility to Hunter's assertion, and gives us occasion to explore further Jesus' attitude toward widows.

The parable of the obstinate widow and the obdurate judge is the first of two passages in Lk. 18 which, according to the Evangelist, deals with prayer. Luke's penchant for male–female parallelism comes to the fore here in that Lk. 18.1–8 has an oppressed woman, and 18.9–14 a despised man (tax gatherer) as prayer models. This procedure betrays much about Luke's purpose in writing his Gospel, since we find this male–female parallelism throughout his work, not just in the pairing parables.[202] 'Other than as a pedagogical device for repetition, there is no apparent reason for stating the same message twice except to choose examples that would make the message clearly understandable to different groups – the female and male listeners.'[203] What emerges is Luke's desire to show that women are equally objects of God's salvation and equally good illustrations of God's dealings with mankind.

The critical problems this parable raises are two-fold and must be dealt with briefly at this point. It is sometimes argued that this parable was not originally or not mainly eschatological in its tenor. This view, while recognizing the clear eschatological statement in 18.8, treats it either as a later addition to the parable (which does not relate to its essential message),[204] or as a specific eschatological warning meant to enforce the more general message about persisting in prayer.[205] Against this view, however, is the fact that the theme of ἐκδίκησις, present throughout the parable and its application, points to an eschatological message as does the central theme of the widow prevailing after a long time (ἐπὶ χρόνον).[206] This tells in favour of seeing this parable as a unity. Further, a recent and thorough form-critical study of this pericope has demonstrated convincingly the inherent unity of 18.2–8[207] and, on the basis of linguistic considerations, Jeremias no longer considers any of 18.6–8 secondary.[208] It is best to recognize the eschatological elements present in both parable and application, while realizing that 18.1 is probably only a general introduction created by Luke, intending to stress the message of persistence in prayer, whether or not one is experiencing the Messianic woes.[209]

The second critical problem raised by the parable is that it is sometimes thought to be a variant or twin of Lk. 11.5–8. Both passages do stress persistence in prayer and its efficacy, but in many other regards they are different: (1) Lk. 11.5–8 is devoid of eschatological elements or context; (2) in that text a friendly neighbour is being asked, not an obdurate judge, and the man asking is not being oppressed, nor is he asking for ἐκδίκησις for himself; in 11.5—8 the problem is not so much the neighbour's real unwillingness to help (unlike Lk. 18.1—8), but the time at which he is asked.[210] Thus, in Lk. 11.5—8 persistence in prayer is inculcated primarily by comparison between the human and divine situation; whereas, in Lk. 18.1—8 persistence in prayer is based on the contrast between the character of the unjust judge and God.[211] One must, however, bear in mind that the Evangelist is possibly shaping this parable in light of Sirach 35.12—18.[212]

Lk. 18.2—8 is important for our study firstly because Jesus' choice of a *woman* in need of help as an *example* for His disciples perhaps indicates Jesus' sympathy and concern for this particular group of people in a male-oriented society, and secondly because the aspect of this woman's behaviour that Jesus focuses on (her perseverance or persistence) is a characteristic that in a patriarchal society was often seen as a negative attribute in a woman (cf. Prov. 19.13*b* M.T.). The parable should be seen as a struggle between the widow and the judge, for the widow's real adversary (ἀντίδικος) plays no part in the story except as a necessary presupposition.[213] If Derrett is correct in holding that we are dealing with a case in an administrative, not religious, court, then it is probable that we are to understand that the widow's opponent has preceded her to the court in order to bribe the judge.[214] The judge, not being a righteous man,[215] not caring about God's or man's opinion of him,[216] was ruled only by self-interest and self-preservation. It is unlikely that the widow had anything to offer the judge, and so her case looked hopeless. Her only asset was her persistence; thus, she ἤρχετο πρὸς αὐτὸν.[217] She did not ask for vengeance, but vindication of her claims to her own belongings, or perhaps protection from her oppressor.[218] The wicked judge successfully resisted her continual pleading for some time,[219] but finally she began to bother him. The judge feared the woman might εἰς τέλος[220] ἐρχομένη ὑπωπιάζῃ με. There are those who think that ὑπωπιάζω is to be taken literally — the judge feared the woman would give him a black eye and he wanted no such conflict or the disgrace that would follow from it.[221] Others believe it means 'to annoy', 'to wear out' — the judge did not relish being bothered continually and was worn out by her pleading.[222] Finally, Derrett believes it is a metaphorical phrase meaning 'to black the face', 'to disgrace',[223] but this presupposes that the judge did care what men thought of him. It is more likely that the judge was tired of being bothered by the widow and, to get rid of her, gives her what she desires.

The case of the widow is like the case of the disciples. Thus, Jesus says, 'Listen to what the unrighteous judge says.'[224] The disciples are continually ($\dot{\eta}\mu\dot{\epsilon}\rho\alpha\varsigma$ $\kappa\alpha\dot{\iota}$ $\nu\nu\kappa\tau\dot{o}\varsigma$)[225] crying to God. They are left alone in a world that oppresses and opposes them, but the attitude of God is not like that of the wicked judge. Jesus argues, if this wicked judge will vindicate this woman, how much more will the good God vindicate His own elect.[226] Jesus indicates that the disciples' only hope of attaining certain vindication is by being persistent at all times, pleading for God's coming and the faith to be ready. For this task, which they have during the interim, they are given only the model of a destitute, resolute woman.[227]

2. The Search for the Lost Coin — Lk. 15.8—10

The second parable of importance to our discussion also comes from Lucan material in chapters 15—19, a section which Manson has labelled 'The Gospel of the Outcast'.[228] Though brief, Lk. 15.8—10 is an interesting example of a parable which involves a woman, since Jesus is drawing an analogy between the activity of a female and that of Himself or of God.[229] Although it is true that we have three parables in Lk. 15, all of which have a similar point about God's redemptive activity and His joy over the repentance of the lost, Plummer is correct in noting that the $\epsilon\dot{\iota}\pi\epsilon\nu$ $\delta\dot{\epsilon}$ in 15.11 clearly separates the story of the prodigal son from the two preceding parables.[230] This is why Jeremias can call the parables of the lost sheep and the lost coin, twin parables — they 'play on the contrast between man and woman, and perhaps between rich and poor'.[231] Indeed, they play on the contrast between the roles men and women assumed in Jesus' time. But this contrast is meant neither to disparage either role, nor to elevate one above the other as more important; rather, it illustrates in a pointed fashion that both the activity of the man and the woman are equally admirable and important, and may equally well serve as analogies to the activity of God in Jesus' ministry.[232]

For various reasons it has been suspected that this parable has been created either by the Christian community before Luke gathered this material,[233] or, as Lk. 15.8—10 is uniquely Lucan, by Luke himself.[234] Against this it must be pointed out, as Bultmann admits, that the doubling of parables or parabolic phrases with similar meaning is a very old and widespread technique found even in the OT (cf. Jer. 2.32, Is. 1.22) and is especially common in Semitic writings.[235] Thus, it is not sufficient as a ground for alleging that verses 8—10 are secondary to note that we have twin parables in verses 4—7, and 8—10. Jesus could easily have been responsible for the duplication and, in view of evidence we have examined elsewhere in this chapter that Jesus made a point of using male and female examples to teach the same point, it is quite plausible that we have another 'pair' formed by Jesus here. In favour of this view is the fact that, 'The thought and situation in the parable are Palestinian.'[236] There are, however, some signs of Lucan editing and stylistic retouching,[237] and the language of this parable is more Lucan than its immediate predecessor in chapter 15. The application in verse 10 is possibly secondary; however, the parable does require some sort of application and we would expect it to end with something like, 'rejoicing over the finding of one lost sinner' rather than with ἐπὶ ἑνὶ ἁμαρτωλῷ μετανοοῦντι (if verse 10 was a later addition). Verses 8–10 then will probably reveal something of Jesus' and Luke's attitude toward women.[238]

At the beginning we are told of a woman who had ten drachmas but had lost one. Jeremias suggests that the ten coins were the woman's dowry and may have been worn by her on her headdress.[239] If so, she was poor and her diligent search for the coin is understandable. It may also mean that Luke wishes to contrast this poor woman with the preceding shepherd who, with his one hundred sheep, would have been financially comfortable. This woman would lose the equivalent of a day's wages if she did not find the coin;[240] thus, she commences a thorough search of her dark, windowless, oriental home. She seeks carefully, leaving no corner uninspected until she finds the coin. The woman's reaction to this discovery was joy so great that despite her impecunity she called her women friends and neighbours because she wished to share her joy with them, perhaps in a small celebration.[241]

To this point, Jesus has presented only His human analogy to the theological point He wishes to make. He concludes by making the point of comparison plain – γίνεται χαρὰ ἐνώπιον τῶν ἀγγέλων τοῦ θεοῦ ἐπὶ ἑνὶ ἁμαρτωλῷ μετανοοῦντι. Is Jesus intending to compare this woman's activities with those of God the Father or His own? While the last verse indicates that the rejoicing takes place in heaven, Hunter remarks, 'the three great parables of Luke 15 ... are all ripostes to scribes and Pharisees who had criticized Jesus for consorting with publicans and sinners'.[242] Thus, it is better not to distinguish the work of the Father and the Son here. God's redeeming activity, especially to 'the lost', was manifested supremely in the person and ministry of Jesus – the fruit of His labour causes joy in heaven.[243]

Summing up what this parable has to say about women, we note that Jesus' choice of this housewife (perhaps a widow)[244] as an example showed that women (15.8–10), as well as men (15.1–7), and their work were considered by Jesus to be equally good points of analogy to describe the activity of the heavenly Father in finding the lost. It also reflects a concern on Jesus' part to convey the Good News in terms with which women could identify.[245]

3. The Leaven and the Dough — Mt. 13.33 (Lk. 13.20—1)

The parable of the leaven follows that of the mustard seed in both Matthew and Luke, but not in Mark. The two parables may have been an original pair from which Mark (and the Gospel of Thomas) chose to use only one member. That Matthew and Luke have them together probably indicates that the mustard seed and the leaven parables were twins in the Q material. Matthew appears to have conflated material from Mark and Q while Luke shows no trace of influence from Mark except perhaps in the double introduction.[246] Kümmel argues that the reasons usually given for assuming that these two parables were not an original pair (that Mark omits a member and that the mustard seed and seed growing secretly are juxtaposed in Mark, and the new introduction) are insufficient and wholly formal.[247] This is probably a correct conclusion, for it is quite possible that Mark created the juxtaposition of the two seed parables in question and an introductory formula was commonly used in Jewish circles to introduce any parable.

As we have them together in Matthew and Luke, these two parables draw analogies between the functions and roles of men and women, and the nature of the Kingdom. The former focuses on the external labour of a man planting a seed; the latter depicts the indoor work of a woman putting leaven in dough. The presence of this complementary male— female parallelism may favour the view that these two parables were told originally as twins since, as Jeremias says, 'Jesus himself favoured the reduplication of similes as a means of illustration.'[248] If such twins do convey the same message, then the reason for telling them would be related to the fact that a man is the focus in one, a woman in the other. This may imply that Jesus deliberately chose His illustrations so as to emphasize that the Good News was equally for men and women, and that their present roles and functions were equally good and positive points of analogy to His work.[249]

Beyond this only a few other remarks need to be made. Firstly, it is a γυνή who puts the leaven in the dough. This is not unexpected considering that it was 'woman's work' to make the bread.[250] Since Jesus is drawing a positive analogy between a woman's work and His own crucial work of preaching (leavening the whole world with the leaven of the Gospel), this would seem to indicate that Jesus presupposed the worth of such 'woman's work'.[251] Secondly, the leaven which this woman took is hidden in σάτα τρία ἀλεύρου. The last word refers to wheat flour or meal,[252] but the surprising thing is the amount of meal — no less than 0.5 bushel,[253] which could probably feed one hundred people.[254] This may be a case of comic exaggeration since normally no housewife would bake so much bread.[255] Jeremias argues that this is an eschatological touch added to the original parable at some point in the transmission of the tradition.[256] It is more likely that the three measures are part of the original parable because it is not the leaven (Kingdom agent) which is qualified here, but the dough, and this may be part of the comic effect.[257] Funk suggests that we see this as a baking for a festive occasion of significant proportions.[258] If Jesus is implying by the huge amount of dough that this is a baking for a special offering or occasion, then reversal of expectations may be intended by mentioning the leaven and the woman, for it is the priest who bakes the unleavened cakes for special offerings.[259] Thus, perhaps not only the dynamic action of the leaven,[260] but also the amount of meal and who prepares it may tell us something of the nature, the participants and the results of the eschatological Kingdom. With this parable Jesus reassures His followers that however small and insignificant the Kingdom may appear now, God/Jesus/Kingdom, like the woman/ leaven, will not cease working until the whole lump is permeated.[261]

4. The Wise and Foolish Virgins — Mt. 25.1—13

If in Mt. 13.33 (Lk. 13.20—1) it is possible that a reference to a Kingdom celebration is implicit, then this celebration is explicit in Mt. 25.1—13, and our discussion of women in Jesus' parables would not be complete without an examination of this uniquely Matthean text. Mt. 25.1—13, from the point of view of a study of women and their roles, is somewhat anomalous — 'It is the only place in the Gospels where Jesus utters any criticism either direct or in metaphorical language against women.'[262] While this is not quite accurate, it is true that this parable is singular in both its commendation of some women (the wise) and its condemnation of others (the foolish).[263]

Mt. 25.1—13 may be a twin to the parable of the talents (Mt. 25.14—30). If so, it involves the complementary male—female parallelism found in Luke, and it intimates the equality of male and female in regard both to God's blessings and banes, and to their ability to be included in or excluded from the Kingdom.[264] W.D. Ridley, remarking on these twin parables, notes the 'contrast between the man-side and the woman-side of human nature pervades the two parables, and appears to have a distinctive purpose'.[265] In the talents parable, the interval is depicted as one of labour; in Mt. 25.1—13 it is a period of waiting. 'There, judgement comes to the slothful; here to those women who are not prepared. There the question is one of the outer life; here of the inner life ... There of action; here of insight.'[266] Thus, we see the Evangelist drawing on the common roles, joys and anxieties which Jewish women had in his day in order to make a point to the followers of Jesus about the eschatological coming of the Bridegroom.[267]

A difficulty arises when one tries to determine what the original form of this parable was and whether any of it derived from Jesus Himself. The parable begins with the word τότε, a favourite of Matthew, which links this pericope back to the time framework in the preceding section and forward to the future coming of the Bridegroom.[268] Many difficulties are solved when one recognizes that verse 1 is an introductory remark of the Evangelist explaining the theme of the parable and not an actual part of the narration itself.[269] Then too, one should perhaps see verse 13 as the Evangelist's moralizing conclusion for his audience.

Klostermann and Bultmann argue that there is 'in der vorliegenden Form eine völlig von Allegorie überwucherte Bildung'.[270] Bultmann claims that the allegory was constructed out of its application but that the creator misinterpreted Jewish wedding customs in doing so.[271] In regard to the latter point it appears that Jeremias has shown that the presentation of the wedding customs is accurate even in details.[272] In regard to the matter of allegory it can no longer be assumed that Jesus Himself did not allegorize some of the parables and stories he told. As R.E. Brown points out, 'there is no really sharp distinction between parable and allegory in the Semitic mind ... Therefore, there is no reason to believe that Jesus of Nazareth in His *meshalim* ever made a distinction between parable and allegory.'[273] Thus, 'there is no ground for denying on principle that these allegorizing features were Jesus' own'.[274] In regard to the parable under discussion we do not wish to deny that later interpreters of this example may have attempted to add allegorical features to it. Indeed, it appears that the addition of καὶ τῆς νύμφης is an attempt to conform this parable to a more conventional and allegorical mode that the Church would recognize. The absence of the mention of any bride in verses 5, 6 make it likely that καὶ τῆς νύμφης is such a later addition.[275] The reference to the Bridegroom in this parable, however, should probably not be taken as a sign that it is a later Church formulation, as Kümmel rightly points out (cf. Mk 2.19*a*).[276] It is entirely possible that Jesus would refer to Himself in a veiled way in this parable as the Bridegroom.

The other major difficulty in seeing this parable in its present form as authentic Jesus material is its eschatological orientation. Dodd and Jeremias both maintain that the parable was originally a 'crisis' parable which has been rewritten to speak to an eschatological problem, i.e., the delay of the Parousia.[277] This presupposes that Jesus Himself could not have foreseen an interval between the completion of His earthly ministry and the eschaton, a matter about which there is no consensus among scholars. Kümmel and Marshall are probably right that in order to adopt the view of Dodd and Jeremias, one must jettison the Bridegroom imagery about a coming person and indulge in wholesale rewriting.[278] Yet this parable has certain features involving the Bridegroom imagery that point to its earliness. Some weight must be given to the fact that it is the bridesmaids, not the bride, that are presented as positive and negative examples for the audience. One must also take seriously the likelihood that Mk 2.19*a* indicates that Jesus did refer to Himself as the Bridegroom and that this self-identification led to the use in 2 Cor. 11.2 and later tradition. Then, too, the joyful nature of the event does not fit in with the idea that the parable is simply warning against a coming crisis; rather, it is an encouragement to be prepared so that one may participate in the Messianic banquet and not be left out.[279] We conclude then that there are enough indications that this parable (minus the Matthean introduction and application, verses 1, 13) is authentic Jesus material about the coming Bridegroom and may be examined to see if incidentally it reveals anything about Jesus' view of women.

The first matter of significance for our purposes is that Jesus chose virgin maidens to illustrate His point about the saints being prepared, a choice possibly made because these virgins actually played a crucial part in the nuptial celebration which constitutes His illustration. They were always given the role of torch-bearers[280] in the torch-light procession to the groom's own house, and the nocturnal torch-light celebration dance held outside that house.[281] Considering this role, the virgins' knowledge that the bridegroom might come at any time, and their marital status, if they are unprepared their negligence is truly inexcusable. Jesus likens their role to that of the joyous role of the saints meeting and celebrating with the Bridegroom in the Kingdom.

The message of preparation is brought home in the illustration because the women were the bearers of torches which could burn for only about fifteen minutes at a time,[282] and thus it was incumbent upon them to bring extra oil because no one knew when the bridegroom would arrive. They were to wait in full preparation at the bride's house until that time. There is no criticism of the fact that these women fell asleep, for that was true of both the wise and the foolish virgins.[283] But one group slept the sleep of those who are prepared to leave at a moment's notice no matter how long the wait; the other group did not.[284] The main criticism is that the foolish virgins failed to come prepared with enough oil. There have been many speculations as to what the oil symbolized, but perhaps this is to over-allegorize. Those who have the extra oil are prepared; those without are not. This meant that the foolish virgins had to go for more oil, and thus they arrived at the groom's house too late to perform the role expected of them as is indicated by the fact that all the others are inside at the feast and the door is closed.[285] Obedience through proper preparation and fulfilling one's appointed role is necessary if one is to enter the feast.

Finally, this feast is not pictured as an all male feast, but one at which both men and women, bridegroom and bridesmaids, attend. This is not in conflict with what we know of Jewish meals of celebration such as a wedding or Passover feast.[286] Nevertheless, the presence of men and women at this feast could symbolize the equal position men and women have and will have in the Kingdom which Jesus brings. Jesus used the foolish virgins as negative examples, and the wise virgins as positive examples for His disciples. The wise virgins' preparedness to perform their roles is to be emulated if one wishes to partake in the marital feast when the Bridegroom returns.

C. Women and Female Imagery in the Judgment Sayings

Our survey of Jesus' attitudes toward women and their roles as reflected in His teaching would not be complete without an examination of how women or female imagery figure in His sayings about the Last Judgment and the judgment on Jerusalem. What is significant about these last days teachings is that they reflect the same male—female parallelism, and the same equality of men and women as objects of God's salvation and judgment that we have found elsewhere in Jesus' teaching.

1. The Queen of the South — Mt. 12.42 (Lk. 11.31)

As we have seen in Mt. 25.1—13, Jesus did not hesitate to use women as both positive and negative examples of God's dealing with mankind.[287] In the course of the presentation of the sign of Jonah, there are two illustrations to punctuate this declaration — the men of Nineveh, and the Queen of the South.[288] Schweizer suggests that the whole group of sayings (Mt. 12.40—2/Lk. 11.29—32) was an original unity to be traced back to Jesus,[289] with the possible exception of Mt. 12.42*b* (Lk. 11.32*b*, καὶ ἰδού). They were found together in the Q material by Matthew and Luke.[290]

The βασίλισσα νότου,[291] because of what follows about Solomon, is clearly the Queen of Sheba of OT fame. She came to Solomon 'to test him with difficult questions' (1 Kgs 10.1, 2 Chr. 9.1).[292] Since Jesus was being tested, His choice of the Queen of the South and Solomon was most apt for this occasion. Because of the way Jesus presents His reply, His listeners as part of this generation are in the end the ones being weighed in the balance: 'The Queen of the South will rise at the judgment with the men of this generation and condemn them.'[293] She will appear in court on Judgment Day as a key witness for the prosecution against this generation.[294] More importantly, her witness will not be thrown out of that final court as it probably would be in rabbinic Judaism; it will be accepted as a decisive testimony condemning this generation.[295] Even a Gentile woman compares favourably with Jesus' audience, for she recognized the favour of Yahweh in Solomon's wise words and ways; yet, this generation cannot understand the greater wisdom which Jesus reveals about the in-breaking Kingdom. Here again is an illustration of a repeated Gospel motif — a woman (in this case, undesirable and foreign) being praised as exemplary in the presence of those who ought to be the examples, the Jews.[296]

2. The Final Separation — Lk. 17.34—5 (Mt. 24.40—1)

The discussion of the final separation in Luke 17 (cf. Matthew 24), probably Q material which both Matthew and Luke have drawn on, provides evidence that the Gospel tradition is concerned to show how eschatological events affect both men and women. Possibly, as Bultmann avers,[297] one Evangelist has changed the original text of the Q material for while both Matthew and Luke give three examples of what will happen on Judgment Day:[298] Matthew's examples involve two in a field and two at a handmill, while Luke has two in a bed and two at a handmill.[299] The First Evangelist may have assimilated his picture to Mt. 24.18. There are several indications of the earliness of the Lucan form of this material: (1) there is a freedom from parenetic expansion about watchfulness in view of the coming Judgment; (2) ὁ εἶς ... ὁ ἕτερος may be a Semitism;[300] (3) ταύτῃ τῇ νυκτί is probably original[301] and reflects Jewish expectations of Jesus' day about the time of day the Judgment would come.[302]

Characteristically Matthew describes the time as τότε ('then'), while Luke has ταύτῃ τῇ νυκτί ('in that night'). In Luke's account, the two examples fit a night-time setting — sleeping in a bed, and grinding with a handmill (which in ancient as in modern times is done by Jewish women shortly before dawn).[303] Though both Matthew and Luke describe their examples in terms of the genderless δύο, Luke probably intends us to see here one pair of men and one pair of women. This is conveyed by his use of ὁ εἶς ... ὁ ἕτερος for the former pair, and ἡ μία ... ἡ ... ἑτέρα for the latter pair.[304] Using complementary parallelism, Luke wishes to make clear here as elsewhere that 'man and woman stand side by side before God. They are equal in honor and grace',[305] and also equal in dishonour and disgrace, as half of each example reveals. Jesus' reference to women grinding is merely a descriptive statement drawing on the common roles women assumed in His own day to illustrate His point — it should not be taken as a prescriptive or even proleptic announcement of what their roles will be in 'that day'.[306] It may, however, tell us that Jesus thought some division of labour between male and female was natural and acceptable both in His own day and in the future.[307] The point of these examples is that both men and women are accountable before God as responsible human beings, and there will come a day when a person will either be taken into God's presence or left behind to face the wrath to come.[308]

3. The Mother and Daughters of Jerusalem — Part I: Mt. 23.37–9 (Lk. 13.34–5)

A judgment saying of a very different sort is to be found in Mt. 23.37–9 (Lk. 13.34–5), and it is relevant for our discussion because it involves the 'Mother' of Jerusalem. In this passage, the role of Jesus is conceived of in terms of feminine, albeit female animal, imagery.

There are three opinions about the origins of this saying: (1) that it came from a Jewish source and is an utterance of a supra-historical being called Wisdom;[309] (2) that it is a Christian formulation based on Jewish wisdom material;[310] and (3) that it is a genuine Jesus saying and that He used wisdom terminology to express His feelings about Jerusalem.[311] Haenchen rightly points out that while a wisdom saying may be in the background (cf. Prov. 4.20–33) it is difficult to argue for a wisdom persona here.[312] The wisdom word is about a future sending of prophets, but here the sending is a past act. Then too the imagery of a bird (not a wisdom persona) gathering in its young is often ascribed to God or the Shekinah in Jewish literature.[313] Bultmann himself admits that the surviving fragments of Jewish wisdom speculation that we have do not say that Wisdom as she departed referred to her coming judgment.[314] The wisdom view is partially based on the questionable assumption that Mt. 23.37–9 is a continuation of Mt. 23.34–6. It is not usually Luke's practice to break up his sources and we find the Lucan version of Mt. 23.34–6 at Lk. 11.49–51.[315] It is Matthew especially who is noted for grouping related material together on a topical or 'Stichwort' basis. Against the view that we have a late Christian formulation is the fact that Burney and Manson have shown that Mt. 23.37–9/Lk. 13.34–5 appears to be a

reproduction of a saying originally in Aramaic with *kina* or *dirge* rhythm.[316]
As M'Neile points out the third view has a certain advantage for, 'there is
nothing which forbids the whole passage to be understood as an excla-
mation by Jesus Himself'.[317] Even the identification of Jesus and the
Coming One in verse 35*b* is cryptic enough to discourage the suggestion
that it originated in the Christian community rather than on Jesus' lips.
It is possible, however, that in the Q material God was the subject of
ἠθέλησα.[318] Apart from this it appears we have a saying of Jesus here
that has come down to us with little alteration.[319]

The expression ὃν τρόπον ('in the manner which', 'just as') in both
Matthew and Luke, makes clear that Jesus is speaking of a comparison of
functions, not natures. He would have gathered in Jerusalem's children
in the same manner as the mother bird gathers in her brood under her
wings.[320] The expression by Jesus of His feminine role of gathering together the lost children of Israel and caring for them comes in the midst
of His lament over Jerusalem. Matthew and Luke have placed this apos-
trophe in very different portions of their Gospel.[321] When Jesus says,
'Jerusalem, Jerusalem, you who kill the prophets and stone those sent to
you, how often I have longed to gather your children together as a hen
gathers her chicks under her wings, but you were not willing',[322] we are
reminded of the lament of God over His wayward children in Hosea, or,
since feminine imagery is used here, Rachel weeping for her lost children.[323]
It should not be overlooked that Jesus takes on a role normally performed
by a Jewish woman of publicly and proleptically mourning for Jerusalem.[324]
Also, Jesus chooses here one of the most proverbially gender distinctive
and instinctive roles a woman or female animal takes when He describes
His desires in terms of a mother's care and protection, which may tell us
something of how He felt about a loving mother's role.[325]

4. The Mother and Daughters of Jerusalem —
   Part II: Lk. 23.27—31

Lk. 23.27—31, a passage unique to Luke, raises several critical problems
which must be discussed before we exegete this material. It has been
argued by Bultmann that verses 29—31 record a Christian prophecy
placed on Jesus' lips. He appears to maintain that this prophecy came
from an Aramaic speaking community and thus is old, though not authentic, Jesus material.[326] Since this is material peculiar to Luke, it could
also be argued that it is his own composition reflecting his interest in
Jesus' attitudes toward women. Against the latter assumption are the
various elements Bultmann points out that indicate an Aramaic original.[327]

In addition, Taylor lists καὶ ὡς (temporal), the vocative θυγατέρες
Ἰερουσαλήμ, ἐρεῖν, ἄρξομαι with infinitive, στραφεὶς κλαίεω (twice), and
the impersonal plural ποιοῦσιν (which is an Aramaism), as elements that
point to a pre-Lucan source.[328] Against the view that we have a Christian
prophecy are two factors. (1) The conduct of Jesus and of the women in
this incident may be described as true to Jewish life in Jesus' day and true
to the characteristic way Jesus showed selfless concern for others.[329] (2)
The saying in verse 31 is most probably proverbial as it has certain parallels
to other Semitic Jewish proverbs of a somewhat enigmatic nature.[330] The
question then becomes, were early Christian prophets in the practice of
citing or adapting enigmatic Jewish proverbs in their prophecies, and did
the early Christian community place such enigmatic sayings on Jesus' lips?
Against answering this last question affirmatively is the fact that many of
the major concerns of the early Church are not addressed in the Jesus
material. If the point of placing such sayings on Jesus' lips was so that the
living voice of Jesus could address current concerns clearly, then this text
does not seem to fulfill that purpose. Thus, it appears that the objections
to seeing this passage as deriving from a *Sitz im Leben Jesu* fall short of
conviction. It must, however, be borne in mind that the saying in verse 30
is based on the LXX version of Hosea 10.8 and it is possible that Is. 54.1
in some form is in the background of verse 29 (though if so, the meaning
is considerably altered).[331] In regard to verse 30, it is likely that Luke
has conformed the quotation to the version of the OT with which he
(and perhaps his audience) was most familiar. The allusions in verse 29
and the proverb in verse 31 could derive from Jesus Himself for He was
well-versed in the Scriptures and traditions of His people.[332]

Jesus, who had lamented and wept over the fate of Jerusalem, now
reaches the point on His own *via dolorosa* where the daughters of Jerusalem
lament for Him. We are told that He was followed by πολὺ πλῆθος τοῦ
λαοῦ καὶ γυναικῶν αἳ ἐκόπτοντο καὶ ἐθρήνουν αὐτόν. These two groups are
seen by Luke as distinct entities. It is the women alone who are said to be
mourning and wailing, and it is to them that Jesus addresses His comments.[333] It was not uncommon for Jews to mourn prior to a death,[334]
especially if they were relatives of the one mourned, or if he was a famous
person whose death would mean a great loss.[335] But we know of no
instance where *professional* mourners were called upon to perform their
task proleptically. Also, it is unlikely that Luke intends us to think that
the θυγατέρες Ἰερουσαλήμ are the women mentioned in Lk. 8.1−3 as
Jesus' travelling companions,[336] though it is conceivable that they were
followers of Jesus who lived in the Jerusalem area and were with Him only
when He visited the city. It has also been suggested that they were local

women who travelled out to witness executions and provide opiates for
the condemned man.[337] It seems most probable that these women were
inhabitants of Jerusalem who were sympathetic to Jesus and grieved at
His present plight. Their act was a spontaneous show of their feelings, but
it was also a dangerous one, for the Jews did not permit such public crying
and wailing for a criminal.[338]

Jesus addresses them as a group that will share the destiny of Jerusalem.[339]
In view of what is about to happen to their homes and families, he suggests
that they should weep for themselves and for their own children, not for
Him. Jesus (perhaps drawing on Is. 54.1–2), says to these women, 'Behold,
the time will come when you will say "Blessed are the barren women, the
wombs that never bore, and the breasts that never nursed!" '[340] He is not
saying that barrenness or childlessness is in itself a blessing, only that in
'that day' one's blessings become one's burdens, and thus those without
children are better off.[341] Jesus knew well that for these daughters of
Jerusalem their children were their greatest delight, and thus His address
to them is dramatic and appropriate. The loss of their children will lead
them to ultimate despair, to cry out for a speedy death. 'They will say to
the mountains, "fall on us", and to the hills, "cover us".'[342]

Jesus leaves these women, who represent the heart of the old Israel,
with a question — If an innocent man cannot escape the Judgment, what
will happen to guilty Israel, a hollow, rotting tree fit only for a fiery
consummation?[343] Even in the waning minutes of His earthly ministry,
Jesus shows His concern for women by identifying with their plight, for
they too must face suffering and Judgment as He does now.

D. Jesus' Attitude Toward Women Reflected in His Words

Having completed our examination of the teaching of Jesus as it bears on
women and their roles, we can draw some conclusions. Some of Jesus'
teaching is provocative and stands in contrast to many commonly held
views of His day. For instance, Jesus' teaching on filial piety, as it relates
to the matter of corban, stands in contrast to what we know of rabbinic
attitudes about vows and oaths. In this teaching Jesus rejects allowing
vows to interfere with one's duty to honour parents, and thus rejects
rabbinic tradition which would not permit the annulment of such vows.
The effect of this teaching is to strengthen the traditional family structure
and intensify a child's obligation to honour both mother and father. That
Jesus affirms the mother's right to respect and material support from her
children reflects Jesus' high estimation and appreciation of both the
personhood and role of the mother. Further, there may be implicit in

Jesus' unreservedly positive attitudes about children a positive estimation of women in their role of child-bearer.

Further evidence of Jesus' appreciation of and desire to strengthen the physical family structure surfaces in Jesus' teaching on marriage, divorce and adultery. In contrast to common rabbinic teaching, Jesus does not warn men against the wiles of loose women, but against their own lust and aggression that leads women into sin (Mt. 5.27–8). Both the responsibility and the onus for such sin is placed on the male, and consideration is given to the woman, the more often suspected party in a male-oriented society. What is intriguing about this teaching is that it is not only a reaffirmation of men's leadership and responsibility for the community welfare, but also an attempt to liberate women from a social stereotype. Jesus does not approve of a system where a man's lust is not taken as seriously as a woman's seduction. As in Matthew 5, we find in Jn 7.53–8.11 a critique of men who fail to live up to their responsibility of being paradigms of virtue for the community. The net effect of Jesus' teaching on marriage and divorce is that the traditional family strucure is not only reaffirmed but also strengthened through the intensification of the demands made on a husband's fidelity and the rejection of divorce outright. This teaching gives women greater security in marriage. By appealing to the creation plan and the one flesh union, Jesus equally rejects male and female promiscuity and freedom to divorce, thus requiring a standard of fidelity and life-long partnership that goes beyond much of the teaching of the rabbis on this subject. No other rabbi spoke of a man committing adultery against his former wife by remarriage.

While Jesus was countering stereotypes of women as temptresses and giving them a more secure basis from which to operate in their traditional roles, He also gave a teaching on singleness which allowed some believers to live and work in roles apart from those involved in the traditional family structure. It is not clear whether or not Jesus ever rejected specifically the rabbinic mandate that all (or at least all men) who are able must be fruitful and multiply; but clearly this teaching on eunuchs for the Kingdom and some of the more radical statements on the cost of discipleship reflect a new attitude toward the single person. We have conjectured that it was Jesus' teaching on eunuchs and the cost of discipleship that allowed some women to be present among Jesus' travelling company (Lk. 8.1–3). It is also possible that the teaching in Mt. 19.10–12 provided the precedent for women in the Christian community to be allowed to remain single and serve the community (Ac. 21.9). It is true that Jesus' views remained patriarchal, but male headship for Jesus meant extra responsibility, not extra privilege (cf. Mt. 5.27–32). Jesus appealed to the creation plan and the new demands of the Kingdom in order to reform common misunderstandings in regard to God's will about marriage, divorce, children and the family.

Lest the impression be given that Jesus wished to strengthen the traditional family structure as an end in itself, it must be affirmed that all His teaching on such subjects is conditioned by the demands of discipleship. The physical family must be seen in light of the context of the higher priorities of the family of faith. As we shall see, the basis of the new Kingdom community is not kinship ties, but association between disciples and Master, disciple and disciple (cf. below on Mk 3.33—5). While some rabbis recognized that discipleship had higher claims than one's family for men, it is doubtful whether anyone before Jesus taught this principle to women (cf. below on Lk. 10.38—42). That Jesus gave positive teaching on the physical family implies that He thought there was no necessary conflict between the demands of the family of faith and of the physcial family so long as the latter was oriented to serve rather than to sever the former. All of this is most significant in its effects on women and their roles since it is clear that they are called to be disciples first and foremost, and their roles as wives or mothers then necessarily become subordinate, or at least oriented so as not to interfere with the demands of discipleship.

It is not clear whether or not Jesus thought that marital relations would cease in the age to come. Probably, He saw marrying and propagating as ceasing when the Kingdom was consummated, but this does not necessarily entail the dissolution of the marital bond in all respects. In any event, it is clear that Jesus rejected those views of the rabbis in which the age to come is envisioned as simply this age on a grander scale. Jesus' sayings involving widows give us a picture of His concern for a particular disadvantaged group of women. Jesus shows equal concern for the plight of widows with property as for those who were impoverished. It is perhaps fair to say that Jesus' concern for widows is not merely one facet of His concern for the poor and disenfranchised (Mk 12.40, 41—4).

A more indirect source of information about Jesus' attitude toward women may be found in His parables, and the eschatological sayings. For instance, in the parable of the obstinate widow and the obdurate judge (Lk. 18.1—8) we see manifested not only a concern for a widow, but also a desire to present even indigent (even nagging or annoying) women as models in at least one regard for the behaviour of the disciples. We noted the elements of reversal of expectations or roles involved in such sayings. In addition, while Luke stresses male—female parallelism more than the other Evangelists, there are good reasons for thinking that Jesus Himself deliberately indulged in the pairings of sayings with a similar message — one directed to females, and the other to males. In this manner, both Jesus and especially Luke indicate their desire to see women as equally worthy to be examples, equally objects of God's grace, and equally an accepted part of their audiences. There are also parables and sayings where Jesus likens God's or even His own redemptive activities to the everyday activities of women (Lk. 15.8—10) and even a female animal (Mt. 23.37—39 and parallels). The parables of the lost coin and the leaven (Lk. 15.8—10, Mt. 13.33/Lk. 13.20—1) show that Jesus took care to express His Kingdom message so that women would be able to identify with it immediately. The parable of the wise and foolish virgins uses women as both positive and negative examples for Jesus' disciples, and there is perhaps a hint of a woman's right to participate in the Messianic banquet when the Bridegroom returns for His own.

If women are envisioned equally with men as objects of God's grace and participants in the community of Jesus and the consummated Kingdom, then it is also true that such sayings as Lk. 17.34—5 reveal that women are equally objects of God's Judgment. Mt. 12.42 and parallels indicates Jesus' readiness to refer even to a Gentile woman as a valid witness against men on the Day of Judgment, and His willingness to stress how God's ways are often the opposite of what men expect. What Jew would expect to be told that a Gentile queen would stand as a witness against his generation? Lk. 23.27—31 may be meant as an example of how Jesus identified with a woman's plight (in this case, a future plight).

Jesus' teaching relating to women and their roles is sometimes radical, sometimes reformational, and usually controversial in its original setting. Even when Luke wrote his Gospel, it is likely that the very reason he felt a need to stress male—female parallelism and Jesus' positive statements about women was that his own audience had strong reservations about some of Jesus' views on the subject. The case for women being seen as equal objects of God's grace and equal examples for disciples, as well as being disciples, had still to be argued when Luke wrote his Gospel. All of this teaching prepares us for an examination of Jesus' actions, and His manner of relating to harlots, widows, small girls, foreign women, mothers and women made unclean through illness or incapacitated through injury.

WOMEN AND THE DEEDS OF JESUS

Considerable space is devoted in the Gospels to Jesus' interactions with women from all walks of life. In some instances, a healing of a woman is involved; in others, Jesus helps certain women by revealing their sins, forgiving their sins, or healing their relatives. After a review of seven pericopes dealing with specific women in the Gospels, we can evaluate Jesus' attitude toward women as reflected in His actions toward them.

A. Stories of Help and Healing

1. The Lucan Anointing – Lk. 7.36–50

Martin Dibelius in his brief discussion of Lk. 7.36–50 contends that this narrative is a product of pious curiosity concerning secondary figures in the Gospel tradition. He believes that, 'the legendary character of the narrative cannot be disputed'.[1] Nevertheless, most scholars have been willing to dispute this judgment at least in regard to a portion of Lk. 7.36–50, and thus its character requires closer scrutiny. One of the minor difficulties this text presents is whether or not it may be pronounced a unified whole or a combination of various traditions and, if it is the latter, which of these traditions is the core to which later additions were made. Bultmann claims that the parable (verses 41–3 with 47a) was the original nucleus to which the remainder has been added at a later date.[2] Essentially the opposite view has been maintained also – that the story was original to which was added the two debtors parable.[3] The fundamental reason for arguing in either of these fashions is that it is thought that the message of the story and that of the parable contradict one another. This conclusion, however, turns mainly on a point of exegesis in regard to the proper interpretation of verse 47. J.J. Donohue has argued that even if the point of the parable is that much forgiveness begets much love, and that of the story that much love for Jesus leads to much forgiveness, the two ideas need not be mutually exclusive.[4] Even if this is so, it seems unlikely that either Jesus or the Evangelist would juxtapose two such potentially confusing messages together. A more viable approach is that which argues that even if the Evangelist or his predecessors have combined two different sources here, it is unlikely that an author such as Luke would allow an obvious contradiction to stand in his narrative. It is even more unlikely that he would create such a difficulty. Thus, if there is a view that can show how the narrative could be perceived by the Evangelist as being a unified whole (without exegetical gymnastics), it would be preferable to any view that conceives of the author as inept in the handling of his sources. Such a view has been advanced by those who have argued that verse 47 should probably be translated, 'Because, I say to you, her many sins are forgiven, she loves much.'[5] The question remains, however, what the historical value of this narrative is, even if it is presenting a unified whole. It is possible that Luke has radically revised the Marcan anointing story (14.3–9) and added a parable to suit his purposes. The view that there is only one original narrative behind all the anointing stories will be discussed in detail in our next chapter.[6] For now it is sufficient to say that a more probable view is that there are two different traditions about Jesus being anointed by a woman which may have interacted with one another in their language and details at the stage of oral transmission.[7] This would not be surprising since the two stories have certain similarities. In regard to Luke's contribution to the narrative, verse 50 may be his addition of a 'typical' remark made by Jesus in such cases, or perhaps his own formulation indicating how he believed Jesus reacted in such circumstances.[8] Verse 48 may also be Luke's addition because he had not mentioned a previous encounter of Jesus or His message with this woman.[9] Further, Luke's ability as a descriptive writer shines through in this narrative.[10] Lk. 7.36–47, 49 was probably an original unity which Luke derived from his special source and has presented in a context and in a way to illustrate the scandal of Jesus' love for sinners (cf. Lk. 7.34) and to show how they reacted to His offer of forgiveness and healing.[11] Thus, we will examine the narrative as a literary unit, taking into account the above considerations and expecting that we may discern something about Jesus' as well as the Evangelist's views on women.

Simon the Pharisee, perhaps in order to discover for himself what kind of man Jesus was, invited Him to a banquet in His honour. The word κατεκλίθη (verse 36) tells us that this is no ordinary meal.[12] At some point after Jesus arrived, an unnamed woman entered the house to perform a deed of loving devotion. This is no ordinary woman coming into the house, but γυνὴ ἥτις ἦν ἐν τῇ πόλει ἁμαρτωλός. In this context, ἁμαρτωλός most likely means 'prostitute' (as verses 47–9 intimate).[13]

We should not be surprised that this woman enters the house uninvited. Considering the openness of Jewish homes and, more importantly, the feeling in Judaism that one should help the poor and hungry, it was not uncommon for a poor or disadvantaged person to come into a house during a banquet to beg or grab something to eat.[14] Thus, Simon is not surprised that the woman comes in during the banquet, but he is shocked at what she does. This woman is carrying an *alabastron* of perfume, much the same as that found in the Matthean and Marcan anointings. This was a common and well-known container for good perfume.[15] By mentioning the perfume at this point in the narrative, Luke intimates that it is the woman's intention to anoint Jesus.

If common banqueting customs were being followed,[16] then the woman probably is visible to Simon as she enters, but not to Jesus. His body is resting on the couch, with His feet turned away from the table toward the wall, and with His left elbow on the table itself. It is not until He later turns toward the woman (verse 44) that Jesus clearly sees her.[17] Thus, this woman is standing behind Jesus' couch near His feet.[18]

Whether or not the woman has met Jesus previously is uncertain. The presentation of her unsolicited act of anointing and her emotional outburst, however, makes it inconceivable that she had not at the very least heard of Jesus' message of forgiveness. Her act is one of loving devotion and possibly gratitude, for she sees in Jesus acceptance, rather than rejection, despite her past life of sin. Just as her tears speak of remorse over sin, so too Jesus' silence speaks of His acceptance of her gift and, more importantly, of this woman herself.[19] She is overcome and weeps on Jesus' feet. In the midst of emotion, perhaps forgetting that it was improper, she quickly wipes Jesus' feet with her hair, a clear violation of rabbinic customs of propriety.[20] By the act of kissing Jesus' feet, she also violates the laws of clean and unclean.[21] There is perhaps an implied contrast between the way she used her perfume to anoint and honour Jesus, and the way she probably used her perfume previously to attract other men.

Simon's reaction is both typical and legally correct. This woman has defiled Jesus. Simon is portrayed as expecting Jesus, as not only a teacher but also a prophet, to know what sort of person this woman is. That Jesus passes over the woman's act in silence proves to Simon's satisfaction that He is not a prophet. The use of the term teacher is intended to show that Simon has some respect for Jesus, and enough interest to invite Him to a banquet;[22] however, he has not performed for Jesus the supererogatory works of kindness (washing the feet, kiss of greeting, anointing with oil) which a gracious host would do or have done for a special guest.[23]

This was so much a part of the system of hospitality Jesus was used to in His day, that He missed it when it was omitted. By contrast, the woman's deed was one of exceptional humility and love, for it was not common in Judaism to kiss someone's feet. Kissing the feet is usually the act of someone, such as a criminal, who has just been freed or whose debt was remitted, and in some sense this was the condition of this woman.[24] That the anointing was also on the feet means that the woman is assuming a servant's function.

The example of two debtors is given in order to lead Simon to see the woman as He sees her.[25] When Jesus asks, 'Who will be more grateful to the money lender?'[26] Simon, not wishing to be trapped in his own words, responds, 'I suppose that it will be the one to whom more has been remitted.' Jesus affirms that he has judged properly. Only at this point (verse 44), in order to apply His illustration to the immediate situation, does Jesus turn to the woman clinging to His feet and, as Marshall notes, 'three aspects of the woman's deeds are contrasted with three expressions of hospitality that Simon had not shown to Jesus'.[27] Jesus says to Simon,

> 'You see this woman: when I came to your house you did not perform for me the gestures of a gracious host — foot washing, the kiss of greeting, or the anointing of my head with oil. By contrast, this woman, whose sins are indeed many,[28] bathed my feet with her tears and wiped them with her hair. Since I came in,[29] she has not ceased to kiss my feet.[30] You did not anoint my head with oil, yet she has anointed my feet with perfume.'

Yet, as Jesus has indicated to Simon at the beginning of this comparison — εἰσῆλθόν σου εἰς τὴν οἰκίαν.[31] Marshall adds, 'not only is Jesus willing to accept the touch of a sinful woman, but he even suggests that her action is more welcome to him than that of his host'.[32] Here we see a clear example of reversal — a sinful woman is praised at the expense of and by comparison to a 'good' Jewish man.

Verse 47 may indicate that he who loves much is forgiven much,[33] but οὗ χάριν need not be merely logical; there is good evidence for seeing it as causal and translating 'because'.[34] We may argue also that ὅτι logically depends on λέγω σοι not ἀφέωνται — 'I can say with confidence that her sins are forgiven *because* her love evidences it.'[35] It appears that there are no substantial difficulties in seeing the point of the parable and the story as one and the same.[36] Gratitude is the *proof*, not the *ground*, of forgiveness.

Jesus has violated the letter of the laws of clean and unclean in the presence of a Pharisee by transcending them because of His own priorities.

He has implied that Simon, by not receiving Him with more graciousness, shows that he does not bear the same grateful and loving heart toward Him that the woman does. The Evangelist concludes this discussion by including a verbal pronouncement that the woman's sins are forgiven;[37] thus, Jesus demonstrates that He is indeed a prophet for He has supernaturally discerned the thoughts of Simon's heart and knows the condition of the woman. He has taken the part of a woman who was the object of scorn and scathing remarks. Possibly He has shown He was more than a prophet by indicating that He previously had forgiven her sin (verse 47).[38] Jesus proclaims a Kingdom where the unclean are cleansed by forgiveness through faith. The breaking down of the barrier of clean and unclean and of social ostracism by forgiveness opened the door for a return of such women to a more normal life and perhaps even a place in His community. This is one reason why women often showed their gratitude and devotion to Jesus; they were finally treated by Him as fellow creatures of God without special restrictions. This same loving and liberating forgiveness is found in two other stories, that of the woman at the well, and that of the woman caught in adultery.

2. The Woman at the Well – Jn 4.4–42

In Jn 4.4–42, the author of the Fourth Gospel proceeds to develop his portrait of Jesus by presenting Him in a new and perhaps surprising setting, while still maintaining a certain continuity with the narrative in Jn 2 and 3 by drawing on some of the elements in those two chapters. In Jn 2, Jesus changes water into wine while interacting with a woman. In Jn 4, in an encounter with another woman, Jesus persuades her to exchange water for living water. Perhaps we see a contrast between Nicodemus of Jn 3, a teacher and representative of orthodox Judaism who fails to understand Jesus, and the common Samaritan woman who gains some insight into Jesus' true character.[39] The theme of Temple worship mentioned in 2.13–22 is now explained more fully in 4.1–26.[40] More significantly,

'The story of the Samaritan woman at Jacob's well (4:4–42) is in marked contrast to the negativism that surrounded those whose faith, if any, rested on signs in the latter part of chapter 2, and in chapter 3. This story deals precisely with the process of coming to faith, but in it faith is a response to Jesus' word, not to any sign.'[41]

Finally, Jesus Himself, who has been shown to be the fulfillment of OT and Jewish expectation, makes clear in this story that though salvation is of the Jews, it is for all who believe and receive it.[42]

The story of the woman at the well raises various critical problems for the student of history. The narrative appears, with the possible exception of 4.31–4, 35–8,[43] to be an original unit,[44] and it appears impossible 'to isolate a pre-Johannine nucleus'[45] from the material in Jn 4.4–30. This does not preclude the possibility that there is such a nucleus since the Fourth Evangelist is a most skilful editor and adaptor of his source material. Nevertheless, some scholars, impressed with the unity of this composition, have deduced that it is almost exclusively a theological composition of the Evangelist or his predecessors.[46] It is argued that the Samaritan woman should be taken as a 'traditional figure' treated by the Evangelist as a symbol or representative type.[47] A further factor which seems to cast doubts on the possibility that this is an historical account is the fact that the central dialogue between Jesus and the Samaritan woman appears to happen without any disciples to witness it.

On the other hand, various factors indicate that we are dealing with an actual occurrence. The story betrays a considerable knowledge of Samaritan beliefs, local colour, geographical factors, and Jew–Samaritan relationships that would seem to point us in the direction of an historical account.[48] Then too, the dialogue between Jesus and the woman seems very fitting for the occasion. It is quite believable that the woman would have understood Jesus' claims 'against the background of the Samaritan expectation of the Taheb'.[49] The difficulty of finding a plausible *Sitz im Leben* in which such a dialogue could have been preserved and passed on has perhaps been overcome by H. Riesenfeld who suggests that the Johannine discourses first took a definite shape 'in the discussions and meditations of Jesus in the circle of his disciples such as certainly took place side by side with the instruction of the disciples proper, with its more rigid forms'.[50] It is plausible that Jesus would have had informal discussions with His disciples about some of His encounters and teachings. If this is the *Sitz im Leben* for this dialogue then the major obstacles to accepting the essential elements and discussion here as a record of historical events are removed. Nonetheless, one must make due allowance for the fact that the Evangelist has made the material his own and has shaped the narrative and dialogue in expert fashion.[51] As for the contention that the Samaritan woman is a traditional or typical figure, the following factors must be said to militate against this view: (1) she cannot be seen as a personification of the Gentile world since the author presents her as a monotheist;[52] (2) she should not be seen as an allegorical figure representing the apostate and adulterous Samaritan nation since she plays an individual's role in summoning her fellow countrymen to Jesus (verse 28–30),[53] and more significantly, since it appears from 2 Kgs 17.30–1 that it was *seven*, not five, strange deities that were introduced into Samaria *simultaneously* (not in succession). 'Again, the allegory would imply that the heathen deities had been the legitimate gods of Samaria while Yahweh, whom she came to worship, was not a true "husband" at all.'[54] Thus, it is not implausible that we are dealing with an historical event in Jn 4. If such phrases as 'salvation is of the Jews' are any indication, then it appears we have here an early tradition that will yield some accurate information about the views of Jesus and the Fourth Evangelist on women.

Following our usual procedure we will first treat this passage as a literary unit. Various factors in our narrative may give us an indication of Jesus' attitude toward women. First, there is His request for a drink of water from the woman who is rightly surprised at this for two reasons: Jesus is both a Jew and a man.[55] John makes an editorial comment to explain why she was surprised – οὐ γὰρ συγχρῶνται Ἰουδαῖοι Σαμαρίταις.[56] It is hard to decide whether συγχρῶνται should be translated 'have dealings with' or 'use together with', but probably the latter is preferable since in this narrative Jews *are* having dealings with Samaritans (the disciples are buying food in town).[57] The Samaritan woman is in a somewhat similar position to that of Martha (cf. pp. 100–3 on Lk. 10.38–42). She supposes that she is the hostess and it is Jesus who needs something; however, it is Jesus who has something to bestow – living water. Thinking on an earthly plane, she believes Jesus is referring to running water, rather than standing water, and thinks she might be saved repeated trips to the well.[58] Her Samaritan pride rises to the surface in this discussion when she asks if Jesus is saying He can give better water than Father Jacob, 'who gave us the well'.[59] Jesus responds in the affirmative by saying that His water satisfies forever.[60] Despite her pride and 'Unlike many of the other people whom Jesus encounters in His ministry, the Samaritan woman wins the reader's admiration because of her openness to the revealing word of Jesus even when she does not understand. Her attitude is one of inquiry, not rejection, and it is this that makes her a suitable subject for faith.'[61]

A second revealing statement is Jesus' command that the woman go and call τὸν ἄνδρα σου. The Evangelist probably intends to indicate at this point that Jesus, through His supernatural insight, knows this woman's life and wishes to bring her sins out into the light so that they may be forgiven. The woman's response is deliberately evasive – οὐκ ἔχω ἄνδρα.[62] Jesus' rejoinder may mean either that the woman had had five legal husbands (all now deceased or divorced from her) and she was now living with a man who was not her legal husband; or that she is now living with a man who, while legally her husband by Mosaic law, is not so according to Jesus' views (cf. Mk 10.11–12). Probably, the former is meant here. In the context of Judaism it was not the custom to have more than three marriages in a life-time – legally, any number might be admissible, but morally more than three would be suspect.[63] If this woman was living with a man other than her husband, she would be ritually unclean, yet Jesus shows no signs of maintaining the distinctions of clean and unclean. He asks for a drink and continues to pursue His discussion so that she may believe, thus violating the well-known Jewish warning against speaking to a woman (especially a known harlot) in public.[64]

A third crucial factor in this interchange comes to light as the discussion turns to the matter of worship. The woman changes the subject from her own personal life to the old debate of whether Gerizim or Jerusalem was the proper place to worship. If Jesus says Jerusalem, then as a Samaritan she will reject the possibility that Jesus is the Messiah.[65] Rejecting her either/or, Jesus says that the crucial issue is not the place but the manner in which God is worshipped – in spirit and truth.[66] The Samaritans may worship the right God but ὑμεῖς προσκυνεῖτε ὃ οὐκ οἴδατε. Perhaps it is this statement that leads the woman to assert, οἶδα ὅτι Μεσσίας ἔρχεται ... ἀναγγελεῖ ἡμῖν ἄπαντα.[67] The Jews by contrast know whom they worship because salvation is from them.[68] Jesus adds, 'The hour is coming and now is' when the worship of God will depend neither on where one is nor who one is. Salvation may be from the Jews, but it is for all those who will worship God in spirit and truth. Thus, Jesus does not exclude this woman from those who may offer such worship. There is no hint of separation of male and female, and no hint of other special restrictions on women, as would apply in the Temple worship in Jerusalem.[69]

After the woman has expressed her belief about the Coming One, Jesus says ἐγώ εἰμι, ὁ λαλῶν σοι. It is possible that this is intended to be the theophanic formula, but more probably it means that Jesus is claiming to be the Messiah.[70] With this statement the Evangelist brings the first dialogue to a dramatic close, just as the disciples return from town.[71]

The disciples arrive to see Jesus talking to a woman and they probably overhear His last remark.[72] They are amazed that He would speak with this strange woman, but they are circumspect enough not to ask questions. The author indicates that they might have wanted to ask, 'What are you seeking?' or 'Why are you talking with her?'[73] The Evangelist, in typical ironic fashion, contrasts the woman who leaves her water jug (forsaking her original purpose at the well) to go into town and speak about Jesus, with the disciples who left Jesus to find mere physical sustenance.[74] He summarizes the woman's witness as follows: 'Come see a man who told me everything I have done. Could he perhaps be the Messiah?'[75] Her witness, which appears to speak openly of her own notoriety, induces the towns-people to leave the village and go in the direction of Jesus and the well.

While this travelling scene develops in the background, Jesus has His second dialogue, this time with the disciples. It is possible, as Dodd argues, that this discussion has been culled from other source(s) in which case the Evangelist has inserted it here perhaps to contrast the disciples and the Samaritan woman.[76] The disciples offer food to Him, but Jesus remarks that He has a source of nourishment unknown to them, namely, bringing this woman to faith and to the point of sharing that faith (a particular example of doing the will of God).[77] The disciples, like the woman, mis-understand Jesus' remark about food by thinking merely on the physical level. Jesus then speaks metaphorically about teaching and witnessing and the fruit it bears when it leads people to faith in Him.[78] In verse 35, Jesus tells them that they do not need to wait for the harvest time in order to do what they were sent to do. They are exhorted, 'Open your eyes and look at the fields! They are ripe for harvest.' Jesus clearly distinguishes between the reaper and the sower in verse 37.[79] The disciples are to be the reapers Jesus has sent.[80] Who then are the ἄλλοι of verse 38? Perhaps the most likely answer is, Jesus and the Samaritan woman. Jesus has sown the Word in her and, in turn, she has sown the Word in the other Samaritans. Thus, the disciples, the reapers, are not to suspect the conversation He had with this woman, or her witness in the town. Rather, the sowers and reapers are to rejoice together.[81] The disciples must not begrudge Jesus His source of nourishment, or the woman the nourishment she has received. They must turn now and see the fruit of the evangelistic work of Jesus and the woman.

The Evangelist makes clear that this woman's witness was fruitful — ἐκ δὲ τῆς πόλεως ἐκείνης πολλοὶ ἐπίστευσαν εἰς αὐτὸν τῶν Σαμαριτῶν <u>διὰ</u> τὸν λόγον τῆς γυναικὸς <u>μαρτυρούσης</u>.[82] This should be compared to Jesus' prayer — περὶ τῶν πιστευόντων διὰ τοῦ λόγου αὐτῶν εἰς ἐμέ (Jn 17.20).[83] This woman is presented as one of Jesus' witnesses, through whom others are led to Him. The Samaritans believed her, but it was necessary that they go further and believe in Him through their own contact with the Lord. The result of their encounter is that they are said to exclaim, 'This man really is the Saviour of the world.'[84]

How are we to evaluate the material in John 4? There are several possible points of view. Some might maintain that it represents exactly what happened, but that would seem not to take into consideration the evidence of redactional work and theological expansion by the Evangelist. If, as we have argued, Jn 4 has *foundations* in an historical encounter of Jesus with a Samaritan woman of ill repute, a claim which does not contend for the accuracy of every detail, then it would seem to indicate various things about Jesus' attitude toward women. It reveals that Jesus rejected various sorts of prohibitions that would have separated Him from those He came to seek and to save, such as the rabbinic warning against talking with women in public places, especially women who were known sinners. While the Evangelist is concerned to make the legal point that Jesus was willing to share a common cup with a Samaritan in contrast to the prevailing views, incidentally this text serves to reinforce what we found in Lk. 7.36–50, that Jesus did not accept the Levitical distinctions between clean and unclean persons. If Jesus did in fact share a common cup with a woman he knew to be immoral and 'unclean' by Jewish standards, it says something to us about His attitude toward the Levitical distinctions in general (though not about female uncleanness in particular). Further, the discussion in John 4 suggests that Jesus rejected the distinctions that separated Jewish and Samaritan worshippers and perhaps those imposed in the Jerusalem cult that separated men and women. This is implicit in His affirmation of worship ('neither on this mountain, nor in Jerusalem, but in spirit and truth') and the fact that He could make such statements to a Samaritan woman. Further, anyone willing to witness to and for Jesus is an acceptable witness. It may be the case that *some* of this portrayal of Jesus is more a 'typical' picture than an actual picture of what took place on this occasion. If so, then the Evangelist would still be intending to convey that these attitudes were characteristic of the historical Jesus. Finally, even if the narrative is *wholly* a creation of the Evangelist, it seems likely that the author is suggesting that the attitude described is theologically grounded in the attitudes and teachings of Jesus.

On the level of the Evangelist's intentions we may note the following: (1) If Jn 4.31–4 and 35–8 is an insertion from a traditional source, then it is the Evangelist who is portraying this woman as a 'sower' and the disciples as somewhat less spiritually perceptive and active in their faith than she. The Samaritans believed because of this woman's witness. With typical irony, the Evangelist paints a contrast between the disciples who bring Jesus physical food that does not satisfy, while a woman brings Jesus His true spiritual food by helping Him to complete God's work. Once again, the pattern of reversal of expectations and of expected male–female roles becomes apparent. (2) The language about Jesus as the 'Saviour of the World' is perhaps the Evangelist's formulation, but this does not preclude the possibility that the woman's witness led some Samaritans to Jesus and that they made some sort of faith affirmation. (3) Some of the staging, the ironic contrast, and the presentation of

Jesus as a supernatural figure may be the Evangelist's work. In the story Jesus' asking for water seems ironic, while in the actual encounter it may have been a simple request from a thirsty man. (4) What the Evangelist intends to convey by this literary unit may be summed up briefly. Jesus and the woman had discussed a more universal source of life and basis of worship. The witness of Jesus and this sinful Samaritan woman bore fruit in Samaria and led to the confession and acknowledgement of the presence of the universal Saviour. 'The hour is coming and now is' when even women, even Samaritan women, even sinful Samaritan women, may be both members and messengers of this King and His Kingdom.

3. The Syrophoenician Woman — Mk 7.24–30 (Mt. 15.21–8)

The story of the Syrophoenician woman has long been recognized as presenting one of the 'hard sayings' of Jesus. It is most unlikely that the Church would have created this saying, given the flow of Gentiles into the community and a growing devotion to Christ. 'If the Evangelist were to yield to the temptation to reconcile his narrative with the current situation, it would certainly have been in this instance. The fact that he did not attests to his having kept faith with the tradition.'[85] This story argues strongly against the view that the Gospel writers were substantive authors in the modern sense of the word. They were a great deal more constrained by tradition and their sources, like their predecessors were in Judaism, than many modern scholars would admit. Each Evangelist, however, has a certain freedom to rearrange and recast his material to stress certain points more or less than the other Gospel writers in accordance with his individual purposes. Even in this pericope there are certain obvious differences between Matthew and Mark which require explanation. Nevertheless, the argument of Derrett that Mark built up a story around a saying of Jesus using the OT, is unconvincing. One must explain why someone writing at a time when Gentiles were already in the Church would create an apparently offensive story, choosing as a character a Syrophoenician woman who would be suspect to Jewish–Christians. Even the 'positive' conclusion of this story does not mitigate the harshness of the majority of the pericope.[86] Accordingly, we can examine this pericope with a certain conviction that it does reflect something of Jesus' own attitude toward Gentiles, especially Gentile women.

This pericope is the only example in Mark's (and perhaps Matthew's) Gospel where the healed patient is definitely a Gentile pagan.[87] It is apparently a story Luke found too offensive for his audience and thus does not follow his Marcan source at this point.[88] The Fourth Evangelist has a story that serves a similar purpose to Mk 7.24—30, i.e., the Samaritan woman in Jn 4. The following points of contact between the two should be noted: (1) In Mark's version of the Syrophoenician woman, Jesus appears to be withdrawing from a predominantly Jewish area because of misunderstanding and possible persecution at the hands of the scribes and Pharisees (7.1—23).[89] The withdrawal in Jn 4.1—3 is for similar reasons. (2) Both narratives may be seen as an illustration of Jesus' dismissal of distinctions of clean and unclean (reading Mk 7.24—30 in the light of the teaching in 7.1—23, cf. Jn 7.7—42). (3) The attitude of the disciples in both stories is the typical Jewish reaction to non-Jews, and in the end it is their attitude that is challenged by Jesus' deeds of mercy to these two women and by the women's own deeds, and faith. (4) In both stories we learn that, though Jesus' earthly ministry was directed to the lost sheep of Israel, He was willing to help those non-Jews who sought His aid.[90] If the Fourth Evangelist knew the Synoptic account, he has chosen not to include it. In any event, the similarities of these two narratives give confirmation to the supposition that there were certain types of narrative in circulation about Jesus' words and deeds, and that stories of the same general type tended to be related with certain common features.

Characteristically, Mark says that immediately after the woman heard Jesus was in the area,[91] she came to implore Him to exorcise an unclean spirit from her daughter.[92] She falls at His feet in a gesture of supplication.[93] Mark then stresses the woman's political and national identity (Ἑλληνὶς Συροφοινίκισσα τῷ γένει), while Matthew possibly may be referring to her religious affiliation (Χαναναία).[94] After her request, the Marcan narrative proceeds directly to the saying of Jesus about the children and their food, while Matthew relates a three-part response by Jesus.

Since the first two parts of the plea and response will at least tell us something of the First Evangelist's views of Jesus, this woman, and the disciples, it is important that we examine it here. First, when the woman says, 'Have mercy on me Lord, Son of David', and then asks for exorcism, Jesus says nothing. Matthew appears to cast Jesus in an uncharacteristically unresponsive role (though cf. Jn 8.6). Possibly, we are meant to think that this woman was trying to curry favour with Jesus by using the title Son of David. Yet, it was precisely because he was the Son of David that she had no claim on Him. The silence of Jesus is perhaps to be understood as a means of testing the woman's faith,[95] or even a means of testing His disciples' character by giving them time to react to the situation.[96] If so, their response is ambiguous: ἀπόλυσον αὐτήν, ὅτι κράζει ὄπισθεν ἡμῶν (Matthew). This may mean, 'Send her away because she is crying after us', or 'Grant her request, for she is crying after us.' In either case, it appears they wish her to leave because she is a nuisance. The former translation, however, better reflects their attitude and the lexical probabilities.[97]

Jesus' second response in Matthew is directed primarily to the disciples and only secondarily (if at all) to the woman,[98] when He says, 'I was sent only to the lost sheep of Israel.' It may be a statement of Jesus' own view of His mission, but if so, then it seems cold comfort and uncharacteristic of Jesus when He is confronted with someone in need.[99] In any case, the woman is not put off, but pleads again, 'Lord, help me.' This saying does not appear to be a Matthean creation even though it is a Matthean addition since the First Evangelist has well-known universalistic tendencies (cf. Mt. 4.15f; 4.24, 12.18, 13.37f). Yet precisely because it is a saying that the Church would not be likely to create, it has high claims to being an authentic Jesus word even if it is not in its original context here.[100]

The response of Jesus found in both Matthew and Mark is even more harsh: 'It is not good to take the food of the children and throw it to the dogs.'[101] No matter how one interprets κυνάριον (as dog or puppy), it is an insult, especially when spoken by a Jew to a Gentile.[102] It is possible that there is a reference here to the practice common among Jews of giving bread not worth saving to puppies.[103] Despite the insult, however, the woman is not to be put off, perhaps because she is desperate and/or because she hears something in Jesus' tone of voice that indicates there is still hope.[104] Such a remark usually would produce a bitter rejoinder unless Jesus' tone or expression belied His words. Thus, she enters into the spirit of the test by accepting Jesus' judgment on her: ναὶ κύριε, καὶ γὰρ τὰ κυνάρια ἐσθίει ἀπὸ τῶν ψιχίων.[105] She may be quoting a well-known proverb.[106] Whether or not the Jews kept dogs as house pets, they did not feed them. By referring to them, the woman shows that even now, though it might only be a by-product, the 'dogs' can be fed.[107] In the end, the woman achieves her desire, not so much by a witty remark, as by a faith that goes on imploring even though it recognizes that it has no claim on the Master. She is similar to the persistent woman of Lk. 18.1–8.

With regard to Jesus' views of women, we may deduce the following from this narrative. Jesus' willingness to talk with and help this foreign woman is proof of His rejection of certain rabbinic teachings concerning discourse with women and the uncleanness of Gentiles. Thus, Mk 7.24–30 both by its content and by its position does draw out the implications of 7.14–23. In Mark, the woman's trust is indicated by the fact that she believes Jesus when He says her daughter is healed and leaves in full confidence. Matthew makes explicit what is implicit in Mark, 'O woman, great is your faith.' Only one other in the Synoptic tradition is praised in these terms, again a non-Jew (Mt. 8.5–13, Lk. 7.1–10). This woman serves as an example to the Evangelists' audiences. In Matthew her great faith contrasts with the disciples' great annoyance with her persistent pleading. How surprised Matthew's audience must have been to hear this Gentile woman's faith called great, when a characteristic description of Jesus' own disciples in that Gospel is that they have little faith (ὀλιγόπιστος, Mt. 6.30, 8.26, 14.31, 16.8). We see that not only in Jesus' own words and deeds, but also in the redactional activity of the Gospel writers, the theme of reversal of expectations brought about by the Gospel message is emphasized.[108]

4. Peter's Mother-in-Law – Mk 1.29–31 (Mt. 8.14–15, Lk. 4.38–9)

Jesus' ministry to diseased women is the subject of several pericopes in the Synoptic tradition. In each instance we are given further evidence of Jesus' outright rejection of various taboos inhibiting His ability to help those in need. In Mk 1.29–31 and parallels, we see Jesus' willingness to heal a diseased woman even on the Sabbath. That this healing is paired with that of a man (Mk 1.21–8, Lk. 4.31–7) may be the Gospel writers' way of saying that Jesus was willing to perform such an act on the Sabbath for both men and women.

Mk. 1.29–31 is the initial part of a section which V. Taylor calls 'a historical unity'.[109] Various scholars have remarked about the primitive character of this narrative and that it probably derives in its original form from one of the eyewitnesses of the event – Peter.[110] The grammatical awkwardness in Mk 1.29 is explained adequately by the supposition that it was changed by Mark from Peter's first person testimony to the third person.[111] Nevertheless, the narrative has apparently been moulded and edited to conform to a pattern common in ancient miracle tales: (1) touch of the healer; (2) sudden cure; (3) action by the person cured confirming the result.[112]

It is in the context of the Sabbath that Jesus performs His first two miracles, as presented in Mark: the healing of the man with the unclean spirit in the synagogue, and the healing of Simon's mother-in-law in her home after the Sabbath service.[113] Matthew does not present this story as a Sabbath healing, perhaps in order to avoid creating unnecessary controversy for some of his Jewish-Christian (?) audience. Mark says that after Jesus preached and healed in the synagogue to the amazement of all, He immediately left and entered a house where Simon Peter's mother-in-law lay sick with a fever.[114] Mark and Luke tell us that some of those in the house speak to Jesus about her, probably asking Him to do something about her illness.[115] Jesus' response is immediate and dramatic.[116] Mark, in contrast to Matthew and Luke, does not say merely that the woman arises and serves, but that Jesus raises her up. This may point forward to more miraculous acts in Jesus' ministry, and to His own Resurrection.[117] Luke, stressing Jesus' confrontation with the effects of Satan as seen here in sickness, states that Jesus rebukes the fever while standing over her.[118] In Mark there is the hint of Jesus' Resurrection power; in Luke the power of the King and His Kingdom over Satan; and in Matthew the awesomeness of Jesus' person in that He can heal by a mere touch.[119]

Though there were precedents for rabbis taking the hand of another man and miraculously healing him, there are no examples of rabbis doing so for a woman, and certainly not on the Sabbath when the act could wait until after sundown.[120] Indeed, a man could be suspected of evil desires if he touched any woman other than his wife. This was true even if it was a cousin, and more true if the woman was no relation at all.[121] At the very least, Jesus could be accused of contracting uncleanness and violating the Sabbath. Jesus, however, was willing to be misunderstood so that women such as Peter's mother-in-law might be healed.

Luke says that immediately[122] after she was healed, she rose, and served them.[123] There is no delay in recovery; Jesus' healing is complete, not only driving out the evil, but also restoring wholeness. Having been freed from servitude to disease, she is now free to serve her liberator and others.[124] What is interesting about her act is that women, according to some rabbis, were not allowed to serve meals to men.[125] It also appears that this may be a violation by the woman of the prohibition against working on the Sabbath. Perhaps she realized that if Jesus was free to heal her on the Sabbath, then she was free from the Sabbath restrictions preventing her from serving and helping others. In this act, she manifests a new freedom and courage similar to that of Mary and Martha in Jn 12, the women in Lk. 8.1–3, or the sinful woman in Lk. 7.36–50, all of whom took upon themselves the role of servant in gratitude to Jesus.[126] It is interesting that Mark and Luke tell us that others in the area cautiously wait until after the Sabbath to receive from Jesus healing and liberation (Lk. 4.40, Mk 1.32).

Mk 1.29–31 and parallels, though brief, give us important information concerning Jesus' attitude toward women. Just as He dismissed the idea that the touch of a sinful woman or non-Jewish woman was defiling, so too He rejected the idea that the touch of a sick woman was defiling. If we may accept Mark's and Luke's placing of this pericope as an indication that we are dealing with an incident near the beginning of Jesus' ministry, then we see that even from the first Jesus showed His concern for women and His willingness to violate the common view of the Sabbath and the standing rules about the uncleanness of a sick person in order to help them. We have conjectured that Mark and Luke may be emphasizing Jesus' equal concern for men and women by placing an example of the healing of each at the beginning of His ministry. Marshall is probably right to say, 'It is unlikely that the use of διακονέω is meant to indicate that this is the appropriate form of Christian service for women; it simply indicates the normal domestic arrangement.'[127] Nonetheless, Jesus accepts such service and it is notable that Peter's mother-in-law is performing a task which some rabbis felt was inappropriate for women, especially the matron of the house. This may be an indication of Jesus' tacit rejection of the prevailing ideas about what was and was not appropriate work for a woman.[128] We will have occasion to say more on this subject when we discuss Lk. 10.38–42.

5. Healing a Cripple on the Sabbath – Lk. 13.10–17

Lk. 13.10–17, a pericope unique to the Third Gospel, illustrates what precedes and prepares for what follows. The unfruitful fig tree (13.6–9), just like the unfruitful approach to the Sabbath (13.10–17),[129] must be cut down, and fruitful attitudes which bring glory to God must be planted, just like the healthy growing tree in 13.19. It is the unhealed woman, like the growing tree, which gives succour to living things and life itself, that is the sign that the Kingdom and the final Sabbath is at hand. In this pericope Jesus is presented as teaching and healing in the synagogue Sabbath service in such a way that He rejects certain rabbinic understandings of the Sabbath. Not the absence of work, but the presence of a creative and healing peace is the essence of the Sabbath. Daube has noted a tri-partite structure within this pericope that is used elsewhere in the Gospels – revolutionary action, protest and silencing of the remonstrants.[130] Thus, Lk. 13.10–17 is placed carefully in relation to its context, and presented carefully in its content and internal structure.

This pericope, like Mk 1.29–31 and parallels, Mk 5.21–43 and parallels, and Lk. 7.11–17, raises certain problems for scholars because of its miraculous content. Dibelius and Bultmann have both maintained that an isolated saying (verse 15) or paradigm has probably been expanded in novelistic fashion.[131] Verse 15, however, could not have stood on its own but at the very least requires verse 16 to explain how the illustration is to be applied. While verse 17 may be a Lucan creation, if one allows verse 16 as original then some such healing or action as we find in verses 10–15 is required to make sense of verses 15–16. Lk. 13.10–17 is an independent narrative probably written by Luke himself. Bultmann points to the fact that the healing precedes the discussion as proof that the story is an artificial composition meant to illustrate Jesus' attitude about the Sabbath. His verdict, however, seems to be predicated on the assumption that Gospel stories must fall into certain structured forms or else they cannot be an original organic unity.[132] The details of the story probably rule out the supposition that this narrative is a secondary variant to Mk 3.1–6.[133] Unless one is predisposed to reject a narrative's historicity simply because of its miraculous content, it is not improbable that we have authentic Jesus material here. At the very least we probably have authentic information here in the kernel of this story (verses 11–16) about Jesus' attitude toward the Sabbath and helping those in bondage.

The narrative opens with Jesus teaching in one of the synagogues on the Sabbath. A woman with a spirit of sickness of eighteen years duration[134] enters the synagogue. We are not told the exact nature of the illness, except that she was bent over and unable to stand up – εἰς τὸ παντελές.[135] Apparently, this sickness did not render her unclean, or at least did not render her ineligible to attend the Sabbath service. There is no indication that she is coming to be healed by Jesus, though this is possible.[136] She possibly did not wish anyone to notice her as she slipped in, for often it was assumed by first-century Jews that long sickness meant great sin.[137] Despite the fact that she is bent over and Jesus is sitting down, He sees her and interrupts His teaching to call her. Jesus says, 'Woman, you are released from your sickness.'[138] He not only heals her, but also lays hands upon her, and immediately she stands upright.[139] Now she truly has a reason to praise God on this Sabbath, and she does so then and there. The congregation no doubt would be stunned at this striking miracle wrought in such close quarters before their eyes on the Sabbath, but the ruler of the synagogue is not at a loss for words. Though he is angry because Jesus healed on the Sabbath, he directs his comments τῷ ὄχλῳ. His objection is not to *where* the miracle took place, but *when*.[140] 'It is necessary (δεῖ) to work six days, but we should not on the Sabbath.' In his mind, healing was a violation of the prohibition against work on the Sabbath; however, as Aquinas says,

> 'But the law has not forbidden all manual work on the Sabbath-day, and has it forbidden that which is done by a word or the mouth? Cease then both to eat and drink and speak and sing ... But supposing the law has forbidden manual works, how is it a manual work to raise a woman upright by a word?'[141]

Apparently, the objection is made on the basis of the rabbinic idea that
such acts of healing should not be performed on the Sabbath unless life
was in danger.[142] The woman who had suffered eighteen years clearly
could wait one more day.

Jesus' reply shows that the coming of the Kingdom will not wait. He
sees the hypocrisy in the ruler's remark and also condemns all who agree
with him.[143] He argues from the lesser to the greater,

> 'If it is acceptable to loose (λύει) your donkey from the manger and
> lead it to drink on the sabbath,[144] how much more proper is it for this
> one who is a daughter of Abraham, whom Satan has bound (in his
> stall)[145] for lo these eighteen long years. Was it not then necessary
> (ἔδει) that she be loosed (λυθῆναι) from this bondage on the day of the
> Sabbath?'[146]

The synagogue ruler has appealed to the necessity of the rabbinic interpretation of the Mosaic law. Jesus appeals to the original purpose of the
Sabbath and the fact that this woman is a daughter of Abraham. This
nomenclature is used nowhere else in the Bible or in rabbinic literature
of an individual.[147]

> 'By giving this woman this rarely-used title, Christ echoes the phrase
> "son of Abraham" and in doing so asserts that this woman is a child of
> Abraham, a member of the people of God, and should be treated as
> such, instead of being valued less than a mere pack animal. The woman,
> then, is not only healed but restored to her true dignity.'[148]

Jesus' use of the term or concept, son/daughter of Abraham, so far as we
know was limited to the poor, despised (cf. Lk. 19.9) and oppressed Jews
(and perhaps Gentiles – Mt. 8.11–12 and parallels) whom He especially
came to liberate. It is these, rather than the religious elite, who are the
rightful bearers of the title and who will gain the places of Abraham's
physical descendants in the Kingdom. In our context, we may note the
specific contrast between the label 'hypocrite' that Jesus places on the
synagogue ruler and those who agree with him, and the title of daughter
of Abraham He gives to the woman.[149] Again we see a woman not only
being used as a positive example as she praises God, and even given a
positive title, but also being defended at the expense of the males and
in particular the synagogue ruler who objects to Jesus' actions. The Gospel
brings healing on the Sabbath and a reversal of expectations. By using
the title, Jesus implies that she is as worthy of His concern and healing
as any Jewish man and has as full a claim to her religious heritage as anyone.

Thus, in the context of Lucan theology, 13.10—17 presents another example of the fulfillment of 4.18—19. The year of the Lord's favour has broken in and this woman is presented as an example of the oppressed set free. The Sabbath is to be a day of release from the effects of the fallen order. It is this which brings rest and peace to God's people, and glory to God. Insofar as this pericope tells us something about Jesus' attitude about women, it indicates that He thought they had an equal right with men to their religious heritage and it shows the lengths to which He was willing to go to help them. He risked outright rejection by religious leaders in order to heal a woman on the Sabbath in their presence in the synagogue.

6. Jairus and the Jewess — Mk 5.21—43 (Mt. 9.18—26, Lk. 8.40—56)

Mk 5.21—43 and parallels is a narrative that has been submitted to widely varying assessments in regard to its historical worth. Some scholars have argued that Mark is here drawing on Petrine reminiscences and thus there is a solid core of historical material in this narrative.[150] Others have argued that we have here a combination of two separate traditions each of which has been built up out of many features which are typical of miracle stories in antiquity.[151] In regard to the structure of the story we probably do not find the technique of the artificial interpolation of one narrative into another here for, as Dibelius, followed by R. Pesch, points out, the delay caused by healing the woman on the road is integral to the Jairus story.[152] It is probably not the case that only isolated, simple stories were originally handed down in the tradition for the examples of 'pure' narratives are in a decided minority in the Synoptics, and it is not proper to dismiss all complex narratives as later combinations or amplifications simply because they are complex.[153] Each narrative must be assessed on its own merits. Mk 5.21—43 has many distinctive characteristics: 'the vivid portraiture of Jairus and his agonized cry for aid, the incident of the woman on the way to his house, the skeptical attitude towards Jesus of the messengers ... the command in Aramaic addressed to the girl, the compassionate regard for her welfare shown by Jesus'.[154] We have evidence from some of the other sections of this chapter that Jesus' passionate regard for women in need is an early feature of the tradition and authentically portrays the Jesus of history. Further, Pesch has made a good case for the view that Jairus' name was originally in the story and later omitted by Matthew and the Western text of Mark.[155] We need look no further than Matthew's version of this story to see what later editors such as this Evangelist would often do to an original and vivid narrative: the name Jairus is omitted as is the Aramaic command; he uses the more general ἄρχων; he telescopes the whole by omitting the messengers altogether; he adds a typical general conclusion (verse 26, cf. Lk. 7.17); and he neatly summarizes Mark's description of the woman's illness with γυνὴ αἱμορροοῦσα. To be sure even Mark has shaped his narrative. The secrecy motif (5.43) may be his own addition and it appears that he has chosen to include those features of these two healings that were often regular components of such stories: mention of length of sickness (verse 25), emphasis on fruitlessness of treatment (verse 26), physical contact for healing (verses 27 ff), the instantaneousness of the healing (verses, 29, 42).[156] This may lead one to conclude that the narrative is merely composed of 'typical' elements, but more probably, in view of the reasons cited above for seeing the narrative as a unified whole and a vivid account of actual events, it shows us that Mark has edited and stylized his historical material in order to conform it to familiar patterns for such stories. If this is correct, while we must examine the small divergences in the three Synoptic accounts for theological significance, we may accept the nucleus of the story as revealing something of Jesus' views of women.

The story of Jairus and the woman with the twelve year flow of blood builds from the healing of one person to the raising of another, and there is an interesting contrast between the elicited witness of the woman and the command to silence of Jairus' family and the three disciples.[157] This pericope illustrates the progress of the Gospel reaching those at the bottom of the Jewish social ladder (the impoverished unclean woman) and those at the top (Jairus and his family). The story opens with Jesus being approached by a synagogue president[158] named Jairus who, because of his desperate need, forgets his pride and position and falls at Jesus' feet begging His aid for his θυγάτριον.[159] The First Evangelist describes Jairus' act of imploring Jesus by the term προσεκύνει. This need not imply worship or special reverence, but rather respect and a sense of special urgency which he has made more explicit than his Marcan source.[160] The condition of the girl is described in three different ways by the Synoptic accounts, but they all probably mean that the girl is dying or at the point of death.[161] Jesus is requested to lay hands on the young girl in order to heal her.[162]

As Jesus sets off to Jairus' home, the crowd pressed in nearly suffocating Him.[163] In the midst of this crowd, a woman with a twelve year flow of blood,[164] in hopes of a cure, touched Jesus' upper garment.[165] Miraculously, her flow of blood immediately dried up.[166] One must ask whether she showed little or great, weak or strong, pure or magic-tainted faith. Undoubtedly, there was an element of superstition in her belief that she might be cured by touching the healer's garment; but the point is that she did have faith enough to believe that Jesus might help her. Perhaps it is because of her ritual uncleanness or natural modesty that she tried to fade into the crowds again. She risked being restrained or cast out, yet she was approaching Jesus in faith.[167]

Instantly, Jesus knew He had been touched in faith and thus He asks, 'Who touched my clothes?' (Mark and Luke only). It is probable that Jesus asks this question in order to educate and elevate the faith of the woman above the belief in a magical power in Jesus and His garments. He wants the unclean woman to bear witness to the crowd of her faith and cure through Jesus. He wishes to make an example of her, in the good sense of the word. Luke, with his special emphasis on the liberation and witness of women, says δι᾽ ἣν ἀπήγγειλεν ἐνώπιον παντὸς τοῦ λαοῦ καὶ ὡς ἰάθη παραχρῆμα. Matthew, as he did in the case of the Syrophoenician woman, makes this woman an explicit example of faith when he presents only these words of Jesus as a climax: θύγατερ ἡ πίστις σου σέσωκέν σε.[168] Though the woman trembled[169] when she was found out, perhaps fearing Jesus' censure, Jesus reacts in a way she would never have expected. Not only was this woman no longer to be avoided, but now in fact she was set forth as a living example of faith for all to emulate. By contrast the disciples are shown to have little faith in Jesus and little understanding of why Jesus would ask who touched Him in such a mob. As was the case with the Samaritan woman and the Syrophoenician woman, Jesus' words mean more than His disciples' superficial interpretation led them to believe.[170]

It is at this point in the Marcan and Lucan accounts that the messengers arrive to report to Jairus, 'Your daughter is dead ... Why bother the Teacher any more?'[171] Jesus overhears[172] these messengers speaking to Jairus and, to prevent him from despairing, interjects μὴ φοβοῦ, μόνον πίστευε.[173] When Jesus arrived at the house He allowed only Peter, James and John to enter with Him, leaving the remaining crowd and group of disciples outside.[174] These three serve as witnesses to the miracle and, as representatives of the disciples, receive this special privilege perhaps in preparation for their leadership role and their commissioning to perform similar acts soon to follow this episode.[175] Already present in the house were mourners, some of whom may have been members of the family. Matthew adds αὐλητάς, perhaps to make the narrative conform to Jewish customs.[176] The scornful or mocking response to Jesus' statement about the girl may indicate the bitter rejoinder of relatives who are grieved and would view such a remark as flippant. The meaning of Jesus' remark has been debated. The mourners clearly interpreted Jesus' τὸ παιδίον[177] οὐκ ἀπέθανεν ἀλλὰ καθεύδει to mean that He thought the girl was still alive. This interpretation is favored by the οὐκ ... ἀλλὰ construction used. It is certainly possible that the Marcan narrative was not originally about a dead girl but one who was in a coma, despite Luke's clear indications that he views this narrative as a raising story (8.53 – εἰδότες; 8.55 – ἐπέστρεψεν τὸ πνεῦμα αὐτῆς).[178] Mark is probably not using the word καθεύδει as a metaphor for death, since he is not saying, 'Yes, she is dead, but death is like a sleep.'[179] Probably, the explanation of the οὐκ ... ἀλλὰ contrast lies in who Jesus is (the Lord of life) and what He is about to do (raise the girl). The girl is dead and her death is not merely like a sleep; in His presence it *is* sleep rather than death. It is not an end, but an interim condition from which she returns healthy and hungry.

In order to perform this act, Jesus casts out[180] all those in the house except the three disciples and the parents. Only those who are closely connected either to the girl or to Jesus can witness this act and interpret it properly through the eyes of faith. Perhaps it is not without significance that Jesus treats the mother as equally worthy with the father and the Apostles of witnessing this act. As in the case of Peter's mother-in-law, Jesus takes the girl by the hand and Mark and Luke record that He adds the command, 'Girl, I say to you arise.' It is Mark alone who records the words ταλιθὰ κοῦμ which are a transliteration from the Aramaic.[181] This probably reflects a Petrine remembrance of Jesus' actual words, not a later attempt by Mark to give the story local colour.

To further a return to normality, Jesus commands a renewal of attention to the girl's physical needs. This was not magic but the power and word of God harnessed in the service of a young girl and of her family.[182]

If there was still room for doubt about Jesus' attitude toward the clean/unclean distinctions accepted in Judaism, an examination of this pericope removes any remaining uncertainties. Bearing in mind Jesus' operative principle that it is only what comes out of a man's heart that defiles him (Mk 7.15, 21 – and thus the view that Jesus simply allowed Himself to be defiled on behalf of others seems unlikely), we have evidence here that Jesus treats neither the touch of the woman with the twelve year blood flow, nor the contact of a dead girl as defiling. Neither woman is viewed as unclean or as a source of uncleanness by Jesus, but rather is treated as a person in need of help. Though not worked out in our text, the implications of Jesus' views are important to this study. If a woman with a blood flow is not defiled or defiling, then the rabbinic reason for not requiring a woman to fulfil all of the Law's positive commandments, and not permitting her to be counted on for all the periodic feasts and functions of the faith is by implication rejected by Jesus' deeds in the first of these two stories. Thus, the way is paved for women to participate more fully in Jesus' own community. In both stories, faith is a key commodity, a commodity which the healed woman is as capable of possessing as Jairus. Since this is also the commodity which is the basis of association in Jesus' community, the woman and perhaps to a lesser extent Jairus, become examples to the Gospel writers' audiences. Certainly, the healed woman is made an example by Jesus when He calls her to centre stage and speaks of her faith. In Mark's presentation of the event, the woman appears in a more favourable light than the exasperated disciples. The Jairus story is also significant in that it shows Jesus' desire to reunite a physical family despite the great obstacle of death. Here is further evidence that the family of faith and the physical family were not mutually exclusive alternatives in Jesus' mind. Indeed, it appears that Jairus' faith is in part the basis of the reunion of his physical family. Had he not believed in Jesus and His power he might not have approached Jesus in the first place. While an ordinary rabbi might have treated the loss of a daughter as less significant than the loss of a son, when one compares this story to that of the raising of the widow of Nain's son, Jesus exhibits an equal concern over the loss of either son or daughter.

7. The Widow of Nain — Lk. 7.11—17

Lk. 7.11—17, beyond all cavil, is a story about the raising of the dead. Perhaps it is significant that every example in the Gospels of Jesus performing such a miracle involves women either as the object of the miracle (Mk 5.21—43 and parallels) or as those for whom the miracle is performed (Lk. 7.11—17, John 11).[183] Luke, with his penchant for pairing male and female stories of similar content and intent, presents the healing of the centurion's servant (7.1—10) followed by the text at hand.[184] Lk. 7.11—17 reflects Luke's general theme of the ministry of Jesus to women, and his special interest in the way the Gospel aided such disenfranchised groups as widows and the poor.[185]

Lk. 7.11—17 creates various critical problems for the scholar. Not only does it involve the miraculous resuscitation of a dead young man, but also it is uniquely Lucan and thus falls under suspicion because it is not attested in any other strand of the Gospel tradition. Some have suspected that the Evangelist (or at least the post-Easter community) created this narrative using the pattern of various OT or even non-Biblical miracles.[186] Schürmann, however, argues that basically we have an old narrative coming from a Palestinian community.[187] Jesus is cast in this narrative as a great prophet, like but even greater than Elijah (cf. 1 Kgs 17.8—16) for he heals by a mere command. This sort of Christology cannot be described as 'Hellenistic Jewish Christian'. The context is clearly 'Jewish' as the cry 'God has visited his people' shows. Jesus is called προφήτης μέγας, not χριστός or κύριος by the crowd, and this too counts against seeing the narrative as a late Christian composition. Further, one may point to the abundant parataxis in this narrative that gives it an Aramaic flavour.[188] The name Nain is not found elsewhere in the NT and is perhaps derived from a local tradition.[189] The narrative should not come under suspicion simply because it is a raising story, for we find these in many strands of the tradition and the multiple attestation creates a presumption that such events with relation to Jesus are not an invention of the post-Easter community.[190] To be sure this miracle story has been schematized so that it has the form of a typical miracle story. It is told in the light and the style of various other miracles particularly that found in 1 Kgs 17.8–16. But, 'eine Nachbildung ... ist unsere Erzählung nicht'.[191] The location of the Elijah miracle is outside Israel, the act is a private one, and the method is wholly different from Lk. 7.11–17. The example in 2 Kgs 4.8–37 does not involve a widow (though it does have an only son) and again the act is a private one performed by means unlike Jesus' and without the significance of Jesus' act. Only the location is reasonably close to our narrative.[192] As for the example from Philostratus,[193] besides the fact that if it is historical it probably post-dates the time of Jesus (Apollonius died *ca* A.D. 98), and was certainly written down after the Gospels were completed, Philostratus himself was sceptical about whether or not a miracle had taken place. Further, in Philostratus' story, 'Das Motiv der Lebensrettung ... ist aber so sehr menschliches Desiderium, dass es immer wieder zum Fabulieren reizt und nicht traditionsgeschichtliche Abhängigkeit angenommen werden muss.'[194] Thus, it is quite possible that we are dealing with an old Palestinian tradition cast in the light of similar OT stories but nonetheless bearing witness to an actual deed of Jesus, and to his compassion for widows. It is possible that verse 17 is Luke's own addition to the story and we probably also see his redactional work in verse 11 and possibly in the use of κυρίος in verse 13. Against Dibelius, however, verse 13 is not Luke's novelistic expansion of the story, for the use of σπλαγχνίζομαι is a feature of his special source (cf. 10.30, 15.20), and he takes over none of Mark's occurrences (Mk 1.41, 6.34, cf. 8.2, 9.22).[195]

Luke sets the scene by indicating that Jesus went to Nain with His disciples and a huge crowd.[196] As they were entering the city gate a funeral procession was leaving. Luke indicates that this was the saddest sort of funeral by saying, 'Behold, a dead person was being carried out — the only son of his mother, and she was a widow.'[197] The mother was left alone and her family line was cut off. Luke says that Jesus felt compassion for this woman in her pitiful state and decided to perform an act solely on her behalf, as the details of verses 12–15 explain.[198] It is an act of mercy and does not involve forgiveness or faith.[199]

Jesus is so certain of the outcome of His actions that He first tells the widow, who would be walking in front of the bier, μὴ κλαῖε.[200] Next, He violates rabbinic practice by stopping the funeral procession and touching the σορός, an act which causes those carrying the bier to stand still.[201] Jesus needs only to speak to raise the young man and addresses him not as a body or soul, but as a person — Νεανίσκε σοὶ λέγω ἐγέρθητι.[202] The dead young man sits up, begins to speak,[203] and is given by Jesus back to his mother, thus defiling Himself in the eyes of some Jews. The mother immediately takes the young man back and 'they were all filled with fear (awe) and praised God'.[204] The crowd interprets this raising as an act of God visiting His people through a great prophet. Luke rounds off his narrative by adding that the news spread ἐν ὅλῃ τῇ Ἰουδαίᾳ περὶ αὐτοῦ καὶ πάσῃ τῇ περιχώρῳ.[205]

Our pericope succinctly illustrates Jesus' concern for women, particularly widows. The raising is a deed of compassion — faith is not a prerequisite, though the deed does engender the praise of Jesus as a great prophet of God. The act was also a practical one since it provided the woman with a means of support as well as a source of joy. It demonstrates Jesus' continual rejection of certain OT and rabbinic distinctions of clean/unclean, and certain Sabbath rules which prevented Him from helping women and others in need, i.e., those with whom according to Luke He especially chose to associate (Lk. 4.18–19, 24–7, 5.30–2, etc.). Luke views this miracle as a demonstration of the inbreaking of the Lord's favour, and indicates both by his introduction (verse 11) and his conclusion (verse 17) that it did not go unnoticed or unreported. In a sense the Evangelist himself, by including this story, made certain that such would be the case.

B. Jesus' Attitude Toward Women Reflected in His Actions

Our study of Jesus' interactions with women has brought to light several fundamental principles which seem to have guided Him in His dealing with the opposite sex. Jesus' outright rejection of rabbinic ideas of sin and sickness leading to ritual impurity or defilement allowed Him to relate to many women He might not have reached otherwise. We have suggested also that Jesus' implicit rejection of the idea that a blood flow in a woman caused her to be defiled or to be a source of defilement removed the rabbinic basis for excluding women from synagogue worship and periodic feasts and functions of the faith. This was perhaps one of the factors which paved the way for women to travel with Jesus and to be full-time followers of their Master without special restrictions (cf. chapter four on Lk. 8.1–3).

Jesus' rejection of certain rabbinic Sabbath restrictions also allowed Him to serve and to accept service at the hands of grateful women when normally such activities were forbidden (Mk 1.29–31 and parallels). In Jn 4.4–42 and Mk 7.24–30 and parallels, we see clear examples of Jesus' willingness to relate openly to women who were not fully Jewish or, in the case of the Syrophoenician woman, perhaps not Jewish at all. This abrogated numerous rabbinic warnings about foreign or Samaritan women, as well as the familiar prohibitions against talking with women, especially sinful women, in public, and opened the door for a more normal and natural basis for relationship. While it is true that Jesus' earthly ministry was directed to the lost sheep of Israel, He did not reject other lost sheep who encountered or sought Him, and perhaps this set a precedent for the acceptance of non-Jewish women in the early days of the Gentile mission. It seems likely that one reason why Luke gives special prominence to women in his Gospel is to explain the influx of women into the Christian community of which he was a part and later wrote about in his book of Acts.

We noted a certain pattern in the Gospels of presenting women as examples of faith, and in one case of witness (Jn 4), often at the expense of either good male Jews or even Jesus' male disciples. We suggested that this pattern of reversal, while certainly owing something to the Gospel writers themselves, nonetheless is to be traced back to Jesus Himself as one manifestation of His teaching that the last and least shall be the first to be liberated as the Kingdom breaks into history with His ministry. We also detected a certain tendency on the part of the first three Evangelists to pair male–female healing stories, perhaps to stress Jesus' equal concern for men and women. This tendency, though less obvious than the male–female pairings of the parables, is perhaps significant and may reflect the purposes of each Evangelist, since there is at least one example in each Synoptic Gospel of a male–female pair not found in the other two Gospels.

Throughout the pericopes we have examined, Jesus' concern for women as persons, rather than as sources of potential temptation or defilement, is obvious. It is significant that Jesus was willing to perform extraordinary miracles (raising the dead), and to violate the rabbinic Sabbath regulations even in the presence of rabbis and in the synagogue in order to help women. Jesus did not pass over a woman's sins, indeed, by bringing some women to confession and pronouncing their sins forgiven He revealed His desire to heal the whole person and His recognition that women were as capable of many sins as men (John 4, Lk. 7.36—50).

All of this reveals Jesus' attitude that women were God's creatures, even daughters of Abraham, and thus as worthy as men to receive the benefits of God's love and salvation. If even a Samaritan woman, in contrast to His male disciples, could bear witness for Jesus and bring Him 'true food', who could dispute a woman's right to a place among His followers? On this note, we turn to an examination of those women most often mentioned in the Gospels as associates of Jesus — His mother Mary, His friends Mary and Martha, and His female travelling companions.

WOMEN IN THE MINISTRY OF JESUS

There were several distinct groups of women who interacted with Jesus during His ministry. After a detailed examination of the material in the Gospels (apart from the Birth narratives) that refers to the mother of Jesus, we will proceed to investigate Jesus' relationship to Mary and Martha, and finally to study those women who travelled with Jesus and played a crucial role in the events surrounding His death. By examining the status and place of these women in Jesus' earthly ministry, we will perhaps discover the background for and the explanation of the new roles women assumed in the primitive Christian community.

A. Mother Mary, Jesus' Disciple

The credal phrase, 'Born of the Virgin Mary', rightly emphasizes that Mary's importance in the NT is due to her relationship to her Son who is the focus of the Gospels. Thus, we must recognize that Mary is not mentioned as a result of an independent interest in her person, but because of the important role she played in Jesus' life.[1] Our concern here will be to examine those passages that may reveal something of the attitudes of the adult Jesus toward His mother.

1. The Wedding Feast at Cana — Jn 2.1–12

The historical value of Jn 2.1–12 is frequently questioned and thus a brief discussion of the major problems this passage raises for the historian is in order. It is often noted that this miracle story is out of character in its content both with the other 'signs' in this Gospel and with the miracles in the Synoptics. The magnitude of the 'miracle' could be seen as comical, especially since it is not required in the situation. It is possible that the Evangelist or his source has adopted or adapted a Hellenistic and pagan miracle story and applied it to Jesus.[2] Dodd has suggested that Jn 2.1–12 may ultimately go back to a parable of Jesus.[3] It has also been argued that the dialogue in verses 3–4 shows Johannine characteristics and thus is probably not part of the pre-Gospel form of this narrative.[4] These arguments will be examined in reverse order.

While it may be granted that the reference to Jesus' hour is characteristically Johannine and thus may well be an addition by the Evangelist, the initial and most problematic sentence of the reply of Jesus cannot be so categorized, apart perhaps from the word γύναι. Even in the case of γύναι, however, it is unusual for a son to use such a term in response to his mother and so one should not be too hasty in assuming that it was not an original part of the narrative. It is, after all, in keeping with a pronouncement such as Mk 3.34–5 which is probably authentic Jesus material.[5] Secondly, there is nothing particularly Johannine about οἶνον οὐκ ἔχουσιν in content or form.[6] In regard to Mary's word to the servants, while the form is Johannine, the content does not reflect any characteristically Johannine ideas. In short, this sentence may simply reflect the Evangelist's tendency to recast the material in his source into his own style and vocabulary. It is possible that the original pre-Gospel form of the dialogue in Jn 2.3–5 included: (1) a statement or plea by Mary indicating the problem; (2) verse 4a, possibly without γύναι; (3) possibly another statement by Jesus (omitted by the Evangelist), for the transition from verses 4 to 5 is awkward on any showing; (4) some form of the final statement by Mary to the servants preparing them to act if Jesus asks them to do something. It is difficult to believe that the Evangelist, who elsewhere (Jn 19) presents a favourable picture of Jesus' mother, could have added verse 4a which could be taken to reflect badly on her.[7] For the same reason, γύναι may well be original to the narrative.

The suggestion of Dodd that this narrative grew out of a parable is possible, but unfortunately we do not have the original parable or anything like it that would substantiate this view. Mk 2.22 and parallels should probably not be adduced at this point since the analogy in the Second Gospel only has its force because the container is a wine skin, whereas in John we are talking about purification jars. Further, in the Johannine narrative the new wine *is* put into the old containers. In its form and brevity, however, this narrative is much like the Synoptic miracles,[8] and as has been noted by Barrett and Schnackenburg (among others) it appears to have only been lightly worked over by the Evangelist.[9] This lends weight to the view that it was originally a miracle story and that it does not derive from the Evangelist.

A more probable suggestion is that this story has in some respects been influenced by (if not derived from) extra-biblical miracle tales involving wine.[10] Even here one must proceed with caution, however.

In most respects our narrative does not bear the hallmarks of a Hellenistic wonder story. We are not told how or when the change from water to wine took place. Indeed, the mention that the miracle had taken place is made indirectly and casually in the course of the narrative (verse 9*a*) and there is no attempt to indicate or create a response to the miracle itself by those present at the time (taking verse 11 or at least 11*b* to be the Evangelist's own addition).[11] The concern in Jn 2 is with the revelation of Jesus' divine glory to those who believe, not with a god's divine assistance or manifestation in the cult.[12]

> 'Moreover, it may be legitimately asked if the Evangelist, who has shown himself to be working within the general framework of the traditional miracles of Jesus in six of his seven narratives, would be likely to introduce a seventh narrative from an extraneous tradition? As for the uniqueness of the miracle, is changing water into wine so different from the multiplication of loaves? Both have echoes in the Elijah-Elisha tradition.'[13]

Perhaps the best explanation of what we find in Jn 2 is that this narrative in its present form has been written-up by someone who was conscious of both the OT miracles and the Hellenistic miracle material and has shaped the story in light of such material. The amount of wine produced, for instance, may be a touch that reflects an attempt to show that Jesus was greater than Bacchus.[14] Nevertheless, the retouching has not been done with a heavy hand and it is possible to produce a plausible pre-Gospel form of this narrative that probably included some form of a dialogue between Mary and Jesus.[15]

In the end, the historical value of the dialogue, which is our prime concern, depends in part on whether or not the Evangelist is drawing on the Synoptics. If so, then the apparent tension and distance between Mary and Jesus could be derived from various Synoptic texts (Mk 3.32–5, Lk. 2.48–50, cf. Jn 7.3–5).[16] If he is not relying on the Synoptics, and we have given reasons above to show that such dependence on the closest parallel subject matter in the Synoptics (Mk 2.22 and parallels) is unlikely,[17] then we have in Jn 2 and in the dialogue in particular independent confirmation of a Synoptic motif that has high claims to historicity since it stands in contrast to later pious legends about Jesus' relations with His family. It is plausible then that Jn 2.3–4*a*, 5 has real historical value, especially since verse 4*a* is not likely to be a product of the Evangelist's imagination and cannot stand alone as an isolated saying. In regard to the rest of the pericope, it is sufficient for our purposes to say that the arguments against this story having in its broad outlines foundations in an historical event in Jesus' life are not decisive.

Jn 2.1–12 is possibly an example of a 'hidden life' story (cf. Lk. 2.41–52) relating an incident that took place before Jesus had broken away from His family.[18] The miracle of Cana and the episode in Jn 19.25–7 frame the public ministry of Jesus, and one expects to find a certain continuity between the two episodes (along with some development). The dialogue between Jesus and Mary is at the heart of both Jn 2 and 19 — both include the address γύναι and both involve Jesus doing something that aids Mary. One should note the significant positioning of the mother of Jesus at the inception and climax of Jesus' ministry (and only in these two places), an indication of the important place Mary is given in this Gospel.[19] Our discussion of Jn 2.1–12 must focus on the central dialogue in verses 3–5 and especially on the crucial and difficult verse 4.

One's view of Mary's role here will be determined to a great degree by how one translates verse 4. We will examine first the easier half of the verse — οὔπω ἥκει ἡ ὥρα μου — which may well derive from the Evangelist. Is this phrase to be taken as a statement or a question? As the Evangelist has painted the scene Mary does seem to think Jesus will do something (verse 5), and in fact Jesus does go on to act in verse 6. It would be a more natural transition to this act if Jesus was saying that it was now time to act.[20] There are two grammatical points in favour of reading it as a question: (1) the οὔπω clause is asyndetic unlike its other eleven occurrences in John; (2) the phrase follows a question which, on the basis of Mt. 16.9, Mk 4.40, 8.17, leads one to expect another question.[21] There are, however, some considerations which make this view untenable. When the Fourth Evangelist has Jesus refer to His hour, no act before the Passion is in view (cf. 7.30, 8.20).[22] The parallels in Mt. 16.9, Mk 4.40 and 8.17 are not true parallels. They do involve two questions in succession and οὔπω, but they are not found in John and they do not follow an idiomatic Greek phrase such as we have in Jn 2.4*a* (τί ἐμοὶ καὶ σοί, γύναι). Other attempts to find parallels in Mk 1.24, Mt. 8.29, and Lk. 8.28 or in the LXX, are unsuccessful because the subject (demons) or the situations are not parallel to Jn 2.4 (cf. Judg. 11.12, 2 Chr. 35.21, 1 Kgs 17.18, 2 Kgs 3.13). The only similarity that all these phrases share with Jn 2.4 is that they are involved contextually with an expression of hostility, warning, or protest.[23]

In favour of taking this phrase as a statement are most of the translations and many notable commentators.[24] Further, verse 4*b* seems to be an explanation of what immediately precedes it: the idiom in 2.4*a* — τί ἐμοὶ καὶ σοί, γύναι — is colloquial and any attempt to render it literally

('What to me and to you.') is not helpful. It involves ellipsis and is best seen as a dative of possession which cannot be rendered literally into English. Nor can it be equated with the phrase πρός plus the accusative.[25] A careful study of Hebrew OT (2 Chr. 35.21) and extra-Biblical (Epictetus, Demosthenes, Suetonius, etc.) parallels reveals that the idiom is often unfriendly. The Hebrew and Greek forms of this phrase seem to deal with persons, but in the Greek it can deal with things.[26] It does not appear that Derrett is correct about the guests providing some of the wine, for it is the bridegroom who is commended when the new wine is sampled (2.9–10).[27] This means that this phrase probably does not refer to a joint obligation of Mary and Jesus, and/or the disciples.

A clue to the translation of verse 4a may be found in the fact that we seem to have a Semitism here.[28] If so, the phrase means, 'That is your business, do not involve me.' Jesus would be disengaging from Mary's concern or request and not necessarily from Mary herself.[29] This, however, fails to explain why Mary did not take Jesus' words as a refusal of her concern, and why Jesus does act.

The most probable explanation of verse 4a is that Jesus is disengaging from Mary in her role of parent in authority over Him (cf. Mk 3.20–35) and not from her concern for the problem at the wedding feast. He sees in her statement, 'they have no wine', an implied imperative, 'Do something.' He does not reject the need, but the authority of the one expressing it, for she has failed to understand her Son's mission and His primary allegiance to the spiritual family.[30] Jesus' heavenly Father, not His earthly mother, must determine when His hour is to come and what He is to do until then.[31]

Probably the Evangelist means, 'My hour has not yet come', to imply that in that hour Jesus will have an obligation to fulfil to Mary and then she will have a claim on Him (cf. Jn 19.25–7).[32] In the Fourth Gospel it is not until the word comes from the cross that the mother of Jesus is ushered officially into the spiritual family of Jesus (those who do have a claim on Him).[33] Two things show that the Evangelist intends verse 4a to be seen as a gentle rebuke, not an irretrievable rejection, and that our interpretation is correct. First, the vocative γύναι is a term of respect or affection. It implies 'neither reproof nor severity'.[34] It is the normal way that Jesus is depicted in the Gospels as addressing women that He either does not know well, or must address in a formal manner (Mt. 15.28, Lk. 13.12, Jn 4.21, 20.13). There are, however, no known uses of this word in either Hebrew or Greek by a son in addressing his mother.[35] It is likely that while it is not intended to carry a derogatory connotation toward Mary's motherhood, 'woman' is Jesus' way of placing His relationship to

Mary on a different basis. He is disengaging from her parental authority.[36]
If, however, as seems less likely, γύναι is the Evangelist's own addition to
the narrative, then it is one way that he has softened the blow of Jesus'
remark. Another way that he softens the blow is by adding, 'My hour has
not yet come', a phrase by which the Evangelist explains that Jesus cannot
relate to Mary as mother or recognize her claim on Him until His hour has
come. For now He must be about His Father's work (cf. Lk. 2.49).[37] They
will be reunited as a spiritual family when His hour comes; however, at
Cana she is not placed among the group that has faith in and travels with
Jesus as disciples.[38] Jn 2.5, if it is an original part of this pericope, may
imply that historically Mary had some faith and knowledge of Jesus'
compassionate nature, and perhaps of His miracle-working power, but her
powers to intercede for others with Him are not stressed here.[39] So far as
its historical worth is concerned, this dialogue reveals both that Jesus
disengaged from Mary in her role as mother and that Mary, unlike Jesus'
brothers (cf. Jn 7.5), was apparently not without some faith in Jesus
long before the post-Easter community was formed. In the schema of
Johannine theology, Jesus' disengagement from Mary is related to the
theme of Jesus' 'hour' and thus the scene at the cross is prepared for and
the blow of disengagement is softened. The Evangelist may intend some
slight hint that Mary is a type of Eve (tempting the new Adam), but the
term γύναι probably should not be taken as an indication that Mary is
seen as the archetypal woman here.[40] Rather, the point would seem to
be that it is as 'woman' that Mary must work out the tensions between
the physical and spiritual family, for later (Jn 19.26) the Evangelist
indicates that it is as 'woman', not as Jesus' mother, that she enters the
community of faith. Before turning to John 19, we must examine the
role of Mary in the Synoptics apart from the Infancy Narratives.

2. Mary in the Synoptics

There is a paucity of material on Mary in the Synoptics apart from the
Birth narratives of Matthew and Luke. Before the Passion narratives there
is only Mk 3.20–35 and parallels, and Mk 6.1–6 and parallels. Both are
for the most part passing remarks, and thus we see that the Evangelists
are not compelled either by controversy or personal interest to develop
a fuller picture of Mary. Probably this reflects the fact that Mary was not
a prominent influence in Jesus' earthly ministry. What references we do
have refer also to Jesus' brothers and sisters, and therefore we will deal
with the question of whether or not these are Mary's children.

Mk 3.21 is the most crucial text and fraught with difficulties. Unique to Mark, it is set in the context of Jesus' exorcisms (3.7–12) and the Beelzebub controversy (3.22–30). The references to Jesus' family seem to serve as a frame for this pronouncement story (3.20–1, 31–5) as well as a setting for Jesus' word about His true relatives.[41] It is likely that we have here an example of the Marcan *Schachteltechnik*.[42] Mark has combined two (or three) originally separate narratives into an effective chiastic structure with three accusations and three answers.[43] Of the material in 3.20–1 Taylor has rightly said, 'The narrative is based on the best historical tradition. No one has the hardihood to suggest that it is a creation of the community, for without the warrant of fact no early narrator would have alleged that the family at Nazareth thought that Jesus was beside Himself and went out to restrain him.'[44] A similar judgment should probably be pronounced on 3.31–5 even if it should prove to be at one time a narrative independent of 3.20–1 for the contrast between Jesus' physical and spiritual family is not likely to be a creation of the post-Easter community.[45]

The textual problems in Mk 3.21 are not major but do reflect what can happen to a 'hard' saying. Codex D, W and *it* read, 'When the scribes and the rest heard concerning Him', thus removing all possible references to Jesus' family.[46] Another set of interesting emendations centres on the word ἐξίστημι. While most manuscripts read ἐξέστη, Θ, 565, and others read ἐξέσταται ('he escaped'). D and it add to ἐξέσταται the word αὐτούς ('he escaped from them'); Codex W and 28 remove all reference to insanity by saying ἐξήρτηνται αὐτοῦ (they were 'adherents of his' or 'dependent on him').[47] These variants, none of which are likely original readings, reflect two concerns: (1) a desire to protect the image of the Holy Family, and (2) a desire to protect the image of Jesus.[48] This tells us that οἱ παρ' αὐτοῦ was taken at a relatively early date in the West to refer to Jesus' family, an interpretation which is correct as we shall see.

Though some commentators conjecture that οἱ παρ' αὐτοῦ may refer to the disciples, this idea is not supported from the context or lexical evidence.[49] Note that when Mark wishes to express the idea of the disciples in general, he uses οἱ περὶ αὐτὸν (4.10), not οἱ παρ' αὐτοῦ. Beyond this fact there is abundant support for seeing this phrase as referring to Jesus' family.[50] It is likely that Mark intended οἱ παρ' αὐτοῦ to be explained in verse 31 (ἡ μήτηρ αὐτοῦ καὶ οἱ ἀδελφοὶ αὐτοῦ).[51] This includes Mary, and it is interesting that recent Catholic scholars agree with this interpretation, but either do not see this entire group as the subject of ἔλεγον in verse 21, or say that the subject of ἔλεγον is indefinite.[52] This is unlikely because when one has a natural plural subject in the immediate context (οἱ παρ' αὐτοῦ), it is normal and natural for it to be related to this plural verb.[53]

The purpose of the family is made clear in the Marcan account; Mary and the brothers have gone forth to seize Him because they thought He was 'beside himself' or not in control of His situation.[54] At the least, verses 20–1 indicate that Mary and Jesus' brothers misunderstood Jesus' mission and ministry at this point.[55] Further, in what may be a separate pericope (verses 31–5) the way Jesus contrasts His physical and spiritual family (verse 34) implies that the former group was not the same as the latter (verses 32–4). Verse 34 reads: περιβλεψάμενος τοὺς περὶ αὐτὸν κύκλῳ καθημένους λέγει Ἴδε ἡ μήτηρ μου ...; this contrasts to the group in verse 31 which is ἔξω στήκοντες. The contrast is made more vivid by the First Evangelist who adds, καὶ ἐκτείνας τὴν χεῖρα αὐτοῦ ἐπὶ τοὺς μαθητὰς αὐτοῦ εἶπεν, Ἰδοὺ ἡ μήτηρ μου ... (12.49). The point is that there are some among those sitting who are, or are more nearly, His spiritual kin at this point than His family outside.[56] In its Marcan context, this contrast would have little force if Jesus' family did not share the opinion expressed by those who were saying ἐξέστη. In the first two Gospels someone other than Mary is identified, at least hypothetically, by Jesus as His spiritual mother. Neither the Matthean nor the Lucan parallels are as strong in tone as Mark. Neither includes Mk 3.21 and thus Jesus' family is spared at this point. The door is left open, however, for Jesus' physical family to join His spiritual family, even in Mark — 'Whoever (Mark, ὃς ἄν, cf. Matthew, ὅστις) does the will of God' will belong to His spiritual family (Mk 3.35, Mt. 12.50, Lk. 8.21).[57] Mark, however, did not want His readers to identify with the relatives of Jesus since they misunderstood His mission. Mark's plan in this pericope is to reveal the nature of true kinship.

Mk 3.20–1 indicates that whether or not Mary led the efforts to seize Jesus, at the very least her faith was not strong enough to resist her own protective instinct or the determination of the others with her.[58] There may be reflected a concern for Jesus'person by His family, but it is due to serious misunderstanding of what He was doing which leads them to think that He is not properly caring for Himself.[59]

In Mk 3.31–5 and parallels, Jesus does not agree to His family's request for an audience, but whether or not He knew their intention is unclear from the text.[60] The pronouncement which closes this pericope, even in its Marcan form, leaves the door open for the inclusion of His family within the family of faith at some future time if they will relate to Him on the basis of faith as His disciples. If some form critics are correct that Mk 3.20–1 and 3.31–5 (and parallels) were originally separate traditions, then we may have two pieces of evidence that reflect negatively on the family of Jesus in their relationship to Him. The First and Third Evangelists attempt to tone this material down by omitting Mk 3.21 and in the case of Luke by presenting a milder form of Mk 3.35 (cf. Lk. 8.21). The main focus of the text, however, is not on Jesus' family but on the nature and basis of Kingdom relationships.[61]

Mk 6.1–6 (and parallels) is another text which requires close scrutiny as we examine the Gospel tradition about Mary. Bultmann has contended that we have in this text a perfect example of an ideal scene probably built out of the Oxyrhynchus form of the saying found in 6.4.[62] The difficulty with this view is that there is no mention of Jesus' kin or home in the Oxyrhynchus saying, and a reference to a prophet without honour in his country (or among those who knew him) does not suggest the sort of narrative about Jesus' relatives we have in Mk 6.1–6. Indeed, it need not suggest a specific reference to Jesus' family at all. Dibelius, who originally agreed with Bultmann, later decided that there is too much special material here for it to be the filling out of a saying.[63] This is probably a correct judgment for, 'The section contains elements which it is particularly hard to imagine the early Church's inventing: the statement in v 5, the reference to Jesus' kinfolk in v 4 which was discreditable to people who had come to be prominent in the Church, and probably also the designation of Jesus as "Son of Mary".'[64] The Marcan form of the tradition then probably preserves material of real historical value.

In Mk 6.1–6, the family of Jesus is not present; however, they are mentioned first by Jesus' listeners and then by Jesus Himself. What connects this pericope with Mk 3.21, 31–5 and parallels is the idea that physical relationship or knowledge of Jesus' physical relations proves to be a stumbling block to seeing Jesus as He truly is. There is also a connection in that Jesus places His relatives and His own household once again in a category other than that of believer or disciple.[65]

Mk 6.3 and its parallel in Mt. 13.55–6 (cf. also Lk. 4.14–30) is of prime concern. The textual problem in regard to Mk 6.3 is not resolved easily because p[45] and f[13], among others, have ὁ τοῦ τέκτονος ὁ υἱὸς τῆς Μαρίας, rather than the generally accepted reading, ὁ τέκτων, ὁ υἱὸς τῆς Μαρίας. The reading which best explains the others on both textual and theological grounds is ὁ τέκτων, ὁ υἱὸς τῆς Μαρίας for the following reasons: (1) Calling Jesus a carpenter would not be seen as demeaning to a Jewish or early Christian audience familiar with the Jew's high estimation of manual labour,[66] while it might be to a later Hellenistic or Roman audience. Thus, this reading could be the earlier form of the two. (2) The reference to Jesus as 'Son of Mary' may reflect a setting of controversy and an insult would be implied by this phrase.[67] Thus, the First Evangelist may have changed this phrase because of its negative connotations. (3) The external evidence of the uncials strongly supports this text. (4) If the phrase 'Son of Mary' is original to Mark, then it reveals one of the reasons why Jesus' wise words were not received. How could a child of undistinguished or dubious origins be able to interpret truly the Torah? It is Mark alone who records that Jesus placed His own family in the group with those who stumbled over His apparently ordinary or mysterious origins. It is difficult to believe that Mark would record such statements if they had no basis in fact, especially with the Church's tendency to revere and respect the family of Jesus after His death.[68]

Mk 6.3 and Mt. 13.55 are the only references in the Gospels where Jesus' brothers are mentioned by name.[69] The vast literature on this subject should be consulted for a fuller treatment.[70] Traditionally, there have been three main views concerning the relation of these brothers and sisters to Jesus, to which have been added various modifications. The view most widely held in the Western Church is that of St Jerome, first put forth in a treatise against Helvidius in A.D. 382. He asserts that the Lord's brethren are cousins, being the children of Mary's sister.[71] The Helvidian view which prompted Jerome's new approach to the problem says that they were Jesus' actual brothers, being the children of Mary and Joseph after Jesus' birth.[72] The third view was put forth by Epiphanius in A.D. 376—7. He held that the brothers of Jesus were children of Joseph by a previous marriage. This latter view drew on certain statements in earlier apocryphal Christian documents but was fully presented first by Epiphanius himself.[73] Each view has problems and all were formulated in their more or less final forms between A.D. 375 and 385. The Hieronymian view seems the least likely for the following reasons: (1) The noun ἀδελφός seldom if ever is used in the NT to mean ἀνεψιός (cf. Col. 3.10), nor in the classical usage of ἀδελφός is there much if any evidence that it was used to mean 'cousin'.[74] (2) This view claims that James, the brother of the Lord = one of the Twelve = James the Less, son of Alphaeus; indeed, it has been claimed by some Catholic scholars that all the brothers of the Lord were among the Twelve or the disciples except for Joses. This contradicts the explicit evidence of Mk 3.21, 31—5, and Jn 7.5.[75] (3) Jerome also inferred from the μικρός used with James (son of Alphaeus?) that this meant James the Less to distinguish him from James, the Apostle and son of Zebedee. The word μικρός, however, is not used in a comparative but a positive sense as 'the little'. Further, there is no Scriptural support for calling James, the son of Zebedee, 'the great'.[76] (4) One must maintain not only a questionable punctuation of Jn 19.25, but also the improbability that two sisters would have the same name in order to assert that Mary of Clopas was the sister of Mary, mother of Jesus.

   The Epiphanian view is more probable than the Hieronymian though
there are convincing reasons for rejecting it as well. (1) If Joseph previously
had other sons, then Jesus could not have been legally his first born or
first in line for the Davidic throne.[77] (2) 'Epiphanius' evidence is wholly
based on apocryphal gospels, and everyone knows that for all his diligence
in collecting fragments of tradition and local gossip, he was not exactly
critical in his assessment of the material collected.'[78] (3) It appears that
Lightfoot or his predecessors in the Epiphanian view may have derived
their view from a misreading of ancient texts.[79] Another view, proffered
by McHugh, deserves closer scrutiny. McHugh argues that the brothers
referred to in the Gospels were in fact the first cousins of Jesus on His
father's side. This entails seeing Mary, the mother of James and Joses,
and Clopas (whose wife, Mary, may have been the mother of Simeon)
as the sister and brother of Joseph respectively. McHugh further suggests
that James and Joses may have been raised in the same house as Jesus,
and that they may have called each other (foster) brother.
   McHugh accepts the fact that ἀδελφός means 'brother', not 'cousin',
and acknowledges that contextual hints are necessary if one is to deduce
that ἀδελφός means something other than full blood-brother in a non-
spiritual context.[80] He believes, however, that he finds such hints in the
NT texts under investigation. He suggests, for instance, that the singular
verb in Mk 3.31 following the reaction of Jesus' mother may indicate
that she is separated from the brothers.[81] It may, however, indicate no
more than that Mark's main concern is to mention Mary and her activity,
the brothers being of secondary importance. The number of this verb
may even be a simple grammatical infelicity and in any case should not
be taken as an indicator of a particular view of the relation of Mary and
these 'brothers'. Further, the view that Mark changed the phraseology of
3.21 when he came to verses 31–2 in preparation for verse 35 does not
explain why Mark has failed at least in verse 31 and probably in verse 32
to mention the sisters at all. There is no difficulty in Mark's applying the
more general phrase οἱ παρ' αὐτοῦ (3.21) to Jesus' immediate family, in
the same way we might in English use the phrase 'my folks' or 'my people'
to refer to parents and blood brothers and sisters. Then, too, Mark may be
using two different sources in 3.20–1 and 3.31–5.
   The arguments of McHugh in regard to Mk 6.1–6 and parallels should
also be rejected.[82] Mark's phrasing 'the Son of Mary' and '(a) brother of
James', etc. is perfectly natural since James had other brothers and Jesus
is *the* Son of Mary in question here. In fact, some scholars argue that the
single article here may imply that Jesus bears the same kind of relationship
to both Mary and the brothers.[83] It probably does not hint at a distinction

between the relation of Jesus to His mother and to these brothers. It is also hard to believe that the First Evangelist's mention of 'all' Jesus' sisters[84] (a qualification not found in Mark) is his attempt to pile up arguments against Jesus' Messiahship since there is no attempt in the rest of the pericope to answer such a charge. Why would he strengthen the case of the opposition and then not strengthen the response of Jesus to counter it? To be sure, neither the First nor the Second Evangelist tries to hide the fact that Jesus' origins were a stumbling block to some but it is hardly likely that they would bolster the case of the opposition. The addition of 'all' in Matthew requires some other explanation, especially in view of the modification of 'the carpenter' to 'the carpenter's son' which indicates that the Evangelist is intent on eliminating potentially offensive material (not adding it). Nothing should be made of the First Evangelist's choice of the verb λεγέται. Interestingly, it is singular and thus wrongly some might even attempt to apply it only to its nearest antecedent, Mary. The reference in Mk 6.4 to 'kinsmen' should probably not be taken as an indication that the brothers in 6.3 were not blood brothers, since it may well be a reference to some of Jesus' audience quite apart from those listed in 6.3, or alternatively it may simply be added for rhetorical effect as the group referred to becomes increasingly smaller.[85] McHugh also suggests that the First Evangelist's phrase, 'the other Mary' (27.61, 28.1) might be used to distinguish her from Jesus' mother. Mother Mary, however, is not mentioned in these two Matthean texts and the reference should and does make sense in context — as a means to distinguish this woman from Mary Magdalene.[86]

A more adequate argument than McHugh presents is required to explain why these 'foster' children are frequently mentioned in the same breath with Mary (cf. Mk 3.21, 31−5 and parallels, Mk 6.1−6 and parallels, Jn 2.12),[87] and why also these brothers and sisters, like Mary, are identified as residents of Nazareth and Jesus' closest relatives.[88] The question is whether or not the Evangelist's audiences would have understood 'foster brother' by the word ἀδελφός, when no clear hints of this meaning are forthcoming in the texts under discussion.[89] The answer to this question must in all probability be no. Thus, McHugh's view is not to be accepted as the best explanation of the data.

We are left with the Helvidian view which admittedly has problems, though none are insurmountable. Bishop Lightfoot's objection that Jesus would never commend His mother to a stranger (Jn 19.26−7) rather than His own physical brother(s) is not obvious. As noted in Mk 3.31−5, Jesus is insistent that the family of faith take precedence over the physical family (cf. Mk 10.29−30), and thus it is more natural (if Jn 19.26−7 is of historical value) for Jesus to entrust His dearest relative to His dearest friend since they were united in the bond of faith.[90]

There is little evidence that tells us whether or not the brothers in Mk 6.3 and the men in Mk 15.40 are different or the same; however, James and Joses are common names and they could easily be two different sets of brothers. Further, perhaps the fact that the James of Mk 15.40 is called μικρός does distinguish him from the James of Mk 6.3 who receives no such title.[91] Finally, it cannot be argued on the basis of the fact that some called Jesus the son of Joseph that Jesus was related to His brothers in the same way as He was related to His legal father (Joseph). This overlooks the fact that in the reference to Jesus as the son of Joseph, none of those on whose lips we find the term were in a position to know about the virginal conception (Mt. 13.55, Mk 6.3 p[45], Lk. 4.22, Jn 1.45, 6.42). In the one reference where the comment comes from a Gospel writer himself (Lk. 3.23), it is tactfully qualified by the phrase ὡς ἐνομίζετο. There are no good reasons to reject the Helvidian view, and many good reasons to commend it, since it allows one to take not only ἀδελφός but also ἕως οὗ in Mt. 1.25 and the meaning of Lk. 1.34 in their most natural sense. As Taylor says, 'It may also be fairly argued ... that the expressions used in Lk. ii.7 and Mt. i.25 would have been avoided by writers who believed in the perpetual virginity of Mary.'[92]

How does accepting the Helvidian view affect our understanding of Mary and her role? It reveals her as a normal Jewish mother who saw her blessedness primarily in bearing children and in raising them properly. It also reveals that she was perhaps subject to the unbeliefs or misunderstandings about Jesus that her other children held. Mk 3.21, 31–5 reveals both her natural concern for and her misunderstanding of Jesus. Mark, and to a lesser degree Matthew and Luke, portray Mary during the ministry as an example of how kinship ties can hinder proper understanding of Jesus as Messiah. They also show that Mary was fully human and struggled with the difficulties of placing her spiritual allegiance to Jesus over her motherly love for Him and her other sons and daughters. In this she may be seen as a point of contact for other married women in the Gospel writers' audiences.

3. Mary at the Cross – Jn 19.25–7

Jn 19.25–7 is without question a crux in the Johannine problem. We have here a scene of which there is no trace in the Synoptic material. It seems likely though, *if* Luke had known the story, he would have used it, for Ac. 1.14 does show that he had some interest in whether or not Jesus'

mother became a member of His community. Again, the scene with
women standing near the cross seems to flatly contradict the Synoptic
account and some have argued that the location is historically improbable.[93] Then, too, the historicity of this incident is in part bound up with
the question of whether or not the beloved disciple was an historical
figure. Finally, the list of women differs from those found in the Synoptics, both in its names and in its position, and it is of particular importance that only the Fourth Evangelist includes Jesus' mother in the list.

There are certain indications that the Fourth Evangelist is relying on a
source for at least part of this material and that the source was not the
Synoptics. In the first place, his list of names varies too much from any
of the Synoptic lists for it to be probable that he derived his own list from
those found in the first three Gospels. It may be that they share only one
name (Mary Magdalene) in common.[94] Secondly, the absence of any
mention at 19.25 of the beloved disciple among those that are standing
at the cross and the mention of two women who are not to be found
elsewhere in the Fourth Gospel and whose mention has little apparent
purpose or significance make it likely that the Evangelist has not created
this list. It is not impossible that he added Jesus' mother's name to a pre-
existing list, but why then did he not also add the beloved disciple in
preparation for 19.26–7? These considerations lead to the suggestion
that he found Jesus' mother's name listed in his source as one of those
present at the cross. As we shall point out, there is nothing historically
unlikely about a few grieving women being allowed near Jesus' cross
especially if it was guarded, and there are reasons for thinking that the
ἀπὸ μακρόθεν of the Synoptics derives from the Psalms and should not be
taken as an historical description of their location.[95]

If the beloved disciple is an historical figure, and it seems unlikely
that the Evangelist or the Johannine community would have made claims
such as we find in 19.35 if they were not relying on the testimony of an
historical figure,[96] it is not at all certain that he was one of the Twelve.
If he was not, then there is no contradiction between his presence at the
cross and the tradition that the Twelve deserted Jesus before He went to
the cross. It must be borne in mind that the Fourth Evangelist probably
bears witness to the desertion (cf. 16.32, 20.10) and yet he saw no incon-
gruity in mentioning the presence of the beloved disciple at the cross.
Again, if the beloved disciple is an historical figure, then it is possible
that the tradition being drawn on in Jn 19.26–7 was originally about
Jesus providing for the ongoing security of His mother by placing her
in the care of a friend he knew and trusted.[97] That He would entrust her
to a disciple is not historically unlikely because: (1) there are strong

reasons for thinking that He considered the family of faith His primary family (cf. Mk 3.34–5); (2) it is likely that at the time of Jesus' death, His physical brothers were unbelievers (cf. Jn 7.5). If the beloved disciple is an ideal figure, then Jn 19.26–7 is probably a Johannine creation meant to affirm various things (which we will soon discuss) about men and women as disciples of Jesus. Even if this is so, it does not preclude the possibility that the Evangelist incorporated into this ideal scene certain historical fragments about what happened to Mary. Perhaps, the Fourth Evangelist simply had access to a traditional list of women who were present at the cross that included the name of Jesus' mother,[98] and he knew that Mary at some point joined Jesus' community. Finally, the entire narrative may be a creation of the Evangelist himself without use of or access to any historical information.

Of these various possibilities the option which will be accepted in the discussion which follows is: (1) that verse 25 is a traditional list to which the Evangelist added a narrative found in his sources;[99] (2) that originally the narrative in verses 26–7 was about Jesus providing ongoing care for His mother — a motif probably based on historical fact; (3) that the Evangelist has transformed his material into a powerful statement about men and women as disciples at the foot of the cross and has used it as a vehicle to affirm the historical truth that at some point (not necessarily at the cross) Mary became a full-fledged disciple of her Son. The other views mentioned are, however, options which cannot be ruled out.[100] There will be no attempt here to claim historical value for more than the substratum which the Evangelist uses in writing his narrative (i.e., Mary's presence at the cross and in the Church, and Jesus' provision for Mary).

The story of Mary witnessing her Son's crucifixion should probably be seen as the climatic episode of the Fourth Evangelist's Passion narrative.[101] Drawing on elements presented in Jn 2.1–12 (mother of Jesus, γύναι, the 'hour', physical family, disciples), the Evangelist presents in Jn 19.25–7 the resolution of the tension or division between Jesus' physical family and His spiritual family in the context of Jesus' 'hour'.

In Jn 19.25 we read of Jesus' mother standing near the cross with three other women.[102] It should not be objected that it is historically unlikely that Mary or these women would be near the cross, for evidence shows that relatives and close friends might be permitted to stand near a crucifixion.[103] In the end, it was the women, not the Twelve, who stayed with Jesus to the last. In the Johannine schema here is the point at which Jesus could not reject His mother's claims. His 'hour' had come, and so too had hers in a different sense of the word.

From among these four women, the Evangelist shows Jesus singling out His mother and addressing her as at Cana — 'Woman'. This time, however, the intention is not disengagement, but rather engagement or unification. The Evangelist wishes to show that Mary is accepted officially into Jesus' spiritual family, yet she is still addressed as γύναι, the same address used in Jn 2.1–12. Where is the point of similarity in these two narratives that warrants such an address? One would have expected the Evangelist to portray Jesus as using a more intimate term to address His mother in her anguish and sorrow.[104] Perhaps the Evangelist is indicating the following: Jesus resolves for Mary the tension between her roles as mother and disciple of Jesus. He is in control of this scene, and He alone speaks and calls His mother γύναι precisely because He does not wish to renew the filial bond, but rather to confirm her in her relationship to Him as disciple. As she loses Jesus both in a physical and spiritual sense, she gains a new family, the beloved disciple being her first 'son' in the faith. She does not cease to be a mother; however, at Jesus' hour she becomes a mother of a different sort and joins with the family of faith.

Mary learns that she is to be a mother as a disciple, not a mother and also a disciple. Discipleship must be the larger context in which her role as mother is delimited and defined. Mary responds in silence and submission. She obeys the word of the Lord and goes with the beloved disciple. In so doing she is the model woman — a testimony to a woman's new freedom in faith and also to a woman's traditional roles of serving under the authority and headship of man. Her new son is the man under whose charge she now is. This is reflected in the fact that, though John is first commended to her, she does not take charge but rather is received into the charge of the beloved disciple. It is not without reason that Jesus calls her 'Woman'. She must enter the family of faith in full recognition of who she is as a sexual being. She will not lose that sexuality for some spirituality in the community of belief. Rather, she will assume both her old role of motherhood and her new roles as witness, prophetess and proclaimer of God's word in relationship to believers. She will orientate her physical nature so as to engender and further the growth of Jesus' true kindred. In this, she is like the many other women who followed Jesus, being liberated by God's word, and serving Jesus and the Twelve in their traditional roles (cf. Lk. 8.1–3, Mt. 27.55 and parallels). This is the Evangelist's theological message. Perhaps Stauffer is closer to the historical truth in this matter when he suggests that Mary needed someone to provide for her after Jesus' death: 'Jesus knew this. And a crucified man had the right to make testamentary dispositions even from the cross. Now Jesus took advantage of this right, and, using the formal language of Jewish family law, he placed his mother under the protection of John: "Woman, behold your son!" And to the disciple: "Behold your mother!" '[105]

Having given an overview of the meaning of Jn 19.25–7, let us see how the exegetical particulars bear on this interpretation. As R.E. Brown and others have noted, the Evangelist probably intends us to recognize a revelatory formula in the phrases, γύναι ἴδε ὁ υἱός σου ... Ἴδε ἡ μήτηρ σου.[106] The formula involves two things: (1) God's messenger sees someone and says, 'Behold!' and, (2) after this, a description or explanation of one's role or task in salvation history is given.[107] An exegetical point which supports our interpretation is the mention of the ὥρα in 19.27, which may refer back to what Jesus said to His mother in Jn 2.4. This is the hour of Jesus which has come and so it is also Mary's hour. After it (ἀπ᾽ ἐκείνης τῆς ὥρας) she will be irrevocably a part of the family of faith.[108]

How are we to take the phrase εἰς τὰ ἴδια? Originally this pericope may have had some reference to the specific provisions Jesus made for Mary's care. In its present context and in light of various other Johannine texts, it appears that this phrase means more. Perhaps a clue is found in Jn 1.11: εἰς τὰ ἴδια ἦλθεν, καὶ οἱ ἴδιοι αὐτὸν οὐ παρέλαβον. This phrase seems to mean, 'He came into His own (or 'His own home') and His own people did not receive Him.' Consider another example found in Jn 16.32: ἰδοὺ ἔρχεται ὥρα καὶ ἐλήλυθεν ἵνα σκορπισθῆτε ἕκαστος εἰς τὰ ἴδια κἀμὲ μόνον ἀφῆτε — 'Behold, the hour is coming and has come whereupon you will be scattered, each to his own (home) and you will leave me alone.'[109] For the disciples this means the time when they abandon Jesus and go home — the Church is scattered leaving Jesus alone. In Jn 19.25–7, however, the Church is re-established in unity. Jesus unites His own family with the family of faith and gives them a home (εἰς τὰ ἴδια) which is the home of the one faithful disciple. The εἰς τὰ ἴδια in Jn 19.25–7 represents the 'Church' gathered, in contrast to Jn 16.32.[110]

The Evangelist intends the scene to be balanced between attention given to the beloved disciple and attention given to Jesus' mother. Both are addressed and both receive a commission. While Mary's importance stands out here (she is addressed first and her future is considered at the end of verse 27),[111] and it may be significant that the beloved disciple is only referred to as a son of Mary (while Mary is addressed as 'Woman' and referred to as mother of this disciple),[112] throughout this scene only the beloved disciple is called ὁ μαθητής and it is he who takes charge of Jesus' mother at the close of this scene. It should be emphasized that this disciple's faith and his role as representative disciple, antedate Mary's role as spiritual mother.[113] Thus, Mary is not depicted here as the mother of the Church, but as a spiritual mother to and in the Church. 'Initially, it is significant that the scene brings together two figures for whom John never gives us personal names. That may mean that the significance of both figures lay in their respective roles.'[114] It also means that the Evangelist's focus is on these two persons as models or types. Not Mary alone, but both Mary and the beloved disciple are in a sense a foreshadowing of the Church, standing beneath the cross of their Lord.[115]

It is to be noted that Mary and the beloved disciple are not depicted simply as representative male and female disciples. Jesus does not refer to them as 'sister' or 'brother'. This is a scene about the new equality of male and female beneath the cross of Jesus, but the way that equality is expressed is by the woman resuming her role as mother with new significance, and the disciple becoming a son. In this scene then the tension between physical family and the family of faith is resolved as Mary is included in the fold. Further, the tension between traditional roles and the role of disciples is resolved as the representative disciple becomes a son again, and Mary a mother. The Fourth Evangelist's vision of male–female equality in the Christian community entails an incorporation of the physical family into the family of faith, and a reinterpretation of physical family roles in light of the priorities of the family of faith. Thus, the new community is served rather than severed by traditional roles and relationships. This scene is not about the replacement of Jesus' physical brothers by His brother in the faith, but the text does imply that the beloved disciple becomes Jesus' brother by sharing the same mother.[116] Also, it is not correct to shift the emphasis of this text to something which is not mentioned here — the care of the mother for the son (i.e., the disciple).[117]

The mother of Jesus is seen as the typical female disciple who struggles with the relationship of her physical and spiritual roles. She is depicted as a spiritual mother to and in the Church, though not as Mother Church that gives birth to spiritual children, since the beloved disciple's faith antedates Mary's role as spiritual mother.[118] If this assessment of Mary as a symbol of woman ($\gamma\acute{v}v\alpha\iota$) in her new relationship to the community of faith is correct, then it appears to be part of the plan of the Fourth Evangelist to show that in Christ the dignity of woman is restored and her place of equality affirmed.[119] Especially significant is that Jesus' mother typifies the traditional role of mother and that she is the symbol of woman in her new roles as spiritual mother and disciple. The Evangelist is indicating that her two types of roles, once confused (cf. Jn 2) are now fused under the cross of Jesus, in service of His community, typified by the beloved disciple.

Having achieved the reconciliation of the physical family and the family of faith, of male and female, the Evangelist intimates that Jesus has accomplished the work the Father had given Him — μετὰ τοῦτο εἰδὼς ὁ Ἰησοῦς ὅτι ἤδη πάντα τετέλεσται ... (Jn 19.28).[120] The Fourth Evangelist saw in the material he drew upon a great deal more than Jesus' act of filial piety. He saw in it an example of male and female standing as equals (though with different roles to play) beneath the cross of Christ.

4. Conclusions

We will not reiterate here the conclusions drawn at the end of various sections involving Mary, but we will make a few concluding remarks. Since our main concern is with Jesus' attitude toward Mary, and only secondarily with how the Evangelists portray her in relation to Jesus, we must first ask what impressions this material leaves on the reader in regard to the former matter. Quite clearly, Mark stresses Jesus' distancing of Himself from His family (Mk 3.21, 31) in favour of an identification with the family of faith (3.31–5), though the possibility of the physical family finding a place within the spiritual one is never ruled out. The First Evangelist follows Mark in indicating that Jesus distinguished His physical and spiritual families, but omits Mk 3.21 to soften the criticism of Mary and Jesus' family. The criticism appears, however, in a somewhat muted form in 13.57 (καὶ ἐν τῇ οἰκίᾳ αὐτοῦ). Luke in even milder fashion shows Jesus indicating that His true mother and brothers are other than His physical mother and brothers at one point in His ministry (8.20–1), but this text is set in the midst of various other Lucan texts which give a generally favourable impression of Mary and of her relationship to Jesus (cf. 1.38, 1.46–9, 2.39, 2.19, 51, Ac. 1.14, though contrast Lk. 2.50). The Fourth Evangelist in his own way likewise indicates that Jesus distanced Himself from His family (cf. 2.4, 7.6–8), or at least from their authority over Him. Thus, we seem to have a rather unanimous testimony to the fact that Jesus' first allegiance was to the family of faith and to doing His heavenly Father's will, not the will of His earthly mother. It is worth noting that Mary appears to be the only woman in the Gospels whom Jesus clearly distanced Himself from when she made requests of Him during the course of His ministry (with the possible exception of the Syrophoenician woman). This is also attested to in uniquely Lucan material (2.49–50). This distancing is apparently to be accounted for by the fact that Jesus believed He had a special mission in life and a special relationship to His heavenly Father, and human relationships and authorities were not to be allowed to interfere with

that mission and relationship. If this is a correct deduction, then it means
that these texts do not necessarily indicate any antipathy of Jesus toward
His mother as a woman or as a mother *per se*, but indicate a rejection
of her authority over Him when that authority was being exercised in
a way that interfered with the principles and priorities of Jesus' mission.[121]

In regard to the Evangelist's portrayal of Mary in her relationship
to Jesus, the portrait painted by Mark and the First Evangelist is quite
different from that in the other two Gospels. The Second Evangelist,
if anything, indicates only Mary's misunderstanding of Jesus' mission
(Mk 3.21, 31). In Mk 6.1–6, Mary appears as someone well-known in
Nazareth, who appears to have other children besides Jesus, and about
whom there is some controversy with regard to the birth of her first
son (hence the term 'son of Mary'). The First Evangelist generally follows
Mark in this matter, though as we have noted Mk 3.21 is omitted and
also the term of reproach 'son of Mary' is omitted. The portrait here
of Jesus' mother is not strongly negative, but Mary is not portrayed
as exemplary either. Even in his Birth narratives, the First Evangelist
merely portrays Mary as a good Jewish woman who is silent and follows
the lead of her husband (2.13, 20).

The portrayal of Mary in Luke is considerably more positive, though
this impression is mainly derived from material in the birth narratives
and thus many will question whether it is of any historical value. The
most that one can say on the basis of the relevant ministry material
(8.20–1) is that Luke has muted somewhat the criticism of the family,
though strikingly it crops up at 2.50. In John, Mary appears to have
some sort of faith in Jesus (2.5). The family and disciples, though distinguished, are pictured together at 2.12. The scene in Jn 19.25–7 is
an idealized one, as Mary is presented as the representative female disciple at the foot of the cross and thus the Fourth Evangelist indicates
that Mary gained a place among Jesus' disciples. As for historical matters,
however, this scene probably only tells us about Jesus' care for His mother
as He was dying.

What is particularly striking is that all four Gospels to one degree
or another indicate both that Jesus' mother failed at some point to completely understand or honour her Son (cf. Mt. 13.57*b*, Mk 3.21, Lk.
2.50, Jn 2.4), and that Jesus distanced Himself from her in the process
of distinguishing His physical family from His spiritual one (cf. Jn 2.4,
Mk 3.31–5 and parallels, Mk 6.4*b*, Mt. 13.57*b*). The overall impression
left by the material in the Gospels about Mary is that no Evangelist made
a concerted effort to give Mary more significance than she actually had
in the ministry of Jesus; that no Evangelist attempted to paint a purely

idealized portrait of her; and that no Evangelist attempted to portray a strictly Christian (i.e., non-Jewish) picture of Jesus' mother.

B. Mary and Martha

1. Hosts or Guests? Lk. 10.38—42

Though it is unlikely they travelled with Jesus, Mary and Martha may have been the most important and prominent women in Jesus' life after His own mother. The Gospels give us three accounts of how these women figured in Jesus' life — Lk. 10.38—42, Jn 11.1—44 and Jn 12.1—11.

The Lucan story is a brief vignette sandwiched between two crucial sections — the Good Samaritan and the Lord's Prayer. It seems possible to see a purpose and progression in this arrangement: the Good Samaritan parable (10.25—37) gives an example of how to serve and love one's neighbour; Lk. 10.38—42 teaches that the 'one thing necessary' is not first service, but listening to and learning from Jesus (allowing Jesus to serve us), and the Lord's Prayer (11.1—4) gives an example of what is to be heard and learned from Jesus.[122]

This uniquely Lucan pericope, the only Synoptic passage on Mary and Martha, appears to be a unitary construction, for the climactic saying of Jesus (10.41—2) could not have stood on its own.[123] The question remains, however, whether this scene is an 'ideal', mainly legendary, construction, or whether it contains good, historical tradition. Bultmann gives no reason for suggesting that this scene is 'ideal',[124] and it is questionable whether the 'legendary' view should stand. The characterization of Mary and Martha is neither highly embellished nor detailed. It involves a simple contrast in activities or attitudes and this characterization is to some extent confirmed in another strand of the tradition (cf. Jn 11.20 ff; 12.2 ff).[125] Secondly, in view of the uniqueness both of Mary's activity and of Jesus' attitude about it when compared to Jewish attitudes about women disciples and their proper role in the home and later attitudes in the Church about a woman's place and role in the Christian community and family (cf. for instance 1 Tim. 2.9—15), it is most unlikely that this scene is an 'ideal' construction.[126] Thirdly, there appears here no interest in Mary and Martha for their own sake. The narrative is presented not to indulge a Christian audience's curiosity about certain well-known early disciples but to relate Jesus' teaching in verses 41—2, to indicate how it arose, and to show how it applied to later Christians as well. Some of the textual problems in verse 42 may have arisen because this text in its original form might have appeared too radical to some, calling even women

away from putting their traditional roles first so that they too might have
the good portion Mary partook of.[127] Thus, it is more probable that this
story has a sound basis in historical fact, even though Luke has written
and presented the narrative in his own language and style.[128]

Martha appears to be the older sister and the mistress of the house, for
she ὑπεδέξατο αὐτόν.[129] It is she who takes charge of preparing for the
guest and she feels she has a right to her sister's assistance.[130] Though this
story primarily focuses on Martha and what she must learn about 'the one
thing necessary', Mary appears to know already, for she 'was listening to
his word'.[131] Contrary to what some commentators have asserted, Mary
is not sitting at her Master's feet at the table.[132] Here the meal is clearly
yet to come. The use of the phrase 'to sit at the feet of' in 10.39 is significant since there is evidence that this is a technical formula meaning 'to be
a disciple of'.[133] If so, then Luke is intimating to his audience that Mary
is a disciple and as such her behaviour is to be emulated. Though we
mentioned previously that women could attend synagogue, learn, and
even be learned if their husbands or masters were rabbis,[134] for a rabbi
to come into a woman's house and teach her specifically is unheard of.
Further, being alone with two women who were not one's relatives was
considered questionable behaviour by the rabbis.[135] Thus, not only the
role Mary assumes, but also the task Jesus performs in this story is in
contrast to what was expected of a Jewish man and woman.

While Mary is taking on the not so traditional role of disciple, Martha
is engaged in what some would call 'woman's work' — providing hospitality for her guest. In a Jewish context, however, women were not allowed
to serve at meals if men were in attendance, unless there were no servants
to perform the task.[136] It is possible that Martha's behaviour is atypical
and reflects her desire and willingness to serve Jesus, even if it meant
assuming a servant's role. Martha, whether because she resents not receiving
help from Mary or because she envies Mary's 'portion', is 'distracted by a
good deal of serving'.[137] Rather than quietly serving without complaint,
she vents her feelings by accusing Jesus of not caring, and indirectly
accusing Mary of neglecting her when she needed help.[138] Jesus does not
respond as Martha expected. His remarks, however, are neither an attempt
to devalue Martha's efforts at hospitality, nor an attempt to attack a
woman's traditional role; rather, Jesus defends Mary's right to learn from
Him and says this is the crucial thing for those who wish to serve Him.
Jesus makes clear that for women as well as men, one's primary task is to
be a proper disciple; only in that context can one be a proper hostess.
His address to Martha shows a recognition that Martha is concerned with
'many things'.[139] Such things as even one's own family, however, must be

seen as of lesser importance, indeed in an entirely separate and subordinate category, to the responsibility of hearing God's word and being Jesus' disciple.

Unfortunately, the rest of Jesus' response to Martha, the climax of this pericope, is clouded with large textual difficulties. There are no less than six possibilities for the text of Lk. 10.42*a*.[140]

(1) ὀλίγων δέ χρεία ἐστιν ἢ ἑνὸς — B

(2) ὀλίγων δέ ἐστιν χρεία ἢ ἑνὸς — p³ ℵ^c C² L f¹ 33 syr^h mg cop^bo eth Origen^1/2 Basil Jerome Cyril

(3) ὀλίγων δέ ἐστιν ἢ ἑνὸς — ℵ*

(4) ἑνὸς δέ ἐστιν χρεία — p⁴⁵ A K P Δ Π Ψ f¹³ 28 565 700 892 *et al.* Byz Lect 160m *et al.* Clement Basil Macarius Chrysostom Antiochus John-Damascus

(5) ὀλίγων δέ ἐστιν χρεία — 38 (syr^pal) Cop^bo ms arm geo Origen 1/2

(6) omit the entire clause — it^a b e ff² i l r¹ syr^s Ambrose Possidius

It is probable that option three should be eliminated as it appears to be either a later simplification of, or a scribal mistake based on, option one or two. It could be argued that variants one and two are the products of a process of conflation and that the original text read either, 'few things are necessary', or 'one thing is necessary'. Scribes who had some manuscripts with one reading and some with the other might have conflated the two rather than take a chance of omitting the original text.[141] Another factor which argues against the longer readings is that they do not have the wide geographical spread of the shorter readings.[142] In addition, the shorter reading with ἑνὸς may claim the support of p⁴⁵ and other important manuscripts.[143] Both scholarly opinion and the evidence of the Fathers appear equally divided between the longer and shorter readings, though the modern English translations are not.[144] Though nearly all the Old Latin manuscripts omit the clause entirely, it appears that only one or two of the Latin Fathers witness this omission, which weakens the evidence for the omission.[145] Contrary to M. Augsten's assertion, the fact that the shorter reading is rather 'secular' in thought is not a basis for ruling it out.[146]

Purely on the basis of external evidence, it is difficult to decide between the longer and shorter readings. Several internal considerations, however, give the shorter reading a slight edge. Though variants one and two are more difficult readings, that is precisely the difficulty. In the context, Jesus is contrasting Martha's 'many' with something else. It does not seem likely that Jesus would contrast many and few here when in fact it is one thing (τὴν ἀγαθὴν μερίδα), Mary's listening and learning, that He is defending. Elsewhere in Luke, the importance of one thing is stressed (15.8, 16.13, 18.19, 22).[147] It is not a matter of contrasting the active to the contemplative life; rather, it is a matter of contrasting the importance of listening to and learning the word of God to anything else.[148] We are dealing with a matter of priorities and only one thing can come first and be absolutely necessary.

If one of the longer readings is preferred, Creed is right that a pun on a 'few dishes' (ὀλίγων) and the 'one portion' Mary has been served is being made.[149] This idea is not ruled out, however, if we only have ἑνὸς and πολλά. The meaning then would be that Jesus did not come to be served, but to serve. He is the host, and Mary and Martha are the guests. Mary has just received τὴν ἀγαθὴν μερίδα.[150] This is not to be taken from her.[151] The phrase τὴν ἀγαθὴν μερίδα is probably not to be seen as a comparative term (such as the better or best portion), for we are dealing with something in a class by itself.[152] It should be noted also that this is something that the Evangelist intimates Mary chose for herself (middle), responding to the Word in faith by placing it first.[153] As in the case of Jesus' relation to His mother Mary, we see once again a reorganizing of traditional priorities in light of Kingdom requirements. Martha's service is not denigrated but it does not come first. One must reorientate one's lifestyle according to what Jesus says is the 'good portion'. It is this universal priority of faith and equality in faith that gives woman a new and equal place under the new covenant. This is the radical nature of the Gospel and why it dramatically affected women's status especially in first-century Palestine. Luke portrays Mary as a disciple sitting and learning at the feet of her Master, and as such she serves as a model for his audience. The appeals to a woman's traditional role, here voiced by Martha, do not prevail against the fact that women (like men) are called to be hearers and obeyers of Jesus' word first. We must now turn to the Johannine portrayal of these two women.[154]

2. A Confession and a Proclamation – John 11

Few would dispute the fact that the story of the raising of Lazarus raises more problems than almost any other miracle recorded in the Gospels for the student of history. It is not possible to deal adequately with all the difficulties this narrative poses in these paragraphs; thus, the most we can hope to do is present a few reasons for the approach taken and explain why other approaches have been rejected.

In our discussion of Lk. 10.38–42 we suggested that it was unlikely that there was a relation of dependence either of Luke on John or the converse so far as their material on Mary and Martha is concerned. Further support for this view can now be given. Clearly, the Fourth Evangelist does not derive the association of Lazarus with Mary and Martha from Luke. Also, he did not derive the connection of Mary with an anointing of Jesus in Bethany from Luke. Yet Jn 11.2 makes clear that the Fourth Evangelist expects his audience to be already cognizant of this tradition. Thus, he himself probably did not create the connection nor did he procure his information on this matter from the Synoptics. This leads to the conclusion that he had a source of information about Mary (and Martha?) other than the Synoptics.[155] Further, the suggestion that the Lazarus narrative derives from Lk. 16.19–30 is implausible. In the first place there is no raising of a man named Lazarus in the Lucan parable; indeed, the conclusion suggests that such a raising would be pointless and thus is not to be undertaken (verse 31). Secondly, the Lazarus in the Lucan parable bears no resemblance to the man who was part of a household that could afford a tomb and entertain house guests such as Jesus (Jn 11).[156] Lazarus was not an unusual name, but it should be noted that it was unusual for a character in a parable to be named.[157] Thus, 'It is the occurrence of the name in the Lucan parable that calls for explanation. Such an explanation would be forthcoming if there existed in pre-Johannine tradition a story about the resurrection of a man called Lazarus, with a general implication that this did not win men to faith in Christ.'[158]

Another of the major difficulties with this narrative so far as its historicity is concerned is that there is no real trace of it in the Synoptics (unless Lk. 16.19–30 evidences it). This is problematic mainly because the raising is of such a dramatic and crucial nature (in John it is the act which precipitates the organized efforts to get rid of Jesus) that, it is contended, the Synoptics could hardly afford to leave it out, if they knew of it. Two things lessen the force of this argument. First, as Morris points out, 'Mark has nothing about Jesus' ministry in Jerusalem before the final week.'[159] Matthew and Luke are fundamentally following Mark. It is thus not at all unlikely that Mark simply had no knowledge of this story. This is especially believable if (1) some of the drama of the narrative is due to the Fourth Evangelist's handling of the material and, more importantly, (2) the positioning of the narrative is the work of the Fourth Evangelist. Brown has provided a very plausible argument for the view that the positioning of this narrative is the Evangelist's own doing, as he intends to provide a dramatic end to the public ministry of Jesus and prepare the way for the Passion and Resurrection narratives.[160]

If this narrative was originally simply another story of the raising of the dead by Jesus, perhaps without the delay motif which heightens the drama, it is quite believable that even if Mark (or any of the Synoptists) knew of the narrative, they could have chosen to omit it and include another raising story since theirs is, after all, a selective presentation of Gospel events.

In regard to the form and content of this narrative it is difficult to separate what may be attributed to the work of the Evangelist and what to his source(s), although Bultmann and Schnackenburg believe they are able to make such a separation. The former argues that the figures of Mary and Martha probably do not belong to the original form of this narrative; the latter concludes that the Mary material was probably in the source and that the Evangelist has constructed the dialogue with Martha as a sort of doublet of the encounter with Mary and as a forum for conveying Christological remarks and a Christian confession.[161] At this point, however, a word of caution is in order. As Dodd remarks: 'Nowhere perhaps, in this Gospel, have attempts to analyze out a written source, or sources, proved less convincing, and if the evangelist is following a traditional story or fixed pattern, he has covered his tracks.'[162] The story as it stands is both a literary unity and thoroughly Johannine.[163] But this may mean no more than that the author has made the story his own, and told of these (possibly historical) events in his own style with a certain amount of poetic license. As for its form, this narrative has certain of the features that are usually found in the miracle narratives in the Synoptics.[164] All other things being equal this may count against seeing this narrative as in the main a Johannine creation.

For our part it should be noted that even if the raising of Lazarus proves to be a legend, or a creation of the Evangelist, the encounters Jesus had with the grieving Martha and Mary may not be, and it is these encounters with which we are concerned in this thesis. There are certain features in these encounters that point toward their basic authenticity: (1) the characterization of Martha and in some respects Mary comports with that in Lk. 10, while probably being independent of the Lucan material; (2) Martha's faith in Jesus is not a full-blown Christian faith, nor does the presentation of Jesus here reflect some later Christo-monistic ideas, but, as Bultmann says, 'her faith in his power is faith in the power of his prayer; ... The Revealer accordingly is removed from the sphere of the θεῖος ἄνθρωπος as the old miracle stories see him; it is recognized that everything he possesses he has from God.'[165] (3) Martha's statement in verse 24 simply expresses a common Jewish idea about resurrection; there is nothing particularly Christian about it.

As for verse 27, while the Evangelist may simply be assembling various Christological titles here (cf. Jn 1.19ff), it is noteworthy that this confession is inadequate and does not include the crucial element of belief in Jesus' present power to raise the dead. Were the construction purely redactional, the Evangelist would perhaps have made the confession more suitable to the occasion. Perhaps Martha made some sort of rudimentary confession, within the parameters of correct Jewish belief and expectation about the Messiah, and the Evangelist has modified the confession in verse 27 just enough to suit his purposes without placing a full-blown Christian confession on Martha's lips (for 27*a*, cf. Mk 8.29 and parallels; for 27*b*, cf. Mk 1.11 and parallels; for 27*c*, cf. Jn 1.9 and Mt. 11.3, etc.). Verse 27*c*, however, may simply be the Evangelist's creation on the basis of Jn 1.9. The proclamation in Jn 11.25–6 in its present form may be assigned to the Evangelist. This, however, does not preclude the possibility that Jesus spoke privately to some of His closer disciples about His life-giving powers. If Riesenfeld is right that the original *Sitz im Leben* for the Johannine 'I am' sayings and proclamations was the informal discussions of Jesus with His closer disciples,[166] then it is possible that even verses 25–6 may in some form go back to Jesus. The use of ἀνάστασις and ἀνιστάναι here may indicate the use of a source for they are not common in John and are used only once of Jesus' own Resurrection (20.9).[167] Perhaps with Brown we may conclude: 'From the contents of the Johannine account then, there is no conclusive reason for assuming that the skeleton of the story does not stem from early tradition about Jesus.'[168] Thus, it seems reasonable to assign the characterization of Mary and Martha, the idea that Martha made a rudimentary confession of a Jewish belief in resurrection and in Jesus as Messiah, the self-proclamation of Jesus as a life-giving source, and the general encounter of Jesus with the grieving sisters to a *Sitz im Leben Jesu*; but that as far as the exact wording, the dramatic delay of Jesus' coming, the setting of the raising at the climax of the ministry, and perhaps even the raising itself, it is best not to go beyond a statement of what these aspects of the narrative say about the Evangelist's own views and theology.

Jn 11.1–44 is the longest continuous narrative in the Fourth Gospel apart from the Passion narrative. This is not without reason, for in the Johannine schema of things it is the climactic and most miraculous episode in the series of signs he presents.[169] In many ways this story parallels the first sign in Jn 2 and serves to bring together and re-emphasize some of John's chief themes. The message Mary and Martha send in 11.3 is similar to the open-ended suggestion of Jesus' mother in 2.3. Further, Martha's remark in 11.22 about 'whatever you ask' resembles Mary's statement in 2.5. In both scenes, the hope is implied that Jesus will act despite the seeming impossibility of the situations.[170] It is fitting that verse 40 (cf. 11.4) mentions glory, for this also relates back to the Cana miracle (2.11) and forward to the climax of this Gospel. In this story, as in Jn 2 and Jn 7, Jesus can only act as the Father wills, not at the request of His mother, sisters, brothers, or friends. This causes the delay in Jesus going to Bethany.[171] It is this fact that explains why He seems to reject mother Mary's request and the plea of Mary and Martha, and then in fact responds as if He had not rejected their suggestion.[172] As the best is saved for last in Jn 2, so in the Gospel as a whole the best miracle is saved for last. In Jn 2 Jesus comes and brings new life and joy to the celebration of the union of two lives; in John 11 He brings new life and reunion to a family He dearly loved. Finally, both narratives involve women whom the Evangelist portrays as being in the process of learning Jesus' true nature and becoming His true disciples. For Mary and Martha and mother Mary there is perhaps knowledge of and belief in Jesus and His miracle working power, but in both cases this knowledge and faith is insufficient. They do not realize that Jesus is able to bring life because He is the Resurrection and the Life.[173]

Realizing that Lazarus is the object and Jesus the subject of this story, it is interesting to note that Mary and Martha play a more prominent part than their brother.[174] The factors in this narrative important to this study are not emotions Mary and Martha express (which are common human reactions to death), but the way the Evangelist portrays these women, the confession of faith by Martha, and Jesus' proclamation to Martha.

The character portrayals of Mary and Martha in Jn 11 are on the whole true to the portrayals we saw earlier in Lk. 10.38–42. Martha appears to be the elder sister and the hostess of the home.[175] She is clearly the more out-going, thus it is she who goes out to meet Jesus first. Martha's out-spokenness, which gives us more knowledge of her than we have of Mary, sometimes makes her appear to have less faith and understanding. The Evangelist portrays Mary as a woman of great devotion. She is always at her Master's feet whether to revere (Jn 11.32) or to anoint (Jn 12.3, cf. Lk. 10.39). Both women are devoted to Jesus and are close friends whom He loved and visited on more than one occasion.

John, in rather balanced fashion, mentions Mary first and then Martha in 11.1; Mary only in 11.2; Martha only (by name) in 11.5; and then both Martha and Mary have a private audience with Jesus in 11.17–37. While Mary gets more prominence in verses 1–5, Martha is the more central figure in verses 17–37. In verse 2 Mary is described by John as ἡ ἀλείψασα τὸν κύριον μύρῳ καὶ ἐκμάξασα τοὺς πόδας αὐτοῦ ταῖς θριξὶν αὐτῆς. It would be this act that would remind John's audience of Mary, thus the story in 12.1–8 must be based on well-known tradition. The statement in Jn 11.5 that Jesus loved Martha and her sister and Lazarus is perhaps more significant than it appears on the surface. First, the order of the names (two women, then Lazarus) is unusual. Perhaps the Evangelist is intimating that these women were closer to Jesus than Lazarus was, or were more prominent or important than Lazarus in the eyes of the Evangelist. It is pointed out frequently that Lazarus is the only male in the Fourth Gospel who is named as the object of Jesus' love (cf. 11.3, 5), but what is overlooked is that Martha and Mary are the only women so mentioned by name. In light of the theological significance of such language elsewhere in John and its use to describe the relationship between Jesus and His disciples, it seems the Evangelist is implying that these women and Lazarus were disciples of Jesus;[176] and that there were women prominent among the disciples even during Jesus' earthly ministry (11.2 hints that Mary should be known).

The Evangelist portrays Martha as one who sincerely believes in Jesus and has faith in His power, for she says, 'I know even now God will give you whatever you ask' (verse 22). This does not seem to imply that she believes Jesus can or will raise her brother since her confession of faith does not go beyond the orthodox Pharisaic view of resurrection on the last day,[177] and since her later comment (verse 39) makes probable she still does not expect Jesus to raise Lazarus. Brown's summary about Martha's faith seems accurate:

'Throughout the incident involving Martha we see that she believes in Jesus but inadequately. In vs 27 she addresses him with lofty titles, probably the same titles used in early Christian professions of faith; yet 39 shows that she does not as yet believe in his power to give life. She regards Jesus as an intermediary who is heard by God (22), but she does not understand that he is life itself (25).'[178]

What is the Evangelist trying to convey by having Martha confess — ἐγὼ πεπίστευκα ὅτι σὺ εἶ ὁ χριστὸς ὁ υἱὸς τοῦ θεοῦ ὁ εἰς τὸν κόσμον ἐρχόμενος (verse 27)? Schnackenburg suggests that this confession is probably a model for the Evangelist's audience.[179] This may well be so, for it is similar to the Petrine confession, especially in its Matthean form (16.6 — Σὺ εἶ ὁ χριστὸς ὁ υἱὸς τοῦ θεοῦ τοῦ ζῶντος). Perhaps it is not too much to say that Martha's confession is the least inadequate to this point in the Fourth Gospel. Certainly, it is more adequate than the Samaritan woman's hopeful question in 4.29, or her affirmation that the Messiah will come into the world (cf. 4.25 to 11.27). Ironically, Martha's confession is also a fuller and perhaps more satisfactory statement than the Petrine confession in Jn 6.68–9. It is possible that the Evangelist has constructed his Gospel so that alongside the crescendo of the miraculous, we have a crescendo of confessions. This would mean that Martha's confession takes on new importance because of its place in the climactic episode of the series of signs. Perhaps a further indication of the importance of Martha for the Evangelist's audience is that she receives a revelation from Jesus about Himself that prompts the confession in verse 27. By giving his audience a story in which a woman is the recipient of one of Jesus' most profound and direct statements about Himself, and in which a woman makes a heart-felt and accurate response to Jesus' declarations, the Fourth Evangelist intimates that women have a right to be taught even the mysteries of the faith, and that they are capable of responding in faith with an accurate confession. In short, they are capable of being full-fledged disciples of Jesus.

In this pericope, the portrait of Mary is not favourable. In her audience with Jesus she makes the same initial remarks as Martha (11.21, 32), though again it is likely this is not so much a complaint as a statement of loss and grief.[180] She makes no confession, and her wailing[181] in Jesus' presence suggests an attitude of hopelessness and lack of trust in Him. This must be balanced against the hint in 11.3 (cf. verses 21, 32) that both Mary and Martha had enough faith to believe that only Jesus could deal with their drastic situation.

In conclusion we have in Jn 11 not an idealized portrait of two women disciples, but a portrait that indicates that women are capable of faith and an accurate confession, and are worthy recipients of the teaching of Jesus about Himself. Martha's confession (verse 27), even if it was in actuality only a rudimentary expression of certain conventional expectations coupled with a belief that Jesus was the one who had been sent to fulfill those expectations is noteworthy. In its present form (accepting that verse 27*b, c* may be the Evangelist's contribution to the confession) the confession rivals and resembles the great Petrine confession (Mt. 16.16 and parallels). By placing it on Martha's lips, the Evangelist makes his own statement about the ability of women to be confessing and exemplary Christians. It is also true that the Evangelist portrays Martha as having her bad moments when she so misunderstands Jesus and His intentions that she questions His reasons for having the stone rolled away and is rebuked. Mary is presented as one who has given herself wrongly over to an all consuming sorrow even in Jesus' presence, though she too has faith, and the Evangelist indicates (11.2) that she will yet honour Jesus by anointing Him (12.1–8). It is to this anointing that we must now turn.

3. Another Anointing — Mk 14.3—9 (Mt. 26.6—13, Jn 12.1—8)

How are the anointing stories in Mk 14.3—9 and parallels and Lk. 7.36—50 to be assessed? Are they two forms of one story, or two distinct stories having similarities perhaps as a result of cross-fertilization at the level of oral tradition?[182] The first similarity between the Lucan anointing story and the story in Mark and Matthew is that the meal is held at the house of a man named Simon (John does not specify). This, however, is a superficial similarity when one considers how many Simons are in the NT and Josephus.[183] A second similarity between the narratives is that a woman anoints Jesus with perfume, and in the Synoptics the perfume is contained in an alabaster jar. This last detail does not prove that we are dealing with the same story because in the first-century Mediterranean world, it was known that 'the best ointment is preserved in alabaster'.[184] We know that dealers in perfumes were exceedingly common in Israel for the rabbis often mentioned them.[185] What then of the fact that a woman is involved in all four of the Gospel accounts of an anointing? Luke says the woman is a sinner, which is contrary to the picture of Mary of Bethany presented in Lk. 10, and the picture we find in Jn 11 and 12.[186] It seems that Luke, who relied on Mark, did not identify the sinner woman with the unnamed woman in the Marcan account. 'The fact that Luke has omitted the narrative in Mk 14:1—9 at the corresponding point in his own Gospel is no proof that he regarded this story as identical with Mark's. It simply indicates that he saw the similarity between the two narratives and avoided repetition.'[187] The Lucan story is set at a different time and place from the Marcan story, and for many scholars these are decisive reasons for not identifying the two stories.[188] Both anointing stories involve an act of devotion and love, but there is no hint in the Lucan story that a prophetic and proleptic burial rite is involved, as could be the case in the other three Gospels. 'The very strong element of sinfulness and forgiveness, that is essential to the Lucan story, is totally missing in the Bethany account.'[189] Finally, the way Jesus uses the act of anointing and a parable of debtors in the Lucan story to teach Simon that he who is forgiven more is more grateful, is completely at variance with the other anointing story. The point and purpose of Luke's narrative is very different from that of the other anointing story. If Luke knew Mark, it seems improbable that he would so thoroughly rearrange the story as to change its essential point and purpose, or leave only fragmentary details of similarity if he intended to relate the same event as Mark.[190] Even a cursory examination of the anointing stories of Mark, Matthew and John makes it apparent that they are dealing with the same event. Between these three accounts the similarities are of the essence of the story.[191] We thus conclude that the Lucan anointing story is not the same as that found in Mk 14.3–9 and parallels, and we are justified in treating the latter as a separate story.

What then is the historical value of Mk 14.3–9 and parallels? It seems clear that the story rests on good tradition. Dibelius calls it a paradigm of noteworthy purity and Bultmann says that it is no ideal scene but in the strictest sense biography, although he contends that verses 8b–9 are probably secondary.[192] This need not be the case if Jn 12.7 is an independent attestation to the same idea expressed in Mk 14.8b (cf. below). Probably the Evangelist's shaping of the material may be seen in the reference to the Gospel and 'the whole world' in verse 9. Perhaps the original form of this prophecy or pronouncement simply spoke of the woman's deed being held in memory continually. The placing of this episode before the triumphal entry in John seems historically more likely than Mark's position, which may be located next to the Lord's Supper narrative for theological reasons. This leads us to ask whether or not the Fourth Evangelist, like the First, is dependent on Mark for this narrative. There are certain verbal similarities that might point in this direction: the use in both Gospels of the rare word πιστικῆς; ἄφετε αὐτήν in Mark and ἄφες αὐτήν in John; the use of ἐνταφιασμόν in both Gospels; the saying about the poor; and the mention of 300 denarii.[193] Against these points must be balanced the following considerations: (1) it is very difficult to believe that the Fourth Evangelist, if he had Mk 14.8, 9 before him, would have introduced in its place the difficult Jn 12.7;[194] (2) while not impossible, it seems unlikely that the Fourth Evangelist would have modified Mark's reference to an anointing of Jesus' head to an anointing of His feet and the wiping of His feet with the woman's hair;[195] (3) it is unlikely that the Fourth Evangelist would deliberately add to Mary's actions the questionable act of loosing the hair if Mark was his source; (4) counting against literary dependence is the fact that there are 'small differences that surround the details in which they are most alike (Mark has *valuable* perfume in contrast to John's *expensive* perfume; Mark has *more* than 300 denarii)'.[196] There seems to be no compelling reason why the Fourth Evangelist would have altered the Marcan account in these ways if he knew of it. This leads to the suggestion that the two Gospels are reporting, independently of each other, two different versions of one sequence of events. It is also unlikely that the Fourth Evangelist is relying on Luke's anointing narrative for one must require that he transfer the description of the act of a woman with an immoral past to Mary of Bethany and embody that description in a narrative that has a wholly different point from the Lucan narrative.[197] The similarities between the Lucan and

Johannine anointing stories (especially the wiping of the feet with her hair) are perhaps best explained by the likelihood that at the stage of oral tradition some of the details of one anointing story have been transferred to the other and vice versa. What then are we to make of the personal references unique to the Johannine account (Mary, Martha, Lazarus, Judas)? It is quite possible that the Evangelist has added these names to a general account of the anointing, possibly on the basis of the narrative being set in Bethany in his source.[198] It is perhaps more likely, if the Fourth Gospel's account is independent of the Synoptics, that the names are original, for Jn 11.2 seems to indicate that the association of Mary with the anointing was already known to his audience (and thus went back to tradition that preceded the Fourth Gospel). It must be remembered that in the Canonical Gospel tradition there is no definite trend to add names at the later stages of the tradition. It was just as common in the polishing of a narrative for practical use that names, places and interesting (but unnecessary) details be omitted in order to generalize the narrative.[199] Thus, in conclusion, it would appear that the Fourth Evangelist presents, in most regards, a form of this anointing story that is closer to the original than Mark's generalized account.

The story contains typical Johannine irony in that the place where Jesus gave life to the dead (12.1) becomes the place where 'Seated beside Lazarus, whom He "called out of the tomb" (xii.17), He is anointed as one would anoint a corpse.'[200] The characterization of Martha and Mary in Jn 12 comports well with the Lucan portrayal. There is one noticeable difference, however, between the portrayal of Martha in Lk. 10 and Jn 12. In Jn 12 there are no complaints by Martha and no hint of a rebuke to Martha — she serves quietly. If Leipoldt is correct, then we may see the process of liberation and Christian service expressed in Martha's life for she is performing the functions a free servant or slave would perform at an all male feast.[201] She apparently violates certain rules of Jewish practice in order to take on the role of servant and show love to her Master for what He has done for her and her family. Liberty in Christ is not only freedom from customs which restrict love, but also freedom to take a lower place, to humble oneself to serve.

Mary also may be taking on the role of servant when she anoints Jesus. There were many reasons for anointing in a Jewish context. As Lk. 7.46 implies, anointing with oil was not of the same order or purpose as anointing with perfume, especially fragrant and expensive perfume. The latter was reserved either for burial rites, or for cosmetic or romantic purposes in small quantities (Song of Solomon 1.12, Jn 19.39—40, Lk. 24.1).[202] What Mary poured on Jesus' feet is called μύρον and is not oil, but perfume, nard being a well-known Eastern ointment with a potent fragrance.[203] The Fourth Evangelist, perhaps with deliberate exaggeration to indicate that this is an act of complete devotion, says Mary used about a pound of nard, a very large amount considering the perfume's worth.[204] It is not true that anointing of the feet is unknown in antiquity.[205] Athenaeus tells us of a man having a female slave smear his feet with μύρον.[206] Though it may not be common practice, Billerbeck cites cases where the rabbis allowed a person to anoint their own feet, and in some places women could anoint rabbis.[207] Thus, the possibility that Mary did anoint Jesus' feet, especially if this was originally intended as an act of humble devotion, should not be dismissed. A plausible explanation of Mary's act of wiping Jesus' feet with her hair might be found in the custom of wiping one's hands on the head or hair of a servant if the hands had excess oil or water on them at dinnertime. Mary could have used her hair to wipe off the excess perfume as she had seen servants do in the past.[208] In a Jewish context, however, for a woman to let down her hair in the presence of unrelated men was scandalous.[209] Thus, it is best to attribute the act to the cross-fertilization of the two anointing stories while the anointing of the feet may well be original to the story. It is easy to see why Mark would change the anointing of the feet to an anointing of the head to emphasize Jesus' royal nature and role. It is not so easy to explain the change to the feet if the anointing of the head was original.[210]

In all three narratives the motive of the woman (unnamed in the Synoptics) appears to be devotional. In all three Gospels, Jesus interprets the act in relation to His burial. In Matthew and Mark it is evident that the act is seen as a proleptic anointing for Jesus' burial.[211] It has been suggested that since the First Evangelist and Mark tell us that the head of Jesus is anointed, it is possible they viewed this act as a kingly coronation rite.[212] If so, then the woman is portrayed as taking on the task of a prophet or priest. Since both the First Evangelist and Mark make clear, however, that Jesus refers the act to His burial, then it is probably to be viewed this way in the main.[213] This means that they viewed the act as prophetic in character, in which case the Synoptists may have been suggesting to their audiences that women could legitimately assume the roles performed by prophets.[214] In Mark and Matthew the act is described as a beautiful deed — which may indicate to the Evangelists' audiences that such extravagant devotion should be seen as an example for all disciples.

Jesus' response to the objection that Mary's extravagant act has wasted about a year's wages of a day-labourer is problematic in the Fourth Gospel.[215] The existence of αὐτήν in John makes it unlikely that we should treat ἄφες as merely an auxiliary.[216] In Mark it seems clear that the sense is 'Leave her alone.'[217] If the ἵνα in John is imperatival,[218] then the translation, 'Let her alone; let her keep it' is necessitated. If not, then we should connect ἄφες to the following phrase and translate 'Allow her to keep it.' Our second difficulty with the Johannine phrase is in the word τηρέω. There is no lexical evidence for the meaning 'keep it in mind'.[219] In John it can mean 'to keep' (as in keep a commandment, cf. Jn 8.51, 55, 9.16, 14.15, 21, 23, 24, 15.10, 20). As Barrett has pointed out, it is most unlikely that John means 'to retain' the ointment since the whole house is filled with the smell and Judas is indignant at the extravagance.[220] Thus, it seems probable that it means 'Let her observe it (the rite) now as though it were (i.e., with a view to) the day of my burial preparation.' The Fourth Evangelist then in essence is saying the same as the First and Second. If this translation is correct, then the implication is that Jesus prophetically sees that Mary will not have an opportunity to prepare Him for burial later, and thus she is allowed to have the opportunity now. We reject the suggestion that αὐτό refers to the ointment itself (as if Mary could save some for the actual burial), and also the suggestion that τηρήσῃ αὐτό refers to Mary 'keeping in mind' on that fateful day that she had anointed Jesus previously.

The first two Evangelists close their presentation of the anointing with the remark, 'Truly I say to you, wherever the Gospel is preached throughout the world, what she has done will also be told in memory of her.' This saying sets up this woman as an example, and if one deletes the clause ὅπου ... τὸν κόσμον, there is no reason why the saying cannot be attributed to Jesus, even though the Fourth Evangelist omits it.[221] The Fourth Evangelist gives evidence in 11.2 that those words were coming true already, and it is possible (though perhaps not probable) that we should take the reference to the odour filling the house in 12.3 as a symbolic way of saying the same thing we find in Mk 14.9 and Mt. 26.13.[222]

4. Conclusions

Several important points come to light in these passages with regard to Jesus' attitude toward women. Firstly, there is the crucial point that Jesus was willing to teach women, as a rabbi would teach his students, and it seems He was not afraid to do this in private when He was alone with women. This appears to indicate that Jesus was willing to go to some lengths and risk a certain amount of public scandal in order to instruct women. Secondly, from the Johannine material we may deduce that Jesus apparently felt free to have close friendship ties with women who probably were not related to Him. If there is any historical substance behind the story in Jn 11, then it serves to illustrate that Jesus was willing actively to aid women, and that He was unafraid to show His love for such people. Finally, it is worth noting that while Lk. 10 and Jn 12 do serve to show that Jesus was willing to accept service that was either typical or perhaps even beneath the level of a woman's usual tasks, Lk. 10 makes quite clear that Jesus thought that even in the case of women, hearing and heeding God's word was the one thing truly necessary in this life, the first task for all who would seek to please God.

Turning to the secondary matter of the Evangelists' portrayal of these women, we may note the striking correspondence between the Lucan and Johannine portrayals of Mary and Martha. As Stauffer remarks,

> 'We learn much concerning the validity of the Gospel tradition and its value as a historical source when we observe that the characters of Mary and Martha, the sisters of Lazarus, are given the same delineation in all the Gospels. Martha appears resolute, energetic, ready of tongue, used to giving orders, as eager to make suggestions as to reprove (Luke 10, 38. 40. 41; John 11, 20 ff. 28. 39 f.; 12, 2); Mary is hesitant, slow, quiet, easily moved, obedient, devoted (Mark 14, 3 ff.; Luke 10, 39. 42; John 11, 20. 29.32f.).'[223]

Interestingly, Mary is the only woman in the Gospels whom Jesus defends twice for her devotion and desire to serve her Master. In Lk. 10, Mary is portrayed as a disciple who has a right to learn from Jesus; in Jn 12, we see her as a disciple who has a right to take the role of servant and honour Jesus in an extravagant and exemplary way. The Fourth Evangelist does not present an idealized portrait of Mary, however, for in Jn 11 he shows that she, like Martha, was capable of misunderstanding and not trusting Jesus sufficiently. It is possible that Mary's act of anointing is presented by the First and Second, and even the Fourth, Evangelist as a coronation ritual,[224] but it is more probable that it is seen as a prophetic burial rite. The Gospel writers may be implying that it was acceptable for women to take on the role or tasks of a prophet.[225]

In comparing the portraits of Martha in Lk. 10 and Jn 12, we note that Martha appears in the same role in both cases. The mention of her household in Jn 11.19 may indicate that she need not have performed these tasks, in which case we see in her life how her devotion to Jesus led her to take on the role of servant. We noted Brown's suggestion that the audience of the Fourth Evangelist would see Martha's activities as corresponding to those that a deacon would perform for the Church community; thus, Jn 12 could be seen as giving precedent for deaconesses.[226]

In any event, it is significant that the Fourth Evangelist portrays Martha as making perhaps the least inadequate confession about Jesus up to this point in this Gospel (11.27), and she in turn receives one of the most dramatic revelations of Jesus' nature. Both of these factors indicate that Martha is to be seen by the Evangelist's audience as someone who is in the process of becoming a full-fledged disciple. By relating this scene, the Evangelist intimates that women were worthy of being taught even the mysteries of the faith (cf. Jn 4.21–6). Confirmation that John is portraying both Mary and Martha as disciples is to be found in the statement in Jn 11.5 that Jesus loved them (cf. 13.1). Indeed, they, together with Lazarus, are the only figures in the Fourth Gospel who are mentioned by name (cf. 10.3) as Jesus' loved ones. In these stories we have pointed out the interesting juxtaposition of women's new freedom to be disciples and be taught by a rabbi with the freedom to take up the roles of a servant, roles which were forbidden by the rabbis to women who had servants (as Mary and Martha probably did). Lk. 10 makes clear that a woman must first orientate her priorities so that the good portion comes first, being the one thing necessary. Having her priorities straight (as in Jn 12) she can assume a role that servants usually performed. This role is given new significance as a means of serving the Master and manifesting discipleship to and love for Him.

Apparently, Mary and Martha did not travel with Jesus, for He always comes to them. This did not make them any less His disciples or His 'followers' who were progressing toward being full-fledged disciples. There were women, however, who took the unprecedented step of leaving their home and family in order to travel with Jesus. It is these women we must now study.

C. Women Who Followed Jesus

1. On the Road with Women Disciples – Lk. 8.1–3

Lk. 8.1–3 is near the middle of a series of pericopes that make special reference to women.[227] Since we have dealt with this passage and its significance for the Third Evangelist's Gospel in some detail in another context, we only need to make a few remarks here about its significance for this study of Jesus' attitudes about women.[228]

Though Lk. 8.1–3 in its form and content is thoroughly and distinctively Lucan,[229] it nonetheless contains material of considerable historical value. The list of women could be traditional and does not appear to be derived from Mark's list (cf. Mk 15.41).[230] Possibly, Luke himself has

added the names of Joanna and/or Susanna as a result of personal knowledge or from a well-informed Palestinian source.[231] There is little reason to
question the authenticity of the information that women travelled with
and served Jesus and the disciples as this was conduct which was unheard
of and considered scandalous in Jewish circles. It is unlikely to have been
invented by a Christian community which contained converted Jews and
which did not wish to appear morally suspect to a Mediterranean world
that was already sexually and morally indulgent.

Lk. 8.1–3 stands in contrast to its historical context in rabbinic Judaism
in other regards as well. We know women were allowed to hear the word
of God in the synagogue but they were never disciples of a rabbi unless
their husband or master was a rabbi willing to teach them.[232] Though a
woman might be taught certain negative precepts of the Law out of
necessity, this did not mean they would be taught rabbinic explanations of
Torah. For a Jewish woman to leave home and travel with a rabbi was not
only unheard of, it was scandalous. Even more scandalous was the fact
that women, both respectable and not, were among Jesus' travelling
companions. Yet it was apparently an intended part of His ministry for
women to benefit from His teaching (cf. Lk. 10.38–42) and healing. While
Jesus rejects much of rabbinic teaching on women's 'flightiness', inferior
nature, and monthly ritual uncleanness, this does not mean He abrogated
all sexual, social, or creation order distinctions recognized under the old
covenant. Indeed, it seems rather clear that He affirmed the headship and
authority of the man when He chose Twelve men from among His disciples
to be leaders of the community.[233]

The first woman mentioned, Mary Magdalene, is the best known among
these women, possibly because her healing was the most dramatic, i.e.,
seven demons indicates a possession of extraordinary malignity.[234] She,
and apparently the others mentioned, were living proof of the Gospel's
power. Mary of Magdala is commonly placed first when listed with other
women (Mt. 27.56, 61, 28.1, Mk 15.40, 47, 16.1, Lk. 24.10). She is undoubtedly important, and Luke wishes to mention her so her special
devotion and witness in Lk. 24 will be seen as the proclamation of someone who has long been one of His disciples. Similarly, Joanna is a long-
standing disciple, present with Mary at the tomb and the upper room, and
thereafter bearing witness. She is very unlike Mary of Magdala who came
from a small town and was undoubtedly avoided by many until Jesus
healed her. Joanna is the wife of Chuza who managed Herod's estate.[235]
Thus, she was a woman of some means and prominence. What is especially
noteworthy about her presence among Jesus' followers is that apparently
she had left her home and family to become a follower and travelling

companion of Jesus. Here Luke gives evidence of how the Gospel breaks down class and economic divisions, as well as social barriers, and reconciles men and women from all walks of life into one community. The third woman, Susanna, though perhaps known to Luke's audience, is unknown to us and is not mentioned elsewhere in the Gospel. Luke intends us to understand that these three women were only the most prominent among ἕτεραι πολλαί[236] women that followed Jesus. Luke indicates that Jesus' actions in behalf of these women freed them to serve both Him and the disciples (αὐτοῖς)[237] ἐκ τῶν ὑπαρχόντων.[238] Though it was uncommon or unknown for women to be travelling disciples of a rabbi, it was not uncommon for women to support rabbis and their disciples out of their own money, property, or foodstuffs.[239] What is unique about the actions of Jesus' women followers is that the traditional roles of hospitality and service are seen by them as a way to serve not only the physical family but also the family of faith. Being Jesus' disciples did not lead these women to abandon their traditional roles in regard to preparing food, serving, etc. Rather, it gave these roles new significance and importance, for now they could be used to serve the Master and the family of faith. The transformation of these women involved not only assuming new discipleship roles, but also resuming their traditional roles for a new purpose.

2. Women at the Cross — Mk 15.40—1 (Mt. 27.55—6; Lk 23.49; Jn 19.25)

We have had occasion to note several trends or patterns in our examination of women to this point. One of these, found in the parables and also in some of the pronouncement stories and elsewhere, involved a reversal of male—female roles, or a reversal of expectations. Another pattern found almost exclusively in Luke and John involves presenting narratives so that certain women are revealed to be or to be becoming disciples (Jesus' mother, Martha and Mary, the women of Lk. 8.1—3). Perhaps the most surprising reversal was that Jesus' women friends and travelling companions, not the Twelve or even the Three, became the primary witnesses to the crucial final events in Jesus' earthly career — the events surrounding His death.

The Passion narrative, it is generally agreed, was one of the first pieces of tradition to become relatively fixed in the course of transmission. Accordingly, few would doubt that the reporting by the Evangelists of the betrayal, failure, or desertion of Jesus' trained male leadership, the Twelve, during the crucial events of the last days of Jesus' ministry is historically

accurate. It is not something that the post-Easter community was at all
likely to invent. Thus, we will take it as an historical given that there was
at least one disciple that betrayed Jesus (Judas), that there was one who
denied him (Peter), and that the general desertion described in Mk 14.50
(cf. verses 32, 37, 43, and Mt. 25.56, Jn 20.10) took place sometime
during those crucial events. Apart from the beloved disciple, who represents the model male disciple (Jn 19.26–7) and may not be one of the
Twelve (if indeed he is an historical figure), no men who were clearly
among the circle of disciples of Jesus perform any good acts during the
events immediately prior to and including the Crucifixion. It is striking
that the Evangelists portray various non-disciples both Jew and Gentile
as assisting or in part accepting Jesus (cf. Mk 15.21 and parallels, Mk
15.42–7 and parallels, Mk 15.39 and parallels, Lk. 23.40–3). Some of
this material may be redactional, but it is not likely that all of it is, and
it is the general pattern we are concerned with here – abandonment by
the Twelve, help or devotion expressed by others (the women or non-
disciples). Even more striking is the fact that this pattern of doubt and
desertion among the Twelve persisted even after the reports of Jesus'
Resurrection reached them. Even in Luke, who is fond of male–female
parallelism, we have a picture of the failure and disintegration of the
trained male leadership during the crisis. Rengstorf comments:

> 'Luke ceases to use μαθητής for the disciples of Jesus at the end of the
> Gethsemane story (22:45). From then on he has οἱ περὶ αὐτόν (22:49;
> cf. also 22:56, 58, 59), οἱ γνωστοὶ αὐτῷ (23:49, based on Ps. 38:11;
> 88:8, 18), οἱ ἕνδεκα καὶ πάντες οἱ λοιποί (24:9), αὐτοί (24:13), οἱ
> ἕνδεκα καὶ οἱ σὺν αὐτοῖς (24:33) ... The only possible explanation is
> that the behaviour of the disciples of Jesus during the passion is equiv-
> alent to a breach of the relationship by them, and that it is the task
> of Jesus to gather disciples afresh after His resurrection.'[240]

While Rengstorf goes too far in claiming that this is the only possible
explanation, it is probably the best. The first have become last or even
lost; and it speaks well for their faithfulness to history that the Evangelists, especially Luke, have not omitted or glossed over this fact. But
what of the last and least among the brethren? We will now examine Mk
15.40–1 and parallels.

In the Synoptics, the brief paragraph about women at the cross follows
the proclamation of the centurion about Jesus. In John, it follows the
story of the soldiers dividing Jesus' garments. Apparently, the women
were not limited in number to those listed in Mark's account.[241] Luke
mentions in addition to the women 'all his acquaintances' (πάντες οἱ

γνωστοὶ αὐτῷ). Since it appears Luke is following Mark at this point,[242] this phrase may be his attempt to create a male group of witnesses to parallel the females. Probably he means us to think of Jesus' friends in Jerusalem or His relatives. One would expect Luke to use the term 'the Apostles' or 'the Twelve' (now 'Eleven') if he meant them by this phrase.[243]

Where were these mourning women standing? The Synoptics use the phrase ἀπὸ μακρόθεν while the Fourth Evangelist uses παρὰ τῷ σταυρῷ (with the impersonal object in the dative, which is unknown elsewhere in the NT). The preposition the Fourth Evangelist uses literally means 'near' or 'beside', but one is not able to determine exactly how near.[244] In this case it must mean within hearing as well as seeing range. On the other hand, the phrase ἀπὸ μακρόθεν normally would mean from a distance, though again this phrase is not exact and in the Synoptics must mean within eyesight. Some of those who stood far off could have made their way to the cross. Perhaps this whole dilemma is one created by a failure to recognize that Ps. 37.12 (LXX) probably stands in the background here, in which case the phrase ἀπὸ μακρόθεν should not be taken as a literal description of their historical position. Luke especially appears to be under the influence of this OT verse which may in itself explain his reference to οἱ γνωστοὶ (cf. Ps. 37.12 LXX – οἱ ἔγγιστα).[245] As we noted earlier, there is probably rabbinic support for the idea that crucified men sometimes were surrounded by relatives and friends.[246] Thus, the Johannine description cannot be considered implausible and the Synoptic one cannot be assumed to be intended as a precise historical statement.

In Mark, we have the following women listed: Mary Magdalene, Mary the mother of James the Little and Joses, and Salome;[247] in Matthew: Mary Magdalene, Mary the mother of James and Joseph, and the mother of the sons of Zebedee. In Luke, we have no specific list; however, the Third Evangelist may have intended us to recall the list of those whom Jesus helped or healed in Lk. 8.1–3, or planned for the reader to find out their names in 24.10. The former is perhaps more probable since he says these women at the cross are those who had followed Jesus from Galilee.[248] In John, we appear to have four women listed: Jesus' mother, the sister of Jesus' mother, Mary of Clopas, and Mary of Magdala. Even though the First Evangelist is almost certainly following Mark, it is not certain whether he has omitted Salome's name and replaced it with another, or if he identified Salome and the mother of the Zebedees. Again, while Mary of Clopas may be the mother of James and Joseph,[249] it may also be that these are two different people and to simply assume their identity is overly harmonistic. This is especially so if Mark is correct that there were 'many other women' present. Luke, if he means us to refer back to 8.1–3 has the additional names of Joanna and Susanna. If he means us to refer to 24.10, then he probably adds but one name, Joanna, who was perhaps important to Luke as one of his sources of information. It is striking that all four Gospels agree in listing Mary of Magdala and it appears that Mk 15.40, Mt. 27.56, Lk. 24.10 share at least two names in common. The Fourth Evangelist has special reason to list Jesus' mother, and it is strange that she is omitted in the Synoptics if she was actually present. Nevertheless, we have argued previously that the reference to her in Jn 19.25 may well be historical, especially if Jn 19.27*b* is, and since some explanation must be given for her presence in the Church (cf. Ac. 1.14). In any event, the mention of various women by name indicates their importance in the eyes of the Evangelists and early Church and argues strongly for the view that historically at least some of these women (Mary Magdalene and another Mary, not Jesus' mother) must have played a crucial role in the Passion and Resurrection events.

The Synoptic lists are arranged perhaps in order of importance or familiarity both in relation to the Gospel writer and to his audience.[250] In every instance in the Gospels where women followers of Jesus are mentioned, Mary Magdalene's name is placed first (except in Jn 19.25 where there is a special interest in Jesus' mother).[251] Mary Magdalene's first place was not only because of her loyalty to Jesus or notable service, but also (and perhaps primarily) because of her witness about the risen Lord. These particular lists of those at the crucifixion may be more like that in 1 Cor. 15.5–8 than is sometimes thought.[252] They may be lists of those who saw and witnessed about the risen Lord. Each of the Synoptic accounts refers to the fact that they witnessed the crucifixion,[253] and the First Evangelist and Mark refer to these women's service specifically to Jesus (διηκόνουν, Mk 15.41, Mt. 27.55) a fact noted earlier in Lk. 8.3 (though there the Twelve are also among those served), and thus not repeated by Luke here. In addition, all three accounts speak of these women as followers of Jesus. In Mark we are told they ἠκολούθουν Him when He was *in* Galilee. The First Evangelist says they ἠκολούθησαν Jesus *from* Galilee, while Luke says they συνακολουθοῦσαι Him *from* Galilee. Let us examine the Marcan account first.

David Flusser notes an intentional contrast in the Marcan account between those who represent the Christian community and those who reject Jesus: 'all the "non-Christian" Jews are enemies of Jesus, and as followers there are only the Christian women from Galilee (and the centurion)'.[254] Thus, Mark wishes to show that except for His women followers, Jesus died amidst a host of enemies.[255] Mark distinguishes between those women who followed Jesus when He was in Galilee, and many other women (ἄλλαι πολλαί) who came up with Jesus into Jerusalem. The long-standing women followers of Jesus are probably referred to in the former category. It may be that the latter was simply a group of women who came up with Jesus into Jerusalem (but cf. Ac. 13.31). Alternatively, these may be Jesus' women followers from Judea. The discipleship status of the named women is indicated by Mark in three ways: they are said (1) to be witnesses of the most crucial events in Jesus' life (θεωροῦσαι); (2) to have served Jesus (διηκόνουν – note this is said only of the women in Mk 15.40–1*a*); and (3) to have followed Him (ἠκολούθουν). The reason why Mark does not use the word μαθητής of any of these women may be because usually he reserves this word for the official witnesses or inner circle of Jesus, i.e., the Twelve.[256] We conclude that Mark intends us to understand that the named women are disciples of long standing, even while Jesus was *in* Galilee.[257] Thus, they are prepared to be reliable witnesses to the events beginning with the Crucifixion.

In the Fourth Gospel we noted that the beloved disciple and Mary at the cross are representative male and female disciples. In Luke we note that ὁρῶσαι is feminine and has the women as its antecedent, in which case there is a stress on women as witnesses. Further, it is the women alone of whom it is said αἱ συνακολουθοῦσαι αὐτῷ in Lk. 23.49. Bauer says that 'follow' here has the connotation of being a disciple.[258] While this verb's other uses in the Gospels (cf. Mk 5.37, 14.51) do not appear to have theological overtones, and as the simple form of this verb is that which usually is used of following as a disciple,[259] the conjunction here of 'following' and 'witnessing' probably indicates that Luke is intending συνακολουθέω to have theological overtones. Further, if we compare this 'from Galilee' phrase to Ac. 1.21–2 (cf. Jn 15.26–7), then it may be that 'from Galilee' in itself is intended to accredit and authenticate the witness of the women to the empty tomb and the message about the risen Lord in Matthew and Luke. If they followed Jesus 'from Galilee', then they were in a position to remember His words and appearance so that they could relate what they were hearing and seeing *now* to what they had known *before*. Thus, the change of Mark's ἐν to ἀπὸ in Luke and Matthew may be motivated by an attempt to indicate the women's credentials. In Matthew as in Mark we have three verbs, at least two of which refer to what disciples do or ought to do – 'watch' Him ('look on'), 'serve' Him, and 'follow' Him. The First Evangelist is unambiguous in that he ascribes these things only to the women (no men are mentioned). Further, he says that these women followed Jesus serving him (διακονοῦσαι αὐτῷ, cf. Mk 15.40–1) perhaps implying that there was a history and a personal relationship behind this grateful service.[260] Thus, some women in the Synoptics

are depicted as faithful disciples of long standing who are being prepared
to bear witness to the things they began to see and take part in at this
time. In John, Mary is portrayed as one who witnessed Jesus' death
and was ushered into the community of faith, thus becoming a full-
fledged disciple. The portrait, though perhaps in many regards an 'ideal'
one, nonetheless indicates that all four Evangelists at this juncture were
concerned to portray the women as disciples who had prior contacts
with Jesus. That the women followers (save Jesus' mother) are specifically named and the men are basically anonymous (or go unmentioned)
may be the Gospel writers' testimony to who had the more crucial roles
and parts in the events of the last days of Jesus' earthly life.

D. The Place of Women in Jesus' Ministry

In chapter four we have examined the pericopes in the Gospels which
depict women who are, or are in the process of becoming, Jesus' disciples. We have seen that this involved a woman who was a member
of Jesus' physical family (His mother Mary), women who were His
friends but did not travel with Him (Mary and Martha), and those
women who followed Jesus in Galilee and to Jerusalem (Mary Magdalene
and others). That Jesus taught women and allowed them to follow Him
reveals how very different He was from other rabbis in His treatment
of women. Probably, it is this precedent that explains why the Gospel
writers, especially Luke and the Fourth Evangelist, include a considerable amount of material revealing women's new freedom and equality
in the presence of Jesus and in the midst of His community. Jn 19.25—
7 also reveals the new equality of male and female disciples beneath
the cross of Jesus. His mother is not idealized in the Gospels, however,
for at least three of the Evangelists reveal that she had some lack of
understanding of her Son and the nature of His mission (cf. Mk 3.21,
31—5, and parallels, Jn 2.1—12, and Lk. 2.50). Mary and Martha also
are depicted as women in the process of becoming disciples. Lk. 10.38—
42 portrays Mary as having a right to learn from and become a disciple
of Jesus. Indeed, this pericope makes clear that even for women, learning
from Jesus takes precedence over a woman's role of preparing a meal
and her responsibility of providing for a guest. While in Luke it is only
Martha who appears to misunderstand the nature and priorities of discipleship, in John we see that both Mary and Martha do not understand fully
Jesus and the extent of His power (cf. Jn 11). Nonetheless, the Fourth
Evangelist also depicts Martha as making the least inadequate confession
of Jesus in his Gospel (11.27), and Mary is presented as one who properly

honours Jesus and perhaps unknowingly performs a prophetic burial rite for Him (12.1—8).

From Lk. 8.1—3 through the Passion narratives we followed the portrayal of the women who travelled with Jesus. These women are remembered chiefly for the crucial role they played during the time of Jesus' death and burial, and the events that ensued thereafter, a time when all the male disciples (with one possible exception) fled and abandoned Jesus. Thus, not only Jesus' teaching and actions, but also the relationships He was involved in and the events surrounding His death and burial led to the acceptance of women as valid witnesses and genuine disciples of Jesus.

In what follows we will try not only to draw some conclusions on the basis of this study but also to look at the implications of this work for some of the relevant material in the rest of the NT. I shall also speak briefly about the efforts of the Third and Fourth Evangelists to portray women in a positive light.

CONCLUSIONS AND IMPLICATIONS

Having completed our investigation of the texts in the Gospels which deal with Jesus' attitudes toward women and their relationship to Him during His ministry, we are now in a position to correlate some of the conclusions of the various chapters of this study. We can now offer some suggestions about their possible implications for the material in the rest of the NT that deals with our subject.

Our study of Jesus' words and deeds leads us to conclude that in many, though not all, regards, Jesus differed from His Jewish contemporaries. This is all the more remarkable when we note that Jesus, so far as we know, never left His immediate Jewish environment for any length of time and, more importantly, directed His mission specifically to His fellow Jews.

Jesus' rejection of divorce outright would have offended practically everyone of His day. Further, Jesus' view that the single state was a legitimate and not abnormal calling for those to whom it was given, went against prevailing views in various parts of the Roman Empire about a man's duty to marry and procreate, but nowhere more so than in His native Palestine. We suggested that it was this teaching which made it possible for women also to assume roles other than those of wife and mother in Jesus' community. That Jesus did not endorse various ways of making women 'scapegoats', especially in sexual matters, placed Him at odds with other rabbis, though doubtless even many Gentiles would have thought that Jesus' rejection of the 'double standard' was taking equality too far. Further, we do not find negative remarks about the nature, abilities and religious potential of women in comparison to men on the lips of Jesus in contrast to various Jewish authors. There is also reason to believe that Jesus' estimation of the worth and validity of a woman's word of testimony was higher than that of most, if not all, of His contemporaries (cf. Jn 4.27—42). Jesus' teaching that the family of faith's claims took priority over the claims of the physical family on both men and women (cf. Mk 3.31—5, 10.29—30), also led to some circumstances that both Jew and Gentile would have found objectionable; for instance, what husband (Jew or Gentile) would willingly have let his wife leave home and family to become a follower of an itinerant Jewish preacher? Yet Lk. 8.3 probably indicates that Joanna, the wife of Chuza, had done this. This teaching, however, did not lead Jesus to repudiate either the traditional family structure outright or, it would seem, the patriarchal framework which existed to one degree or another in all the various Mediterranean cultures of that day. Jesus' teaching on the matter of corban, on honouring parents, on divorce, and on children makes clear that He was not advocating a rejection of the traditional family structure. If Mt. 5.27–32 and Jn 7.53–8.11 are any indication, then Jesus reaffirmed the responsibility of the husband and male leaders to be moral examples for the community. Jesus' choice of twelve men to be leaders of His new community also leads one to think that He was attempting to reform, not reject, the patriarchal framework under which He operated.

Certain of Jesus' words and deeds, such as His teaching on the laws of uncleanness, His healing of a woman on the Sabbath, and His willingness to converse with a strange woman in public, while obviously offensive to His fellow Jews, would probably not have raised many eyebrows outside Jesus' native context. Then, too, Jesus' attitude toward a woman's right to religious training and to be a disciple of a religious leader, while no doubt shocking to Jews, would not have seemed radical to many Romans or Greeks of that day.

Jesus' views of women and their roles do not fit neatly into any of the categories of His day. He was not a Qumranite, nor was he a traditional rabbi in these matters, though he had certain things in common with both groups. His use of women, both fictitious and real, as examples of faith for His followers, and His teaching on honouring parents, is not without precedent in rabbinic literature. His calling of men and women to radical commitment to God, in view of the inbreaking of the Kingdom, has certain affinities with the teachings of both John the Baptist and Qumran. Yet, on the whole, and especially in view of His Jewish context, Jesus appears to be a unique and sometimes radical reformer of the views of women and their roles that were commonly held among His people. Further, it appears that the case for new and more open attitudes toward women had still to be argued when the Evangelists wrote their Gospels. Perhaps this is the very reason why the Third and Fourth Evangelists take pains to present various women as religious models for their audiences. What then was the effect of these new attitudes about women and their roles on the women who participated in the community of Jesus? What was the community of Jesus offering women in terms of status and roles in comparison to what was offered them in Judaism?

To begin with, it is apparent, not only in the Gospels but also in Acts and the Epistles (e.g., Rom. 16), that the impact of the Christian message on women was considerable. It is probable that Jesus' teachings, in a somewhat similar fashion to the teachings and practices of the cult of Isis, attracted women in part because of the new roles and equal status they were granted in the Christian community. There were many cults in Greece and Rome that were for men only or, at best, allowed women to participate in very limited ways. Further, it is easy to see why women who were on the fringe of the synagogue community became Christian converts. Judaism offered women proselytes a circumscribed place at best, for they were faced with the rabbinic restrictions that limited their participation in religious functions. While women were able neither to make up the quorum necessary to found a synagogue, nor to receive the Jewish covenant sign, these limitations did not exist in the Christian community. The necessary and sufficient explanation of why Christianity differed from its religious mother, Judaism, in these matters is that Jesus broke with both biblical and rabbinic traditions that restricted women's roles in religious practices, and that He rejected attempts to devalue the worth of a woman, or her word of witness. Thus, the community of Jesus, both before and after Easter, granted women *together* with men (not segregated from men as in some pagan cults) an equal right to participate fully in the family of faith. This was a right that women did not have in contemporary Judaism or in many pagan cults. Jesus' teachings on the priorities of discipleship, His willingness to accept women as His disciples and travelling companions (cf. Lk. 8.1–3, 10.38–42), and His teaching on eunuchs and what defiled a person, effectively paved the way for women to play a vital part in His community. *Anyone* could have faith in and follow Jesus – He did not insist on any other requirements for entrance into His family of faith.

In regard to the roles women could and did assume in Jesus' community, Luke particularly shows us that a variety of tasks were assumed by women, especially in the post-Easter community. The Third Evangelist gives evidence (cf. Lk. 8.3, Ac. 9.36–42) that women often enough simply resumed their traditional roles of providing hospitality or material support, though now it was in service to the community of Jesus. Such roles were acceptable so long as they did not hinder a woman from choosing or learning more about the 'one thing needful' (Lk. 10.38–42). It is interesting and perhaps significant that the major female figures in the Gospels are depicted as being in the process of becoming full-fledged disciples, a process which involved their learning how to reorientate their traditional roles so that the priorities of the family of faith were heeded. Thus, we saw Mary learning to be a mother *as* a disciple, Martha learning to be a hostess *as* a disciple, and Mary Magdalene and others providing material aid as they followed Jesus. In the post-Easter community we find women assuming a greater variety of roles, some of which were specifically of a religious nature (e.g., the prophetesses of Ac. 21.9), and some of which would have been forbidden to a Jewish woman (e.g., being a teacher of men in Ac. 18.24—6). From evidence in the Pauline corpus and elsewhere we know that in the case of Priscilla and probably some of the other women set forth as examples in Acts (mother of John Mark, Tabitha, Lydia) Luke has in all probability presented a picture of women that is faithful to the actual historical circumstances.

While the teaching and community of Jesus was perhaps more easily and more naturally embraced by Gentile women than by Jewish women, it offered Jewish women more in terms of status and roles than it did to Gentile women. For a Jewish woman, the possibility of being a disciple of a great teacher, of being a travelling follower of Jesus, of remaining single 'for the sake of the Kingdom', or even of being a teacher of the faith to persons other than children, were all opportunities that did not exist prior to her entrance into the community of Jesus. Nonetheless, the Christian faith and community offered Gentile women a great deal also. As well as the roles mentioned above, the offer of salvation from sin, of starting life with a new self-image and purpose, of actively participating in a community whose Master had directed His mission especially to the oppressed, were offers that appealed greatly to Gentile, as well as Jewish, women. This new status and these new roles, some of which had not been available to these women before, are factors which explain the influx of women into the community of Jesus.

The implications of this study lead us to conjecture that Paul's appeal to the creation order in his discussion of matters involving men and women (cf. 1 Cor. 11.7—9, and possibly 1 Cor. 14.34 and 1 Tim. 2.13) is a technique that he may have derived from the teaching of Jesus (Mt. 19.4—6 and parallels). Further, Paul's belief that singleness for the Kingdom was not only a legitimate but also a preferable option to being married may well be derived from the attitude and teaching of Jesus about 'eunuchs' for the Kingdom (cf. Mt. 19.10—12 and 1 Cor. 7). Paul's concept of continent singleness (and fidelity in marriage) as a gift (χάρισμα, 1 Cor. 7.7) seems to echo the οἷς δέδοται of Mt. 19.11. Paul openly states that his teaching about the indissolubility of marriage is derived from 'the Lord' (1 Cor. 7.10—11). This leads one to suppose that the exceptive clauses are the First Evangelist's redactional expansion on the words of Jesus. It should also not go unnoted that structurally 1 Corinthians 7 (cf. also 1 Cor. 11.1—12) is a grand exercise in male—female parallelism on a scale and to a degree that even Luke did not pursue. In all these matters (singleness, the indissolubility of marriage, the gift concept) Jesus and Paul stand together and in contrast to their own Jewish backgrounds. The precedent set by Jesus of allowing women to travel with Him to hear and heed His words and to serve the community may also have borne fruit in Paul's ministry, for there were several women with whom Paul travelled or whom he considered his συνεργοί (cf. Ac. 18.1–3, 18–26, Rom. 16.1–4, 6, 7(?), 12, 15, 1 Cor. 16.19).

If we are right that Jesus was attempting to reform, not reject, the patriarchal framework of His culture, then it is understandable why Paul and other NT authors sought to redefine, not reject, concepts of male headship and leadership in light of Christian or biblical ideas (cf. especially Eph. 5.21–33, 'as the Church submits ... as Christ loves'; 1 Cor. 11.3–12, 'in the Lord'; and 1 Pet. 3.6, ὡς Σάρρα ... κύριον αὐτὸν καλοῦσα). The work of the Spirit in women's lives led some of them to prophesy (Ac. 21.9). If the gift gave a person a certain leadership status (cf. also 1 Cor. 12.28), then there may be an integral connection between 1 Cor. 14.1–33a and 33b–36. Paul may be exhorting women prophetesses in 1 Cor. 14.33b–36 to exercise their gifts in a way that did not involve the violation of their husband's headship (cf. 1 Cor. 11.3–5, 14.34–5). It is possible that the tensions in Paul's thought between the concept of male headship and his willingness to allow women to exercise new roles in the Christian community are tensions that were inherent in the attitudes and teachings of Jesus, and do not reflect, as some have suggested, tensions between ideas drawn from Paul's non-Christian rabbinic past and theological concepts that he had learned since becoming a Christian.

The effects of Jesus' teachings and attitudes also appear to be in evidence in Luke's second volume as well as in his Gospel. Luke especially seems determined to drive home his point about the equal place and new roles of women in the community of Jesus by utilizing the techniques of male–female parallelism (not only in the pairing of parables but also elsewhere), male–female role reversal, and by giving space to stories about women not found in the other Gospels. Luke's five vignettes in Acts presenting women assuming various roles in the primitive Christian community must not be passed over as though they were only descriptive accounts of history (cf. 9.36–42; 12.12–17; 16.12–15, 40; 18.1–3, 24–6; 21.9). Their choice, position and content reveal a deliberate attempt on the author's part to indicate to his audience how things ought to be. Further, there is evidence that Luke's message was all too clear, for the editors of the Western text of Acts recognized the implications of these narratives and attempted to tone down the language in them which spoke of women's new freedom and roles in the Christian community (cf. the variants for 1.14, 17.4, 17.12, 17.34, and chapter 18 *seriatim*). It is also of interest that both Luke and the Fourth Evangelist wished their audiences to know that the tensions between the claims of the physical family and the family of faith on a woman could be resolved so long as the physical family allowed itself to be defined and directed by the dictates and priorities of the family of faith. Thus, in their own way, they present episodes in the life of Jesus' mother to reveal both the difficulties of hearing and heeding the call to discipleship faced by a mother, and how these difficulties could be successfully overcome as Mary learns to become a mother *as* a disciple (cf. Ac. 1.14, Jn 19.25–7). The stories about Mary and Martha, especially Lk. 10.38–42, also reflect this theme.

Another motif that comes to light in the Gospels is the presentation of women as valid witnesses of the truth about Jesus (Jn 4 for instance), and especially about His death, burial, empty tomb and appearance as the risen Lord. Though it may have been a matter of necessity, it is significant that a crucial part of the Christian kerygma is based on the testimony of Jesus' female followers. It is to the credit of the Evangelists that, far from trying to gloss over this fact, it is highlighted in different ways by the First Evangelist, Luke, the Fourth Evangelist, and probably Mark. Worthy of special mention is Luke's way of revealing the validity of the testimony of Jesus' female followers by showing that it was confirmed by the Apostle Peter (cf. Lk. 24.1–10, 12). Also notable is the Fourth Evangelist's presentation of Martha's confession as, to some extent, a model for his audience (cf. Jn 11.27, 20.31). Whatever the historical value of the Resurrection narratives they, like other portions of the Gospels, tend to bear witness to the effect of Jesus' attitudes toward women on the Christian community, as women appear in these narratives as well as elsewhere as witnesses and participants in that community.

There are other possible points of contact between the insights brought to light by this study and the material found in the rest of the NT. One avenue worth exploring is the possible relationship between the household codes found in various NT Epistles and the teachings of Jesus. It is often assumed that these household codes were adopted and adapted by Christians from non–Christian writings or teachings on ethics. If this is the case, then it might be evidence of how the Church began to accommodate its Christian teaching about women and the family to the conventions of its environment. On the other hand, Jesus Himself had something to say about such matters as honouring of parents, the treatment of children, and other relevant subjects that might be classified as general ethics. Could there be a connection between this teaching and that found in the Epistles on these matters? This question must wait until a further study is undertaken before it can be answered.

As for this study, it is not intended to be the last word on its subject, but rather the first part of a larger effort that I am undertaking to understand the whole of the New Testament's teaching on women and their roles. Only after a comprehensive exegesis of all the New Testament material can the hermeneutical question of its applicability to the modern Church situation be approached. Thus, it is hoped that this study will be judged for what it is: an open-ended beginning, rather than a self-contained end.

NOTES

1 Women and their Roles in Palestine

1 G.F. Moore, *Judaism in the First Centuries of the Christian Era* vol. II (New York, 1971), 126, 131; R. Loewe, *The Position of Women in Judaism* (London, 1966); I.J. Peritz, 'Women in the Ancient Hebrew Cult', *JBL* 17 (1898), 111–48. Cf. C. Klein, 'Jewish Women in the Time of Mary of Nazareth', *Bible Today* 60 (1972), 746–52; Jacques Pirenne, 'Le Statut de la Femme Dans la Civilization Hébraïque', in *La Femme*, Recueils de la Société Jean Bodin XI (Bruxelles, 1959), 107–26; 'Women', in *Encyclopedia Judaica* vol. XVI (Jerusalem, 1971), cols. 623–30; S. Schechter, *Studies in Judaism* (1st ser.; Philadelphia, 1945), 313–25; S.W. Baron, *A Social and Religious History of the Jews* vols. I, II (New York, 1952); J. Jeremias, *Jerusalem in the Time of Jesus* (trans. F.H. and C.H. Cave; Philadelphia, 1969); L. Swidler, *Women in Judaism: The Status of Women in Formative Judaism* (Metuchen, New Jersey, 1976); J. Donaldson, *Woman: Her Position and Influence in Ancient Greece and Rome, and Among Early Christians* (London, 1907); G. Delling, *Paulus' Stellung zu Frau und Ehe* (Stuttgart, 1931); J. Leipoldt, *Die Frau in der antiken Welt und im Urchristentum* (Leipzig, 1955); J.P.V.D. Balsdon, *Roman Women: Their History and Habits* (London, 1962).

2 Cf. relevant material from endnote 1 above.

3 Material of extremely late date has been avoided. Of the passages used here with an author's name attached only the sayings of R. Phineas b. Hannah, R. Nahman, R. Joseph and R. Hisda could be assigned to a period after the middle of the second century.

4 We may well ask why the section on the suspected *adulterer* is nowhere to be found in rabbinic literature.

5 M. Ket. 4.1–12, Danby, 249–51.

6 M. Ned. 9.10, Danby, 277.

7 M. Ket. 4.4, Danby, 250.

8 M. Ket. 4.1, Danby, 249.

9 M. Ket. 4.4, Danby, 250; M. Kid. 2.1, Danby, 323.

10 M. Yeb. 13.1–2, Danby, 237–8.

11 B.T. Kid. 2*b*, Nashim VIII, Kiddushin, pp. 2ff.

12 M. Kid. 1.1, Danby, 321.

13 M. Ned. 9.5, Danby, 276.

14 Cf. M. Ket. 7.6, Danby, 255, on loss of *ketubah* due to violation of rabbinic law or tradition. Also M. Sot. 4.3, Danby, 297–8, says that a barren, sterile, or old woman does not receive her *ketubah* upon divorce.

15   M. Git. 5.1, Danby, 312.
16   M. Yeb. 13.3, Danby, 238.
17   M. Yeb. 14.1, Danby, 240.
18   M. Git. 9.10, Danby, 321.
19   M. Ket. 10.1–6, Danby, 259–60; M. Kid. 2.6, 3.9, Danby, 324, 326.
20   S. Lowy, 'The Extent of Jewish Polygamy in Talmudic Times', *JJS* 9 (1958), 129–30.
21   Lowy, 115–6.
22   M. Yeb. 3.10, Danby, 223.
23   Aboth de Rabbi Nathan II, 5a, extra-canonical tractate, *The Fathers According to Rabbi Nathan* (*'AbotDe-Rabbi Natan*) (trans. J. Goldin; New Haven, 1955), 16–26; cf. Lowy, 117ff.
24   M. Ned. 9.1, Danby, 275; Genesis Rabbah 1, 15, end, *Midrash Rabbah* vol I, Genesis, (ed. H. Freedman and A. Simon; trans. H. Freedman; London, 1951), 14.
25   M. Kerithoth 6.9, Danby, 572–3; cf. Mekilta Bahodesh 8, *Mekilta de Rabbi Israel* vol. II (trans. G. Z. Lauterbach; Philadelphia, 1933), 257ff.
26   B.T. Yeb. 62b, Nashim I, Yebamoth I, pp. 419ff.
27   M. Kid 1.1, Danby, 321.
28   M. Ket. 5.5, Danby, 252; M. Git. 7.6, Danby, 316; B.T. Ket. 60a, Nashim III, Ketuboth I, pp. 356ff, on breast feeding.
29   B.T. Ket. 4b, 61a, Nashim III, Ketuboth I, pp. 12–13, 364–5. Also. B.T. Ket. 96a, Nashim IV, Ketuboth II, p. 610.
30   M. Ket. 5.5, Danby, 252.
31   M. Yeb. 6.6, Danby, 227; B.T. Yeb. 65b, Nashim I, Yebamoth I, pp. 436ff.
32   M. Git. 1.6, Danby, 307–8.
33   B.T. Ket. 77a, 107a, Nashim IV, Ketuboth II, pp. 482ff, 685ff.
34   M. Ket. 4.4, 4.8, 4.9, Danby, 250–1.
35   M. Ket. 5.6, Danby, 252; B.T. Ket. 62a, Nashim III, Ketuboth I, p. 279. B.T. Ned. 15b, Nashim V, Nedarim, pp. 41–2; B.T. San. 75a, Nezikin VI, Sanhedrin II, pp. 505ff. These same references show that a woman had a right to marital union even beyond menopause, or if she was sterile. A woman was allowed to practice contraception if pregnancy endangered her health. Cf. B.T. Yeb. 12b, Nashim I, Yebamoth I, pp. 62ff.
36   M. Yeb. 6.6, Danby, 227.
37   B.T. Babba Bathra 141a, Nezikin IV, Babba Bathra II, pp. 599–600.
38   There is some evidence that women could occasionally divorce their husbands even in Palestine. Cf. R. Yaron, 'Aramaic Marriage Contracts – Corrigenda and Addenda', *JSS* 5 (1960), 66–70. There is similar evidence from Elephantine papyri as well as some Karaite and Samaritan documents. Cf. Ernst Bammel, 'Markus 10.11 f. und das jüdische Eherecht', *ZNW* 61 (1970), 95–101. P. Sigal, 'Elements of Male Chauvinism in Classical Halakhah', *Judaism* 24 (2, 1975), 226–44.
39   M. Ned. 11.12, Danby, 280; M. Ket. 5.5, 7.2–5 and 7.9–10, Danby, 252, 254 and 255.
40   B.T. Ket. 57b, Nashim III, Ketuboth I, pp. 338ff.
41   M. Git. 2.5, Danby, 308.
42   M. Git. 3.1, Danby, 309.
43   B.T. Git. 90b, Nashim VII, Gittin, p. 439.

44   Danby, 277.
45   M. Yeb. 14.1, Danby, 240.
46   M. Git. 6.2, Danby, 314.
47   Cf. Aulus Gellius, *Attic Nights* 10.23 (LCL II; trans. J.C. Rolfe; London, 1927), 278–9, and the helpful survey by B. Cohen, 'Concerning Divorce in Jewish and Roman Law', *PAAJR* 21 (1952), 3–34, espec. 31.
48   Y. Yadin, 'Expedition D – the Cave of Letters', *IEJ* 12 (1962), 235ff.
49   M. Ket. 4.2, Danby, 249.
50   M. Ket. 6.4, 8.5, Danby, 253, 256.
51   M. Ket. 8.1, Danby, 246.
52   M. Ket. 13.3, Danby, 262.
53   M. Ket. 12.3, Danby, 262.
54   The quotation is from a Midrash on Gen. 2.18 most conveniently found in Moore, *Judaism*, vol. II, 119. Cf. B.T. Yeb, 62*b*, Nashim I, Yebamoth I, p. 418.
55   M. Tanhuma Wayyishlah sec. 36, most conveniently found in ML, *Anthology*, 508, num. 1434.
56   B.T. Kid. 31*b*, Nashim VIII, Kiddushin, p. 153.
57   B.T. Yeb. 23*a*, Nashim I, Yebamoth I, p. 137.
58   Genesis Rabbah 17.7, *Midrash Rabbah* vol I, Genesis I, p. 138. Cf. Swidler, *Women in Judaism*, 214, n. 49.
59   Sotah 3.4, Danby, 296; 'Women', *Encyclopedia Judaica*, vol. XVI, col. 626; Freedman, in *The Babylonian Talmud*, Nashim VIII, p. 141, n. 1, says that R. Eliezer's statement probably refers to advanced Talmudic education only, because women had to have some instruction in Torah to say their prayers properly.
60   M. Sotah 3.4, Danby, 296. This comment is given with R. Eliezer's.
61   Danby, 269. In this case it is a permission to teach someone else's sons and daughters. The implication of this text may be that they could be taught Scripture but not Mishnah, etc.
62   M. Kid. 4.13, Danby, 329.
63   M. Sotah 3.4, Danby, 296. 'May the words of Torah be burned, they should not be handed over to women.' From Midrash Rabbah Numbers (Naso 9.48), *Midrash Rabbah*, vol. V, 'Numbers' I (trans. J.J. Slotki, 1951), 327.
64   M. Sotah 7.4, Danby, 300.
65   Midrash Tanhuma Mesora, end, Loewe, *Position of Women*, 49; cf. ML, *Anthology*, 510–11.
66   On Beruriah, cf. Swidler, *Women in Judaism*, 97–104, and A. Goldfeld, 'Women as Sources of Torah in the Rabbinic Tradition', *Judaism* 24 (2, 1975), 245–56.
67   Moore, *Judaism*, vol. II, 128.
68   Cf. Loewe, *Position of Women*, 30; 'Women, Right Of', *Jewish Encyclopedia*, vol. XII (ed. I. Singer; New York, 1906), 556–9. This study will not attempt to treat such atypical figures as Alexandra Salome or Julia Bernice who, as Hellenized Jewish princesses, tell us little about the status of Jewish women outside certain royal circles. Cf. G.H. Macurdy, 'Julia Bernice', *AJP* 56 (1935), 246–53.
69   B.T. Kid. 70*a*, *b*, Nashim VIII, Kiddushin, pp. 355ff.
70   M. Yeb. 7.5, Danby, 228–9; M. Yeb. 8.1, Danby, 229.

71 M. Ned. 11.5, Danby, 270; M. Naz. 9.1, Danby, 291–2; M. Naz. 3.6 (cf. 4.2), Danby, 284.
72 M. Naz. 6.11, Danby, 289.
73 M. Sotah 2.1, Danby, 295.
74 Danby, 471.
75 B.T. Hagigah 16*b*, Mo'ed VII, Hagigah, pp. 108–9; cf. Moore, *Judaism*, vol. II, 130, n. 6.
76 M. Sotah 3.1, Danby, 296; M. Kid. 1.8, Danby, 322.
77 M. Sotah 3.7, Danby, 297.
78 B.T. Shabbath 23*a*, Mo'ed I, Shabbath I, p. 98.
79 Moore, *Judaism*, vol. II, 46, 130, for differing opinions on this matter. Also, Jeremias, *Jerusalem*, 365; Peritz, 'Women in the Ancient Hebrew Cult', 114; Baron, *History of the Jews* vol. II, 240–1; M. Middoth 2.5, Danby, 592; B.T. Suk. 51*b*, Mo'ed VI, Sukkah, pp. 245–6. E.L. Sukenik, *Ancient Synagogues in Palestine and Greece* (London, 1934), 47–8, cites *Jerusalem Talmud* Sukkah 51*b*, end, and 55*b*, to prove that galleries existed in Trajan's time. He appears to have proved his point; however, his references are not correct and should read, p. Tal. Sukkah 5, 1, end f. Cf. *Le Talmud de Jérusalem* (trans. M. Schwab; Paris, 1933), Tome VI, 43–4. On the issue of when women began to be separated from the men, cf. Loewe, *Position of Women*, 44, 49. Cf. Jeremias, *Jerusalem*, 374, n. 78. One must also ask why women originally were separated from men in the Temple and in the synagogue. The separation may not have implied anything negative originally about a woman's nature or religious rights.
80 Jeremias, *Jerusalem*, 363; Moore, *Judaism*, vol. II, 130.
81 B.T. Mo'ed VIII, Megillah, p. 140; Jeremias, *Jerusalem*, 374, n. 79 on Tosephta Meg. 4.11, 22*b*.
82 Jeremias, *Jerusalem*, 374; Moore, *Judaism*, vol. II, 122ff on the relevant passages.
83 M. Shab. 2.6, Danby, 102.
84 M. Berakoth 3.3, Danby, 4. There was no uniform opinion on whether or not women should say benediction after a meal. M. Ber. 3.3, Danby, 4, Moore, *Judaism*, vol. II, 129, and Loewe, *Position of Women*, 32, say yes; however, M. Ber. 7.2, Danby, 7, says no.
85 As Peritz, 'Women in the Ancient Hebrew Cult', 115–19, has noted.
86 Danby, 322. One must also remember the famous benediction recited by a Jewish man each day thanking God He has not made him 'a heathen, a woman, or a brutish man'. B.T. Menahoth 43*b*, Kodashim, Menahoth, 264. It may well be that this blessing was originally said because a normal man, unlike any of these other groups, had the privilege of fulfilling all the positive ordinances of the Law and of full participation in the cult. This is a conjecture of Loewe, *Position of Women*, 43. In the context of other negative evaluations, it seems likely that whatever the saying may have denoted originally, it certainly connoted a negative view of women.
87 M. Hag. 1.1, Danby, 211; M. Ber. 3.3, Danby, 4; cf. Lowy, 'Extent of Jewish Polygamy', 115–35. Schechter, *Studies in Judaism*, 320, says that women could make up the quorum, if it is only comprised of women, in order to say the grace.
88 Despite Jeremias' statement (*Jerusalem*, 374) that women, except in rare cases,

had no right to bear witness since they were considered to be liars. Jeremias
cites M. Sheb. 4.1 (Danby, 413–14) which refers specifically to the oath of
testimony, a particular type of oath. But in M. Sheb. 3.10–11 (Danby, 413)
we are told of laws which pertain to the oaths of both men and women.
Further, in Sanhedrin 3.3 (Danby, 385) the section of the Mishnah which
tells us who is *not* qualified to be a witness or judge, women are not included.
Cf. S. Mendelsohn, *The Criminal Jurisprudence of the Ancient Hebrews* (New
York, 1968), 116.

89   M. Ket. 9.8, Danby, 258–9.
90   M. Yeb. 16.5, 7, Danby, 244; M. Ket. 1.6, Danby, 246.
91   M. Yeb. 13.13, Danby, 239–40.
92   Danby, 280.
93   Danby, 291–2. I do not agree with Jeremias (*Jerusalem*, 375) that women
were in general religiously on a par with minors and Gentiles. It is true that
the three are often grouped together in distinction from Jewish males who
could participate fully in the cult. This does not imply that distinctions were
not made between these three groups (the stipulations for Naziritic vows argue
against such a view). Cf. J. Pirenne, 'Le Statut de la Femme', 125, who says,
'La femme n'est pas une perpétuelle mineure.'
94   M. Ned. 11.9, Danby, 279–80.
95   M. Sot. 9.8, Danby, 304; M. Sot. 6.4, Danby, 299–300.
96   M. Ket. 2.9, Danby, 247, reads, 'None may testify of himself.' M. Ket. 2.5–7,
Danby, 247, makes clear that a woman's uncorroborated word about someone
else might be accepted. Cf. M. Yeb. 15.1, Danby, 241.
97   R. Akiba was of this opinion; M. Yeb. 16.7, Danby, 244–5. Cf. B.T. Babba
Kamma 88*a*, Nazikin I, Babba Kamma, p. 507.
98   Jeremias, *Jerusalem*, 375.
99   M. Ket. 1.8, Danby, 246; cf. M. Kid. 4.12, Danby, 329.
100   Danby, 258; M. Ket. 7.8, Danby, 255.
101   B.T. Ket. 62*b*–63*a*, Nashim III, Ketuboth, pp. 378–9.
102   Loewe, *Position of Women*, 49.
103   Genesis Rabbah 15.2, Midrash Rabbah I, Genesis I, 141ff. Cf. 'Women',
Encyclopedia Judaica, vol. XVI, col. 626; B.T. Kid. 49*b*, Nashim VIII, Kiddushin, p. 249; The Letter of Aristeas, sec. 250, *APOT* vol II (1913), 116;
M. Aboth 1.5, Danby, 446; B.T. Shab. 152*a*, Mo'ed II, Shabbath II, p. 777;
B.T. Kid. 82*b*, Nashim VIII, Kiddushin, p. 425. Philo, *Questions and Answers
on Genesis*, ques. 27 (LCL Supplement I; trans. R. Marcus; 1953), 16; also
ques. 29 (LCL), pp. 17–18. Philo, *On Drunkenness*, 58–9 (LCL III; trans.
F.H. Colson and G.H. Whitaker; 1930), 347; cf. Richard A. Baer, *Philo's Use
of the Categories of Male and Female* (Leiden, 1970), 40ff; Philo, *On the
Special Laws* III.169–71 (LCL VII; trans. F.H. Colson; 1937), 580–3;
Josephus, *Against Apion* II.201–3 (LCL I; trans. H. St. J. Thackeray; 1926),
372–5.
104   Cf. n.1 above; Moore, *Judaism*, vol. II, 126, 131; Roland de Vaux, *Ancient
Israel, Its Life and Institutions* (trans. J. McHugh; London, 1973), 40. In
relation to the cult and the *patria potestas* Jewish women compare unfavour-
ably with Babylonian women, though favourably with Assyrians. Cf. E.M.
MacDonald, *The Position of Women as Reflected in Semitic Codes of Law*
(Toronto, 1931), espec. 31–2, 48–9, 69–73. Cf. P. Cruveilhier, 'Le droit de

la femme', *RB* 36 (1927), 353–76. As a result of foreign influences, women in the Jewish colony at Elephantine and at Alexandria had certain civil rights not granted them in Palestine. Cf. W.A. Meeks, 'The Image of the Androgyne: Some Uses of a Symbol in Earliest Christianity', *HR* 13 (3, Feb., 1974), 176, n. 64.

105   Cf. Jeremias, *Jerusalem*, 375, who says, 'We have therefore the impression that Judaism in Jesus' time also had a very low opinion of women', to J. Bonsirven, *Palestinian Judaism in the Time of Jesus Christ* (New York, 1964), 100, who says, 'Misogyny is another widespread characteristic in Israel.' This is also the view of S. Zucrow, *Women, Slaves, and the Ignorant in Rabbinic Literature* (Boston, 1932), 74–84. For a more balanced treatment, cf. J. Hauptman, 'Images of Women in the Talmud', in *Religion and Sexism, Images of Women in the Jewish and Christian Traditions* (ed. R.R. Ruether; New York, 1974), 184–212.

2 Women in the Teaching of Jesus

1   For a general introduction to this subject, cf. the following: V.R. Mollenkott, *Women, Men, and the Bible* (Nashville, 1977); K. Stendahl, *The Bible and the Role of Women* (FBBS; Philadelphia, 1966); F. Leenhardt and F. Blanke, *Die Stellung der Frau im Neuen Testament und in der alten Kirche* (Zürich, 1949); Leipoldt, *Die Frau*; I. Brennan, 'Women in the Gospels', *New Black-friars* 52 (1971), 291–9; J.A. Grassi, 'Women's Liberation: The New Testament Perspective', *Living Light* 8 (2, 1971), 22–34; C.F. Parvey, 'The Theology and Leadership of Women in the New Testament', in *Religion and Sexism*, 117–49; J. Sanderson, 'Jesus and Women', *The Other Side* 9 (4, July–August, 1973), 16–21, 35–6; L. Swidler, 'Jesus was a Feminist', *Catholic World* 212 (1970–1), 177–83; S. Terrien, 'Toward a Biblical Theology of Womanhood', *Religion in Life* 42 (1973), 322–33.

2   There are no real difficulties in taking the essence of the Marcan form of this story as authentic. Cf. V. Taylor, *The Gospel According to St. Mark*, 2nd ed. (New York, 1966), 424–5; C.E.B. Cranfield, *The Gospel According to St. Mark* (CGTC; London, 1972), 325. Martin Dibelius, *From Tradition to Gospel* (trans. B.L. Woolf; London, 1934), 50ff, does assign verses 17–22 to the category of paradigm 'of a less pure type'; however, the impurity (i.e., later accretions) he sees has to do with certain details that do not affect our assessment of verse 19 as an affirmation by Jesus.

3   Notice that Jesus speaks of 'following Me' (Mk 10.1–12 and parallels). Jesus is not talking about a Jewish requirement for obtaining eternal life.

4   Cf. pp. 25ff on Mk 10.1–12 and parallels. Luke also has the pericope on children before that of the rich man, but has omitted the discussion on divorce found in Mk 10.1–12 (but cf. Lk. 16.18).

5   Taylor, *Mark*, 339; but cf. R. Bultmann, *History of the Synoptic Tradition* (trans. John Marsh; Oxford, 1963), 17–18.

6   Dibelius, *From Tradition*, 220–1; Cranfield, *Mark*, 230 takes 7.1–23 as a single unit.

7   In view of the content of this saying it is highly probable that in his original audience was a group of Jewish leaders, and possibly some Pharisees.

8   It is possible that we should read στήσητε ('establish') here with D, W, Θ,

among others, instead of τηρήσητε with אּ, A, K, L, *et al.* So Metzger, *TC*, 94; Taylor, *Mark*, 339; W. Michaelis, 'κρατέω', *TDNT*, vol. III, 911–12.

9   Cf. M. Ker. 6.9, Danby, 466. For Jesus, to honour one's parents is a commandment which involves providing them with financial support. Cf. J. Schneider, 'τιμή', *TDNT*, vol. VIII, 178–9; G. Schrenk, 'πατήρ', *TDNT*, vol V, 982. This is what 'honouring' was commonly thought to imply. Cf. J.D.M. Derrett, KOPBAN, Ο ΕΣΤΙΝ ΔWPON, in *Studies in the New Testament*, vol. I (Leiden, 1977), 112–17 (cf. Prov. 28.24).

10   The idea of speaking evil or reviling rather than cursing is probably what is being conveyed by this word. Cf. BAG, 298; Taylor, *Mark*, 340; C. Schneider, 'κακολογέω', *TDNT*, vol. III, 468.

11   Cf. K.H. Rengstorf, 'κορβᾶν', *TDNT*, vol. III, 862; Danby, 794, 'the usual term introducing a vow to abstain from anything, or to deny another person the use of anything'.

12   For the ossuary inscription with κορβᾶν dating from the late first century B.C., cf. M.-E. Boismard, 'Chronique Archéologique', *RB* 65 (1958), 400–23, espec. 409; J.A. Fitzmyer, 'The Aramaic Qorbān Inscription from Jebel Hallet et-Tûri and Mark 7.11/Matt. 15.5', *JBL* 78 (1959), 60–5. The development of κορβᾶν into a course formula seems to be later than the NT. Cf. Derrett, 'KOPBAN', 115. For Mishnaic parallels, cf. M. Nedarim 5.6, Danby, 271; M. Baba Kamma 9.10, Danby, 345. Cf. Philo, *On the Special Laws* 2.16 (LCL VII), 314–17; Josephus, *Antiquities* 4.73 (LCL IV; trans. H. St. J. Thackerary; 1930), 510–11; Josephus, *Against Apion* 1.167 (LCL I), 230–1.

13   κορβᾶν is not an imprecation, but a technical term in an oath formula. Cf. J. Bligh, 'Qorban!', *HeyJ* 5 (1964), 192–3; Z.W. Falk, 'Notes and Observations – on Talmudic Vows', *HTR* 59 (3, 1966), 311–12.

14   Str-B, vol. I, 714; Rengstorf, 'κορβᾶν', *TDNT*, vol. III, 865, W.G. Kümmel, 'Jesus und der jüdische Traditionsgedanke', *ZNW* 33 (1934), 105–30, espec. 122–4, says that such means of declaring a vow invalid probably were not known in Jesus' time, but cf. M. Nedarim 9.1, Danby, 275.

15   Cf. J.H.A. Hart, 'Corban', *JQR* 19 (July, 1907), 648–50; Philo, *Hypothetica* 7.3–5 (LCL IX; trans. F.H. Colson; 1941), 424–5.

16   Notice how Matthew (15.6) has altered Mark at this point, substituting μὴ τιμήσει for οὐκέτι ἀφίετε ... ποιῆσαι.

17   But cf. Derrett, 'KOPBAN', 115, and Falk, 'Notes and Observations – on Talmudic Vows'. It is oral tradition or Halakah that is being rejected by Jesus; cf. J. Jeremias, *New Testament Theology, The Proclamation of Jesus* (trans. J. Bowden; New York, 1971), 210.

18   On the basis of rabbinic interpretation of Deut. 23.21, Num. 30.2, *et al.* In some cases, such vows might be classified as vows of exaggeration and could be annulled. Cf. M. Nedarim 3.2, Danby, 266; M. Nedarim 9.1, Danby, 275. Also, C.G. Montefiore, *The Synoptic Gospels*, vol. I (London, 1909), 165–6.

19   Mt. 21.15–16 will not be treated in this section as there is considerable doubt about its authenticity. It may simply be a creation of the First Evangelist out of the LXX of Ps. 8.3. If so, it could intimate that the First Evangelist wished to characterize Jesus as one who appreciated children and their qualities (cf. Mt. 18.3).

20   Taylor, *Mark*, 422, quotes J.V. Bartlet as saying, 'Hardly anything is more

characteristic of Jesus than his attitude to children.' J.V. Bartlet, *St. Mark* (Edinburgh, 1922), 292.

21   A. Oepke, 'παῖς', *TDNT*, vol. V, 640, 642–3. On papyri examples of exposure of children in Jesus' age, cf. W.L. Lane, *The Gospel According to Mark* (Grand Rapids, 1974), 361; C.K. Barrett, *New Testament Background: Selected Documents* (New York, 1961), 38.

22   Cf. pp. 3–6 of text.

23   Oepke, 'παῖς', *TDNT*, vol. V, 646. Apparently some rabbis did hold that children were innocent; cf. Str-B, vol. I, 773–4.

24   Cf. Bultmann, *History*, 142, 149; Taylor, *Mark*, 403–4.

25   Cf. Cranfield, *Mark*, 307–8; I. Howard Marshall, *The Gospel of Luke. A Commentary on the Greek Text* (NIGTC; Exeter, 1978), 394–5.

26   On the disciples' wrangling, cf. Lk. 14.8–10; and on Jesus' response, cf. Mk 10.13, 10.31, Mt. 20.16, Lk. 13.30, and Marshall, *Luke*, 395.

27   Bultmann, *History*, 147, believes that such sayings originated in Jewish statements about kindness to children. There is, however, no implausibility in supposing that Jesus adopted popular Jewish ideas, phrases and proverbs for His own purposes.

28   E. Schweizer, 'Matthew's View of the Church in his 18th Chapter', *AusBR* 21 (1973), 7–14, here 9–10.

29   Cf. Taylor, *Mark*, 404: 'The teaching on true greatness (35), the indispensability of the attitude of childlike trust (Mt xviii.3), and the mind which esteems the lowly as in some sense Jesus Himself (37) are some of the most authentic and characteristic elements in His thoughts.'

30   In Mark and Luke there is evidence of an argument; cf. pp. 14–16 on Matthew's modification at this point.

31   Cf. Oepke, 'παῖς', *TDNT*, vol. V, 637–8; W.K. Lowther Clarke, 'Studies in Texts', *Theology* 16 (1928), 161–3. The word παῖς can mean 'servant' as well. Cf. M. Black, 'The Marcan Parable of the Child in the Midst', *ET* 59 (1947–8), 14–16; T.F. Glasson, 'The Marcan Parable of the Child in the Midst', *ET* 59 (1947–48), 166. The suggestions of Black and Glasson that involve a play on the Aramaic *talya* (servant/child) can only be maintained if verses 35–7 are originally a unity, relating one occurrence – this is uncertain and perhaps improbable.

32   Luke, perhaps in an attempt to link the saying more closely to the example, is very specific. It is not 'a child of this sort' but 'this little child' (τοῦτο τὸ παιδίον). Mark's expression indicates that Jesus is referring to a certain kind of child as a model not just any child. Cf. L. Vaganay, 'Le schématisme du discours communautaire à la lumière de la critique des sources', *RB* 60 (1953), 217–20.

33   Cf. Mt. 10.40, Lk. 10.16. The obligation of hospitality to a guest in Judaism is well-known. Cf. Str-B, vol. I, 588ff. One is to entertain his guest before going to learn Torah. Cf. M. Shabbath 18.1, Danby, 116. Further, there is the obligation to charity in the case of orphans; cf. Str-B, vol. I, 774.

34   It could mean 'with my authority or power' or even 'according to my will' but the situation does not favour either of these as it would in the context of exorcism. A. Plummer, *A Critical and Exegetical Commentary on the Gospel According to St. Luke* (ICC; Edinburgh, 1922), 258; Marshall, *Luke*, 396; David Hill, *The Gospel of Matthew* (New Century Bible; Greenwood,

1972), 273, all favour something like 'for my sake'. If this is the meaning, then there is no need to see this phrase as a secondary Christological addition meant to focus on Jesus' person and power.

35 Some have argued that Jesus sees the child as His representative here. Cf. Lane, *Mark*, 341; T.H. Darlow, 'Divorce and Childhood, A Reading of St. Matt. xix.3–15', *Exp*, 4th ser. 7 (1893), 294–9. This overlooks the fact that the pericope is concerned with the behaviour of the adult disciples to whom Jesus is speaking. There is no hint that the child is acting as Jesus' agent.

36 It is doubtful that the texts on little ones (Mt. 10.42, 18.6, Mk 9.42) bear on our subject, for in these texts the least among the believers are meant by the Gospel writers. Cf. S. Legasse, *Jésus et L'Enfant* (Paris, 1969), espec. 337–41.

37 Cf. Taylor, *Mark*, 421–2; Cranfield, *Mark*, 322; A.H. M'Neile, *The Gospel According to St. Matthew* (London, 1965), 276. Otherwise Bultmann, *History*, 32, who considers this an ideal construction with its basis in the Jewish practice of blessing. J. Jeremias, *Infant Baptism in the First Four Centuries* (trans. D. Cairns; London, 1960), 49–50, states that it was the custom for rabbis to bless children on Yom Kippur and argues (*pace* Bultmann) that this narrative indicates that Jesus probably did so as well. Cf. E. Lohse, 'χείρ', *TDNT*, vol. IX, 432. Plummer, *Luke*, 421, says that rabbis blessed children on their first birthday but gives no references. Cf. Str-B, vol. I, 807–8.

38 Dibelius, *From Tradition*, 43.

39 Bultmann, *History*, 32.

40 Cf. Marshall, *Luke*, 681. The catechetical arrangement in Matthew and Mark is noteworthy (cf. Mk 10.1–12, 13–16, 17–31 to Mt. 10.1–9, 13–15, 16–30). Matthew also includes a short section on eunuchs (19.10–12) but, as if to indicate that the eunuch teaching did not rule out having children, returns immediately to the Marcan order and section on children. Cf. Hill, *Matthew*, 272–3.

41 The αὐτοῖς of Mk 10.13 and parallels is significant for it indicates that it was not only mothers bringing their children, but also fathers or older children. Cf. Lane, *Mark*, 358–9, n. 22; E. Hampden-Cook, 'Whom did the Disciples Rebuke?', *ET* 17 (1905–6), 192. The point of Luke's change to τὰ βρέφη is perhaps to bring out that here were persons totally dependent on God. Cf. Cranfield, *Mark*, 324.

42 For typical Jewish attitudes about the immaturity of children, cf. M. Aboth 4.20, Danby, 455; M. Aboth 3.11, Danby, 351.

43 Plummer, *Luke*, 421.

44 Marshall, *Luke*, 682; M'Neile, *Matthew*, 277; C. Brown, 'Child', *NIDNTT*, vol. I, 284.

45 G.R. Beasley-Murray, *Baptism in the New Testament* (Grand Rapids, 1962), 327.

46 This last view is suggested by F.A. Schilling, 'What Means the Saying About Receiving the Kingdom of God as a Little Child (τὴν βασιλείαν τοῦ θεοῦ ὡς παιδίον, Mk x.15, Lk xviii.17)', *ET* 77 (2, 1965) 56–8; cf. A.R.C. Leaney, 'Jesus and the Symbol of the Child (Luke ix.46–48)', *ET* 66 (1954–5), 91–2.

47 So Cranfield, *Mark*, 323; Taylor, *Mark*, 423 (genitive of possession); but cf. MHT, vol. III, 214.

48 This is not to say that children were considered the ultimate divine blessing

by Jesus (cf. Lk. 11.27–8), as they seem to have been by some Jews. Jesus also saw that in the Day of Judgment what would normally be a blessing would become a curse. Both of these sayings show how Jesus' eschatological teaching conditioned His teaching on other subjects. For Him, the physical family must live under the guidelines of the Kingdom ethic, always realizing that it was only part of a larger and more fundamental community – the family of faith.

49   Cf. Taylor, *Mark*, 494; Cranfield, *Mark*, 383.

50   Though the Scribes would not charge for their teaching, they could accept hospitality or free-will offerings. Cf. Jeremias, *Jerusalem*, 111–16. M. Aboth 1.13, 4.5, Berakoth 4.5–6, Danby, 447, 453, 534.

51   καὶ ὀρφάνων in D, W, f¹³, and other mss., is probably a later addition. Cf. Metzger, *TC*, 111; Taylor, *Mark*, 495. Mt. 23.13 is an interpolation based on Mk 12.40. Cf. Metzger, *TC*, 60.

52   Derrett, ' "Eating up the Houses of Widows": Jesus's Comment on Lawyers?' *Studies in the NT*, vol. I, 118–27; H.B. Swete, *The Gospel According to St. Mark* (London, 1898), 274; O. Michel, 'οἰκία', *TDNT*, vol. V, 131, n. 3.

53   Jeremias, *Jerusalem*, 114; Taylor, *Mark*, 495; Swete, *Mark*, 274; Cf. the description of the wicked scribes in *The Assumption of Moses* 7.3ff, *APOT*, vol. II, 419–20. Also, Lk. 8.3 and pp. 116–18.

54   Derrett, ' "Eating up the Houses of Widows" ', 120ff; M. Sotah 3.4, Danby, 296; Str-B, vol. II, 33; Josephus, *Antiquities* 17.34–47 (LCL VIII; trans. R. Marcus and Allen Wikgren; 1963), 388–95; *Antiquities* 18.81ff (LCL IX; trans. by L.H. Feldman; 1965), 58–9; *Antiquities* 13.400–4 (LCL VII; R. Marcus; 1943), 428–33, may argue more for the view expressed by those in n. 53 above. F.W. Danker, *Jesus and the New Age, According to St. Luke* (St. Louis, 1972), 208, argues that the scribes were seizing the widows' property because they could not pay their debts. This is possible since regulations about the seizure of property if one defaulted on a debt had changed since OT times. Cf. Baron, *History of the Jews*, vol. II, 270, 303.

55   Cf. Stählin, 'χήρα', *TDNT*, vol. IX, 449; L. Simon, 'Le Sou de la Veuve – Marc 12/41–44', *ETR* 44 (2, 1969), 115–26.

56   Marshall, *Luke*, 750–1; J.M. Creed, *The Gospel According to St. Luke* (London, 1969), 251.

57   Cf. Bultmann, *History*, 32–3; Dibelius, *From Tradition*, 261; Jeremias, *Jerusalem*, 109.

58   Taylor, *Mark*, 496.

59   It is not certain whether γαζοφυλακίον is meant to represent the treasury itself or one of the offering receptacles; cf. Lane, *Mark*, 442, n. 83.

60   Luke simply uses the collective πλουσίους and stresses the gift aspect (τὰ δῶρα αὐτῶν); while Mark speaks of χαλκὸν. Note the present participle in Luke (βαλλόντας) indicating an ongoing activity. Mark makes a strong contrast between the continual action of the rich and the punctiliar action of the widow (πάντες ἔβαλλον – αὕτη δὲ ἔβαλεν). Cf. Robertson, 833, 838.

61   Stählin, 'χήρα', *TDNT*, vol. IX, 449, n. 81. Mark describes her as χήρα πτωχὴ; Luke, perhaps with his stress on the woman's plight, intensifies the description saying she is needy – πενιχρὰν. As Jeremias, 'Zwei Miszellen: 1. Antik-Jüdische Münzdeutungen. 2. Zur Geschichtlichkeit der Tempelreinigung', *NTS* 23 (2, 1977), 177–80, points out, we are dealing with free-will offerings and thus the widow's example is all the more striking.

62 Cf. D. Sperber, 'Mark xii.42 and its metrological background', *NovT* 9 (3, 1967), 178–90. Mark's mention of the Roman quadrans, not minted in the East, probably points to his Western audience. Cf. the debate between F. Blass, 'On Mark xii.42 and xv.16', *ET* 10 (1898–9), 185–7, also 'On Mark xii.42', *ET* 10 (1898–9), 286–7, and W.M. Ramsay, 'On Mark xii.42', *ET* 10 (1898–9), 232, also 'On Mark xii.42', *ET* 10 (1898–9), 336. The assertion that giving less than two coins of the smallest denomination was not permitted is based on a misunderstanding of B.T. Baba Bathra 10*b* by Plummer, *Luke*, 375, *et al*. Cf. Marshall, *Luke*, 752; Str-B, vol. II, 45. Thus, the sacrifice is greater than it might have been.

63 Luke has only two other sayings introduced by 'Truly' – 9.27 and 12.44. He reserved the third to emphasize this woman's example. Cf. Danker, *Jesus*, 209.

64 πλεῖον πάντων may mean 'more than any', or probably 'more than all combined'. So B. Reicke, 'πᾶς', *TDNT*, vol. V, 889; Cranfield, *Mark*, 386. The point is that though the rich gave much, the widow gave all. Swete, *Mark*, 276. This may reflect Jesus' supernatural knowledge in the situation; *or* the amount of the widow's giving (and this saying attributed to Jesus) may be a later addition intended to raise the Christological significance of the story. Finally, if this was originally a story told by Jesus, then there are no problems raised by this remark.

65 Luke is more dramatic at this point – πάντα τὸν βίον ὃν εἶχεν ἔβαλεν. βίος indicates means of subsistence, property, living. BAG, 141; Str-B, vol. II, 46.

66 Mark has πολλοὶ πλούσιοι; Luke, πλουσίους.

67 Cf. Stählin, 'Das Bild der Witwe. Ein Betrag zur Bildersprache der Bibel und zum Phänomen der Personifikation in der Antike', *JAC* 17 (1954), 13, F.C. Fensham, 'Widow, Orphan, and the Poor in Ancient Near Eastern Legal and Wisdom Literature', *JNES* 21 (1962), 129–39. As Fensham shows, Jesus is reaffirming and returning to their rightful place the obligations of the Jewish society to the widow originally enjoined in the OT (cf. Exod. 22.22ff).

68 D.R. Catchpole, 'The Synoptic Divorce Material as a Traditio-Historical Problem', *BJRL* 57 (1974–5), 92–127.

69 It is possible that the isolated logia and the controversy dialogues both go back to a common saying.

70 There are some rabbinic parallels to the content of verse 28 but they all appear to post-date Jesus' ministry. Cf. C.G. Montefiore, *Rabbinic Literature and Gospel Teachings* (New York, 1970), 41–2; W.D. Davies, *The Setting of the Sermon on the Mount* (London, 1964), 252. Jeremias, *NT Theology*, 251, says, 'We may take it as quite certain that in the antitheses we are hearing the words of Jesus himself ... because this has neither Jewish nor early Christian parallels.'

71 Jeremias, *NT Theology*, 18.

72 Bultmann, *History*, 131, gives 5.27–8 as an example of an older (i.e., non-redactional) formulation of the antithesis and admits the 'I' saying here can be historical (p. 147).

73 So T.W. Manson, *The Sayings of Jesus* (London, 1957), 157. The assumption of two sources is probable considering the differences in 18.8–9 and 5.29–30 in form and order and also in view of the fact that the Evangelist includes the same material twice.

74 Taylor, *Mark*, 408–9.

75 Davies, *Sermon on the Mount*, 227, n. 2.
76 Cf. pp. 20–1, and nn. 83, 84, below.
77 For the view that Mt. 5.29–30 is an edited and less authentic version of a fuller saying, cf. Bultmann, *History*, 311–12, and Hill, *Matthew*, 123. Manson, *Sayings*, 157, maintains that Matthew has reversed the order of the reference to eye and hand in 5.29–30 to improve a bad connection. But the order may have been more subject to manipulation in a catechetical collection of isolated sayings such as we have in Mk 9.37–50 than in Matthew's special source.
78 Cf. LSJ, 1141; BAG, 528; A-S, 295; MM, 416; F. Hauck, 'μοιχεύω', *TDNT*, vol. IV, 729–35. Derrett, *Law in the New Testament* (London, 1970), 367ff, rightly notes that μοιχεία and πορνεία can both be used in the same context without πορνεία excluding μοιχεία. It may be that the two terms are distinct here.
79 Cf. NIV, KJV, NEB, RSV, NASB, Phillips, Moffatt.
80 The ἐν τῇ καρδίᾳ αὐτοῦ is perhaps awkward in this interpretation, nevertheless, Jesus is talking about the initial act, the sinful gazing, which amounts to the man leading the woman astray to adultery in his heart (even if the act is never carried out). Jesus was not shy of speaking of a man's adultery (cf. Mt. 5.32*b*, Lk. 16.18). Cf. Lk. 18.1 and Ac. 3.19. Haacker's interpretation has the apparent support of several early scribes. Cf. the variant αὐτῆς at Mt 5.28 in אֱ¹, M, etc. Cf. K. Haacker, 'Der Rechtssatz Jesu zum Thema Ehebruch (Mt. 5,28)', *BZ* 21 (1, 1977), 113–16.
81 Cf. the related idea in B.T. Ned. 90*b*, Nashim V, Nedarim, 279; cf. Str-B, vol. I, 299ff, and Swidler, *Women in Judaism*, 127.
82 Jesus is advocating a reformation of patriarchal culture, but there is no indication that He advocated the abandonment of such a culture. In Jesus' eyes, male headship or authority was a call for male self-restraint and community responsibility, not a licence for self-indulgence or sin. This view of purged and purified male headship and responsibility becomes more apparent in Mt. 5.32.
83 M'Neile, *Matthew*, 64ff; Hill, *Matthew*, 123ff.
84 Derrett, 'Law in the New Testament: *Si scandalizaverit te manus tua abscinde illam* (Mk IX.42) and Comparative Legal History', *Studies in the NT*, vol. I, 4–31, argues that 'eye' refers to giving bribes to women in exchange for illicit sex. Perhaps this is an overstatement. It is more plausible that the right hand reference would be to a man handling or forcibly taking another's wife. In Jewish circles, adultery and other sexual sins were considered sins, not so much because of infidelity, as because of the theft involved. Cf. Hill, *Matthew*, 123. F.J. Leenhardt, 'Les femmes aussi ... à propos du billet de répudiation', *RTP* 19 (1, 1969), 31–40, suggests that Mt. 5.28 concerns covetousness rather than lust and proposes to translate the verse, 'He who looks at a woman for the purpose of possessing her'. The principle of punishing the offending member is well-known in Jesus' day. Cf. Str-B, vol. I, 302–3; G. Stählin, 'ἀποκόπτω ἐκκόπτω', *TDNT*, vol. III, 853, 857, 859.
85 Derrett, 'Law in the New Testament ... (Mk IX.42)', 25–6; M. Niddah 2.1, Danby, 746; cf. K. Weiss, 'συμφέρω', *TDNT*, vol. IX, 75.
86 It is crucial to remember that all of Mt. 5.27–32 is directed toward the male who looks at (verses 27–9) or takes (verse 30) or divorces (verses 31–2) a woman. So, too, Lk. 16.18.

87   That p[66], [75], א, B, L, *et al.* omit this pericope is fatal to any view that it was originally part of John's (or Luke's) Gospel. Cf. Metzger, *TC*, 219–22. This does not preclude the possibility that it is authentic Johannine or Lucan material. The case for Lucan authorship is impressive. Cf. H.J. Cadbury, 'A Possible Case of Lukan Authorship', *HTR* 10 (1917), 237–44; F. Warburton Lewis, 'The Pericope Adulterae', *ET* 29 (1917–18), 138. In part, this view is based on the fact that f[13] includes this pericope after Lk. 21.38, and 1333[c] includes it after Lk. 24.53. For an argument for Johannine authorship, cf. A.F. Johnson, 'A Stylistic Trait of the Fourth Gospel in the Pericope Adulterae?' *BETS* 9 (2, 1966), 91–6. Though D, G, H, K, Didascalia, Apostolic Constitutions, Ambrosiaster, and most mss. include this pericope in the traditional place after Jn 7.52, Jn 7.53 and the 'again' of 8.2 argue against this placement.

88   D. Daube, 'Biblical Landmarks in the Struggle for Women's Rights', *JR* (in press), 14.

89   Cadbury, 'A Possible Case of Lukan Authorship', 243, n. 12; cf. C.K. Barrett, *The Gospel According to St. John*, 2nd ed. (London, 1978), 590.

90   Eusebius, *Ecclesiastical History* III, xxxix 17 (LCL I; trans. K. Lake; 1926), 298–9, indicates that Papias recorded a narrative that is probably the same as Jn 7.53–8.11 with small variations. The evidence of Apostolic Constitutions II, 24, also appears to point to an early knowledge and use of this story in the Christian community. Cf. Barrett, *John* (1978), 589–90; R.E. Brown, *The Gospel According to John*, 'i-xii' (New York, 1966), 335–6. Perhaps even earlier evidence of the existence of this narrative is found in the language and ideas of *Hermas*, Mand. IV.I.4.11 (LCL; trans. K. Lake; 1913), 78–81; cf. also IV.I.3.2, and 3.4 (LCL), 82–5. Cf. C. Taylor, 'The Pericope of the Adulteress', *JTS* 4 (1902–3), 129–30.

91   Cf. E.C. Hoskyns, *The Fourth Gospel* (ed. F.N. Davey; London, 1940), vol. II, 676–7.

92   Cf. Brown, *John*, 'i-xii', 335.

93   Barrett, *John* (1978), 590; Leon Morris, *The Gospel According to John* (NICNT; Grand Rapids, 1971), 833ff; cf. Lk. 7.36–50, Mk 12.18–23.

94   There was no other place in the Temple to which this woman could be brought without impropriety. Cf. G. Schrenk, 'ἱερεύς', *TDNT*, vol. III, 236–7.

95   ἐπὶ μοιχείᾳ κατειλημμένην. It is reasonably certain that ἁμαρτία is a later correction of μοιχεία to conform this phrase with verse 11. Cf. Metzger, *TC*, 222. It seems probable that the scribes and Pharisees were accompanied by the witnesses and perhaps a lynching mob. So Derrett, 'Law in the New Testament: The Story of the Woman Taken in Adultery', *NTS* 10 (1963–4), 1–26.

96   Daube, 'An Attack on Discrimination Against Women: the Adulteress of John 8', unpublished essay of 25 pages, by permission of the author (an abbreviated form will appear in 'Biblical Landmarks'), 14–23. Since this may be a lynching mob, willing to take matters and stones into their own hands, one cannot insist that, since stoning is mentioned, a betrothed woman must be involved. *Pace* E.F. Harrison, 'The Son of God Among the Sons of Men. VIII. Jesus and the Woman Taken in Adultery', *BSac* 103 (1946), 431–9. J. Blinzler argues persuasively that μοιχεία would not be used of a woman who was only betrothed and that the death penalty in Jesus' day generally meant stoning. Cf. his 'Die Strafe für Ehebruch in Bibel und Halacha. Zur Auslegung von Joh. VIII.5', *NTS* 4 (1, 1957), 32–47.

97 Derrett, 'Law in the New Testament ... Adultery', 5ff.

98 M. Sotah 1.1ff, Danby, 293ff.

99 This was a necessary prerequisite, as Derrett, 'Law in the New Testament ... Adultery', 5ff, notes.

100 The position of οὐ makes it emphatic.

101 Cf. Barrett, *The Gospel According to St. John* (London, 1955), 492. Probably it is not the case that this woman is being taken either to or from a court, since the only Jewish court which could try this woman was closed by this time. So Derrett, 'Law in the New Testament ... Adultery', 9ff. *Pace* Jeremias, 'Zur Geschichtlichkeit des Verhörs Jesu vor dem Hohen Rat', *ZNW* 43 (1950–1), 145–51. Further, the word 'condemn' in verse 10 argues against Jeremias' case. The Romans would not try an adulterous woman.

102 Cf. E. Power, 'Writing on the Ground', *Bib* 2 (1921), 54–7. P. Humbert, 'Jesus Writing on the Ground (John viii.6–8)', *ET* 30 (1918–19), 475–6; D.S. Margoliouth, 'Jesus Writing on the Ground', *ET* 31 (1919–20), 38; Daube, 'An Attack on Discrimination ... John 8', 25; Barrett, *John* (1978), 592; R.H. Lightfoot, *St. John's Gospel, A Commentary* (Oxford, 1960), 347; Derrett, 'Law in the New Testament ... Adultery', 9ff.

103 Cf. Brown, *John*, 'i-xii', 337–8.

104 Daube, 'An Attack on Discrimination ... John 8', 6. This implies that Jesus suspects there is other serious sin involved (in addition to the woman's). On ἀναμάρτητος meaning 'without serious sin', cf. Josephus, *The Jewish War* 7.329 (LCL III; trans. H. St. J. Thackeray; 1928), 596–7; Herodotus 5.39 (LCL III; trans. A.D. Godley; 1922), 42–3.

105 Derrett, 'Law in the New Testament ... Adultery', 25–6.

106 πρεσβύτερος could be either 'elders' or 'older men'. Morris, *John*, 890, suggests both; Brown, *John*, 'i-xii', 334, translates it as elders.

107 This is Daube's main point ('An Attack on Discrimination ... John 8', 23ff). I endorse his view with some hesitation since it is conceivable that this is simply an attack on injustice rather than discrimination. Cf. Barrett, *John* (1978), 590–1.

108 As Morris, *John*, 890, says, 'The form of the command implies a ceasing to commit an action already started.' Brown, *John*, 'i-xii', 334, states that Jesus is saying 'avoid *this* sin'. If so, then His statement in 7*b* has a limited scope as well.

109 Lightfoot, *John*, 348.

110 Probably the narrative has been touched-up by editors and/or the Evangelist to heighten the effect; for instance, by adding αὐτόφωρος in 8.4, the second writing on the ground in 8.8, and the editorial comment in verse 6. Cf. Bultmann, *History*, 63.

111 For our purpose, however, it is unnecessary to debate here the issue of the exceptive clauses since we are focusing on Jesus' view. If they are later additions, regardless of their content, they are of no concern to us. If they are original and the view advocated by Fitzmyer and others is correct (that we are talking about an exception for an incestuous or zenût relationship which Jesus saw as not really a legitimate marriage in the first place), then the prohibition against divorce in cases of legitimate marriages is still absolute. An increasing number of scholars think this is the meaning in Matthew 5 and 19. So E.E. Ellis, *The Gospel of Luke* (New Century Bible; Greenwood; 1974

rev. ed.), 203; W.K. Lowther Clarke, 'The Excepting Clause in St. Matthew', *Theology* 15 (1927), 161–2; H. Baltensweiler, 'Die Ehebruchsklauseln bei Matthäus', *TZ* 15 (1959), 230–56; Baltensweiler, *Die Ehe im Neuen Testament – Exegetische Untersuchungen über Ehe, Ehelosigkeit und Ehescheidung* (Stuttgart, 1967), espec. 87–107; J. Bonsirven, ' "Nisi fornicationis causa" Comment résoudre cette "crux interpretum"?' *RSR* 35 (1948), 442–64; J.A. Fitzmyer, 'The Matthean Divorce Texts and Some New Palestinian Evidence', *TS* 37 (2, 1976), 197–226; H.J. Richards, 'Christ on Divorce', *Scr* 11 (13, 1959), 22–32; Zerwick, 43, n. 8; and this author's forthcoming article on the exceptive clauses, 'Mt 5.32/19.9 – Exception or Exceptional Situation', *NTS* (in press). Finally, if the exceptions are real exceptions, then it is extremely difficult to doubt they are later additions in view of the relevant Pauline texts and the other Synoptic material.

112 ποιεῖ αὐτὴν μοιχευθῆναι. In Lk. 16.18 we have πᾶς ὁ ἀπολύων τὴν γυναῖκα αὐτοῦ καὶ γαμῶν ἑτέραν μοιχεύει. Again, it is the male who is the subject of the action, but here he is called the adulterer, a more radical statement for its day than Mt. 5.32*a* (and there is no exceptive clause in Luke). Luke has juxtaposed this statement with one about the Law not passing away, and thus Lk. 16.18 is intended to indicate Jesus' intensification of the eternally valid Law. It does not appear that Mt. 5.32 implies that divorce itself is adultery; rather, the adultery that the woman is forced to commit comes if she remarries. Adultery is associated only with a further marriage union in Lk. 16.18. Mt. 5.32*b* and Lk. 16.18*b* are both more radical statements than the rabbis were willing to make, since marrying a divorcee was frowned on but not prohibited in rabbinic Judaism. Cf. Str-B, vol. I, 320ff, and Marshall, *Luke*, 630–2.

113 D, it[a],[b],[d],[k], and other mss. omit καί through μοιχᾶται in Mt. 5.32*b*. Metzger, *TC*, 13–14, suggests that some scribes felt that if the divorced woman is made an adulteress by illegal divorce, then anyone marrying such a woman also commits adultery. Alternatively, this omission may reflect the tendency of the Western text to highlight and protect male privilege, while also relegating women to a place in the background. In this case, the omission here is of material that reflects badly on men. Cf. the variant readings in Ac. 1.14, 17.4, 12, 34, 18.26, and elsewhere in Acts 18.

114 B.H. Streeter, *The Four Gospels. A Study of Origins* (rev. ed.; London, 1964), 259. He allowed, however, that Mark's order of pericopes was still being followed by the First Evangelist and perhaps also his content at some points (260).

115 It cannot be ruled out that some Jews might have asked Jesus about the legitimacy of divorce perhaps because they had heard that He opposed it, and they wished for Him to state this openly and so demonstrate that He was at variance with the mainstream of tradition. Thus, they *could* have asked this testing question as we find it in Mark, but it seems almost certain that someone *would* have asked Jesus the question about the grounds of divorce since it was part of the current debate, perhaps to force Him to show that He sided with the stricter view (and thus not with the majority of Pharisees).

116 Even though the Mosaic legislation was given in the form of an imperative; cf. E. Lohmeyer, *Das Evangelium des Markus* (Göttingen, 1951), 199. It is also possible that ἐντέλλομαι/ἐντολή in Mk 10.3, 5 (cf. Mt. 19.7) has the somewhat milder force of instruct(ion) (cf. Ac. 17.15).

117   The 'ἐπ' αὐτήν in Mk 10.11 also looks like an explanatory addition by the Evangelist.

118   See n. 111 above.

119   But cf. Jeremias, *NT Theology*, 225, 251–3; Bultmann, *History*, 134–5.

120   Catchpole, 'Synoptic Divorce Material', 113.

121   Manson, *Sayings*, 137.

122   Cf. Mk 12.18–27, Jn 7.53–8.11.

123   Cf. the parallels to this form in rabbinic sources in Daube, *The New Testament and Rabbinic Judaism* (London, 1956), 141ff. It may well be that Mark has modelled his discussion on this form as it gave him an opportunity (in 10.10) to use his 'in house' and private teaching motif again.

124   This phrase means 'for any reason' and may reflect the Hillel–Shammai debate. Cf. B. Reicke, 'πᾶς', *TDNT*, vol. V, 888; MHT, vol. III, 268. The Hillelites held that virtually any cause was grounds for divorce. Cf. M. Gittin 9.10, Danby, 321. Davies, *Sermon on the Mount*, 104, argues that the phrase is redactional, but cf. M.R. Lehmann, 'Gen. 2.24 as the Basis for Divorce in Halakhah and New Testament', *ZAW* 72 (1960), 263–7, on its authenticity. The Marcan debate is centred on the lawfulness of divorce; the Matthean on the grounds (the lawfulness being taken for granted).

125   Cf. Fitzmyer, 'Matthean Divorce Texts', 211ff; pp. 3–5 of this study. The meaning of ἀπολύω must be constant throughout the pericope, since there is no external or internal evidence to lead us to think otherwise. *Pace* J. Dupont, *Mariage et Divorce dans l'Évangile Matthieu 19, 3–12 et parallèles* (Bruges, 1959).

126   On σκληροκαρδία cf. K. Berger, 'Hartherzigkeit und Gottes Gesetz. Die Vorgeschichte des antijüdischen Vorwurfs in Mk 10.5', *ZNW* 61 (1–2, 1970), 1–47. E. Haenchen, *Der Weg Jesu* (Berlin, 1966), 339, rightly points out that in the Marcan form of the interchange (where Jesus asks, 'What did Moses command you?'), He places Himself in a difficult (and historically improbable?) situation since He is appealing to an authority that speaks against Himself.

127   The wording on the *Get* was to read, 'Lo, thou art free to marry any man'. Cf. M. Gittin 9.3, Danby, 319.

128   So B.W. Powers, 'Marriage and Divorce: The Dispute of Jesus with the Pharisees and Its Inception', *Colloquium* 5 (1, 1971), 37: 'there might be dire consequences if she or her family wrongly believed divorce had taken place'. Cf. Daube, '*Repudium* in Deuteronomy', *Neotestamentica et Semitica: Studies in Honour of Matthew Black* (ed. E.E. Ellis, M. Wilcox; Edinburgh, 1969), 238. Contrast H. Greeven, 'Ehe nach dem Neuen Testament', *NTS* 15 (1968–9), 377–8. Jesus' teaching implies that the bill of divorce does not lighten the husband's responsibility for his wife because by giving the bill to her he gives her opportunity to commit adultery. Cf. F.J. Leenhardt, 'Les femmes aussi ... à propos du billet de répudiation', *RTP* 19 (1, 1969), 34–5.

129   Mark has ἀπὸ δὲ ἀρχῆς κτίσεως which in its explicitness in explaining the reference of ἀρχῆς may be later than the Matthean form. Lehmann, 'Genesis 2.24', 263–7, argues that 'from the beginning' in Matthew refers to the pre-Noahic state of the Jews, and that there is no allusion to a mythical bisexual first human being. *Pace* P. Winter, 'Genesis 1.27 and Jesus' Saying on Divorce',

ZAW 70 (1958), 260–1. Hill, *Matthew*, 280, says it refers to the book of Genesis over the claims of Deuteronomy. A. Van Gansewinkel, 'Ursprüngliche oder grundsätzliche Unauflösbarkeit der Ehe?', *Diakonia* 3 (2, 1972), 88–93, points out rightly that the background to ἀπ' ἀρχῆς may be the Hebrew ШΝ7 in which case ἀπ' ἀρχῆς refers to the original (or fundamental) plan (or design). Cf. similarly, G. Aicher, 'Mann und Weib – ein Fleisch (Mt. 19,4ff.)', *BZ* 5 (1907), 159–65.

130   Cf. Moule, *I-B*, 71. As A. Plummer, *An Exegetical Commentary on the Gospel According to S. Matthew* (London, 1909), 260, says, the point of appealing to Gen. 1.27 is that God originally did not create more women than men so as to provide for divorce.

131   On the textual difficulty in Mk 10.7, cf. Metzger, *TC*, 104–5.

132   J.D.M. Derrett, *Law in the New Testament* (London, 1970), 363–88, rightly argues that the irreversible and indissoluble one flesh union is the basis of Jesus' teaching on marriage. But it must not be overlooked that Jesus also says, 'Let no man put asunder', implying that it is possible for a third party to put a marriage asunder. Powers, 'Marriage and Divorce', 37, notes that the text says *what* God has joined together (i.e., the bond of marriage He has created between them), not *those* whom God has joined together. Cf. K. Barth, *Church Dogmatics,* vol. III, 4 (Edinburgh, 1961), 207; T.A. Burkill, 'Two into One: The Notion of Carnal Union in Mark 10:8; 1 Kor 6:16; Eph 5:31', *ZNW* 62 (1971), 115–20; W. Brueggemann, 'Of the Same Flesh and Bone (Gn.2,23a)', *CBQ* 32 (1970), 532–42.

133   I see no trace of the rabbinic idea of an androgynous Adam in Mt. 19.3–12 and parallels. *Pace* Daube, *NT and Rabbinic Judaism*, 72ff. Cf. R. Pesch, *Das Markusevangelium*, vol. II (Freiburg, 1977), 124–5. Jesus speaks of the two becoming one, but makes no reference to a one that was originally bisexual. It is not man's original unity, but their one flesh union that in Jesus' view disallows divorce and polygamy.

134   This joining and separating refers to marriage and divorce, not the one flesh union and its dissolution. So G. Delling, 'σύξυγος', *TDNT*, vol. VII, 748, n. 1; MHT, vol. I, 140; Str-B, vol. I, 803–4.

135   ἄνθρωπος. Thus, both potential male and female intruders are warned.

136   Cf. J. Murray, *Divorce* (Philadelphia, 1975), 33.

137   There were various concessions in the OT to the fallen order and man's sinful nature (e.g., monarchy, 1 Sam. 8.7). Cf. Daube, 'Concessions to Sinfulness in Jewish Law', *JJS* 10 (1959), 1–13. Jesus implies that these concessions have come to a halt in the new covenant community. Jesus' demands are not new; rather, they are the old demands interpreted in the light of God's original plan, not in the shadow of man's sin. As H.J. Schoeps, '*Restitutio Principii* as the Basis for the *Nova Lex Jesu*', *JBL* 66 (1947), 453–64, concludes, the appeal to God's original plan and order, which sees the end as restoring the original design and uses that truth as a hermeneutical key to the OT, probably derives from Jesus Himself, for the rabbis saw Mosaic law as fulfilling pre-Sinai laws. The citation of Gen. 1.27 in favour of monogamous marriage by the Qumranites is more a matter of proof-texting than hermeneutics. Cf. CD 4.13–5.5, Vermes, *DSS*, 36–7, 101–2.

138   Quite possibly Mt. 19.8*b* (ἀπ' ἀρχῆς ...) is the Evangelist's own addition based on verse 4. Verses 8*a* and 9 go naturally together as an antithesis, and 8*b* is unnecessary.

139　A modified form of the second half of the antithesis formula. cf. M'Neile, *Matthew*, 274.

140　N. Turner, 'The Translation of Μοιχᾶται 'επ' Αὐτήν in Mark 10.11', *BT* 7 (1956), 151–2, and B. Schaller, '"Commits adultery with her", not "against her", Mk 10.11', *ET* 83 (4, 1972), 107–8.

141　Creed, *Luke*, 207; G. Delling, 'Das Logion Mark X.11 (und seine Abwandlungen) im Neuen Testament', *NovT* 1 (1956), 263–74; J.J. O'Rourke, 'A Note on an Exception: Mt 5:32 (19:9) and 1 Cor 7:12 Compared', *HeyJ* 5 (3, 1964), 299–302.

142　For a good survey of the problem, cf. Taylor, *Mark*; 420–1. The divorce reading is probably the more original. So Swete, *Mark*, 206; Cranfield, *Mark*, 321–2; A. Plummer, *The Gospel According to St. Mark* (London, 1914), 230.

143　Cf. E. Bammel, 'Markus 10.11f.', 95–101, and 'Is Luke 16, 16–18 of Baptist's Provenience?', *HTR* 51 (1958), 101–6. The evidence is admittedly not vast. Cf. pp. 5–6 and 133, n. 38. Cf. Josephus, *Antiquities*, 15.259 (LCL VIII), 122–3. Various rabbis recognized the validity of a pagan divorce instituted by a wife through a *repudium*. Cf. B. Cohen, 'Concerning Divorce in Jewish and Roman Law', *PAAJR* 21 (1952), 3–34. Billerbeck (Str-B, vol. II, 23–4) suggests that Mk 10.12 is simply a strong way of saying a woman could forcibly end a marriage by separation or appeal to the courts.

144　In which case the variant might be right. J.N. Birdsall, in an unpublished paper presented at the Tyndale Fellowship (Cambridge, July, 1979) and in a personal communiqué, has pointed out the following: Burkitt saw Mk 10.12 as an explicit reference to the adulterous relationship of Herodias and Herod. He noted the variant of the Ssʸ (supported by miniscule 1) which reverses the order of the declaration, thus placing the offence of the deserting woman first. Birdsall points out that the related ms. 209 omits the male clause by homoioteleuton. W and the idiosyncratic Adis ms. of the Old Georgian also evidence the reversal. Burkitt argues that the true order was Mk 10.12, and then 10.11. Cf. F.C. Burkitt, *The Gospel History and Its Transmission* (Edinburgh, 1906), 100–1, and n. 1. Some rabbis had declared that Gentiles had no divorce because the permission was given only to the Jews. Cf. Str-B, vol. 1, 312; Lehmann, 'Genesis 2.24', 264–6.

145　As Cranfield, *Mark*, 321, says, 'According to Rabbinic law, a man could be said to commit adultery against another man, and a wife could be said to commit adultery against her husband, but a husband could not be said to commit adultery against his wife.' Thus, Jesus equalizes matters.

146　Cf. M. Sotah 5.1, Danby, 298. Catchpole, 'Synoptic Divorce Material', 113, believes that a redefinition of adultery has been formulated: 'such a redefinition involves a higher estimate of the status of women than was current in his environment, but a considerable amount of supporting material, suggesting just such a revaluation of the role of women by Jesus, exists'.

147　Str-B, vol. 1, 320, says that the provision 'he who marries a divorced woman commits adultery' was completely unknown in Judaism except in the case of remarriage to the original wife (cf. Deut. 24.1–4).

148　Montefiore, *Rabbinic Literature*, 269. As Hill, *Matthew*, 282, notes, however, the sectarian group that made up the Qumran community 'may have provided the spiritual milieu which nurtured the ideal of a self-consecration to a holy life and warfare which included celibacy'. Cf. n. 157 below.

149 Bultmann, *History*, 26, calls 19.12 a 'dominical saying' in the midst of a Matthean transitional passage. A. Isaksson, *Marriage and Ministry in the New Temple: A Study with Special Reference to Mt. 19.13–12 [sic] and 1 Cor. 11.3–16* (Lund, 1965), 151, argues plausibly that this tradition derives from Jesus in dependence on Is. 56.3–5. On the authenticity of this saying, cf. Jeremias, *NT Theology*, 224.

150 In the Lucan parallel to Mk 10.28–30 (Lk. 18.29) note the addition of ἡ γυναῖκα perhaps reflecting Luke's interest in and concern for women. The addition of 'wife' may intensify the saying, since it would perhaps be conceivable to a Jew that a man might make an unconditional and possibly permanent commitment to leave his home, parents, cousins and even children, but not the one person to whom he had a biblical obligation 'to cleave'.

151 Cf. M. Yeb. 8.4ff, Danby, 230.

152 Davies, *Sermon on the Mount*, 393, cf. 394–5, 400.

153 συμφέρω can mean 'to be profitable', 'to be better (of gain)'. Cf. BAG, 787–8; LSJ, 1686–7; K. Weiss, 'συμφέρω', *TDNT*, vol. IX, 75, n. 13.

154 Cf. Cohen, 'Concerning Divorce', 3ff; Davies, *Sermon on the Mount*, 393–5, and pp. 344–5, 400.

155 It is probable that the solemn 'this word' refers to something Jesus Himself has said. Mt. 19.22–6 should be compared to Mt. 19.10–12, as J.-M. van Cangh, 'Fondement évangelique de la vie religieuse', *NRT* 95 (6, 1973), 639–40, points out. In both pericopes Jesus does not answer the disciples' question directly but gives a further explanation of what He has said previously. In 19.22, τὸν λόγον τοῦτον or τὸν λόγον (Metzger, *TC*, 49–50) refers to Jesus' teaching. Robertson, 1190, remarks that the γάρ in 19.12 is not causal but indicates that an explanation of 'not everyone, but those to whom it is given' is to follow. Thus, the eunuch saying explains why Jesus' marriage teaching is only given to some. The possibility cannot be ruled out that verse 11 is the Evangelist's own addition (based on the end of verse 12). If so, then it represents a qualification of Jesus' marriage teaching for His own community. To claim that the eunuchs in verses 10–12 are those having put away their wives for πορνεία is to ignore the likelihood that the juxtaposition of 19.1–9, 10–12 is the Evangelist's. Cf. Q. Quesnell, ' "Made Themselves Eunuchs for the Kingdom of Heaven" (Mt 19,12)', *CBQ* 30 (1968), 335–58.

156 In both cases we are talking about someone actually castrated. A. D. Nock, 'Eunuchs in Ancient Religion', *ARW* 23 (1925), 25–33, notes that eunuchs had no place in purely Greek or Roman cults, but are found in various fertility cults of Asia Minor and Syria. As Ac. 8.27 indicates, eunuchs of royal courts could be placed in charge of more than just concubines.

157 The evidence of the Qumran scrolls, Josephus and Philo is difficult to decipher, but it appears that at least some Qumranites were celibate as part of their service to Yahweh. It is doubtful that this entailed actual castration. Cf. J. Galot, 'La motivation evangélique du célibat', *Greg* 53 (4, 1972), 731–57; T. Matura, 'Le célibat dans le Nouveau Testament', *NRT* 97 (6, 1975), 481–500.

158 Cf. Josephus, *Antiquities* 4.290–1 (LCL IV), 614–15. Paradoxically, Josephus, Herod and others made use of eunuchs for teachers, chamberlains, etc. Cf. Josephus, *The Life* 429 (LCL I), 156–7; *Jewish War* 1.488 (LCL II; 1927), 230–1; J. Schneider, 'εὐνοῦχος', *TDNT*, vol. II, 765–8; pp. 3–4 of this study.

159 Cf. J. Blinzler, 'εἰσὶν εὐνοῦχοι – Zur Auslegung von Mt. 19.12', *ZNW* 48 (1957), 254–70, espec. 258.

160 While Jesus was probably not speaking in Greek, it is likely that He was using the Semitic equivalent of εὐνοῦχος – סריס (cf. Is. 56.3, LXX, and MT). Cf. BDF, 710.

161 Even Origen later changed his mind. Cf. J. Schneider, 'εὐνοῦχος', *TDNT*, vol. II, 765–8; Blinzler, 'εἰσιν εὐνοῦχοι', 258ff. MHT, vol. I, 139, says that if εὐνούχισαν referred to a single event, then Origen's original interpretation would be correct. The single event could be the decision to renounce marriage or family for Jesus' sake. Cf. M'Neile, *Matthew*, 276. For the view that Jesus was giving a *Mashal* intending the third class of eunuchs to be understood physically, while Matthew later added 'for the Kingdom's sake' to give a transferred sense to eunuchs of the third type, cf. H. Zimmerman, 'μὴ ἐπὶ πορνεία (Mt 19,9) – ein literarisches Problem – Zur Komposition von Mt 19,3–12', *Catholica* 16 (4, 1962), 295–6.

162 Cf. Clement's *paed.* 3.4 quoted in Manson, *Sayings*, 215–16. Notice, however, that Clement finds it necessary to qualify the word εὐνοῦχος with ἀληθής.

163 These last two suggestions were made by J. A. Kleist, 'Eunuchs in the New Testament', *CBQ* 7 (1945), 447–9.

164 Cf. similarly the NEB. Blinzler's suggested translation ('εἰσὶν εὐνοῦχοι', 259) is based in part on the fact that the Jewish classification of eunuchs was made to denote those unfit for marriage. Possibly, Jesus would have said that even real physical eunuchs can be given the gift of making their state a blessing, rather than a curse, by accepting the call to be a eunuch for the Kingdom. Cf. Isaksson, *Marriage and Ministry*, 148–52; J. Moingt, 'Le Divorce (Pour Motif d'Impudicité) (Matthieu 5,32; 19,9)', *RSR* 56 (1968), 337–84.

165 J. Blenkinsopp, *Sexuality and the Christian Tradition* (London, 1970), 91.

166 Blenkinsopp, 91–2; Galot, 'La motivation', 142–3; J.B. Lightfoot, *St. Paul's Epistles to the Colossians and to Philemon* (London, 1879), 411–12. It is true that some Qumranites married, but there also existed in the Qumran community a sexual taboo and association of holiness with ritual purity. Jesus clearly rejected this connection in His teaching about clean and unclean, and in His repeated association and physical contact with harlots, lepers, etc.

167 Cf. Jeremias, *NT Theology*, 32–3, 224.

168 Blinzler, 'εἰσιν εὐνοῦχοι', 260ff, is wrong to identify so closely the decision spoken of in Mt. 19.10–12 and that mentioned in Mk 10.28–30.

169 E. Schweizer, *Das Evangelium nach Matthäus. Das Neue Testament Deutsch* (n.s. ed. G. Friedrich; Göttingen, 1976), 250.

170 It is possible that Jesus gave this teaching originally to the Pharisees and/or the disciples as a justification of His own singleness for the Kingdom. Cf. Matura, 'Le célibat', 496. That Jesus' marital status is a non-issue in the Gospels probably indicates that He was never married, and that in His community marriage was not an obligation. *Pace* W.E. Phipps, *Was Jesus Married?* (London, 1970). Phipps' book makes the mistaken assumption that Jesus would not have differed from other rabbis about the obligation to procreate; however, Mt. 19.12 is evidence that He did differ from the common view.

171 The belief in an obligation to procreate and thus the duty to marry was one shared by Jews (cf. pp. 3–4 and nn. 31–2, p. 133 of this study), Greeks and Romans. D. Daube, *The Duty of Procreation* (Edinburgh, 1977), 9ff, has

shown that in a Greek context it was common to emphasize the duty to marry and propagate. Cf. Plutarch, 'Lysander' 30.5, *The Parallel Lives* (LCL IV; trans. B. Perrin; 1916), 320–1; Dinarchus, 'Against Demosthenes' 99.71, *The Minor Attic Orators* (LCL II; trans. J.O. Burtt; 1954), 224–5; Plutarch, 'Lycurgus' 15.1ff, *The Parallel Lives* (LCL I; trans. B. Perrin; 1914), 246ff.

172   Cf. Swete, *Mark*, 264; Creed, *Luke*, 249; Plummer, *Matthew*, 306; and W. Manson, *The Gospel of Luke* (MNTC; London, 1930), 225.

173   G.E. Ladd, *A Theology of the New Testament* (Grand Rapids, 1974), 69. Oepke, 'γυνή', *TDNT*, vol. I, 785: 'holding out a prospect of sexless being like that of the angels'.

174   Cf. Bultmann, *History*, 26; Schweizer, *Das Evangelium nach Markus. Das Neue Testament Deutsch* (ed. P. Althaus and J. Behm; Göttingen, 1949), 140.

175   Pesch, *Markusevangelium*, vol. II, 2, 235, cf. 229.

176   *Ibid.*, Jeremias, *NT Theology*, 184, n. 3.

177   By the time the Mishnah was written some were asking that it cease, and before this it was probably in disuse. Cf. M. Eduyoth 4.8, Danby, 429–30; M. Berkoth 1.7, Danby, 429–30; M. Berakoth 1.7, Danby, 531; M. Sanhedrin 2.2, Danby, 384.

178   Cf. Daube, *NT and Rabbinic Judaism*, 158–69.

179   Cf. the *boruth* on resurrection in B.T. Sanhedrin 90*b*, Str-B, vol. I, 888–90. The popular belief seems to have envisioned a resurrection of only the righteous to a state without sin or death in which one will neither eat, nor drink, nor propagate, nor travel. Cf. B.T. Berakoth 17*a, The Babylonian Talmud* Berkot (trans. A. Cohen; Cambridge, 1921), 112; Str-B, vol. I, 888–91. There were, however, rabbis (notably R. Gamaliel) who believed women would bear children daily in the new age to come; cf. B.T. Shabbath 30b, Mo'ed I, Shabbath I, 137–8; Enoch 10.17; *APOT*, vol. II, 194.

180   Ellis, *Luke*, 234; Creed, *Luke*, 249.

181   Cranfield, *Mark*, 373; Taylor, *Mark*, 480.

182   Marshall, *Luke*, 738; Ellis, *Luke*, 234.

183   παρ' ἡμῖν, found only in Mt. 22.25, may indicate that the First Evangelist thought otherwise. M'Neile, *Matthew*, 321.

184   Rengstorf, 'ἑπτά', *TDNT*, vol. II, 630. The possible background to this story in Tobit 3.8, 6.9–12, 7.12–13, suggests this as well. Cf. *APOT*, vol. I, 209, 218, 222.

185   σπέρμα is used in the general sense of a child, but usually the Levir was required to raise up a male. Swete, *Mark*, 262; S. Schulz, 'σπέρμα', *TDNT*, vol. VII, 545. Perhaps there is an intended contrast between the Sadducees who believe in raising up a seed and Jesus who believes in raising up a body – two different means of immortality. Cf. Hill, *Matthew*, 304.

186   Stählin, 'χήρα', *TDNT*, vol. IX, 442, 447, n. 60, 457. Marshall, *Luke*, 739, is only partially correct in saying that Levirate marriage was intended as a means of keeping property in the family.

187   Ellis, *Luke*, 234–7.

188   J. Denney, 'The Sadducees and Immortality', *Exp*, 4th ser. 10 (1894), 402. ἔσχον in Mk 12.23 and parallels may mean not just 'had' as a marriage partner, but 'had' intercourse with. Cf. MHT, vol. I, 134; Zerwick, sec. 289, 98; H. Hanse, 'ἔχω', *TDNT*, vol. II, 817, n. 5. This fits the Levirate marriage contract and the textual variant in Lk. 20.34 (beget and begotten).

189   Cf. Grundmann, 'δύναμαι', *TDNT*, vol. II, 304–6; E.H. Blakeney, 'A Note on St. Matthew xxii.29', *ET* 4 (1892–3), 382.

190   The 'sons of this age' is a Semitic phrase with a similar connotation to the modern idiomatic expression 'a product of his time'. Cf. E. Schweizer, 'υἱός', *TDNT*, vol. VIII, 365; Danker, *Jesus*, 205.

191   E. Stauffer, 'γαμέω', *TDNT*, vol. I, 651, n. 15, states: 'Jesus keeps closely to the traditional modes of Jewish thought and expression when here and in Mk 12.25 He uses the act. (γαμεῖν) for the man and the mid. (γαμίζεσθαι) for the woman.' Further (650), 'The husband is the active partner in the conclusion and direction of marriage. This is self-evident for Jesus.' This is a somewhat surprising statement since it is doubtful that Jesus spoke Greek on this occasion. It is probable that the Gospel writers believed that on this point they were reflecting faithfully Jesus' views on marital customs in their own language.

192   Jeremias, *NT Theology*, 225.

193   Ellis, *Luke*, 204–5, 236–7, notes the possible conflict with Mk 10.6–8 and conjectures that Mk 10 must mean that marriage is intended to be indissoluble in this life. So Jeremias, *NT Theology*, 225. There need be no conflict if Jesus is not speaking of the dissolution of marriages or the dissolution of all kinds of marriages here. Cf. pp. 32–5.

194   The γάρ indicates that here we have the reason why marrying ceases in the age to come. Plummer, *Luke*, 469; J. Reiling and J.L. Swellengrebel, *A Translator's Handbook on the Gospel of Luke* (Leiden, 1971), 654.

195   Jesus and some rabbis rejected the idea that the age to come is just this age on a grander and more carnal scale; cf. Str-B, vol. I, 888–91.

196   Luke coins a word – ἰσάγγελος. Ladd, *Theology of the NT*, 195, rightly remarks, 'It is important to note that Jesus does not say that men will become angels – only that they will be like angels.'

197   Plummer, *Luke*, 469, remarks, 'They do not marry, because they cannot die; and they cannot die, because they are like angels; and they are sons of God, being sons of the resurrection.'

198   Denney, 'Sadducees and Immortality', 403. Marshall, *Luke*, 741, says, 'It is more likely, however, that the marriage relationship is transcended in a new level of personal relationships, and the basic point being made is that marriage as a means of procreation is no longer necessary.'

199   Cf. E.E. Ellis, 'Jesus, the Sadducees, and Qumran', *NTS* 10 (1963–4), 274. The Sadducees have tailored their argument and its textual basis to fit their own purposes which is in itself grounds to reject their question. Cf. Deut. 25.5–10; Taylor, *Mark*, 481; Swete, *Mark*, 262.

200   I.H. Marshall, *Eschatology and the Parables* (London, 1963), 5.

201   A.M. Hunter, *The Parables Then and Now* (London, 1971), 56.

202   H. Flender, *St. Luke – Theologian of Redemptive History* (London, 1967), 9–10, notes that this parallelism is most often seen in special Lucan material. Note his list: Lk. 1.11–20, 1.26–38, 1.46–55, 1.67–79, 2.25–38, 4.25–8, 4.31–9 (cf. Mk 1.21–31), 7.1–17, 7.36–50, 13.18–21, 10.29–42, 15.4–10, 18.1–14, 23.55–24.35, 17.34–5 (cf. Mt. 24.40–1); and Ac. 5.1–11, 9.32–42, 17.34. Flender (10) concludes, 'Luke expresses by this arrangement that man and woman stand together and side by side before God. They are equal in honour and grace, they are endowed with the same gifts and have the same responsibilities.' J. Drury, *Tradition and Design in Luke's Gospel – A Study*

in Early Christian Historiography (London, 1976), 71, argues that Jairus and his daughter, and the widow of Nain and her son make a 'neat pair'.

203   Parvey, 'Theology and Leadership', 139.

204   Among others, D. Buzy, 'Le juge inique (Saint Luc, xviii, 1–8)', *RB* 39 (1930), 378–91.

205   B.B. Warfield, 'The Importunate Widow and the Alleged Failure of Faith', *ET* 25 (1913–14), 69–72, 136–9; Buzy, 'Le juge inique', 378ff; Hunter, *Parables*, 80ff.

206   C. Spicq, 'La parabole de la veuve obstinée et du juge inerte, aux décisions impromptues (Lc. xviii, 1–8)', *RB* 68 (1, 1961), 69–70; G. Delling, 'Das Gleichnis vom gottlosen Richter', *ZNW* 53 (1962), 11ff; Creed, *Luke*, 222.

207   D.R. Catchpole, 'The Son of Man's Search for Faith (Luke xviii.8b)', *NovT* 19 (2, 1977), 81–104; Marshall, *Eschatology*, 45ff; W.G. Kümmel, *Promise and Fulfilment – The Eschatological Message of Jesus* (London, 1957), 59.

208   J. Jeremias, *The Parables of Jesus* (2nd rev. ed.; trans. S.H. Hooke; New York, 1972), 155–7; R. Deschryver, 'La parabole du juge malveillant (Luc 18,1–8)', *RHPR* 48 (4, 1968), 355–66. Deschryver points out that the parataxis, the sudden change of subject in verse 4, the expression 'in himself' in verse 4, the 'judge of unrighteousness' in verse 6, and the general Aramaic tone all argue strongly that this parable is archaic and a literary unit (although he excepts verses 1 and 8b). Verse 8b perhaps is a later addition; cf. Bultmann, *History*, 189, 193, 199; Ellis, *Luke*, 213.

209   The 'crying' of the elect in verse 7 may intimate a context of persecution or oppression. In any case, Luke intends us to see this parable in an eschatological light. Cf. Cranfield, 'The Parable of the Unjust Judge and the Eschatology of Luke–Acts', *SJT* 16 (1963), 297–301; Stählin, 'Das Bild der Witwe', 56.

210   Delling, 'Das Gleichnis', 23; Spicq, 'La parabole', 86ff.

211   Possibly, the original audience was Jesus' opponents or some pious Jews; cf. Delling, 'Das Gleichnis', 22. It is more probable, however, that it was His disciples. Cf. Jeremias, *Parables*, 156, and n. 19; Cranfield, 'Parable of the Unjust Judge', 298; Manson, *Luke*, 200; Plummer, *Luke*, 411. Luke's αὐτοῖς in 18.1 shows clearly whom he sees as the audience.

212   *APOT*, vol. I, 438–9.

213   The ἀντίδικος is a technical term for an opponent in a lawsuit. Cf. BAG, 73; LSJ, 155; A–S, 41. It can refer either to the defendant or to the plaintiff. Cf. Str-B, vol. II, 238; Derrett, 'Law in the New Testament: The Parable of the Unjust Judge', *Studies in the NT*, vol. I, 32–47.

214   Derrett, 'The Unjust Judge', 32–5, 37, n. 1, is right in saying that it was common for Jews to go to civil courts because, unlike religious courts, they could act without trial, witnesses, or evidence, and thus they were used commonly to gain illegal advantage of another person. This is not the widow's motive here. Clearly, someone has got to the judge before her, for she would not have turned to a κριτὴς τῆς ἀδικίας if she had initiated the proceedings. It is probably not true that the judge was legally required to give precedence to a widow's case. *Pace* Stählin, 'χήρα', *TDNT*, vol. IX, 450, n. 86; Marshall, *Luke*, 672. The example in B.T. Yeb. 100a, Nashim I, Yebamoth I, 684–5, is from the fourth century A.D. But cf. G.B. Caird, *The Gospel of St. Luke* (PNTC; Harmondsworth, 1963) 203.

215   ὁ κριτὴς τῆς ἀδικίας – a Hebraic genitive of quality. Cf. MHT, vol. III, 213;
       Jeremias, *Parables*, 45. For rabbinic parallels, cf. Str-B, vol. II, 239.

216   The phrase, 'neither fearing God, nor caring (about the opinion) of man'
       (*pace* Derrett, 'The Unjust Judge', 45, n. 1) does *not* mean this judge was
       'no respecter of persons' in the sense that no one could influence his judgment.
       Rather, as in the extra-biblical examples, the phrase implies that he does not
       care what anyone thinks, and thus he does whatever best suits his own interests.
       Cf. Josephus, *Antiquities* 10.83 (LCL VI; trans. R. Marcus; 1937), 202–3;
       Danker, *Jesus*, 184.

217   The iterative imperfect probably indicates her persistence. Cf. Plummer,
       Luke, 412; Jeremias, *Parables*, 153, n. 4.

218   Derrett, 'The Unjust Judge', 41, says that ἐκδίκησόν με means 'be my advocate';
       others prefer 'vindicate me'. Cf. Jeremias, *Parables*, 153; Spicq, 'La parabole',
       70; Warfield, 'The Importunate Widow', 71, suggests 'deliver or protect me'.

219   ἐπὶ χρόνον implies here 'for a long time'. Cf. Delling, 'Das Gleichnis', 11.

220   Does εἰς τέλος go with ἐρχομένη or ὑπωπιάζῃ? If the former, then it is to be
       translated 'continually (or perhaps finally) coming'. So Plummer, *Luke*, 413;
       Zerwick, sec. 249, p. 81. Spicq, 'La parabole', 75, however, says εἰς τέλος
       usually is used in classical and Hellenistic literature to mean the completion
       of a process – she will finally ὑπωπιάζῃ. So Delling, 'τέλος', *TDNT*, vol.
       VIII, 56; similarly, Jeremias, *Parables*, 154.

221   Spicq, 'La parabole', 76, citing examples from the papyri where a frustrated
       woman finally hits someone. Cf. BAG, 856; Delling, 'Das Gleichnis', 12ff.;
       Zerwick, sec. 249, p. 81.

222   Jeremias, *Parables*, 154; Creed, *Luke*, 223; Buzy, 'Le juge inique', 380; A–S,
       463; LSJ, 1904; MM, 661; Plummer, *Luke*, 413; cf. 1 Cor. 9.27.

223   Derrett, 'The Unjust Judge', 43–6; Marshall, *Luke*, 673. Plummer, *Luke*,
       413, objects that for the meaning 'black my face', ἐλθοῦσα ὑπωπιάσῃ would
       be required.

224   If we take εἰς τέλος as 'finally', as seems probable, and take seriously Jesus'
       enjoinder to listen to the judge's last remark, then Jesus is intimating not only
       vindication for God's elect, but also a delay in God's actions.

225   This is in contrast to the normal Jewish practice of praying at certain times of
       day. Cf. Str-B, vol. II, 237.

226   Thus, the argument is by contraries, or as C. Colpe, 'ὁ υἱὸς', *TDNT*, vol.
       VIII, 435, n. 265, says, *a peiore ad melius*.

227   There is possibly a hint of allegory here in that the widow may represent
       God's people in an oppressive and evil world. Cf. Stählin, 'χήρα', *TDNT*, vol.
       IX, 458–9; Delling, 'Das Gleichnis', 24. It is perhaps worth noting that God's
       people are characterized as one or another sort of woman depending on
       whether Jesus is present (bride, bride-to-be, or even bridesmaid, cf. Mt. 25.1–
       13), or absent (widow). If it is true that the role of the community of faith is
       characteristically feminine, then perhaps women's roles and natures are
       better human models for Jesus' disciples than men's. Perhaps, Jesus intimates
       as much by His association with, teaching about, and His examples involving,
       women.

228   Manson, *Sayings*, 282. The title is particularly fitting for the material just
       discussed in Lk. 18 since there we have a desperate widow (1–8) and a despised
       tax collector (9–14). Manson is right that one of the reasons this material has

been chosen and so arranged is to demonstrate God's care for those whom man condemns or despises. Lk. 15.1–2 shows that this is certainly part of the purpose in presenting the three parables that we have in 15.3–32 as well.

229 This parable is intended to show God's love for and seeking of the lost, and His joy over their salvation. Thus, we should not see it as an analogy between a woman searching for a lost coin, and a person seeking the Kingdom (unlike Mt. 13.44–5).

230 Plummer, *Luke*, 371.

231 Jeremias, *Parables*, 133.

232 The analogy is between the seeking activity of God and these two human beings, and between the rejoicing activity of God and these human beings when they recover the sought after object. Thus, it is not correct to say that God is described as a man or woman in 15.3–10 (*pace* Swidler, 'Jesus was a Feminist', 177–83).

233 Cf. Bultmann, *History*, 194, though it is not clear in the end that Bultmann accepts this view.

234 H. Conzelmann, *The Theology of St. Luke* (trans. G. Buswell; New York, 1961), 111; Drury, *Tradition and Design*, 158–9.

235 Bultmann, *History*, 194.

236 Marshall, *Luke*, 603; cf. Jeremias, *Parables*, 132–6.

237 Cf. Jeremias, 'Tradition und Redaktion in Lukas 15', *ZNW* 62 (3–4, 1971), 172–89, espec. 181–4. Cf. for instance the addition of οὗ after ἕως in verse 8 (cf. verses 4, 7, 8, 10).

238 Cf. Marshall, *Luke*, 603; Jeremias, *Parables*, 9; and contrast C.H. Dodd, *The Parables of the Kingdom* (New York, 1961), 92. If Jeremias, *Parables*, 135, n. 12, is right about an Aramaic imperfect underlying γίνεται and that the reference is to God's future rejoicing at the eschaton, then perhaps we have here evidence that this application is not secondary, in view of Luke's eschatological viewpoint.

239 Jeremias, *Parables*, 133–5; similarly, Hunter, *Parables*, 57. This has been challenged since the text reads simply ἔχουσα δέκα ... ἀπολέσῃ δραχμὴν μίαν. Cf. Danker, *Jesus*, 169; Plummer, *Luke*, 370.

240 BDF, sec. 5, p. 4; Ellis, *Luke*, 197; Manson, *Sayings*, 284, suggests that this is the woman's savings, not her housekeeping money.

241 A, D, W, λ, φ, pm have συγκαλεῖται instead of συγκαλεῖ. Jeremias, 'Tradition und Redaktion', 182–3, suggests συγκαλεῖ is pre-Lucan and reflects the incorrect use of the active in Luke's special source. Cf. BDF, sec. 316.1, 165. K.L. Schmidt, 'συγκαλέω', *TDNT*, vol. III, 496, n. 2, suggests συγκαλεῖται is to be preferred.

242 Hunter, *Parables*, 12; cf. Dodd, *Parables*, 93.

243 Dodd, *Parables*, 92.

244 That she has money at all may support the idea that she is a widow. Cf. pp. 3–4 of this study.

245 It is perhaps significant that this woman has lost this drachma. She could have been used as an example of carelessness. That Jesus chooses to use such an example in a positive manner indicates His desire to present even a fallible man (who loses his sheep) and a fallible woman (who loses her money) as equally good examples of God's activity.

246 Cf. Marshall, *Luke*, 560; Streeter, *Four Gospels*, 246–8, appears to believe

that Luke used solely Q material but the double introduction form appears only here in Lucan parables.

247 Kümmel, *Promise*, 132, n. 98; cf. Bultmann, *History*, 195; Dodd, *Parables*, 154; J. Dupont, 'Les paraboles du sénevé et du levain', *NRT* 89 (1967), 911.

248 Jeremias, *Parables*, 92. Were this a uniquely Lucan pairing one might suspect that the connection was originally his.

249 This is a secondary interest, since the main point concerns the nature of the Kingdom. It is probably wrong to overemphasize the fact that many or most parables have one or two main points. While this is true, there are probably no details given which are wholly meaningless and therefore entirely superfluous, though not all the elements in the picture are of equal value and over-allegorizing is to be avoided. Cf. O.T. Allis, 'The Parable of the Leaven', *EvQ* 19 (1947), 255; R.W. Funk, 'Beyond Criticism in Quest of Literacy: The Parable of the Leaven', *Int* 25 (1971), 149–70, rightly warns (151): 'Methodology is not an indifferent net; it catches what it is designed to catch.'

250 M. Ket. 5.5, Danby, 252. Interestingly, sy^c labels this woman φρονίμη at Mt. 13.33.

251 I am not saying that this is the main point of the analogy, but it is perhaps a reason why Jesus chose to draw an analogy between this woman's work and the working of the Kingdom and/or His own work. Cf. Hunter, *Parables*, 44–5; Jeremias, *Parables*, 149.

252 A–S, 20; BAG, 35; MM, 21.

253 Funk, 'Beyond Criticism', 159; Str-B, vol. I, 669–70. Marshall, *Luke*, 561, remarks, 'The quantity is surprisingly large but the figure is traditional (Gn. 18.6; cf. Judg. 6:19; 1 Sa. 1:24).'

254 Jeremias, *Parables*, 147, n. 71; Marshall, *Luke*, 560; cf. M. Peah 8.7, Danby, 20. As Jeremias suggests, the proportions could indicate that a supernatural action is involved.

255 Jesus seems to have used the technique of comic exaggertion elsewhere (workmen hired at the eleventh hour, amount of forgiving, etc.). Cf. Funk, 'Beyond Criticism', 160.

256 Jeremias, *Parables*, 147.

257 Funk, 'Beyond Criticism', 160.

258 Jesus could have made a connection between Gen. 18.6 and our passage; cf. Funk, 'Beyond Criticism', 160; Jeremias, *Parables*, 31–2; M'Neile, *Matthew*, 199.

259 It is true that in the Feast of Unleavened Bread, as apparently in the case of the Feast of Weeks, people baked their own bread; cf. Lev. 23. 5–8, 17.

260 There is no mention of the amount of leaven in Matthew or Luke, which militates against the idea that the point is simply the contrast between small beginnings and great results in the parable of the leaven. This may be implied by the verb ἐνέκρυψεν, or one may argue it was proverbial (1 Cor. 5.6) but, if so, it remains an implication and probably not the main point. Cf. Dodd, *Parables*, 155; H. Windisch, 'ζύμη', *TDNT*, vol. II, 905–6, n. 27.

261 It is true that this phrase places a strong emphasis on results; however, note that it is a subordinate clause and it does not say, until the whole lump *rises*, but until the whole lump is *leavened*. If the emphasis is on the main verb and the woman's actions, then this parable is more of a growth or dynamic permeation parable than a contrast parable. Cf. H. Thielicke, *The Waiting Father*

(New York, 1959), 61; Marshall, *Eschatology*, 28; and contrast Jeremias, *Parables*, 147. It appears that we have a complete process of taking and hiding until leavened. The word ὅλον, being a predicate adjective (cf. Robertson, 656), makes an additional point about the successful conclusion of the process.

262 J. Massyngberde Ford, 'The Parable of the Foolish Scholars, Matt. xxv.1–13', *NovT* 9 (1967), 107.

263 There are the negative remarks in Mk 3.21, 33–5 about Jesus' mother and family, and we note Lk. 11.27–8 among other possible texts.

264 Now that we have found complementary male–female parallelism in both Matthew and Luke (and in uniquely Matthean and Lucan material), the probability that this male–female pairing (or at least the precedent for it) derives from Jesus Himself is greatly enhanced.

265 W.D. Ridley, 'The Parable of the Ten Virgins', *Exp*, 5th ser. 2 (1895), 342.

266 Ridley, 343.

267 Oepke, 'γυνή', *TDNT*, vol. I, 784. Either Matthew 23–5 or 24–5 is a unit; if the latter, then 24.3 indicates whom Jesus is instructing. The τότε, possibly verse 5, and certainly verses 12–13, indicate that the Evangelist envisions this parable as relating something about the Parousia.

268 Jeremias, *Parables*, 82, n. 52; M'Neile, *Matthew*, 360; Zerwick, sec. 65, 22.

269 Jeremias, 'LAMPADES – Mt. 25.1, 3f, 7f', *ZNW* 56 (1965), 198–9; Dodd, *Parables*, 19; Schweizer, *Matthäus*, 304.

270 E. Klostermann, 'Das Matthäusevangelium' (*HzNT*, vol. IV; 2nd ed., H. Lietzmann; Tübingen, 1927), 199; Bultmann, *History*, 119.

271 Bultmann, *History*, 176.

272 Cf. Jeremias, *Parables*, 171–5; A.W. Argyle, 'Wedding Customs at the Time of Jesus', *ET* 86 (1974–5), 214–15. Even the bridegroom's delay in verse 5 is explicable because it was customary for the bridegroom and the bride's parents to haggle at length over the *mohar* to show the bride's worth.

273 R.E. Brown, *New Testament Essays* (Garden City, 1968), 323. As Massyngberde Ford, 'The Parable of the Foolish Scholars', 120–3, has shown, in rabbinic exegesis and illustration, the literal and allegorical went hand-in-hand and often the literal sense of a word or phrase was used to reinforce allegory.

274 Kümmel, *Promise*, 55.

275 Metzger, *TC*, 62–3; Jeremias, 'νύμφη', *TDNT*, vol. IV, 1100–1; E. Hoskyns and N. Davey, *The Riddle of the New Testament* (London, 1958), 46–8. On the other hand, Professor Barrett has pointed out to me that it may be questioned whether or not the later Christian scribes would have spoken of the *coming* of the Church (bride).

276 *Pace* Jeremias, *Parables*, 52, n. 13; with Kümmel, *Promise*, 57, n. 123.

277 Cf. Dodd, *Parables*, 136–7; Jeremias, *Parables*, 52–3. Similarly, Schweizer, *Matthäus*, 304, takes this parable without verses 5, 6 as authentic, speaking originally, 'vom Himmelreich, nicht vom kommen des Menschensohns'.

278 Marshall, *Eschatology*, 40ff; Kümmel, *Promise*, 54–9.

279 Marshall, *Eschatology*, 41.

280 Jeremias, 'LAMPADES', 200–1.

281 Cf. H.P. Hamann, 'The Ten Virgins: An Exegetical-Homiletical Study', *LTJ* 11 (2, 1977), 68–72; Jeremias, 'LAMPADES', 200–2.

282 Jeremias, 'LAMPADES', 196ff; Str-B, vol. I, 510, 969; M. Sukkah 5.4, Danby, 180; Stauffer, 'γαμέω', *TDNT*, vol. I, 654, n. 42.

283 Thielicke, *Waiting Father*, 172; R. Winterbotham, 'The Second Advent', *Exp*, 1st ser. 9 (1879), 67–80.

284 Thielicke, *Waiting Father*, 177.

285 Hunter, *Parables*, 102, notes that in modern Palestinian weddings, once the bridegroom arrived and the door was shut, latecomers were not admitted. Perhaps this was the rule in Jesus' day as well. Theologically, closing the door means that all opportunities for participation in the Kingdom's consummation are over.

286 Cf. B.T. Berakoth 51*a*–*b*, Cohen, 329; Jeremias, 'LAMPADES', 100–1; F.A. Strobel, 'Zum Verständnis von Mat. xxv.1–13', *NovT* 2 (1957–8), 199–227.

287 Lk. 17.32 is perhaps to be taken as an illustration created and added by Luke, with his interest in women, bringing out the force of the preceding illustration. If so, then it shows that Luke was not reluctant to use a woman as a negative example even though he is concerned to portray various women disciples of Jesus in a positive light; cf. Marshall, *Luke*, 665.

288 The order of these two illustrations differs in Matthew and Luke. The former has: (1) sign of Jonah (12.40) (2) men of Nineveh (12.41) (3) Queen of the South (12.42); and the latter has: (1) sign of Jonah (11.30) (2) Queen of the South (11.31) and (3) men of Nineveh (11.32, omitted by D). Plummer, *Matthew*, 184, remarks, 'With improved chronology, and also with better rhetorical effect, Luke places the case of the Ninevites after that of the Queen of the South.' But cf. Marshall, *Luke*, 486.

289 Cf. Schweizer, *Matthäus*, 188–90.

290 Cf. Bultmann, *History*, 112–13. Bultmann, however, is probably wrong in commenting that these sayings did not originally have an indirect reference to Jesus. Cf. Kümmel, *Promise*, 44, 84.

291 Cf. Str-B, vol. I, 651, where the rabbis attempt to demote this Queen to a royal envoy.

292 Cf. 1 Kgs 10.8 and Lk. 11.27–8 for an interesting contrast between blessed wives and blessed believers.

293 Jeremias, *Jesu Verheissung für die Völker* (Stuttgart, 1956), 43, n. 170, argues that the word ἐγερθήσεται in both Matthew and Luke, with μετά τινος, does not refer to resurrection but is a Semitism for 'join together with someone to plead before a court'. This may be so, though the context lends itself to speaking of resurrection since Jesus is speaking of a long dead person and future judgment, and since the example of Jonah and the Son of Man in Mt. 12.40 implies resurrection. If Jeremias is correct, then this does not argue against taking ἐν τῇ κρίσει to refer to that Day of Judgment yet to come. That p[45] and D omit this phrase in Luke is not decisive.

294 After μετά Luke has τῶν ἀνδρῶν, unlike Matthew, which may be intended to draw a contrast with this Queen. This may reflect Luke's tendency to stress male–female reversal, or to feature prominent women at the expense of certain men. Cf. Marshall, *Luke*, 486, and n. 296 below. The word κατακρίνω here means 'to give judgment against', i.e., to accuse and thus condemn. God alone is the Judge, but the Queen is the key witness for this age. Cf. Jeremias, *Jesu Verheissung*, 43, n. 171; A–S, 235; BAG, 413; Büchsel, 'κατακρίνω', *TDNT*, vol. III, 951, n. 1.

295   One woman's word against that of many men would have carried little if any weight. Cf. pp. 9–10 of this study.

296   On the original audience, cf. Bultmann, *History*, 112–13. The most notable parallel is to Simon the Pharisee and the sinner woman (Lk. 7.36–50). Sometimes it is the disciples, sometimes Jesus' opponents, that are the dark background to the light of a woman's faith, understanding, or witness. Cf. Jn 4.27, Lk. 13.10–17, Mt. 15.21–8.

297   Bultmann, *History*, 117, cf. 126.

298   Probably not three in Luke. Verse 36 could be a later addition attempting to harmonize with Matthew. It is supported only in D (pm, lat.sy.). Cf. Metzger, *TC*, 168. The arguments of Manson, *Sayings*, 145–6, do not outweigh the strong external evidence against including verse 36. This evidence militates against (but does not rule out) the view that Luke (verses 34–6) is trying to depict the whole household – husband, wife, female and male servants. Cf. Marshall, *Luke*, 668.

299   BAG, 531, may be correct in suggesting that we should translate 'with the handmill' not 'at the mill', since this was the common practice of the day. Cf. M. Shebiith 5.9, Danby, 45. A. Strobel, 'In dieser Nacht (Luke 17,34) – zu einer älteren Form der Erwartung in Luke 17,20–37', *ZTK* 58 (1961), 20–1, argues for a metaphorical sense. Strobel mentions, however, the expectation of late Judaism was that the time of tribulation and judgment would begin at night (cf. 1 Thess. 5.2, Mt. 25.1–13).

300   Marshall, *Luke*, 667.

301   Kümmel, *Promise*, 43.

302   Cf. 1 Thess. 5.2, Mt. 25.1–13; Strobel, 'In dieser Nacht', 20–1.

303   Strobel, 'In dieser Nacht', 21; Str-B, vol. I, 966–7. To some rabbis, grinding was a despicable job to be left to slaves if possible. Cf. M'Neile, *Matthew*, 357, and Exod. 11.5. There is no indication that servants are in view in our text, and in any case it was the wife who did this work in most homes. Cf. M. Ket. 5.5, Danby, 252. This argues against Manson's whole family view of Lk. 17.34–36. Cf. n. 298 above.

304   It is possible that husband and wife are meant by ὁ εἷς ... ὁ ἕτερος, since it is inevitable that both pronouns be masculine. Cf. Marshall, *Luke*, 667–8; Manson, *Sayings*, 146. It is conceivable that a father and son might sleep in the same bed (cf. Lk. 11.7).

305   Flender, *St. Luke*, 10.

306   This is true of many of His statements about the roles men and women assume. His concern is more with which Master one serves, not how.

307   It may be significant that Jesus did not argue *against* or refrain from using examples that relied on the traditional division of labour.

308   Manson, *Luke*, 200.

309   Bultmann, *History*, 114ff; similarly, Ellis, *Luke*, 191.

310   Cf. the material discussed in Marshall, *Luke*, 574.

311   Kümmel, *Promise*, 79–81; Marshall, *Luke*, 573–4; Manson, *Sayings*, 102–3.

312   E. Haenchen, 'Matthäus 23', *ZTK* n.s. 48 (1951), 55–63.

313   Cf. Is. 31.5; Str-B, vol. I, 107, 929, 943. In our text the close association of God's and Jesus' presence or absence is implied. Cf. Daube, 'Biblical Landmarks', 5–6; Is. 66.13.

314   Bultmann, *History*, 115.

315 Manson, *Sayings*, 102–3; Kümmel, *Promise*, 80.
316 C.F. Burney, *The Poetry of Our Lord* (Oxford, 1925), 146, cf. 137–46; Manson, *Sayings*, 126. There is no suggestion of *kina* rhythm in Lk. 11.49/ Mt. 23.34–46, which supports our view that the two sayings were not originally together.
317 M'Neile, *Matthew*, 341.
318 Creed, *Luke*, 187.
319 It may be, as Manson and Burney maintain (cf. n. 316 above) that Matthew is closer to the original Aramaic form of this saying than Luke. Cf. n. 322 below.
320 Luke has τὴν ἑαυτῆς νοσσιάν – 'her own brood' (collective); Matthew has τὰ νοσσία αὐτῆς – 'her chicks'. Cf. Deut. 32.11, Ps. 17.8, 36.7; Manson, *Sayings*, 127.
321 Matthew's position seems more logical than Luke's; it makes the ἀπ' ἄρτι refer to a future coming of Jesus (Parousia) and the εὐλογημένος to a post-Resurrection response. Cf. E. Stauffer, *New Testament Theology* (London, 1955), 191. Luke has placed this saying much earlier in the ministry (in Galilee) and perhaps by omitting ἄρτι and having ἕως ἥξει ὅτε he means for us to refer the εὐλογημένος at least in part to the Palm Sunday events. He has placed it at Lk. 13.34 to connect it with 13.33. Cf. Ellis, *Luke*, 191; Kümmel, *Promise*, 79–82.
322 Ἰερουσαλήμ represents the Aramaic form of the name and probably represents very old tradition, for only here does Matthew keep this older form. Cf. Kümmel, *Promise*, 81; Lohse, 'Σιών', *TDNT*, vol. VII, 327, n. 220.
323 Cf. Hos. 11.1–6, Jer. 31.15. The children share the character of their mother, Jerusalem.
324 Stählin, 'κοπετός', *TDNT*, vol. III, 838; M. Ket. 4.4, Danby, 250.
325 Otherwise, He would not have used this imagery to make a positive point about His own desires and role. This saying gives strong incidental evidence of Jesus' appreciation of a mother's role.
326 Bultmann, *History*, 115–16.
327 *Ibid.*
328 V. Taylor, *The Passion Narrative of St. Luke – A Critical and Historical Investigation* (SNTS Monograph 19; Cambridge, 1972), 90.
329 Cf. K.G. Kuhn, 'ξύλον', *TDNT*, vol. V, 38, n. 7: 'It may be seen plainly that the Gospel depiction of the conduct and saying of Jesus on His last journey corresponds in every point to what, on the basis of Rabbinic accounts, we should expect in such a situation of pious Jews aware of God's requirement. This is a strong point in favor of the historical fidelity of Lk.'
330 Cf. Str-B, vol. II, 263; Manson, *Sayings*, 343.
331 Cf. W. Käser, 'Exegetische und theologische Erwägungen zur Seligpreisung der Kinderlosen Lc 23:29b', *ZNW* 54 (1963), 240–54; Marshall, *Luke*, 864.
332 Cf. R.T. France, *Jesus and the Old Testament* (London, 1971), 176–222.
333 καί may mean 'including' here (Marshall, *Luke*, 863), but the αἵ separates the women from the rest (in that only they are weeping and mourning), as does Jesus' address to them. In the NT θρηνέω is used always of a general rather than a formal lament, thus, it is likely that these were not paid professionals. Cf. Stählin, 'θρηνέω', *TDNT*, vol. III, 148–50.
334 Josephus, *Antiquities* 8.273 (LCL V; trans. H. St. J. Thackeray and R. Marcus, 1934), 718–19; *Antiquities* 13.399 (LCL VIII), 428–9.
335 Josephus, *Jewish War* 3.436 (LCL II), 698–9; B.T. Mo'ed Qatan 25a, in Str-B,

vol. IV.1, 599 O and R. All are to be mourners of a famous man, and it was customary to mourn him for thirty, not seven, days.

336   *Pace* Manson, *Luke*, 258; with Plummer, *Luke*, 528. The OT background for the term 'daughter of Jerusalem' (Song of Songs 1.5, Is. 37.22, Zeph. 3.14), as well as the way Jesus addresses these women as one with Israel (not the family of faith) makes it more probable that they are not disciples of Jesus. For a similar instance of the daughters of Israel weeping over a beloved rabbi who had been sympathetic to their plight, cf. M. Ned. 9.10, Danby, 277.

337   Marshall, *Luke*, 864; Brennan, 'Women in the Gospels', 297; Str-B, vol. I, 1037.

338   M. San. 6.6, Danby, 391; Str-B, vol. I, 1049; Str-B, vol. II, 686.

339   Jerusalem and its fate are major themes in Luke's Gospel. Cf. Conzelmann, *Theology of Luke*, 132ff, and Lk. 19.42ff. Probably, not the Day of Judgment, but an eschatological judgment as a foretaste and foreshadowing of that day is in view here. Cf. Danker, *Jesus*, 236−7; Ellis, *Luke*, 266.

340   The imagery develops from the barren, to those who have never conceived (which could include virgins and single women), to those who have never breast fed a child. Käser, 'Exegetische', 251, insists that στεῖραι must be taken metaphorically for spiritually barren, and the contrast is between a fleshly barren and spiritual Israel. This is to read the passage in light of later Christian interpretations. Cf. Marshall, *Luke*, 862.

341   Thus, this saying has no significant bearing on Jesus' view of motherhood or children apart from such exceptional circumstances. The statement must not be isolated from its context of catastrophe. This is also true of Mk 13.17 (Mt. 24.19, Lk. 21.23). It is worth noting that this saying probably is not directed to disciples but to those who reject the Kingdom. It is thus not a radically new statement about the non-physical nature of the Kingdom and its blessings.

342   This is not a desire to be hidden and protected, but a desire for a quick death in preference to such terror and misery. πέσετε here means 'fall down upon', and thus to crush and kill. Cf. Plummer, *Luke*, 529; Michaelis, 'πίπτω', *TDNT*, vol. VI, 162; Oepke, 'καλύπτω', *TDNT*, vol. III, 557, adds that καλύπτω may mean 'to bury', not just 'to hide'.

343   There are at least four possibilities for the meaning of verse 31: (1) If the Romans treat innocent Jesus in this way, what will they do to guilty Israel? (2) If the Jews deal harshly with their Saviour, what treatment shall they receive for destroying Him? (3) If the Jews behave in this way before their cup of wickedness is full, what will they do when they are completely rotten? (4) If God judges the innocent One now in this fashion, what will He do to the guilty Jews? Because of the similar proverb in Seder Elij. Rabbah 14 (65) (cf. Str-B, vol. II, 263), and the phrase ἐν τῷ ξηρῷ (Mt. 3.10, 7.19), Delling argues that the dry wood is the Jewish people that will experience the fire of judgment (not necessarily the Day of Judgment in this case) for rejecting Jesus. Cf. Delling, 'βάπτισμα, βαπτισθῆναι', *NovT* 2 (1958), 110. Jesus, being the fresh wood, still goes through the fire of judgment for others. If Delling is right, then the 'they' of ποιοῦσιν is a more general reference to God (Lk. 12.40). This view seems to be supported by Jesus' comparison between the daughters' fate and His own, though neither judgment nor fire is explicitly mentioned in verse 31.

3 Women and the Deeds of Jesus

1   Dibelius, *From Tradition*, 114.

2   Bultmann, *History*, 21–2.

3   Creed, *Luke*, 109–10, and the authors cited in Marshall, *Luke*, 205.

4   J.J. Donohue, 'The Penitent Woman and the Pharisee: Luke 7.36–50', *AER* 142 (1960) 414–27.

5   Cf. pp. 53–7 of this study and n. 36 below.

6   Cf. C.H. Dodd, *Historical Tradition in the Fourth Gospel* (Cambridge, 1963), 171–3.

7   Cf. Marshall, *Luke*, 306; Brown, *John*, 'i-xii', 450–2; P. Gardner-Smith, *Saint John and the Synoptics* (Cambridge, 1938), 48.

8   Marshall, *Luke*, 307.

9   Without some previous contact being presupposed with Jesus' message or person, the woman's conduct in Lk. 7 is inexplicable. Cf. Marshall, *Luke*, 306–7.

10   Ellis, *Luke*, 121.

11   Marshall, *Luke*, 306.

12   κατακλίνω in the passive means 'to recline' at table; cf. BAG, 412; LSJ, 894. Jews at a normal daily meal would sit or squat, but at banquets they would recline in Graeco-Roman fashion. Cf. Str-B, vol. IV.2, 617–18; J. Jeremias, *The Eucharistic Words of Jesus* (trans. N. Perrin; London, 1966), 48, n. 4; Josephus, *Antiquities* 6.163 (LCL II), 248–9.

13   Cf. Str-B, vol. II, 162; BAG, 43; R.K. Orchard, 'On the Composition of Luke vii.36–50', *JTS* 38 (1937), 243–5. The point seems to be that this woman was well-known in the city as a sinner ('a woman who was a sinner in the city'); Simon expects Jesus to know of her notoriety.

14   Ellis, *Luke*, 122; Str-B, vol. IV.2, 615; Str-B, vol. I, 726.

15   Thus, it may or may not be an indication of cross-fertilization; cf. Pliny, *Natural History* 36.23.60 (LCL X; trans. D.E. Eicholz; 1962), 48–9; Herodotus 3.20 (LCL II; trans. A.D. Godley; 1921), 26–7; A. Edersheim, *The Life and Times of Jesus the Messiah* (Grand Rapids, 1971), vol. I, 565, n. 1, 566; Michaelis, 'μύρον', *TDNT*, vol. IV, 801, n. 10; Josephus, *Jewish War* 4.561 (LCL II), 166–7.

16   Edersheim, *Life and Times*, vol. I, 564; Plummer, *Luke*, 211. Sandals are removed before the meal.

17   Caird, *Luke*, 114, suggests that Jesus reads the progress of events in Simon's shocked face.

18   She is not under the table; but cf. the illustrations in E.E. Platt, 'The Ministry of Mary of Bethany', *TT* 34 (1, 1977), 29–39.

19   Edersheim, *Life and Times*, vol. I, 566.

20   M. Sotah, I.5, Danby, 294, mentions the loosing of hair as a way of disgracing a suspected adulteress. Cf. Jeremias, *Parables*, 126, n. 56.

21   A prostitute was considered defiled and thus ritually unclean, and her touch was in turn defiling. M. Sotah 1.3, Danby, 293.

22   διδάσκαλος is a term of respect; cf. Marshall, *Luke*, 310.

23   Str-B, vol. I, 427, 986; Str-B, vol. IV.2, 615; H. Schlier, 'αλείφω', *TDNT*, vol. I, 230. On the ubiquity of the custom of the kiss of greeting, cf. Str-B, vol. I, 995–6. Feet washing perhaps was not customary in all situations but it was

done frequently if the guest came off the highway. Cf. L. Goppelt, 'ὕδωρ', *TDNT*, vol. VIII, 324, n. 63; Edersheim, *Life and Times*, vol. I, 568.

24   Xenophon, *Cyropaedia* 7.5.32 (LCL II; trans. W. Miller; 1914), 272–5; Polybius, *The Histories* 15.1.7 (LCL IV; trans. W.R. Paton; 1925), 464–5. Cf. Str-B, vol. I, 996; Aristophanes, *Wasps* 605ff (LCL; trans. B.B. Rogers; 1924), 466–7: 'Returning home at the close of day, O then what a welcome I get for its sake: my daughter, my darling is foremost of all, and she washes my feet and anoints (ἀλείφη) them with care, and above them stoops and a kiss lets fall.' Here the act is an attempt to extract money.

25   On the Socratic form of this discussion (question and answer), cf. C.H. Dodd, 'The Dialogue Form in the Gospels', *BJRL* 37 (1954–5), 59–60. The form may be a Lucan construction but it was in use among rabbis and Jewish teachers and may well have been used by Jesus. Cf. Ellis, *Luke*, 121.

26   The harder word 'money lender' rather than 'creditor' is used here. Cf. W.M. MacGregor, 'The Parable of the Money-Lender and his Debtors (Lk vii.41– 47)', *ET* (1925–6), 344–7. ἀγαπάω in this context probably means an expression of gratitude or thanks, though love is involved. Cf. H.G. Wood, 'The Use of ἀγαπάω in Luke vii.42, 47', *ET* 66 (1954–5), 319–20; Josephus, *Jewish War* 1.10.2 (LCL II), 92–3.

27   ἅπτω in the middle means 'to cling to' or 'to lay hold of' in the NT and the papyri. In view of the present tense of the verb here, 'to cling to' is the proper translation. Cf. BAG, 102; A–S, 56; MM, 72; Marshall, *Luke*, 311.

28   This is a statement of fact, not a disparaging remark. Jesus is not concerned with keeping His own skirts clean, as is Simon.

29   ἀφ' ἧς is possibly an abbreviation for ἀφ' ἡμέρας ἧ ('since the time when') or more probably for ἀφ' ὥρας. Cf. Robertson, 717, 978. The εἰσῆλθον of L', Vulgate is a later improvement. Cf. Jeremias, 'Lukas 7.45 εἰσῆλθον', *ZNW* 51 (1960), 131.

30   The verb tense indicates continuous action. Cf. BAG, 184.

31   Note the emphatic position of σου. Cf. Edersheim, *Life and Times*, vol. I, 568, n. 4.

32   Marshall, *Luke*, 310.

33   So Creed, *Luke*, 109–12; A.H. Dammers, 'Studies in Texts', *Theology* 49 (1946), 78–80; Orchard, 'Composition', 243–5.

34   H.G. Meecham, 'Luke vii.47', *ET* 38 (1926–7), 286, citing Papyrus Tebtunis 2.410 and 2 Maccabees 4.16. J. Dublin, 'οὗ χάριν', *ET* 37 (1925–6), 525–6, says οὗ χάριν = χάριν τοῦ ὅτι ('in acknowledgement of the fact that'). Cf. other similar phrases such as ἀνθ' ὧν (Lk. 1.20, Ac. 12.23, 2 Thess. 2.10) and οὗ εἵνεκεν (Lk. 4.18, Gen. 18.5 in the LXX) which mean 'because'. Cf. also Robertson, 647; BDF, sec. 456.4, 239; Conzelmann, 'χάρις', *TDNT*, vol. IX, 391, n. 143; MHT, vol. III, 319.

35   This has been argued well by Moule, *I-B*, 147; Zerwick, sec. 422, 144–5 and sec. 427, 147. For the traditional Catholic view, cf. M.-J. Lagrange, *Évangile selon St. Luc* (Paris, 1948), 230ff. Verse 47*b* argues against this view as does the woman's conduct. The woman is said to be 'saved' by her faith, not her love (cf. Marshall, *Luke*, 306–7). Jesus' words are directed primarily to Simon to teach him a lesson, not to tell the woman about a forgiveness she had responded to already with great emotion. There is nothing improbable about the assumption that this woman had prior contact with Jesus or His message,

though it is somewhat surprising that Luke fails to mention it. Such contact is the best explanation of her conduct.

36 If we take οὗ χάριν as causal, we may read, 'Because I say to you, her sins are forgiven, she loves much'. By this interpretation οὗ χάριν anticipates ὅτι. If the ὅτι is to be stressed, we may read with Moule, *I-B*, 147, 'I can say with confidence that her sins are forgiven, because her love is evidence of it.'

37 This may be Luke's addition based on a deduction from verse 47 or he may be adding a remark that typified what Jesus usually said in such cases.

38 Jesus' listeners understood Him to mean that her sins had been forgiven by Him, which from their point of view was blasphemy since God alone can forgive sins. ἀφέωνται is in the perfect, and the act of anointing and the woman's tears point to a prior act of forgiving.

39 Cf. Morris, *John*, 254; Marshall, 'The Problem of New Testament Exegesis', *JETS* 17 (2, 1974), 67–73. R.E. Brown, 'Roles of Women in the Fourth Gospel', *TS* 36 (4, 1975), 691, suggests a progression in chapters two to four from disbelief (2.18–20) to inadequate belief (2.23ff) to more adequate belief (4.25–9).

40 Lightfoot, *John*, 120ff.

41 G.W. MacRae, *Faith in the Word – The Fourth Gospel* (Chicago, 1973), 38.

42 Cf. Jn 1.31, 49, 3.14–15; Barrett, *John* (1955), 190. John may be consciously modelling his narrative on some aspects of several OT well stories (Gen. 24, 29, Ex. 2.15–22). Cf. N.R. Bonneau, 'The Woman at the Well, John 4 and Genesis 24', *Bible Today* 67 (1973), 1252–9.

43 Cf. Dodd, *Historical Tradition*, 325–7, 391–405.

44 R. Schnackenburg, *The Gospel According to St. John*, vol. I (trans. K. Smyth; New York, 1968), 419.

45 Barrett, *John* (1978), 229.

46 So apparently C.M. Carmichael, 'Marriage and the Samaritan Woman', *NTS* 26 (1980), 332–46. On 4.10–15 as the Evangelist's composition, cf. R. Bultmann, *The Gospel of John: A Commentary* (trans. G.R. Beasley-Murray; Oxford, 1971), 175.

47 Barrett, *John*, 229.

48 Cf. L. Morris, *Studies in the Fourth Gospel* (Grand Rapids, 1969), 146–51; R.D. Potter, 'Topography and Archaeology in the Fourth Gospel', in *Studia Evangelica* (ed. K. Aland *et al.*; Berlin, 1959), vol. I, 329–37, here 331: 'No passage could show better that our author knew this bit of Samaria well.' Cf. n. 65 below.

49 Brown, *John* 'i-xii', 176.

50 H. Riesenfeld, *The Gospel Tradition and its Beginnings* (London, 1957), 63.

51 Probably the Fourth Evangelist exercised greater freedom with his material than did the first three Evangelists because his was an 'informal' rather than formal and relatively fixed tradition. Nevertheless, the evident skillful editing and assembling of this material 'is no reason for doubting the historicity of the narrative' (Schnackenburg, *John*, vol. I, 420).

52 Morris, *Studies*, 147.

53 Schnackenburg, *John*, vol. I, 420.

54 J.H. Bernard, *A Critical and Exegetical Commentary on the Gospel According to St. John* (ICC; Edinburgh, 1928), vol. I, 144.

55 The woman identified herself both by ethnic group and by gender. This leads

one to suspect that she was sensitive about being part of both these groups
(Samaritan and woman).

56   The evidence for omitting this whole parenthesis is not strong enough to rule
it out of the original text. Cf. Metzger, *TC*, 206; *pace* BDF, sec. 193.5, p. 104.

57   Despite the strong arguments of D.R. Hall, 'The Meaning of συγχράομαι in
John 4.9', *ET* 83 (2, 1971), 56–7, for the traditional view. Daube, *NT and
Rabbinic Judaism*, 373–82, is more convincing in his plea for the translation
'use together with' and he has been followed by Barrett, *John* (1978), 232;
Brown, *John* 'i-xii', 170; Morris, *John*, 259, n. 25. Cf. Jeremias, 'Σαμάρεια',
TDNT, vol. VII, 91, n. 25. For an example in the NT of a following dative
being dependent solely on the συν- of the verb to which it relates, cf. Ac.
13.31. In the Mishnah and Talmuds there are various views recorded on
whether Jews would have dealings with Samaritans and whether Samaritans
and their possessions and land were unclean. Cf. Str-B, vol. I, 540–1; M. Ber.
7.1; Danby, 7, 9; M. Demai 5.9, 7.4, Danby, 25, 27; M. Sheb. 8.10, Danby,
49. The famous M. Niddah 4.1, Danby, 748, probably dates from A.D. 65 or
66, though such views probably were held widely in Jesus' day. As Jeremias,
Jerusalem, 352–8, indicates, it is difficult to assess the data, though it is
probably true to say that most good Jews considered Samaritans as ritually
and cultically unclean many years before M. Niddah 4.1 was codified. The
reaction of the disciples to Jesus' encounter with this woman is perhaps
evidence of this fact. Cf. E.F. Harrison, 'The Son of God among the Sons
of Men. VI. Jesus and the Woman of Samaria', *BSac* 103 (1946), 176–86,
espec. 179.

58   The usual meaning of 'living water' is running water. Cf. L. Goppelt, 'ὕδωρ',
TDNT, vol. VIII, 326; Brown, *John*, 'i-xii', 170. The woman has no inti-
mation of whom she is talking to at first, as Jn 4.15 shows. The Evangelist
is using his usual style of *double entendre* and irony to carry the discussion
along.

59   J.R. Diaz, 'Palestinian Targum and the New Testament', *NovT* 6 (1963),
75–80, mentions a story which tells of Father Jacob removing the stone
from a well and its overflowing for twenty years.

60   This 'gift' is probably the Holy Spirit (in view of 6.63, 7.38), not His teaching. So Morris, *John*, 260–1; Barrett, *John* (1955), 195; Brown, *John*, 'i-
xii', 178–9.

61   MacRae, *Faith in the Word*, 39.

62   This may be the technical phrase for 'I have not had intercourse with a man.'
Cf. Mt. 14.4, 1 Cor. 5.1. The phrase can mean, however, 'I have no husband.'
Cf. Mt. 22.28, Mk 12.23, 1 Cor. 7.2. The latter meaning is more probable
here in view of ὅν ἔχεις οὐκ ἔστιν σου ἀνήρ in verse 18. *Pace* H. Hanse, 'ἔχω',
TDNT, vol. II, 817, n. 5.

63   Cf. Str-B, vol. II, 437. The various suggestions about the five husbands standing for five false religions introduced into Samaria seem improbable. John
gives no hint of allegory here. Cf. Brown, *John*, 'i-xii', 171.

64   Cf. p. 136, n. 103 of this study.

65   The Fourth Evangelist seems to reflect an intimate and accurate knowledge
of the beliefs and practices of the Samaritans. Cf. J. Bowman, 'Samaritan
Studies', *BJRL* 40 (1957–8), 298–329. The Samaritans did not expect a
Davidic Messiah, but rather a *Taheb* which means either 'the one who returns'

(Moses *redivivus*) or 'the one who restores' (a prophet like Moses). For them, Moses was the only prophet and thus only of him or the expected one could it be said θεωρῶ ὅτι προφήτης εἶ σύ. Josephus, *Antiquities* 18.85–7 (LCL IX), 60–3, tells us that the Samaritans had Messianic expectations of the *Taheb* returning even during Jesus' day. Our scene and the discussion which ensues is not improbable as an event in the life of Jesus. For a possible Samaritan parallel to Jesus' statement about living waters, cf. J. Bowman, 'Early Samaritan Eschatology', *JJS* 6 (1955), 63–72; Jeremias, 'Μωυσῆς', *TDNT*, vol. IV, 862–3.

66 The single preposition indicates we are dealing with only one concept. So C.H. Dodd, *The Interpretation of the Fourth Gospel* (London, 1953), 314, n. 2; Brown, *John*, 'i-xii', 180–1. True worship is determined by God's nature, not man's prejudices. This phrase then means true or proper worship as God would have it.

67 οἴδαμεν may have been the original reading, as it has good support from p66c, אc, L, Origen, Cyril, etc. but it is more probable that οἶδα would have been changed to οἴδαμεν considering ἡμῖν in 4.25b and the frequent use of οἴδαμεν in John (cf. 3.2, 4.42, 7.27, 9.20, 24, 29, 31). The woman reflects accurately the Samaritan expectation, for they viewed the *Taheb* as more of a prophet or revealer than a deliverer. Cf. Martha's confession in Jn 11. Bowman, 'Samaritan Studies', 299ff, notes that with the Samaritan tenth commandment is the discussion of worship on Mt Gerizim to which is appended a discussion on the *Taheb*. Could this be why the Samaritan woman makes the statement about the Messiah at the point in the discussion that she does?

68 ὅτι seems to be causal (Morris, *John*, 270), but it could be result (Barrett, *John* (1955), 198). If it is the latter, then the meaning would be 'we were given insight into whom we worship in order that the Messiah might come from the Jews'.

69 Brennan, 'Women in the Gospels', 294.

70 Perhaps the reason it is only here in John's Gospel that we have such a clear statement by Jesus of His Messiahship is that the idea would not connote a political kingship in a Samaritan context and thus could be used without fear of the sort of misconceptions such labels were liable to in Judea. Cf. Morris, *John*, 273; Brown, *John*, 'i-xii', 172–3. The use of the emphatic pronoun is in the style of deity. Cf. BDF, sec. 277, 145; BAG, 216; Jn 8.58. For arguments in favour of the theophanic formula here, cf. E. Stauffer, *Jesus and His Story* (New York, 1974), 186–8. J. Bligh, 'Jesus in Samaria', *HeyJ* 3 (1962), 329–46, notes the dramatic shift in discussion from conventional expectation to self-revelation in Jn 4.24–5. This view, however, requires that Jesus' statement be unconnected to the immediately preceding remark of the woman.

71 Note that the second dialogue also ends with people arriving from town (the Samaritans). Cf. M.P. Hogan, 'The Woman at the Well (John 4:1–42)', *Bible Today* 82 (1976), 663–9.

72 ἐπὶ τούτῳ may imply this; cf. Moule, *I-B*, 50; MHT, vol. III, 272.

73 These two questions would be directed to Jesus though some variants show the first as addressed to the woman. As Brown, *John*, 'i-xii', 173, points out (following Bultmann), 'they were more shocked because he was talking with a woman than because he was talking with a Samaritan'. Cf. J. Foster, 'What

seekest thou? John iv.27', *ET* 52 (1940–1), 37–8; W.G. White, 'St. John iv.27', *ET* 26 (1914–15), 180.

74 Lightfoot, *John*, 125; Barrett, *John* (1955), 201 (following Daube), suggests that the jug is left so Jesus may drink.

75 There is a natural amount of hyperbole in her first statement. Her question shows that her faith is not yet complete (μήτι probably introduces a hesitant question). Cf. MHT, vol. I, 170, n. 1, 193; Robertson, 917. The question here implies hope and expectation rather than tentativeness; Cf. Dodd, *Interpretation*, 315.

76 Cf. n. 43 above.

77 Lightfoot, *John*, 125.

78 There may or may not be two traditional proverbs being used here. The point is the harvest is now – there is no interval between sowing and reaping and thus the disciples must get to work.

79 The repetition of the article – ὁ σπείρων καὶ ὁ ... θερίζων (verse 37*b*, cf. verse 36*b*) indicates the two actions are distinct. Cf. Robertson, 786; F. Hauck, 'θερίζω', *TDNT*, vol. III, 133.

80 ἐγὼ ἀπέστειλα ὑμᾶς probably does not refer to the great commission. The reference probably is a general one referring to the mission to the world. Cf. Lightfoot, *John*, 126; Barrett, *John* (1955), 203.

81 Cf. Lightfoot, *John*, 126; L.H. Bunn, 'John iv.34–42', *ET* 41 (1929–30), 141–2.

82 There is probably not a contrast between λόγος and λαλία here since both words are used of the woman's witness. *Pace* Brown, *John*, 'i-xii', 174–5. R. Walker, 'Jüngerwort und Herrenwort, Zur Auslegung von Joh 4.39–42., *ZNW* 57 (1–2, 1966), 50, rightly says, 'Der λόγος der Samariterin in 4.39 ist kein unverbindliches Menschenwort, keine private Mitteilung, sondern aüsdrucklich λόγος im Sinne des Zeugenworts.' Cf. Barrett, *John* (1978), 243, who remarks, 'To bear witness ... is the task of a disciple. The woman joins with John the Baptist as witness, and in fact precedes the apostles.'

83 So Brown, 'Roles of Women', 691.

84 As Dodd, *Interpretation*, 371, notes, κόσμος for John means 'the world of human kind' (cf. 3.16, 17, 4.42). The term 'Saviour of the World' was an imperial title especially under Hadrian but probably it is not used in this sense here. Cf. Morris, *John*, 285, n. 101.

85 R.A. Harrisville, 'The Woman of Canaan. A Chapter in the History of Exegesis', *Int* 20 (3, 1966), 274–87.

86 Derrett, 'Law in the New Testament: The Syrophoenician Woman and the Centurion of Capernaum', *NovT* 15 (3, 1973), 161–86. Cf. n. 94 below. There was no love lost between Jews and Phoenicians, especially those from Tyre. Cf. Josephus, *Against Apion* 1.71 (LCL I), 190–1: 'among the Phoenicians, the Tyrians are notoriously our bitterest enemies'. This may explain the disciples' reaction to the woman, especially if they knew she was from Tyre.

87 The Roman centurion (Mt. 8.5–13) was possibly a God-fearer; the Gerasene demoniac (Mk 5.1–20, Mt. 8.28–34) lives in a foreign country but his religion is not made clear. Cf. T.A. Burkill, 'The Syrophoenician Woman, The congruence of Mark 7.24–31', *ZNW* 57 (1966), 33.

88 Dibelius, *From Tradition*, 261, and n. 1, maintains that Matthew and Mark

are drawing on a common source and that possibly we have a case of a saying
which was built up into a narrative (in two different ways). Bultmann, *History*,
38, and n. 3, toys with the possibility that Matthew used an older version than
Mark but rules it out because of Jesus' dialogue with the disciples in Matthew.
He maintains the somewhat complicated view that Matthew derived 15.24
from a logion collection and that πρῶτον or all of ἄφες πρῶτον χορτασθῆναι
τὰ τέκνα is a secondary addition to Mark's text (presumably after Matthew
used Mark), a view for which there is no real textual support. Matthew probably used the Mark we now have but expanded and edited it at certain points
in order to emphasize on the one hand how great Jesus' charity was, even to
those He was not purposely setting out to help (thus he omits ἄφες πρῶτον
χορτασθῆναι τὰ τέκνα and includes 15.24), and on the other hand to emphasize the woman's great faith (by the three-fold pleading and the Ὦ γύναι
μεγάλη σου ἡ πίστις in verse 28). The source of these additions may be the
Evangelist himself though in some cases other (oral?) sources seem to be
involved (cf. n. 97 below).

89   It is not clear whether Jesus crossed the border or merely went to it (probably
the former). So Hill, *Matthew*, 253; Lane, *Mark*, 260; Taylor, *Mark*, 348;
Cranfield, *Mark*, 246.

90   During the days of Jesus' earthly ministry and the earliest days of the post-
Resurrection Christian community we can speak only of the 'reception of
Gentiles' and not a 'Gentile mission'. Cf. J. Jeremias, *Jesus' Promise to the
Nations* (trans. S. H. Hooke; London, 1958), 25, n. 2. It is not proper, however, to dismiss these narratives as simply exceptions that tell us nothing about
Jesus' fundamental attitude toward a Gentile mission. *Pace* Jeremias, *Jesus'
Promise*, 30–1. If Jesus was willing in the end to help the Syrophoenician
woman in the presence of His disciples and in the face of their request to
dismiss her, then the narrative tells us much about Jesus' present acceptance
of non-Jews and His willingness to help them despite the fact that His earthly
mission was directed intentionally to Jews. Some of His actions prepared the
way for the Gentile mission that began after the Resurrection (whatever one
makes of Mt. 28.19). Burkill, 'The Historical Development of the Story of
the Syrophoenician Woman (Mark vii.24–31)', *NovT* 9 (3, 1967), 161–77,
rightly says that Jesus' dealing with the Syrophoenician prefigures, not in-
augurates, the Gentile mission.

91   Both the woman's coming and her address to Jesus indicate that He was
known widely for His miracles. Cf. J. Ireland Hasler, 'The Incident of the
Syrophoenician Woman (Matt. xv.21–28, Mark vii.24–30)', *ET* 45 (1933–4),
459–61; Taylor, *Mark*, 349.

92   The ἀκάθαρτος in Mark here indicates the spirit's ritual effects as is appropriate
in the Marcan discussion of clean and unclean. Mk 7.17–23 indicates that
Jesus taught in terms of moral, not ritual, defilement.

93   Only Matthew has προσεκύνει αὐτῷ, but even in his version this is probably
not an act of worship, but rather a reflection of the woman's need. *Pace* K.
Weiss, 'πούς', *TDNT*, vol. VI, 630.

94   Possibly Matthew differs here because he wants to point out that in spite of
her religious background she has a great faith in Jesus. Mark seems to be
contrasting the woman's Greek speech and her Phoenician extraction. So
Swete, *Mark*, 148.

95 F.G. Cholmondeley, 'Christ and the Woman of Canaan', *ET* 13 (1901–2), 138; M'Neile, *Matthew*, 230.

96 Cf. D. Smith, 'Our Lord's Hard Saying to the Syro-Phoenician Woman', *ET* 12 (1900–1), 319–21; J.D. Smart, 'Jesus, the Syro-Phoenician Woman – and the Disciples', *ET* 50 (1938–9), 469–72.

97 The translation preferred here is ambiguous since 'send her away' could be with or without her request. Cf. BAG, 96; A–S, 53; LSJ, 208; MM, 66–7. It is very curious that Matthew, who normally spares the disciples more than Mark by omitting some of the Marcan material that reflects badly on them, has here included this reaction when there is no trace of the disciples' presence, much less their reaction, in Mark's account. This leads one to suspect that it is possible that Matthew, as a member of a community in which the Gospel stories were a living legacy, did occasionally have access to additional (oral?) information about some of his Marcan narratives. It should be noted that this is no novel conjecture since it is generally recognized that Matthew had more than one source on other occasions for the same material (i.e., where Mark and the Q material apparently overlapped). Mark, however, is his primary and in many cases sole source, otherwise he would not have taken over 90% of Mark's material and well over half of his exact wording.

98 B. Horace Ward, 'Our Lord's Hard Sayings to the Syrophoenician Woman', *ET* 13 (1901–2), 48. Jesus' response explains why He does not grant her request. As M'Neile, *Matthew*, 231, says, He intends the woman to overhear though He is speaking to the disciples.

99 Cf. Jeremias, *Jesus' Promise*, 34–5. Probably the lost sheep here are all Israel since they are being contrasted to all non-children.

100 Cf. Bultmann, *History*, 38, n. 3.

101 The whole saying as recorded in Mark may reflect a Jewish proverb on the seniority system dictating who eats first in a Jewish house. Cf. Derrett, 'The Syrophoenician Woman', 168.

102 It is not clear that the diminutive softens Jesus' remarks. *Pace* Taylor, *Mark*, 350; Cranfield, *Mark*, 248. There are examples where κυνάριον is a diminutive of contempt. Cf. Smith, 'Our Lord's Hard Saying', 319; Derrett, 'The Syrophoenician Woman', 169. Diminutives are frequent in Mark and it is not certain that they really mean anything even in our passage (does θυγάτριον in verse 25 mean 'little daughter' or ψιχίων in verse 28 mean 'little food'?). Cf. Zerwick, sec. 485, p. 162.

103 M. Hallah 1.8, Danby, 84; Derrett, 'The Syrophoenician Woman', 170; Jeremias, *NT Theology*, 164, n. 2. It is not clear that Jews domesticated dogs, though there are examples of Jews playing with puppies; cf. Str-B, vol. I, 726.

104 That the woman is not crushed by these remarks seems to imply that more is happening than words can tell; cf. Smart, 'Jesus', 472. This, however, may be to read more into the narrative than the Evangelist intended.

105 The woman's response implies submission to Jesus' judgment and initial refusal. So Harrisville, 'The Woman of Canaan', 284; Jeremias, *Jesus' Promise*, 30. Her inventiveness is not so much her verbal play as placing herself in the dog category which allows her into the house. As W. Storch, 'Zur Perikope von der Syrophönizierin Mk 7,28 und Ri 1,7', *BZ* 14 (2, 1970), 256–7, points out, in Jesus' final response to the woman (διὰ τοῦτον τὸν λόγον) it is what

she says, not how she says it or the cleverness, that Jesus mentions as the reason she gains her desire. Is Judg. 1.7 in the background here?

106   Derrett, 'The Syrophoenician Woman', 172; Smith, 'Our Lord's Hard Saying', 321. The maxim in Philostratus, *Life of Apollonius of Tyana* 1.19 (LCL I; trans. F.C. Conybeare; 1912), 52–5, is of uncertain date. It is possible that it originated in the first century A.D., unless it is Philostratus' own creation which would place it in the second or third century A.D.

107   Indeed, her faith is so great that she believes she can be fed now, not just second. Cf. Jeremias, 'παράδεισος', *TDNT*, vol. V, 772, n. 63.

108   Again, in this case it is a matter of male–female role reversal since the woman, instead of the disciples, is depicted as having great faith and serves as the model for the Evangelist's audiences (espec. in Matthew).

109   Taylor, *Formation*, 70.

110   Taylor, *Mark*, 178; Cranfield, *Mark*, 81.

111   C.H. Turner, 'Notes and Studies – Marcan Usage: Notes Critical and Exegetical on the Second Gospel', *JTS* 26 (1924–5), 226, suggests the original oral form – 'We left the synagogue and came into our house with our fellow disciples James and John.'

112   Cf. Schrage, 'τυφλός', *TDNT*, vol. VIII, 288; Dibelius, *From Tradition*, 74–90. That the form is conventional does not necessarily impugn the historicity of this incident, for facts as well as fiction can be presented in a popular pre-existing form. In the case of Mk 1.29–31 the pre-existing form probably only affects *how* the facts are presented, and perhaps *which* facts are included and emphasized.

113   The setting in Luke, considering the non-Marcan sections on the birth and on the rejection in Nazareth preceding 4.38, is essentially the same as Mark. While it is intimated in Lk. 4.3 that Jesus has performed miracles in Capernaum before, the first two Luke presents as a fulfillment of the paradigmatic speech in 4.18–21 are the same as the first two in Mark. Mark and Luke, by placing this healing between the time Jesus left the synagogue (Mk 1.29, Lk. 4.38) and sunset (Mk 1.32, Lk. 4.40), clearly imply that this is a Sabbath healing. The First Evangelist, grouping his material topically, presents this pericope as he sets forth examples of Jesus' healing miracles (ch. 8). Notably, he appears to have maintained a setting of Capernaum for this event. He also calls Simon by his Christian name of Peter. It is possible that this Evangelist is presenting Peter's mother-in-law as a type of a Christian who is healed, since her cure is grouped with the healing of a Jewish leper and a Gentile centurion's servant.

114   πενθερά must mean mother-in-law. Cf. BAG, 648; LSJ, 1360; MM, 502; 1 Cor. 9.5. We do not have enough information to identify the disease. In the first century A.D., fevers were viewed as diseases, not as symptoms of diseases. Cf. K. Weiss, 'πυρέσσω', *TDNT*, vol. VI, 958–9.

115   It is not clear who 'they' are in either Mark or Luke. Matthew records no consultation. Cf. Turner, 'Notes and Studies – Marcan Usage: Notes Critical and Exegetical on the Second Gospel', *JTS* 25 (1923–4), 378.

116   Cf. G.A. Chadwick, 'Peter's Wife's Mother', *Exp*, 4th ser. 6 (1892), 357.

117   ἤγειρεν αὐτὴν κρατήσας τῆς χειρός is probably referring to only one action; cf. Taylor, *Mark*, 179; Swete, *Mark*, 22; Lane, *Mark*, 77. On the possible preparation in this text for later events, cf. P. Lamarche, 'La guérison de la belle-mère de Pierre et le genre littéraire des évangiles', *NRT* 87 (1965),

515–26; Danker, *Jesus*, 62. Matthew may also be pointing forward by his use of the term ἠγέρθη.

118 Chadwick, 'Peter's Wife's Mother', 357, notes that Jesus' reaction to disease here is like that of Jn 11.33, 38. Luke may have included this remark to indicate Jesus' typical reaction to disease rather than His actual response in this case.

119 Danker, *Jesus*, 62; Lamarche, 'La guérison', 520–6.

120 Cf. Str-B, vol. II, 2–3; B.T. Berakoth 5*b*, Cohen, 24–5, and Cohen's notes. It is possible that Peter's mother-in-law was in danger of dying before sundown, but even Luke's 'great fever' need not imply death was at hand (cf. Lk 8.42).

121 Cf. Str-B, vol. I, 299; Hill, *Matthew*, 160.

122 By παραχρῆμα Luke stresses that the cure is sudden and complete, and the woman's gratitude is expressed immediately; cf. Plummer, *Luke*, 37.

123 Here διακονέω has its natural non-technical sense of 'waiting on a table', or to serve in the capacity of hospitality. This probably weighs in favour of seeing this as its meaning in Lk. 8.3 as well. This is significant if Luke's audience was primarily Greek or Hellenistic, for the Greeks saw such serving as demeaning and undignified for anyone but slaves; cf. H.W. Beyer, 'διακονέω', *TDNT*, vol. II, 82. Luke's audience would probably see these actions (here and in Lk. 8.3) as particularly self-sacrificial. Matthew with his Christological focus has διηκόνει αὐτῷ.

124 X. Léon-Dufour, 'La Guérison de la Belle-Mère de Simon Pierre', *EstBib* 24 (1965), 193–216, here 216.

125 Cf. Str-B, vol. I, 480; and p. 172 and n. 136. Obviously, someone had to serve the Sabbath meal, so the woman's actions may not have been considered a Sabbath violation as long as the meal was prepared before the Sabbath, but, due to illness, she probably was unable to make such preparations. There is no indication of any other woman or servants helping when she serves. The 'they' of Mk 1.30 (λέγουσιν) may or may not involve other family members.

126 It is striking that these women all respond in ways that were conventional, and serve in capacities that were traditional for women or, in Mk 1.31, perhaps even 'beneath' the traditional roles for women who were not servants. Cf. K. Weiss, 'πούς', *TDNT*, vol. VI, 631.

127 Marshall, *Luke*, 195.

128 Cf. pp. 2–5 of this study on a wife's rabbinically prescribed tasks. Jesus seems to accept women in traditional roles but rejects the idea that these roles are the only tasks appropriate for them.

129 Cf. Creed, *Luke*, 182. This contrast between 13.6–9 and 13.10–17 was often noted by the Fathers. Cf. Aquinas, *Commentary on the Four Gospels Collected Out of the Works of the Fathers*, vol. V, 'St. Luke', Part II (Oxford, 1874), 479–87.

130 Daube, *NT and Rabbinic Judaism*, 170–83, espec. 181–2.

131 Cf. Dibelius, *From Tradition*, 97; Bultmann, *History*, 12–13.

132 Marshall, *Luke*, 557.

133 *Ibid*.

134 The connection of sickness with demonic activity was common in Jesus' day, but as Marshall, *Luke*, 557, says, we probably should not give too definite a meaning to πνεῦμα here as it may mean simply an evil influence,

in view of the cure not being described as an exorcism. Cf. Ellis, *Luke*, 186.

135 The woman probably had a spinal disease which produces fusion of the joints. Cf. J. Wilkinson, 'The Case of the Bent Woman in Luke 13.10–17', *EvQ* 49 (4, 1977), 195–205. The phrase εἰς τὸ παντελές may be taken with δυναμένη or ἀνακύψαι, but it probably goes with the latter since it follows immediately. Thus, we translate 'not able to stand up fully'. Cf. MHT, vol. III, 266; Creed, *Luke*, 183.

136 Plummer, *Luke*, 342.

137 Cf. Lk. 13.1–5. Jesus rejects this thinking and removes all excuses which might be advanced for discriminating against the sick by treating them as outcasts. Marshall, *Luke*, 559, suggests that perhaps this woman was being denied her status as a descendant of Abraham because her long sickness was taken as a sign of sinfulness.

138 Note the perfect tense of ἀπολύω which prepares us for the play on words in 13.15–16. Cf. RS, *Translator's Luke*, 505.

139 Perhaps speaking and laying on of hands are to be seen as simultaneous. Cf. RS, *Translator's Luke*, 505. If Danker, *Jesus*, 158, is correct that the woman would be suspected or regarded as ceremonially unclean, then Jesus' laying on of hands is all the more significant and unexpected.

140 Some rabbis are said to have performed miracles but not on the Sabbath and not in the synagogue, though the latter would not violate Jewish custom as far as we know. Cf. W. Schrage, 'συναγωγή', *TDNT*, vol. VII, 847ff.

141 Aquinas, *Commentary* V.2, 485. Though Jesus violates the rabbinic stipulations about healing a non-critical case on the Sabbath, it does not seem correct to say with Jeremias (*NT Theology*, 94–5, 208–9, 278, n. 8) that Jesus violated the Sabbath in this instance (as it was set up in the OT). Elsewhere it appears certain that He did violate the OT Sabbath laws.

142 'Whenever there is doubt whether life is in danger this overrides the Sabbath.' (M. Yoma 8.6, Danby, 172); cf. Str-B, vol. I, 622–9.

143 The plural ('Ὑποκριταί) points not only to the ruler but also to those who agreed with him; cf. Plummer, *Luke*, 342.

144 It was lawful to lead an ox or ass to water and to draw the water so long as one did not carry the water to the animal. Cf. Str-B, vol. II, 199–200; Edersheim, *Life and Times*, vol. II, 225. The Qumranites had the following rulings: 'No one is to follow his beast to pasture for more than a distance of two thousand cubits from his city ... If the beast be stubborn, he is not to take it outdoors. No one is to take anything out of his house, or bring anything in from outside ... Even if it drop its young into a cistern or a pit, he is not to lift it out on the Sabbath.' (Zadokite Document between X,14, and XI,18.) Cf. Gaster, *DSS*, 89.

145 This is Danker's amplification (*Jesus*, 159).

146 Jesus is refering to the divine necessity of His mission to bring in the Kingdom and conquer sin (Lk. 4.43, 9.22). Ellis, *Luke*, 186, says, 'From the beginning the Sabbath was prophetic of the consecration of creation to its good and proper end ... This will be accomplished by the deliverance of God's creation from Satan's power.' Thus, the Sabbath was the perfect day to present an example of God's perfect will for His creatures.

147 The examples in Str-B, vol. II, 200, are used of Israel as a community or in a

general sense, but only here is it used of a specific individual. RS, *Translator's Luke*, 508, notes the emphatic position of 'this woman, a daughter of Abraham'. It may be significant that Jesus says a daughter of Abraham rather than, for instance, a daughter of Sarah (cf. 1 Pet. 3.6), implying His acceptance of the idea of a patriarchal head and fountainhead of the Israelite community of faith. It may also imply that this woman should benefit as a rightful heir of Abraham and participate in such a patriarchal religious structure. Again, Jesus intimates not an overthrow of patriarchy, but a new and rightful place for women within such a structure. As N.A. Dahl, 'The Story of Abraham in Luke-Acts', *Studies in Luke-Acts* (ed. L.E. Keck and J.L. Martyn; London, 1968), 150, says, the story with its use of the term daughter of Abraham illustrates 'how God's promise to Abraham was fulfilled to his children through the ministry of Jesus'.

148   Brennan, 'Women in the Gospels', 296–7.

149   Besides the contrasts between the woman and the hypocrites, we may note also the contrast in verse 17 between Jesus' humiliated opponents and πᾶς ὁ ὄχλος who were delighted with Jesus' deeds.

150   Cf. Cranfield, *Mark*, 182; Taylor, *Mark*, 285–6; Marshall, *Luke*, 341–2.

151   Cf. Bultmann, *History*, 214–15, and to a lesser extent E. Klostermann, 'Das Markusevangelium' (*HzNT*, vol. III; ed. H. Lietzmann; 2nd ed., Tübingen, 1926), 58–9.

152   Dibelius, *From Tradition*, 72; R. Pesch, 'Jairus (Mk 5,22/Lk 8,41)', *BZ* 14 (2, 1970), 255–6.

153   Cf. Marshall, *Luke*, 341–2.

154   Taylor, *Mark*, 285.

155   Pesch, 'Jairus', 255–6. The textual evidence strongly favours the belief that the name is original (p45, אֲ, A, B, cf. Metzger, *TC*, 85–6). *Pace* Bultmann, *History*, 215; Taylor, *Mark*, 287. Cf. H.J. Cadbury's crucial admission in 'Between Jesus and the Gospel', *HTR* 16 (1923), 89, n. 6. It is doubtful that the name is derived from the events in the story since Jairus is neither 'awakened' nor 'awakens'. Cf. Cranfield, *Mark*, 183.

156   Cf. Bultmann, *History*, 214–15.

157   The contrast could be explained perhaps by the fact that in the first story Jesus desires that the woman (and perhaps others) be led to understand that she was not healed by a magic trick but through faith in Jesus and His power. In the second incident, however, the miracle is performed in the presence of only a few people and is of such a startling nature that any report of the deed was bound to further the idea of Jesus as a great wonder worker, while overlooking the purpose of the deed. Perhaps, as Chadwick suggests, Jesus wished to preserve at least one place where the girl would be treated as a normal human being. Cf. G.A. Chadwick, 'The Daughter of Jairus and the Woman with an Issue of Blood (Mt. ix.18; Mk. v.22; Lk. viii.41)', *Exp*, 4th ser. 8 (1893), 309–20. As we have stated above, however, verse 43 may well be part of the redactional work of Mark as he adds the secrecy motif.

158   ἀρχισυνάγωγος probably refers to the president of the local synagogue though it could be just an honorary title. Cf. B. Lifshitz, 'Fonctions et titres honorifiques dans les communautés juives', *RB* 67 (1960), 58–9. Str-B, vol. I, 519, and IV.1, 145–6, point out that ἀρχισυνάγωγος has the same meaning as ἄρχων τῆς συναγωγῆς (Luke's term) and he could thus be one

of the ἄρχοντες (Matthew's less specific term). Cf. W. Schrage, 'ἀρχισυνάγωγος', *TDNT*, vol. VII, 847, n. 26.

159 Perhaps the age twelve is mentioned to clear up the fact that the girl is not as young as the diminutive might lead one to think, in which case it is not extraneous information linking the two stories by the number twelve. Cf. Chadwick, 'The Daughter of Jairus', 313; Klostermann, 'Markusevangelium', 58.

160 *Pace* BAG, 724; H. Greeven, 'προσκυνέω', *TDNT*, vol. VI, 763. On this word as a customary form of respectful greeting, cf. Str-B, vol. I, 519; A–S, 386; LSJ, 1518. Alternatively, it could be Matthew's attempt to introduce a stronger Christological emphasis into the story. That Jesus is 'worshipped' at the outset of the story prepares the reader for what is to follow and focuses on who Jesus is.

161 Mark uses the idiomatic ἐσχάτως ἔχει ('at the point of death'); Luke has αὐτὴ ἀπέθνῃσκεν ('she was dying'). Matthew's ἄρτι ἐτελεύτησεν probably means 'she has just now died', in which case, Matthew, to emphasize the magnitude of Jesus' deed, has compressed the narrative leaving out the later word of the messengers. On the other hand, Chadwick, 'The Daughter of Jairus', 310, suggests that a man full of anxiety might say, 'She is dead by now' and mean the same as ἐσχάτως ἔχει.

162 It was common to lay hands on the sick in Jesus' day; cf. E. Lohse, 'χείρ', *TDNT*, vol. IX, 431 and n. 43; Daube, *NT and Rabbinic Judaism*, 224–33.

163 Luke uses the more dramatic συνπνίγω ('to choke', 'to suffocate'); Mark has the milder συνθλίβω.

164 This is probably a uterine haemorrhage making the woman religiously unclean for that whole period; cf. Marshall, *Luke*, 344. Luke, perhaps because of his profession, chooses to omit the derogatory remark of Mk 5.26; cf. Ellis, *Luke*, 130. Twelve years is probably a round number for an illness of long standing; cf. Taylor, *Mark*, 290.

165 All three accounts say Jesus was wearing a ἱμάτιον which is the square upper garment or mantle on the corners of which any good Jew would have tassels. Cf. Num. 15.38–40, Deut. 22.12, Mk 6.56, Jn 13.4, 19.23, Ac. 18.6. In one of the rare minor agreements of Matthew and Luke against Mark, they add that it was the tassels which the woman touched. Cf. Plummer, *Luke* 235; Manson, *Luke*, 98. If, as is possible, Luke did not use Matthew (or vice versa) at this point, this additional detail in both Gospels may reflect: (1) coincidence of redactional activity; (2) additional information derived from oral sources because the story was still being passed on by word of mouth even after it was written down. The latter possibility cannot simply be dismissed since this addition serves little obvious theological purpose, but tassels were so common that both the First and the Third Evangelists could have added this feature independently based on their knowledge of Jewish customs in order to make the narrative more explicitly 'Jewish'.

166 Mt. 9.21 and Mk 5.28 make it apparent that her faith was tainted by a magical notion about Jesus' garments. Luke tells us that this touch immediately caused the blood flow to cease. In Mark, πηγή is used metaphorically to mean that the flow, not its source, dried up. Cf. W. Michaelis. 'πηγή', *TDNT*, vol. VI, 116, n. 18.

167 C. Neil, 'The Throng and the Touch', *ET* 10 (1898–9), 123. It is faith that distinguishes her touch from the crowds. Cf. Lane, *Mark*, 193.

168 The less formal θύγατερ is used rather than γύναι perhaps to indicate tenderness, or to show that she was now a daughter of faith worthy of respect and concern. Cf. Danker, *Jesus*, 110; Plummer, *Matthew*, 142. Notice how Matthew spares the disciples by omitting Mk 5.31 and seems to indicate in verse 26*b* that the woman was healed not immediately after touching Jesus' garment but after Jesus' pronouncements (contrast Mk 5.29, Lk. 8.44). This and the omission of Mk 5.30 serve to take the magical tinge out of Mk 5.27–30.

169 τρέμουσα in both Mark and Luke. Luke presents the woman as if she was afraid of being noticed (verse 47). All three Evangelists in different ways indicate that her fears were allayed: in Matthew by θάρσει; in Mark by ὕπαγε εἰς εἰρήνην καὶ ἴσθι ὑγιὴς; in Luke more simply by πορεύου εἰς εἰρήνην. The remark in Mark (and with some alteration in Luke) may well be original as it is in part a rendering of לשום טב. Cf. BDF, sec. 206, p. 111; MHT, vol. II, 463.

170 Perhaps we may now speak of a motif in the Gospels where the disciples or such leading figures as Simon the Pharisee or the synagogue ruler in Lk. 13.10–17 are contrasted with women in the area of faith or understanding with the latter cast in a more favourable light. In Mark's account, it is Jesus' disciples who answer Him and reveal an attitude of exasperation with His seemingly stupid question; in Luke it appears to be Peter alone, as representative of the disciples, who responds (καὶ οἱ σὺν αὐτῷ is probably a secondary addition). Cf. Metzger, *TC*, 146. We should note that the role change of this woman (as with the woman of Samaria or the sinner woman of Lk. 7) was from that of outcast to that of a normal member of the community, except in cases where witnessing for or being a disciple of Jesus became involved. Cf. pp. 116–18 on Lk. 8.1–3.

171 There was certainly no doubt in the messengers' or the mourners' minds about the state of the girl when Jesus arrived at her home.

172 Mark's παρακούω ('overhear') is replaced by Luke's ἀκούω. Jesus is not ignoring the messengers' sad news, but is responding to it by telling Jairus to have faith. Cf. BAG, 624; LSJ, 1314.

173 In Mark it is πίστευε ('keep on believing'); in Luke πίστευσον ('believe', 'start believing'). The μὴ φοβοῦ may be redactional. Cf. Mk 6.50, Lk. 2.30, Mt. 28.10, etc.

174 Except Jairus. Luke's account seems to indicate that the mother was standing outside the house when Jesus and the others arrived. Cf. Lk. 8.52. Matthew omits the disciples to focus on Jesus and His work.

175 Oepke, 'γυνή', *TDNT*, vol. I, 784; 'Jesus seems to observe the Jewish proprieties. Thus, he does not approach the bed of Jairus' daughter without witnesses.' Also, He is careful to have adequate witnesses when there is a mixed audience of followers and non-followers lest He be suspected of sorcery or necromancy.

176 αὐλητής means flute player; cf. BAG, 121. On the requirement to hire two flute players for mourning, cf. Str-B, vol. I, 521*a*.

177 Matthew has τὸ κοράσιον (= the Aramaic טליתא). Cf. BDF, sec. 111, p. 61 and sec. 147.3, p. 81. Mark has the same at 5.41*b*; Luke has no extra noun at 8.52*b* and calls the girl παῖς at 8.54.

178 Swete, *Mark*, 102; Taylor, *Mark*, 285–6; C. Armerding, 'The Daughter of Jairus', *BSac* 105 (1948), 56–8, and 'Asleep in the Dust', *BSac* 121 (1964),

156—7. Armerding makes much of the contrast between Jn 11.14 and Mk
5.39 and the use of different words for sleep in the two contexts (καθεύδω,
κομάω) in order to prove that the girl was asleep only. His arguments about
1 Thess. 5.10, however, are unconvincing. The most probable explanation is
that in our text and in 1 Thess. 5.10 καθεύδω is used of actual death, but
death as seen from God's point of view. Cf. Marshall, *Luke*, 347; Taylor,
Mark, 295. What Jesus says and does, as well as the reaction which follows,
seems to indicate that Mark saw it as a resurrection story.

179 There is evidence in rabbinic literature for speaking euphemistically of death
as sleep, but this does not seem to be the case here. Cf. Str-B, vol. I, 523;
H. Balz, 'ὕπνος', *TDNT*, vol. VIII, 548—55; Oepke, 'καθεύδω', *TDNT*, vol.
III, 436.

180 Cf. Marshall, *Luke*, 347; and the Matthean and Marcan accounts at this point.

181 The reading in W, 28, 245, 349, etc. is due to scribal confusion with the
woman's name in Ac. 9.40. Metzger, *TC*, 87. That Mark translates ταλιθά
κοῦμ shows his desire to emphasize that Jesus did not use a magic formulation,
and this distinguishes the narrative from many pagan healing stories. Cf. Kittel,
'λέγω', *TDNT*, vol. IV, 107. It also probably shows his own closeness to the
Aramaic original and his audience's distance, since they apparently needed a
translation. Luke's omission of the transliteration probably reveals that he
or his audience or both are yet a step further removed than Mark from the
original source.

182 Plummer, *Luke*, 238, says, 'He intimates that nature is to resume its usual
course; the old ties and old responsibilities are to begin again.' Faith is as much
a part of (if not the necessary prerequisite to) restoration in the case of
Jairus' daughter as of the Jewess (Mk 5.36, Lk. 8.50). It is only when the
Gospel and its call, not sickness or death divides the physical family that
the family of faith must replace physical family relationships. Here, as in Mk
1.29—31, we have instances where the physical family is restored so that it
can see itself in light of the priorities of faith. Yet neither Jairus nor the
Jewess is urged to give up all and follow Jesus. This evidently was not a
requirement for all who believed in Jesus and His power. What this suggests
is that Jesus as often endorsed a transformed perspective on women's traditional roles and the given family structure, as created new roles for women
in the family of faith.

183 Cf. Swidler, 'Jesus was a Feminist', 177—83; Sanderson, 'Jesus and Women',
19—21.

184 The practice of male—female parallelism in healing is a phenomenon found in
all three Synoptics: Cf. Mk 1.21—8, 29—31, 7.24—30, 31—6; Mt. 8.1—13,
14—15; Lk. 7.1—10, 11—17. The difference in the members in some of the
pairs and the fact that no one pairing is shared by all three writers intimates
that all of the first three Evangelists were interested in presenting this parallelism, not simply in reproducing a parallelism found in their source(s). Luke has
two healings (7.11—17, 13.10—17) of or involving women not found elsewhere in the Gospels. Undoubtedly, Luke has a special desire to draw attention to Jesus' concern for women, but in uniquely Lucan material he may
in part be reproducing a motif found in his special source. Cf. Marshall, *Luke*,
285—6.

185 Cf. Lk. 2.36—8, 18.2—5, 20.47, 21.1—4; Stählin, 'χήρα', *TDNT*, vol. IX, 449—52.

186 Cf. E. Klostermann, 'Das Lukasevangelium' (*HzNT*, vol. V; ed. H. Lietzmann; Tübingen, 1929) 87; Bultmann, *History*, 215; R.H. Fuller, *Interpreting the Miracles* (London, 1963), 64. Bultmann argues that the narrative was created in Hellenistic Jewish circles.

187 Cf. H. Schürmann, 'Das Lukasevangelium' (*HTKzNT*, vol. III; ed. A. Wikenhauser; Freiburg, 1969), 1.404–5.

188 Cf. Schürmann, 'Lukasevangelium', 1.45.

189 Cf. Marshall, *Luke*, 283–5.

190 Cf. Caird, *Luke*, 109–110; 'The resuscitation of the dead is as well attested as any of the other miracles of Jesus. Luke drew this story from his private source L, the story of Jairus' daughter from Mark, and from Q a saying of Jesus which includes the raising of the dead among the achievements of the ministry (7.22).'

191 Schürmann, 'Lukasevangelium', 1.405.

192 Cf. Danker, *Jesus*, 93; Creed, *Luke*, 102–3; Marshall, *Luke*, 284.

193 Cf. Philostratus, *Life of Apollonius of Tyana* 4.45 (LCL I), 456–9, and the other parallels cited in Marshall, *Luke*, 283, most of which post-date both Jesus' life and the time when the Gospels were written. Indeed, it is possible that the Apollonius story is an imitation of a Gospel miracle such as this, but cf. Creed, *Luke*, 102–3.

194 Schürmann, 'Lukasevangelium', 1.405.

195 Contrast Dibelius, *From Tradition*, 75–6, and Schürmann, 'Lukasevangelium', 1.401. Cf. Marshall, *Luke*, 285–6. Schürmann argues that the desire to show Jesus' concern for women is characteristic of Luke's special sources; cf. 7.11–17, 36–50, 8.1–3.

196 Jesus is rejected at home in Nazareth (Lk. 4.18–20) but is accepted in a village that is only a few miles south. Cf. Ellis, *Luke*, 118. Elijah had to go further (Sidon) for such acceptance.

197 The widow's family appears to have been rather prominent in the town since a large crowd went with her in the procession. The widow may have been recognizable to Jesus by her clothing. Cf. Stählin, 'χήρα', *TDNT*, vol. IX, 449, n. 81.

198 Cf. Caird, *Luke*, 109, and these features: (1) he is an only son; (2) she is a widow; (3) Jesus has compassion on her ('επ' αὐτῇ); and (4) He gave the son to his mother.

199 Schweizer, 'υἱός', *TDNT*, vol. VIII, 364.

200 This is an extraordinary command considering that it was customary among the Jews for the grieving process to last thirty days and to involve loud wailing (cf. Lk. 7.13, Jn 11.33) and dramatic expressions of grief, especially on the first three days, which were the days of most intense feeling when expression of irretrievable loss was at its peak. Cf. Danker, *Jesus*, 93; Str-B, vol. IV, 1, 578–607; Edersheim, *Life and Times*, vol. I, 554–8 and II, 316ff; Brown, *John*, 'i-xii', 424; Stählin, 'κοπετός', *TDNT*, vol. III, 845–6.

201 The σορός is probably a bier in this case. Cf. BAG, 766; MM, 581; *pace* LSJ, 1621. By touching the bier, Jesus acquired second grade uncleanness (one day) and by lifting the man and giving him to his mother, first grade uncleanness (seven days). Cf. M. Oholoth 1.1–5, Danby, 649–50, n. 3, 800–1. It appears from M. Mo'ed Katan 3.8, Danby, 211, that stopping a funeral procession or setting down the bier was illegal. Cf. Str-B, vol. I, 522, and II, 161.

202 Νεανίσκε indicates he was between twenty-five and forty years old and probably the head of the household. Cf. Philo, *On the Creation* 105 (LCL I; trans. F.H. Colson and G.H. Whitaker; 1929), 84–7.

203 The response to Jesus' λέγω is καὶ ἤρξατο λαλεῖν – the communication brings life and is the sign of its certain return. Resuscitation, like resurrection, is a sure sign of the presence of the Kingdom and its King actively triumphing over death. Cf. Oepke, 'ἐγείρω', *TDNT*, vol. II, 335.

204 The parallel in Josephus, *The Life* 148 (LCL I), 56–7, suggests it means just fear. Marshall, *Luke*, 286, says, 'Fear ... is the natural reaction of men to a demonstration of unearthly power; but the recognition of the source of that power leads also to a glorifying of God.' Cf. BAG, 871; A–S, 472.

205 'In Palestine and surrounding areas'. Cf. BDF, sec. 218, p. 117; MHT, vol. III, 257. Judea probably means Palestine. Cf. Creed, *Luke*, 104; Plummer, *Luke*, 200–1. περίχωρος means the areas immediately outside Palestine. Cf. Marshall, *Luke*, 287.

4 Women in the ministry of Jesus

1 Additional factors may help explain the amount of attention Mary receives in the Gospels: (1) the important role the traditions involving Mary's relation to Jesus began to play in the early Christian community (notice that Matthew, Luke and John give a significant amount of space to some of these traditions); (2) the important role at least one member of Jesus' family had in the early Christian community (cf. Gal. 1.19, Ac. 1.14, 15.13, etc.); (3) various apologetic purposes, including a defence of Jesus' origins by the First and Third Evangelists.

2 Cf. Bultmann, *John*, 118–19; Dibelius, *From Tradition*, 101–2.

3 Dodd, *Historical Tradition*, 226–7.

4 John McHugh, *The Mother of Jesus in the New Testament* (London, 1975), 388–90; Raymond E. Brown and K.P. Donfried, *et al.*, eds., *Mary in the New Testament* (Philadelphia, 1978), 184–5.

5 Cf. pp. 84–5 of this study.

6 As McHugh, *Mother*, 463–4, recognizes.

7 Cf. Bultmann, *John*, 114–15, who does not see the dialogue as a later addition. Cf. Brown, ed., *Mary in the NT*, 185, n. 416. Brown, *John*, 'i-xii', 103, notes as a viable possibility the option that the Evangelist has excerpted portions of an original dialogue according to what suited his theological purposes.

8 Cf. Dodd, *Historical Tradition*, 223; Schnackenburg, *John*, vol. I, 323–4.

9 Cf. Barrett, *John* (1978), 8, 189; Schnackenburg, *John*, vol. I, 324: 'None of the usual criteria of Johannine style are to be found in it.'

10 Cf. the review of the evidence in Barrett, *John* (1978), 188–9.

11 Cf. Schnackenburg, *John*, vol. I, 324; Bultmann, *John*, 114–15. It might be argued that the lack of indication of a response makes this narrative somewhat unlike many Synoptic miracles, yet there are some Synoptic miracle stories (cf. Mk 7.29–30) that omit any real response to the miracle.

12 Schnackenburg, *John*, vol. I, 340.

13 Brown, *John*, 'i-xii', 101.

14 Dodd, *Historical Tradition*, 225, may be right, however, that: 'The time was not yet when apologists could safely draw parallels between Christ and figures

of pagan mythology.' If so, then the influence may be more indirect, as Dodd suggests, and not a matter of conscious borrowing.

15 I adhere to McHugh's reconstruction (*Mother*, 463) except that I would add verse 4*a* and possibly verse 5 in some form.

16 Cf. Dodd, *Historical Tradition*, 226, for a list of the similarities this narrative has to various Synoptic motifs. It will be noted that there are parallels not only to the narrative ideas, but also to the substance of the dialogue (which is probably another argument against the Johannine creation of verses 4*a* and 5).

17 This is not the place to present arguments for or against Johannine dependence on the Synoptics; suffice it to say that I find the arguments in favour of the independence of John from the Synoptics weightier than those that oppose such a conclusion. Cf. among others, Gardner-Smith, *Saint John and the Synoptics*; D.M. Smith, 'John and the Synoptics: Some Dimensions of the Problem', *NTS* 26 (1980), 425–44; L. Morris, *Studies in the Fourth Gospel*, 18ff; and both of C.H. Dodd's classic studies on John.

18 There are some reasons to doubt that this is a 'hidden life' story since in John it takes place after the record of the encounter of Jesus with John (1.32ff) and also after the gathering of at least some of the disciples (1.35–51, 2.2).

19 Cf. M. Vellanickal, 'The Mother of Jesus in the Johannine Writings', *Biblebhashyam* 3 (4, 1977), 278–96, espec. 279.

20 If it is taken as a question, then the Evangelist is trying to give a reason why Jesus must dissociate Himself from her request, i.e., He has begun His ministry and can only follow the dictates of His heavenly Father. Cf. Brown, ed., *Mary in the NT*, 191, and n. 427; Zerwick, sec. 447, p. 151; A. Vanhoye, 'Interrogation Johannique et exégèse de Cana (Jn 2,4)', *Bib* 55 (1974), 157–67; M.-E. Boismard, *Du Baptême à Cana (Jean 1.19–2.11)* (Lectio Divina XVIII; Paris, 1956), 133–59.

21 Vanhoye, 'Interrogation Johannique', 159–66.

22 Barrett, *John* (1955), 159, citing 12.23, 27, 13.1, and 17.1. Morris, *John*, 181; Dodd, *Interpretation*, 365, however, says that in some sense Jesus' hour has come in part at this juncture.

23 E.J. Goodspeed, 'The Marriage at Cana in Galilee, a Reply', *Int* 1 (1947), 487ff.

24 Cf. KJV, RSV, NASB, NEB, Phillips, NIV, JB, TEV; Barrett, *John* (1955), 159; Brown, *John*, 'i-xii', 99–100. Morris, *John*, 181, points out in n. 22 that the expected answer after a question introduced by οὔπω is 'no'.

25 Goodspeed, 'Marriage at Cana', 487–8; H.E. Dana and J.R. Mantey, *A Manual Grammar of the Greek New Testament* (Toronto, 1927), 85: 'This is an idiom for which we have no exact equivalent in English.'

26 C. Lattey, 'The Semitisms of the Fourth Gospel', *JTS* 20 (1919), 330–6, sees this phrase as Semitic and translates it, 'Let me be', but cites the following parallels: Demosthenes, *Contra Aphobum*, ch. 12; Suetonius, *Lives of the Caesars*, Otho 7; Synesius, *Epistle 105* (this is not really a parallel since it does not involve the dative of possession). Cf. MM, 180, citing BGU IV (14 B.C.); BAG, 216; Robertson, 539, 736; Epictetus, *The Discourses as Reported by Arrian, The Manual and Fragments* 1.4.28 (LCL; trans. W.A. Oldfather, 1928), 309, cf. 1.22.15, 1.27.13, 2.19.19.

27 J.D.M. Derrett, 'Water into Wine', *BZ* 7 (1963), 80–97. The interpretation offered below does not rule out Derrett's point (though Jn 2.9–10 seems to).

It is, however, possible that the Evangelist could be out of touch with what the usual procedure was.

28 Brown, *John*, 'i-xii', 99; Lattey, 'Semitisms', 335–6; Zerwick, sec. 221, p. 70, and n. 7.

29 Cf. the Greek usage cited in n. 26 above; JB, NEB, NIV.

30 Barrett, *John* (1978), 191, notes: 'In the same way Jesus refuses to act upon the instructions of his brothers (7.6).' Yet He does go up to the feast; thus, it is not the advice but the motives involved in their suggestion (cf. 7.4) that is rejected. Brown, *John*, 'i-xii', 102, rightly says that it is Mary's role, not her person or advice, that is being rejected here.

31 Cf. Jn 8.28, 42, 10.18, 25, 29, 30, 12.49, etc. Jesus' negative answer to Mary is in harmony with the Synoptic passages that deal with Mary in relation to Jesus' mission. Cf. Lk. 2.49, Mk 3.33–5, Lk. 11.27–8.

32 Barrett, *John* (1955), 159, rightly says, 'the reply of Jesus seems to mean: "You have no claims upon me – yet"'.

33 The phrase ἡ μήτηρ τοῦ Ἰησοῦ is almost a technical term in John. Mary is never called by her own name, only by this phrase by the Evangelist. This shows that her significance is wholly in relation to her Son. As Brown, *John*, 'i-xii', 98, remarks, ' "the Mother of X" is an honourable title for a woman who has been fortunate enough to bear a son'. It is, however, a title that implies no veneration of Mary's person, but focuses on her role. Cf. Michaelis, 'μήτηρ', *TDNT*, vol. IV, 643. The Fourth Evangelist is usually very explicit in his use of names with the exception of two people – Mary and the beloved disciple.

34 A–S, 96; cf. Barrett, *John* (1955), 159; LSJ, 363.

35 Cf. Brown, *John*, 'i-xii', 99; Morris, *John*, 180.

36 Oepke, 'γυνή', *TDNT*, vol. I, 777, states, 'When Jesus addresses His mother in this way ... it excludes the filial relationship.' Cf. Morris, *John*, 181, n. 20.

37 Cf. McHugh, *Mother*, 365–9.

38 There are several textual variants at 2.12 that are of significance for our discussion of whether or not Jesus was Mary's only child. The two second-century Bodmer papyri and B omit 'his' before brothers, and more significantly Codex Sinaiticus and some early versions omit 'and his disciples', while A, f¹, 565, 1241 favour the single 'he stayed'. Was there a pre-Gospel form of this Cana story that involved only Jesus and His family, or were the 'brothers' originally disciples, and someone added 'and his disciples' thinking the brothers were blood brothers? Cf. Brown, ed., *Mary in the NT*, 194–6. Barrett, *John* (1978), 194, thinks 'his disciples' is an addition that arose to emphasize that the mother and brothers stayed in Capernaum while Jesus left to begin His ministry. This may explain why ἔμεινεν is read for ἔμειναν in some mss. For a fuller discussion, cf. Brown, 'The Problem of Historicity in John', *CBQ* 24 (1962), 1–14. If we accept the best attested text, then John, like the Synoptics, associates Mary with Jesus' brothers. Further, in John, as in the Synoptics, Mary and the brothers are not numbered among Jesus' travelling disciples. There is, then, a uniform picture in all the Gospels of the separation of Jesus' family from His disciples. There may be a slight hint in Jn 2.3 that Mary has some faith in Jesus, whereas Jn 7.5 says the brothers did not believe in Him during the ministry. Cf. Brown, ed., *Mary in the NT*, 195–6; and A. Meyer and W. Bauer, 'The Relatives of Jesus', *NTAp*, vol. I, 418–32.

39   Cf. Brown, *John*, 'i-xii', 103: 'it must be honestly noted that the Evangelist
      does nothing to stress the power of Mary's intercession at Cana ... Mary's
      final words, "Do whatever he tells you," stress the sovereignty of Jesus and
      not Mary's impetration.'

40   On Mary as the archetypal woman, cf. McHugh, *Mother*, 373–8; Brown, ed.,
      Mary in the NT, 189–90; Vellanickal, 'Mother of Jesus', 286–7. 'Why ...
      should "Woman" be symbolically more important in John when addressed to
      the mother of Jesus than when addressed to the Samaritan woman or to Mary
      Magdalene?' (Brown, ed., *Mary in the NT*, 190). If such typology is present in
      our text, then it is not developed to any degree. The use of γύναι to refer to
      Mary 'may mean that he places no special emphasis on her physical mother-
      hood' (Brown, ed., *Mary in the NT*, 189). But there is also no attempt to
      divorce Mary's sexual identity as woman from her potential discipleship status.

41   J.D. Crossan, 'Mark and the Relatives of Jesus', *NovT* 15 (1973), 81–113, is
      probably wrong to argue that 3.20 goes with what precedes rather than with
      what follows.

42   Cf. Brown, ed., *Mary in the NT*, 55–6.

43   Cf. McHugh, *Mother*, 237, n. 3; Brown, ed., *Mary in the NT*, 56. This structure
      parallels οἱ παρ' αὐτοῦ with Jesus' family (3.21, 31–5) and perhaps compares
      their motives with those of the scribes (3.21*b*, 22*a*, *b*).

44   Taylor, *Mark*, 235; Bultmann, *History*, 50.

45   Bultmann, *History*, 29, suggests 3.20–1, 31–5 belong together; Dibelius,
      From Tradition, 37, is probably wrong to contend that 3.20–1 was written
      as preparation for verses 31–5.

46   Cf. Lane, *Mark*, 138, n. 76; *NTGNA*, 91.

47   BDF, sec. 342, p. 176, 'they are attached to him'.

48   Metzger, *TC*, 81; Oepke, 'ἐξίστημι', *TDNT*, vol. II, 459, n. 2.

49   As Crossan, 'Mark', 85, points out, the οἱ παρ' αὐτοῦ cannot refer to the
      Twelve because αὐτοὺς of 3.20 can hardly be the ἀκούσαντες of 3.21, nor can
      they be Jesus' followers in a wider sense because the ὄχλος of 3.20 is presum-
      ably the ὄχλος of 3.32, and these are approved as οἱ περὶ αὐτόν in 3.32, 34.
      Pace H. Wansbrough, 'Mark iii.21 – Was Jesus out of his mind?' *NTS* 18 (2,
      1972), 233–5. Cf. D. Wenham, 'The Meaning of Mk. iii.21', *NTS* 21 (2, 1975),
      295–300.

50   Especially Papyrus Grenfell II, 36, 9 – οἱ παρ' ἡμῶν πάντες – 'all our family'.
      Cf. J.H. Moulton, 'Mark iii.21'. *ET* 20 (1908–9), 476; MM, 479; Moule,
      I-B, 52 (2nd ed. only).

51   Lane, *Mark*, 139; Cranfield, *Mark*, 133; Taylor, *Mark*, 236.

52   McHugh, *Mother*, 238–9, attempts to limit the subject of ἔλεγον to Jesus'
      'foster' brothers. Cf. C.H. Turner, 'Marcan Usage: Notes, Critical and Exegeti-
      cal, on the Second Gospel', *JTS* 25 (1924), 383–6; MHT, vol. III, 292. Brown,
      Birth, 520, however, accepts the probability that Mark includes Mary among
      'his own', who thought Jesus was beside Himself. As Crossan, 'Mark', 85, says,
      even if ἔλεγον is impersonal, the οἱ παρ' αὐτοῦ concur in the judgment that
      Jesus is beside Himself enough to act on it. The parallelism between ἔλεγον
      in verses 21, 22 suggests that it is 'his own' that is the subject of this verb in
      verse 21. So Brown, ed., *Mary in the NT*, 57; cf. J. Lambrecht, 'The Relatives
      of Jesus in Mark', *NovT* 16 (4, 1974), 248–9.

53   Cranfield, *Mark*, 124; cf. McHugh, *Mother*, 238, n. 9.

54   As Crossan, 'Mark', 85, notes, κρατέω in 3.21 probably does not refer back
       to the ὄχλος of 3.21, nor should it be taken in a metaphorical sense here. The
       meaning probably is 'to seize', or 'to apprehend' and take into custody. Cf.
       BAG, 449; MM, 358. The reason why Jesus' family was going to seize Him is
       explained by the γάρ clause – they said ἐξέστη. The meaning of ἐξίστημι in
       this context would seem to be 'out of control', or 'beside himself', rather than
       'insane'. But cf. BAG, 276; LSJ, 595; Zerwick, sec. 4, p. 2; to Oepke, 'ἐξίστημι',
       TDNT, vol. II, 459; W.C. van Unnik, 'Jesus the Christ', *NTS* 8 (2, 1962),
       101–16.
55   Brown, ed., *Mary in the NT*, 58.
56   Cf. McHugh, *Mother*, 236–7. The real contrast is between physical kinship
       standing without and some of the spiritual kinship which is closer to Jesus
       literally and spiritually.
57   The suggestion in Brown, *Birth*, 371–8, that Lk. 8.21 is in praise of the faith
       of the members of Jesus' physcial family is not convincing. Reading Lk. 8.21
       resumptively, though grammatically possible, is improbable in view of the fact
       that even Mary is depicted by Luke as misunderstanding Jesus (2.48–50).
       There is no preparation for a reversal of this fact before 8.21. Brown's view
       fails to explain why even in Luke there is no indication that Jesus complies
       with his family's wishes for an audience, and why Luke makes a mild contrast
       between the physical family standing ἔξω (8.20), and the crowd who are
       implied to be the hearers of the word since they are listening to Jesus. Rather,
       in Lk. 8.21 we have an abstract statement that Jesus' spiritual family are those
       who hear and do God's will. Only this view comports with various other Lucan
       texts (cf. 12.49–53, 14.26).
58   Cranfield, *Mark*, 134–5; Lane, *Mark*, 139.
59   *Pace* McHugh, *Mother*, 238; with Taylor, *Mark*, 236.
60   Cranfield, *Mark*, 145; Lane, *Mark*, 147.
61   Danker, *Jesus*, 105, sees in Lk.8.19–21 a continued criticism of Mary (cf.
       2.48–51), working out the theme of the sword piercing Mary and the sword
       of Jesus' rejection of her. This theme is interrelated to the theme of true
       blessedness at 11.27–8. Verses 27–8 may not deny that parenthood is a
       blessing, but rather affirm by hyperbolic contrast that in comparison to the
       blessedness of faith in action, all other forms of blessedness pale in significance.
       Cf. Brown, ed., *Mary in the NT*, 172.
62   Bultmann, *History*, 30–1. If Mark had received a saying, it could have had
       differences in the key clauses from the Oxyrhynchus form, but we have no
       evidence that provides a basis for this conjecture, and Bultmann's argument
       is that the scene in Mark 6 was derived from the Oxyrhynchus form. Cf. now
       the Coptic Gospel of Thomas.
63   Dibelius, *From Tradition*, 110, cf. 43.
64   Cranfield, *Mark*, 192.
65   The phrase ἐν τοῖς συγγενεῦσιν αὐτοῦ καὶ ἐν τῇ οἰκίᾳ αὐτοῦ which follows
       ἐν τῇ πατρίδι αὐτοῦ in Mk 6.4, which all mss. except א,* have, refers to Jesus'
       relatives in a more general sense. However, Taylor, *Mark*, 301, says that many
       mss., but *not* B, Θ, 13, fam[1] and fam[13] pc have συγγενέσιν, not συγγενεῦσιν
       (cf. *Synopsis*, 195). The three part grouping of those among whom Jesus has
       no honour is an ever narrowing circle – His town, His kinsmen, His own house.
       It is this last phrase, ἐν τῇ οἰκίᾳ αὐτοῦ, unless it is a reference to the synagogue,

which makes clear that Jesus' immediate family (Mary and the brothers and sisters) are among those who do not honour or understand Him properly. As Crossan, 'Mark', 103, notes, 'own relations'/'own house' is redundant if both mean those associated with Jesus' family. Probably, Mark intends to give us a list of who are ἐν τῇ οἰκίᾳ αὐτοῦ at 6.3. Cf. Taylor, *Mark*, 301.

66   Cf. Str-B, vol. II, 10–11; Cranfield, *Mark*, 195–6.

67   Cf. E. Stauffer, 'Jeschu Ben Mirjam – Kontroversgeschichtliche Anmerkungen zu Mk 6:3', *Neotestamentica et Semitica: Studies in Honour of Matthew Black*, 119–28; Marshall, *Luke*, 186. Normally, when one was called the 'son of a woman' in a Jewish context, it did have an insulting connotation. Cf. J.K. Russell, '"The Son of Mary" (Mark vi.3)', *ET* 60 (1948–9), 195. The insulting connotation is supported by Jn 8.41, 9.29 which suggest there were questions about Jesus' origins at least as early as the composition of the Fourth Gospel. There is evidence that there was a polemic against Mary among the rabbis. Cf. Str-B, vol. I, 41–2, 147. There was a Jewish legal principle which may have been extant in Jesus' day – 'A man is illegitimate when he is called by his mother's name, for a bastard has no father.' Cf. E. Stauffer, *Jerusalem und Rom im Zeitalter Jesu Christi* (Berne/Munich, 1957), 118, 158, n. 62. Stauffer shows that in the extra-biblical history of the phrase 'son of Mary', it is used almost exclusively in a polemical sense. But cf. McHugh, *Mother*, 271ff; H.K. McArthur, 'Son of Mary', *NovT* 15 (1, 1973), 38–58; Brown, *Birth*, 541.

68   Perhaps the earliest evidence of the respect Jesus' family commanded in the Church is the rather abrupt ascendancy of James to a position of importance in the Jerusalem Christian community (cf. Gal. 1.19, Ac. 12.17, 15.3) and this after we are told that Jesus' brothers did not believe in Him during His earthly ministry (Jn 7.5). Ac. 1.14 and such documents as the Proto-Evangelium of James presuppose a growing reverence for the family during the first and second centuries.

69   Lk. 4.16–30 is only partially parallel, and it omits the names of the brothers. The lists of names in Matthew and Mark are nearly identical save that Matthew reverses Mark's order of the names of Simon and Judas. Also, Mark has a Hellenized form of Joseph (Joses), while Matthew gives the name in its more familiar form. Cf. J.B. Lightfoot, *St. Paul's Epistle to the Galatians* (London, 1896), 268, n. 1, to McHugh, *Mother*, 201, n. 4.

70   The following works are some of the most helpful on this matter, and should be consulted for a full presentation of the various views. Space prohibits us from giving *more* than a few reasons for rejecting all but the Helvidian view, and for accepting that same view. A. Meyer and W. Bauer, 'The Relatives of Jesus', *NTAp*, vol. I, 418–32; McHugh, *Mother*, 200–54; J.B. Mayor, *The Epistle of St. James* (London, 1910), v-lv; Lightfoot, *Galatians*, 252–91; J.H. Ropes, *The Epistle of St. James* (ICC; Edinburgh, 1916), 53–74; J. Blinzler, *Die Brüder und Schwestern Jesu* (Stüttgart, 1967); S. Chapman, 'The Brothers of the Lord', *JTS* 7 (1905–6), 412–33; H. von Soden, 'ἀδελφός', *TDNT*, vol. I, 144–6.

71   The prominence of this view in Church history after Jerome is largely due to the fact that he and Augustine both advocated it strongly, though in their day it was still a matter of debate. Cf. Lightfoot, *Galatians*, 289–90; Blinzler, *Die Brüder*, 130–44.

72 This view is not without patristic support, in the main from Tertullian. It is interesting, however, that before Helvidius it was held by the Antidicomarianitae in Agaria or Arabia, by Bonosus in Sardica, by Jovinian in Milan. This may be significant in that out of the way places are usually the last to relinquish ancient views. These places also represent good geographical spread which tells in favour of the antiquity of this tradition. Cf. Ropes, *James*, 54–5.

73 The first clear statements of this view are in the Gospel of the Hebrews, the Gospel of Peter, and the Proto-Evangelium of James. The later patristic support Lightfoot cites is little more than the endorsement or embellishment of the statements of these apocryphal works or the traditions behind them, except perhaps for the case of Clement of Alexandria. Cf. Lightfoot, *Galatians*, 274, 291.

74 It is possible that there is one example in the NT (Mk 6.17–18) where ἀδελφός means 'step-brother'. Cf. Brown, ed., *Mary in the NT*, 65, n. 121. The evidence of Gen. 14.14–16, Lev. 10.4, 1 Chron. 23.21–2, where the LXX is influenced by the usage in Hebrew of the term אח (which may refer to full or half-brothers or even more distant degrees of kinship), may or may not be relevant to our investigation. It must first be shown that Semitic influence is probable in the NT texts we are investigating. MM, 8–9 (cf. 42) point out that ἀδελφός is sometimes used wrongly in the LXX of relatives other than full brothers. The evidence Blinzler, *Die Brüder*, 44–5, cites from Josephus does not support his case. In Josephus, *Antiquities* 1.207 (LCL I) 102–3, an obvious deception is involved; in *Jewish War* 6.356–7 (LCL II) 478–9, Blinzler wrongly assumes that 'brothers' is equated with 'kinsmen'. Rather, it appears that Josephus means that the brothers involved *are* kinsmen, but from this it does not follow that Josephus means kinsmen by brothers. There is little or no evidence that ἀδελφοί was used to mean kinsmen in Koine Greek. The evidence cited by J.J. Collins, 'The Brethren of the Lord and Two Recently Published Papyri', *TS* 5 (1944), 484–94, of two Egyptian papyri (dated between 134 and 89 B.C.) shows that such usage was possible but, as Collins admits, probably Semitic influence was involved. Lightfoot, *Galatians*, 261, is right in saying, 'But it is scarcely conceivable that the cousins of anyone should be commonly and indeed exclusively styled his brothers by indifferent persons; still less, that one cousin in particular should be singled out and described in this loose way, "James the Lord's brother".'

75 Cf. Lightfoot, *Galatians*, 248, n. 1, 259–61; McHugh, *Mother*, 226, and n. 9; Chapman, 'Brothers', 412. It should be noted that Paul is probably using the term 'apostle' in Gal. 1.19 in a broader sense than of the Twelve or, alternatively, εἰ μή may mean 'but only'.

76 Lightfoot, *Galatians*, 262; McHugh, *Mother*, 231.

77 Cf. Plummer, *Luke*, 224; McHugh, *Mother*, 210.

78 McHugh, 221.

79 McHugh, 210–22.

80 McHugh, 254.

81 McHugh, 239, n. 11.

82 McHugh, 239ff.

83 Robertson, 285; Michaelis, 'μήτηρ', *TDNT*, vol. IV, 642.

84 McHugh, 240, 248.

85 McHugh, 241.

86 McHugh, 246–7.

87 Note that in Jn 7.1–12 these brothers are apparently old enough to go up to the Feast of Tabernacles on their own (cf. 1 Cor. 15.7). de Vaux, *Ancient Israel*, 22, remarks on how small the homes were and adds that even in OT times we rarely hear of a parent surrounded by more than his or her un-married children (Neh. 7.4). It appears that these brothers would have been at least 18–20 years old and probably married. Cf. Moore, *Judaism*, vol. II, 119.

88 Here the whole argument turns on the crowd's knowledge of who these brothers, sisters and parents are. Their argument has no force if these are foster brothers, for Jesus could not be presumed to be the same as them since they had different parents. Nor could they be said to be ordinary in the same way. We note that the ὧδε probably means Jesus' sisters are not merely in town but among the audience. Cf. Schrage, 'συναγωγή', *TDNT*, vol. VII, 818. This makes Jesus' remarks in Mk 6.4 more pointed. The contrast here and in Mk 3.35 is not nearly so forceful if in fact these are not Jesus' actual sisters and brothers.

89 If the usual Protestant exegesis of Mt. 1.25 and Lk. 1.34 is correct, then this also militates against both the Epiphanian and McHugh's view. Possibly, but not probably, the πρωτότοκος in Lk. 2.7 implies that Mary had further children. Cf. Ropes, *James*, 54; Mayor, *James*, xiv-xv; McHugh, *Mother*, 203ff. The view advocated by McHugh was rejected by Lightfoot, *Galatians*, 254 and n. 3.

90 If the children in Mk 6.3 were those of Mary of Clopas, then why are they with Mary, Joseph's wife? Cf. BAG, 523; Brown, ed., *Mary in the NT*, 71–2.

91 McHugh, *Mother*, 205; Lightfoot, *Galatians*, 258–9, finds nearly twelve Josephs in the NT, two James' among the Twelve alone, while in Josephus we have nineteen Josephs.

92 Taylor, *Mark*, 249.

93 Cf. Barrett, *John* (1978), 551; R. Schnackenburg, *Das Johannesevangelium* (HTKzNT IV; ed. A. Wikenhauser and A. Vögtle; Freiburg, 1975), vol. III, 323.

94 Cf. Brown, ed., *Mary in the NT*, 207.

95 Cf. n. 103 below on the objections raised in Barrett, *John* (1978), 550–2, on the historicity of this material. Dodd, *Historical Tradition*, 138, n. 2, mentions as possible that 'the Evangelist had a form of Passion tradition which, like those of Mark and Luke, included a note of the presence of women, and their names, but was not, as were theirs, associated with the *testimonia* from Ps. xxxvii.12, lxxxvii.9.'

96 Cf. Bultmann, *John*, 673, n. 2; Brown, ed., *Mary in the NT*, 209, n. 463: 'he is the human witness par excellence for the Johannine community (19:35, 21:24) and how do we explain this emphasis if the evangelist knew that the beloved disciple really was not present at any of the events he is supposed to have witnessed?' It is also possible, though not probable, that the one referred to in 19.35 is not the beloved disciple, but someone else.

97 It is most probable that He would make such provisions for His mother especially if she was a widow, in view of His teaching on the matter of corban. Cf. pp. 12–13 of this study.

98   Cf. Schnackenburg, *Johannesevangelium*, vol. III, 320–1; Brown, *John*, 'xiii-
     xxi' (1970), 922.

99   Possibly the list was originally mentioned after the death of Jesus (cf. the
     Synoptics) and the Evangelist has moved it forward to prepare for verses 26–
     9 (Bultmann, *John*, 671). Dodd, *Historical Tradition*, 127–8, points out how
     this pericope breaks the unities of time and place (cf. 19.27, 35) and looks
     like an insertion. This counts against Johannine creation of verses 26–7. Cf.
     Barrett, *John* (1978), 547–8: 'The probability must remain that John was
     using what was already in his day traditional material.' Was this tradition
     originally about an unnamed disciple and Mary, and the Evangelist has labelled
     that disciple, 'the beloved'? Cf. Dodd, *Interpretation*, 428.

100 Cf. Schnackenburg, *Johannesevangelium*, vol. III, 319–28; Brown, ed., *Mary
     in the NT*, 209–10.

101 Certainly the μετὰ τοῦτο εἰδὼς ὁ Ἰησοῦς ὅτι ἤδη πάντα τετέλεσται in 19.28
     points in that direction. Cf. Brown, *John*, 'xiii-xxi', 911; Stauffer, *Jesus*, 138.

102 Two is not a valid option for it involves identifying the sister of the mother
     of Jesus with Mary of Clopas, which is not Johannine. Cf. Brown, *John*,
     'xiii-xxi', 905–6. The following considerations argue against seeing three
     women: (1) such a view requires having two Marys in one family, cf. BAG,
     437; (2) it is often the case that names are presented in pairs connected by
     καί when listed in the Gospels, cf. Mt. 10.2–4, Lk. 6.14–16, G.E. Evans,
     'The Sister of the Mother of Jesus', *RevExp* 44 (1947), 475; (3) the Synoptics
     testify to three women other than Mother Mary at the Crucifixion; (4) to
     maintain that there were only three women one must resort to a rather un-
     natural punctuation at 19.25 and ignore the two καίs which divide the names
     into two pairs, cf. B. Schwank, 'Das Christusbild im Zweiten Teil des Johannes-
     evangeliums (XIX) – Die ersten Gaben des erhöhten Königs: Jo 19,23–30',
     SS 29 (7, 1964), 299.

103 Cf. Stauffer, *Jesus*, 136, 229 note for p. 136, 1.10. The example of R. Eleazar
     b. Shimeon (*ca* A.D. 180) standing and weeping near a crucified man may be
     cited (cf. Str-B, vol. II, 580), and compared to our text (Schwank, 'Das
     Christusbild', 298). The objections of Barrett, *John* (1978), 551, to Stauffer's
     view, based mainly on the military requirements of the execution of a rebel
     king and on Josephus, *Life* 420–1 (LCL), 154–5, are unconvincing for the
     following reasons: (1) E. Schürer, *The History of the Jewish People in the
     Age of Jesus Christ (175 B.C. – A.D. 135)* vol. I (Edinburgh, 1973), 370–2,
     does not make clear how the military requirements of the execution of a rebel
     king affected the standing of friends or relatives near the cross; (2) the text
     being cited from Josephus does not say anything about permission being
     required to approach a crucified person, though it may imply that permission
     was required to get someone released from his cross (these are two different,
     though not unrelated, matters); (3) the evidence cited by Stauffer and Str-B
     argues against Barrett's view (J.T. Gittin 48c and Tosephta Gittin 7.1 (cf.
     Lane, *Mark*, 576) may refer to mass executions, not to public or state ex-
     ecutions where there would be guards); (4) it is not certain that what applied
     to men crucified along a roadside would apply also to someone crucified just
     outside Jerusalem in the presence of Roman guards. Cf. Josephus, *Life* 420
     (LCL), 154 (ὡς ἐκεῖθεν ὑποστρέφων εἶδον ... probably implies it is not in a
     city). The very presence of the guards in Jesus' case meant there was no need

to prohibit or hinder a few grief stricken women (and one man?) from being near His cross. They would not be perceived by armed guards as a real threat.

104 Though it is possible, as Professor Barrett has suggested to me, that γύναι may be used because the term 'mother' is about to be used in a different sense, this does not explain its use in John 2. It is better to find an answer that explains the use of γύναι in both John 2 and 19.

105 Stauffer, *Jesus*, 138. Thus, what I am suggesting is that the Fourth Evangelist has not simply drawn out the implications of what actually happened at the cross, but reinterpreted this tradition to serve his own theological purposes. The Evangelist appears to have transformed a simple and historically credible narrative about Jesus' care for His mother into a pregnant statement about Mary and about man and woman beneath the cross.

106 On the revelatory formula, cf. Jn 1.29, 36, 47; 1 Sam. 9.17; Brown, *John*, 'xiii-xxi', 923. Was this originally an adoption or testamentary disposition formula modified by the Evangelist? Cf. Stauffer, *Jesus*, 138; Barrett, *John* (1978), 552.

107 Cf. M. de Goedt, 'Un schème de révélation dans la Quatrième Évangile', *NTS* 8 (1961–2), 145–9.

108 A. Feuillet, 'L'heure de la femme (Jn 16,21) et l'heure de la Mère de Jésus (Jn 19,25–27)', *Bib* 47 (3, 1966), 361–80, attempts to link Jn 16.21 and 19.25–7. But Mary's hour of pain is unlike that of the disciples, for hers is an hour of arrival, theirs an hour of departure, dispersion and grief. Jn 16.21 is a general metaphor, not a veiled allusion to Mary.

109 The phrase τὰ ἴδια can mean 'his house', or 'his home', or even 'his own property and/or possession'. Cf. BAG, 370; LSJ, 818; MM, 298, who translate εἰς τὰ ἴδια as 'into, among his own'. 'Home' then perhaps is not what the phrase usually connotes, but rather 'one's own (something)', the something being determined by the context. It is probably best to translate all the uses of τὰ ἴδια in John the same way, i.e., 'his own house', with the understanding that the phrase is used in a broader sense in 1.11a and 16.32 (where it is a dwelling), and in the narrow sense in 19.27. McHugh, *Mother*, 278, is probably incorrect in saying that εἰς τὰ ἴδια means 'as a spiritual possession of (his) heart'.

110 Barrett, *John* (1955), 458–9.

111 Vellanickal, 'Mother of Jesus', 288.

112 Schwank, 'Das Christusbild', 302.

113 Cf. Jn 1.35–9, 18. 15–16, 19.25–7, 13.23, 20.2, 6–9, 21.7, 20; Vellanickal, 'Mother of Jesus', 289; Brown, ed., *Mary in the NT*, 217.

114 Brown, ed., *Mary in the NT*, 212.

115 Cf. Schwank, 'Das Christusbild', 302.

116 It is pointed out rightly in Brown, ed., *Mary in the NT*, 213–14, that there is no mention of 'brother' in 19.26–7.

117 Brown, ed., *Mary in the NT*, 215–16.

118 To be a spiritual mother to or in the Church and to be 'mother Church' are two different things. Brown, *John*, 'xiii-xxi', 925, states, 'the concept of the personal spiritual motherhood of Mary makes its appearance ... in the 9th century in the East with George of Nicomedia'. If seeing Mary as Daughter of Zion is dependent on linking Jn 16.21 and 19.25–7 (cf McHugh, *Mother*, 384–5), then this is unlikely (cf. Brown, *John*, 'xiii-xxi', 925–7). The same

difficulty faces the Eve symbolism and it becomes even less probable if there is no (or no primary) reference to Mary in Revelation 12. Cf. Brown, ed., *Mary in the NT*, 216–17.

119 Cf. Gospel of Bartholomew IV.5, *NTAp*, vol. I, 495. Perhaps we may speak of the Fourth Evangelist's tendency to depict women as 'first class' disciples when we consider the mention of: (1) Jesus' love for Mary and Martha (11.5, cf. 13.1 and pp. 104–6 of this study); (2) the Evangelist's portrayal of Mary Magdalene as first witness of the risen Jesus and as a sheep who knows the Shepherd's voice when she is called by name (cf. 20.16, 10.2–4); (3) the Samaritan woman who believes and to some extent bears witness (John 4); (4) Jesus' mother as a model with the beloved disciple of male and female members of Jesus' true family (cf. 19.25–7). All of this becomes significant when (with Brown, 'Roles of Women', 699) we recognize that disciple is 'the primary Johannine category'.

120 It is probable that πάντα τετέλεσται alone refers to what precedes and the ἵνα clause goes with what follows as an example of a final clause which precedes. So MHT, vol. III, 344; BDF, sec. 478, 253.

121 M.N. Maxey, 'Beyond Eve and Mary – A Theological Alternative for Women's Liberation', *Dialogue* 10 (1971), 112–22, advocates that Mary's role as mother is not to be seen as the norm or model for women believers today. As Brown, *Birth*, 342, rightly points out, Mary's blessedness in the Gospels is derived in part because the fruit of her womb is blessed. This reveals her subordination, as Brown notes. One must also say that Mary's faith is blessed and is in fact the prerequisite to her being the Mother of Jesus.

122 Cf. Danker, *Jesus*, 133; Marshall, *Luke*, 450. Luke is progressing from 'love your neighbour' to 'love your God with your whole heart', and then on to an example of how devotion to God is manifested by the Lord's Prayer.

123 So Bultmann, *History*, 33; Marshall, *Luke*, 451.

124 Cf. Bultmann, *History*, 33, 60–1, 67.

125 I take it that John is not dependent on Luke here and vice versa. Cf. Creed, *Luke*, 154, on the characterization; cf. p. 112–13 of this study.

126 Cf. Dibelius, *From Tradition*, 293, who speaks of Mary and Martha as holy persons and intimates that we have a legend here which had its final basis in historical reality.

127 Cf. n. 148 below.

128 Cf. Jeremias, *NT Theology*, 226; Marshall, *Luke*, 451. Luke's placing of the story indicates that he is mainly including it because of its spiritual, rather than social, implications. Cf. n. 122 above.

129 The shorter reading (αὐτόν) is to be preferred, for there is no good reason why 'into her house' would have been omitted if it was a part of the original form of our text. Cf. Metzger, *TC*, 153; Marshall, *Luke*, 451–2; contrast 9.53.

130 Plummer, *Luke*, 290; Caird, *Luke*, 149–50.

131 Note the imperfect tense – ἤκουεν. Cf. Plummer, *Luke*, 291.

132 *Pace* Ellis, *Luke*, 162; cf. Plummer, *Luke*, 291.

133 We find indications of this in Ac. 22.3 and possibly Lk. 8.35 (cf. verse 39). Cf. Aboth 1.4, Danby, 446; Tanhuma Genesis Bereshith 2a, ML, *Anthology*, 474; Grassi, 'Women's Liberation', 27–8; Brennan, 'Women in the Gospels', 292–3. In rabbinic Judaism, a woman was expected to stay at home to mind

family affairs so that her sons and husband could study. Cf. B. T. Berakoth
17*a*, Cohen, 112.

134 Cf. pp. 9–10 of this study.

135 Such behaviour on Jesus' part may be one reason why Jesus may have been
thought to have loose sexual morals. Cf. Mt. 9.11; Ellis, *Luke*, 162. It is not
clear what happened to the other disciples (verse 38, αὐτούς) but it appears
that only Jesus entered the house (ὑπεδέξατο αὐτόν, cf. Metzger, *TC*, 153).
Possibly, the plural αὐτούς is Luke's redactional work to fit this story into
the context of Jesus' travelling with and teaching of His disciples.

136 Cf. p. 67 of this study. B. T. Kid. 70*a*, Nashim VIII, Kiddushin, 335–6;
Swidler, *Women in Judaism*, 125. In Jn 11.19 we find the phrase πρὸς τὴν
Μάρθαν καὶ Μαριάμ. The variant reading, τὰς περὶ Μάρθαν, though it has
some substantial support in p[45] vid and A, is rather un-Johannine in style
and probably secondary. The preferred reading probably refers to Mary,
Martha and their household (servants, friends, relatives). Certainly, the scribes
who altered it to the more elegant τὰς περὶ Μάρθαν thought so. Cf. Metzger,
TC, 234. If we may take this as an accurate statement, then it probably was
not necessary for Martha to prepare and serve this meal; Martha's deed then
would have been a labour of love.

137 The δέ in verse 40 seems to be adversative, contrasting Mary and Martha;
thus, 'distracted' is probably the appropriate word to translate περισπάω.
Martha is pulled in several directions at once. Cf. BAG, 656; Moule, *I-B*, 62.
The word διακονία is used in its common sense of providing hospitality. Cf.
BAG, 183. The πολλήν here prepares us for the πολλά in verse 41 and the
contrast there between many and one.

138 Cf. Caird, *Luke*, 150; Danker, *Jesus*, 133.

139 The repetition of the name may express affection or concern (cf. Lk. 22.31;
BDF, sec. 493.1, p. 261), or even reproach (cf. Ac. 9.4). θορυβάξῃ not τυρβάξῃ
is the correct reading here; cf. Metzger, *TC*, 153–4.

140 I owe the idea for this chart to A. Baker, 'One Thing Necessary', *CBQ* 27
(1965), 127; cf. M. Augsten, 'Lukanische Miszelle', *NTS* 14 (1967–8), 581–3.

141 Marshall, *Luke*, 453.

142 The longer readings seem largely confined to the area of Alexandria (B, S,
and other less important mss.), while the shorter readings are attested in
Egypt, Antioch, Caesarea and Syria. Cf. Baker, 'One Thing Necessary', 131.

143 Cf. the apparatus in *UBSGNT*, 254–5; cf. Baker, 'One Thing Necessary',
130.

144 For the longer reading: *Synopsis* (1967); *NTGNA*; Ellis, *Luke*, 162; Danker,
Jesus, 133; Plummer, *Luke*, 292; NIV (margin); RSV (margin); JB; G. Schrenk,
'ἐκλέγομαι', *TDNT*, vol. IV, 172. For the shorter reading: *UBSGNT*; Caird,
Luke, 149; RS, *Translator's Luke*, 426–7; Phillips; TEV; NEB; RSV; KJV;
E. Stauffer, 'εἷς', *TDNT*, vol. II, 435. For the omissions: Creed, *Luke*, 154
(with hesitation); Manson, *Luke*, 132. On the evidence of the Fathers, cf.
Baker, 'One Thing Necessary', 131–5.

145 Tertullian and Cyrian are silent; cf. Baker, 'One Thing Necessary', 134.

146 Augsten, 'Lukanische Miszelle', 581–2.

147 Baker, 'One Thing Necessary', 136.

148 Ellis, *Luke*, 162; Caird, *Luke*, 149. The copyists who decided in favour
of the longer reading or option five may have been of the persuasion that

stressing only one thing as necessary was not being single-minded, but simple-minded.

149   Creed, *Luke*, 149–50; Plummer, *Luke*, 292.
150   Danker, *Jesus*, 133.
151   The conjecture of Wellhausen that ἧς should be substituted for ἥτις is rejected by MHT, vol. II, 435. It is the portion, not Mary, that is not to be taken away. Cf. MHT, vol. I, 92; Robertson, 728.
152   Caird, *Luke*, 149–50; Plummer, *Luke*, 292.
153   *Pace* F. Jeffrey, 'Martha and Mary', *ET* 29 (1917–18), 186–8; cf. Robertson, 810.
154   F. Stagg, 'Biblical Perspectives on the Single Person', *RevExp* 74 (1, 1977), 14, says, 'There may be significance in the fact that their marital status is a non-issue in the Gospels. This does not imply indifference to marriage, but it does mean that individuals have identity apart from marriage.' Jesus' teaching on eunuchs (Mt. 19.10–12) may have had the effect of allowing women to have a choice in regard to marriage. That Luke focuses on single women without comment on their marital status may reveal that by the time he was writing it was acceptable for women to remain single for the sake of the Kingdom. Mary and Martha, presuming they were single, could then be models for such people in Luke's audience, and this may be one reason why he includes this story.
155   Cf. Schnackenburg, *Johannesevangelium* (1971), vol. II, 401, 430–1.
156   Cf. Lk. 10.38–42 and n. 136 above. Jn 11.9 points to this conclusion.
157   Dodd, *Historical Tradition*, 229, says that it is totally unique in giving its character a name.
158   *Ibid*.
159   Morris, *Studies*, 169.
160   Brown, *John*, 'i-xii', 429–30.
161   Cf. Bultmann, *John*, 394–405; Schnackenburg, *Johannesevangelium*, vol. II, 400–1, 430–1.
162   Dodd, *Historical Tradition*, 230.
163   So Hoskyns, *Fourth Gospel*, vol. II, 461.
164   Dodd, *Historical Tradition*, 221–32; Jeremias, *NT Theology*, 89–90; Dibelius, *From Tradition*, 72.
165   Bultmann, *John*, 402.
166   Cf. n. 175 below.
167   Cf. Barrett, *John* (1978), 395.
168   Brown, *John*, 'i-xii', 429. J.N. Sanders, 'Those whom Jesus loved, John xi.5', *NTS* 1 (1954–5), 29–41, argues well for a reconsideration that the narrative is historical in its foundation and life-like details. He is right in noting that the Fourth Evangelist depends here on a source (possibly eyewitness?) that knows Jerusalem and its neighbouring towns well.
169   Brown, *John*, 'i-xii', 429.
170   Brown, *John*, 'i-xii', 433, 436.
171   Barrett, *John* (1955), 325–6; Lightfoot, *John*, 218; Morris, *John*, 540.
172   Cf. pp. 81–2 of this study.
173   Dodd, *Interpretation*, 255.
174   Brown, 'Roles of Women', 694, n. 19, points out that Lazarus is identified through his relationship to Mary and Martha perhaps because the women, but

not Lazarus (who appears as an historical figure only in John), were known in the wider Gospel tradition. Cf. Lk. 10.38−42; Jn 11.2.

175 This is the impression given in Lk. 10.38−42 and Jn 12.2. Cf. Morris, *John*, 539, 578; Lightfoot, *John*, 221, 228. That Mary appears to have less faith and fortitude in the Master's presence than her sister probably is due to her emotional state (cf. pp. 58−61 of this study). John 12 may give us a clearer indication of her usual attitude toward Jesus.

176 Cf. 13.1, 23, 34, 14.15, 21−8, 15.9, 12, 17, 19.26, 21.7, 15−16. So Brown, 'Roles of Women', 694. It seems unlikely that there is a real difference in our text between φιλέω and ἀγαπάω. So Brown, *John*, 'i-xii', 423; *pace* Sanders, 'Those whom Jesus loved', 33.

177 Dodd, *Interpretation*, 147, 364. The καὶ νῦν (verse 22) here, in view of verse 39, does not seem to suggest a hope of present resurrection. But cf. Stählin, 'νῦν', *TDNT*, vol. IV, 1110; Barrett, *John* (1955), 328.

178 Brown, *John*, 'i-xii', 433.

179 Cf. Jn 20.31; Schnackenburg, *Johannesevangelium*, vol. II, 416.

180 Lightfoot, *John*, 221; Barrett, *John* (1955), 328. Possibly the portrayal in 11.32 is a creation of the Evangelist on the basis of the saying of Martha in 11.21, and Mary's place at Jesus' feet in 12.3.

181 κλαίω means not merely 'cry', but 'wail'. Cf. LSJ, 955; Brown, *John*, 'i-xii', 425. It is possible that the Evangelist has somewhat embellished the sorrow and misunderstanding motif (e.g., by doubling the 'Lord, if you had been here ...' remark?) in order to heighten the narrative's tension so that the raising comes as a shock and surprise.

182 For this last suggestion about cross-fertilization, cf. A. Legault, 'An Application of the Form-Critique Method to the Anointings in Galilee (Lk 7,36−50) and Bethany (Mt 26,6−13; Mk 14,3−9; Jn 12,1−8)', *CBQ* 16 (1954), 131−45; cf. Marshall, *Luke*, 306. The table in Brown, *John*, 'i-xii', 450, should be consulted to see the similarities and differences in the two narratives.

183 Plummer, *Luke*, 209, notes some ten or eleven Simons in the NT, and about twenty in Josephus.

184 Pliny, *Natural History* 13.3.19 (LCL IV; trans. H. Rackham; 1945), 108−11; cf. p. 163 n. 15 of this study.

185 Jeremias, *Jerusalem*, 8−9.

186 The tenuous idea that Mary Magdalene = the sinner woman of Luke 7 overlooks the fact that demon possession and sexual sin are not synonymous in the Gospels (note in Lk. 9.1−2 the mention of two ministries). On ἁμαρτωλός cf. pp. 54−5 of this study. In Luke 7 the unnamed sinner woman is forgiven and goes her way; in Lk. 8.2 Mary Magdalene is introduced as one among several new persons. The idea that Mary of Bethany = Mary Magdalene is equally tenuous. Mary Magdalene is a travelling disciple; Mary of Bethany is always associated with a home and with Martha. It is very doubtful that the same woman would be known as both Mary of Magdala and Mary of Bethany. It appears that the confusion of the sinner woman, Mary Magdalene and Mary of Bethany arose after NT times. For additional arguments, cf. F.C. Burkitt, 'Mary Magdalene and Mary, Sister of Martha', *ET* 42 (1930−1), 157−9.

187 Marshall, *Luke*, 306.

188 So Plummer, *Luke*, 209; Ellis, *Luke*, 121−3; Morris, *John*, 571−3; Creed, *Luke*, 109; Burkitt, 'Mary Magdalene', 159.

189   Brown, *John*, 'i-xii', 450–1.

190   Cf. Sanders, 'Those whom Jesus loved', 37; Creed, *Luke*, 109; Burkitt, 'Mary Magdalene', 159.

191   The Fourth Evangelist does *not* say that Jesus dined with Lazarus six days before Passover, though this might be implied by 12.12. He simply says, ὁ οὖν Ἰησοῦς πρὸ ἐξ ἡμερῶν τοῦ πάσχα ἦλθεν. Zerwick, sec. 71, p. 26, says we do not have 'six days before the Passover' because the preposition is governing the distance itself, not the point from which the distance is measured. MHT, vol. III, 248, suggests that it means 'before six days of the Passover', but cf. BDF, sec. 213, p. 114.

192   Cf. Dibelius, *From Tradition*, 43; Bultmann, *History*, 36–7; Taylor, *Mark*, 529.

193   Cf. Schnackenburg, *Johannesevangelium*, vol. II, 464–5.

194   Cf. Dodd, *Historical Tradition*, 166–8.

195   So Gardner–Smith, *St. John*, 47–8; cf. Bernard, *John*, vol. II, 410.

196   Brown, *John*, 'i-xii', 451. But note how Matthew handles his Marcan source at this point.

197   Dodd, *Historical Tradition*, 167.

198   If this is the case, then it must be asked why he has suppressed the name of Simon found in Mark.

199   Cf. E. P. Sanders, *The Tendencies of the Synoptic Tradition* (SNTS Monograph 9; Cambridge, 1969), 22–6, 151–83.

200   Dodd, *Interpretation*, 370, cf. p. 369. D. Daube, 'The Anointing at Bethany and Jesus' Burial', *ATR* 32 (1950), 186–99, suggests that the Gospel writers had an interest in showing that Jesus' body was treated reverently and duly anointed. As Barrett, *John* (1978), 409, says, it is difficult to see how this is reflected in John 12 since Jesus' body is provided for in Jn 19.38–42 in more than adequate fashion.

201   Cf. Leipoldt, *Die Frau*, 145, 259–60; and pp. 67–8 of this study. Brown, 'Roles of Women', 690, suggests that by the time the Evangelist wrote, Martha's activity would be recognized as the function of an ordained office in the Church, i.e., deaconess. If so, then the Evangelist might be suggesting that women were capable of performing diaconal ministries in the Church and should be authorized to do so.

202   On anointing for burial, cf. Str-B, vol. I, 426–9, 986; de Vaux, *Ancient Israel*, 102–4; ML, *Anthology*, 486; cf. Leipoldt, *Die Frau*, 142–5, 259–60, n. 9 on social and royal anointings.

203   Cf. BAG, 531, 535–6; MM, 419; Michaelis, 'μύρον', *TDNT*, vol. IV, 800–1; Barrett, *John* (1955), 343; B. T. Shab. 62*a*, Mo'ed I, Shabbath I, 291. The word πιστικός probably means 'pure' or 'genuine', deriving from πιστός (cf. LSJ supplement, 121; MM, 514–15; A–S, 362), but it could be derived from a name of some sort (pistachio?). Cf. Barrett, *John* (1955), 343; BAG, 668; Max Zerwick and Mary Grosvenor, *A Grammatical Analysis of the Greek New Testament* (Rome, !974), vol. I, 323.

204   λίτρα = twelve ounces = one Roman pound; cf. BAG, 476.

205   *Pace* Brown, *John*, 'i-xii', 454; Morris, *John*, 573, n. 6.

206   Athenaeus, *The Deipnosophists* 12.553 (LCL V; trans. C.B. Gulick; 1933) 512–13 (though this is somewhat later than our period).

207   Str-B, vol. I, 427–8, 986; Hill, *Matthew*, 334, says, 'The gesture of the woman would not be extraordinary in an eastern home.'

208 This practice was customary in the first-century Roman empire. Cf. Petronius, *Satyricon* 27 (LCL; trans. M. Heseltine; 1913), 46ff. Leipoldt, *Die Frau*, 145; Licht, *Sexual Life in Ancient Greece*, 435, 519. Jews had adopted various Graeco-Roman habits such as the practice of reclining at banquets; cf. p. 54–5 of this study. F. Büchsel, 'ἀνάκειμαι', *TDNT*, vol. III, 654; Str-B, vol. IV, 56–76, 611–39, espec. 615–19; BAG, 55; H. Achelis, 'Altchristliche Kunst', *ZNW* 17 (1916), 87.

209 A good Jewess might pride herself in never letting anyone but her husband see her hair. Cf. Jeremias, *Jerusalem*, 360. For a woman to unloose her hair was shameful in the eyes of the rabbis. Cf. ML, *Anthology*, 108–9; M. Baba Kamma, 8.6, Danby, 343.

210 One possible explanation would be that the Fourth Evangelist is portraying the anointing story as a proleptic Last Supper which in John includes a foot washing by Jesus. Cf. E.E. Platt, 'The Ministry of Mary of Bethany', *TT* 34 (1, 1977), 29–39. For another possibility, cf. n. 224 below.

211 The use of ἐνταφιασμόν (verse 8) in Mark, and ἐνταφίασαι (verse 12) in Matthew makes this clear.

212 Platt, 'Mary of Bethany', 29–39; Lightfoot, *John*, 235.

213 It is possible that the woman was doing more than she realized at the time. Women normally performed the ritual of anointing for burial. Here, the woman probably intended it simply as an act of gratitude.

214 Cf. Brown, *John*, 'i-xii', 454; J.K. Elliott, 'The Anointing of Jesus', *ET* 85 (1974), 105–7.

215 It is clearly the extravagance of the act that causes the angry objection. On the value of 300 denarii, cf. BAG, 178; MM, 145; Morris, *John*, 578; Mt. 20.2.

216 Cf. MHT, vol. I, 175; Robertson, 932; BDF, sec. 364, 183–4.

217 Brown, *John*, 'i-xii', 449; Barrett, *John* (1955), 345.

218 MHT, vol. I, 178, 248; Robertson, 931.

219 Cf. BAG, 822; A–S, 445; LSJ, 1789. The primary meaning in the papyri seems to be 'to observe'. CF. MM, 633.

220 Barrett, *John* (1955), 345; G. Bertram, 'συντρίβω', *TDNT*, vol. VII, 925, n. 41.

221 Cf. Cranfield, *Mark*, 415–18; Lane, *Mark*, 494–5; and contrast Jeremias, *NT Theology*, 133–4. It is unlikely that εἰς μνημόσυνον αὐτῆς is referring to a memorial by Mary to Jesus. *Pace* J.H. Greenlee, εἰς μνημόσυνον αὐτῆς "For her Memorial" (Mt. xxvi.13; Mk xiv.9)', *ET* 71 (1960), 245.

222 The rabbinic saying from Ecclesiastes Midrash Rabbah 7.1 probably dates from a time after the era of Jesus and the NT writers. Cf. Barrett, *John*, (1955), 344.

223 Stauffer, *Jesus*, 223–4.

224 Barrett, *John* (1955), 341, thinks that the Fourth Evangelist may be implying that this is a royal anointing in preparation for Jesus' entry into Jerusalem. But, as Brown, *John* i-xii, 454, points out, Mary anoints Jesus' feet and in the next scene the Evangelist casts the narrative so that it appears Jesus does not accept the royal acclamations of the crowd (cf. Brown, 461–3). Barrett, *John* (1978), 409, says that the anointing of the feet need not point away from a coronation ritual since Jesus is glorified in death and is anointed with the spices of burial. Still, if the Fourth Evangelist intended to paint a kingly ritual anointing, then it would seem probable that he would have brought the matter a little more to the foreground.

225 One of the notable attributes of a prophet in both the OT and NT is that he or she performs symbolic acts such as we have in our text. Cf. Ezek. 4.1–5.5; Ac. 21.10–11.

226 Cf. pp. 114–16 and n. 201, p. 193.

227 Manson, *Luke*, xii-xix, notes 7.11–17, 36–50, 8.1–3, 10.38–42, 13.10–17, and more distantly 23.27–32.

228 This section of my study appears in another form in *ZNW* 70 (1979), 243–8.

229 Note Luke's fondness for parallelism: (1) κηρύσσω and εὐαγγελίζομαι; (2) θεραπεύω and διακονέω; (3) πνεῦμα and δαιμόνιον. Creed, *Luke*, 112–13, lists the following elements as characteristically Lucan: (1) καὶ ἐγένετο ἐν τῷ ... καὶ αὐτὸς; (2) καθεξῆς; (3) διώδευεν; (4) εὐαγγελιζόμενος; (5) ἀσθενειῶν.

230 Cf. Caird, *Luke*, 116; M. Hengel, 'Maria Magdalena und die Frauen als Zeugen', in *Abraham Unser Vater, Festschrift für Otto Michel* (Leiden, 1963), 243–56.

231 Cf. Klostermann, *Lukasevangelium*, 96; Caird, *Luke*, 116; and n. 235 below.

232 There are *no* known cases of a woman scholar who did not gain her knowledge through contacts in her own home (the servants of R. Judah, the wife of R. Meir). What they learned at home and in the synagogue was the minimum necessary to remain good Jews. We do not read of them going to any of the rabbinic study houses for more scholarly education.

233 Cf. pp. 118–23 of this study. Jesus broke with Jewish tradition in having women disciples and travelling companions, and there is no reason why He could not have continued this revolutionary trend by choosing some women to be among the Twelve. It appears then that male headship as a pattern of leadership, if refined and redefined according to the dictates of discipleship and Jesus' example, was acceptable to Him. Jesus' choice of twelve men to be His special companions and to receive special teaching, and the fact that He recommissioned these men after the Resurrection to be leaders of His community, is inexplicable on the supposition that Jesus was a 'feminist', i.e., one who rejects a patriarchal framework outright. Such a person would have felt it necessary to include at least one woman among the Twelve. Cf. Schürmann, *Lukasevangelium*, vol. I, 446–8.

234 Rengstorf, 'ἑπτά', *TDNT*, vol. II, 630–1.

235 Danker, *Jesus*, 101, says that the mention of Joanna not only shows a possible source of Luke's information, but also that the Gospel has 'penetrated Herod's own establishment'. ἐπίτροπος here probably means 'manager' or 'steward'. Cf. BAG, 303; MM, 249; LSJ, 669; Michel, 'οἰκονόμος', *TDNT*, vol. V, 150.

236 RS, *Translator's Luke*, 327, says that these are to be distinguished from the 'some women' of Lk. 8.2 who had been healed and were part of the group of disciples travelling with Jesus. The word αἵτινες seems to indicate that all these women provided for Jesus and the Twelve.

237 The variant αὐτῷ probably was a later Christocentric correction. Cf. Metzger, *TC*, 144. The word διακονέω has its most common sense here of providing material aid. Cf. Beyer, 'διακονέω', *TDNT*, vol. II, 85. Could this be the background or precedent for the later order and functions of deaconesses? Cf. Conzelmann, *Theology of Luke*, 47, n. 1; Ellis, *Luke*, 124.

238 τὰ ὑπάρχοντα literally means 'substance' as in one's belongings (money, property). Cf. RS, *Translator's Luke*, 328; BAG, 845; A–S, 457; MM, 650–1. Probably, some of these women could give only their time and talents, perhaps

in making meals or clothes. Cf. Arndt, *Luke*, 223. Caird, *Luke*, 116, says that the well-to-do women underwrote the expenses of the group.

239 Cf. ML, *Anthology*, 415–16, 423–5; B.T. Shab. 62*a*, Mo'ed I, Shabbath I, 290; B.T. Ber. 10*b*, Cohen, 64; pp. 16–18 of this study; Josephus, *Antiquities* 18.81ff (LCL), 9; B.T. Babba Kamma 119*a*, *Der Babylonische Talmud*, vol. VI (trans. L. Goldschmidt; Haag, 1933), 453ff; Baron, *History of the Jews*, vol. II, 240, 412–13. Str-B, vol. II, 164, rightly mentions that women in parts of the Roman Empire could be called *mater synagogae*. Cf *CII*, vol. I, n. 523, p. 384; n. 606, p. 436; n. 639, pp. 457–8. They could be called ἀρχισυνάγωγοι because of their financial support or their respectability, not their leadership. Cf. *CII*, vol. I, no. 638, p. 457. Schrage, 'ἀρχισυνάγωγος', *TDNT*, vol. VII, 846, and n. 20.

240 Rengstorf, 'μαθητής', *TDNT*, vol. IV, 446–7. When one realizes that it is Rengstorf who has recognized perhaps more clearly than anyone the significance of the Twelve Apostles for Luke, this is a most revealing statement.

241 The ἐν αἷς in Mk 15.40 = Mt. 27.56 indicates this. The First Evangelist has γυναῖκες πολλαί (Mt. 27.55), probably based on Mk 15.41 – ἄλλαι πολλαί.

242 Taylor, *Passion Narrative of Luke*, 94–5.

243 Cf. Danker, *Jesus*, 242; RS, *Translator's Luke*, 738; Marshall, *Luke*, 877; Bultmann, 'γνωστός', *TDNT*, vol. I, 718–19; BAG, 163; A–S, 94. D. Flusser, 'The Crucified One and the Jews', *Imm* 7 (1977), 30, argues, 'Luke has given us an historically probable description of who mocked and who mourned the Crucified One, and it seems as if this is what was written in his source.'

244 Cf. BAG, 615; BDF, sec. 238, 124; Robertson, 615; MHT, vol. III, 273, says that it does not imply 'the immediate neighbourhood'.

245 Cf. BAG, 489; A–S, 276; Swete, *Mark*, 367; M'Neile, *Matthew*, 425; Creed, *Luke*, 288; Hoskyns, *Fourth Gospel*, vol. II, 630.

246 Cf. pp. 91–2 and n. 103 of this chapter.

247 Plummer, *Mark*, 361, says ὁ μικρότερος would have been used if 'the Less' rather than 'the Little' was meant. Cf. pp. 116–18 of this study.

248 So Marshall, *Luke*, 877; Danker, *Jesus*, 242; cf. 23.49*b*.

249 Cf. p. 94 and n. 102 of this chapter.

250 Hengel, 'Maria Magdalena', 250, argues that John's principle of arranging names is by degree of kinship to Jesus, while in the Synoptics they are listed according to their importance to and in the family of faith.

251 The mention of Mary's sister and Mary Clopas before Mary Magdalene in Jn 19.25 is possibly a matter of mentioning relatives before acquaintances. Jn 19.26–7 is about how Jesus' closest relative is to relate to Him. The mention of Mary Magdalene in Jn 19.25 may be intended to imply that as Mary will receive a special mention in what follows (19.26–7) so will Mary Magdalene (20.1–18).

252 There are several possible reasons why no women are mentioned directly in Paul's list that do not reflect in a negative way on their witness: (1) Paul's main concern is to mention the apostolic witnesses commissioned by the risen Lord (note the specific mention of Peter, the Twelve, James, all the Apostles and then Paul); (2) Paul may be quoting a traditional list of official witnesses; (3) the omission of the appearances to women may be for apologetic reasons (i.e., in view of the common attitude toward a woman's witness) and need not imply anything about Paul's or the original list maker's view of

women's witness. Paul does not say that Jesus appeared first to Peter, he simply says ὅτι ὤφθη Κηφᾶ. The εἶτα which follows probably indicates that this is a chronological list, but it may be a chronological list of the appearances to the official witnesses. Cf. Stagg, 'Biblical Perspectives', 14. Brown, *John*, 'xiii-xxi', 971, rightly says of Paul's list: 'There is no reason why such a tradition should have included an appearance to a woman who could scarcely be presented as either an official witness to the resurrection or as an apostle.' Cf. Brown, 'Roles of Women', 692, n. 12.

253   Matthew and Mark have θεωροῦσαι, while Luke has ὁρῶσαι. The gender of ὁρῶσαι as well as the position of the verb, indicates that, as Danker, *Jesus*, 242, says, 'The women are mentioned almost as a separate group.'

254   Flusser, 'The Crucified One', 32.

255   Flusser, 34. Is this an Isaiah 53 motif?

256   This appears especially to be the case in the Passion and Resurrection narratives in Mark. Cf. 14.13, 16.17, 20, 32, 33, 43, 50 and 16.7. R.P. Meye, *Jesus and the Twelve. Discipleship and Revelation in Mark's Gospel* (Grand Rapids, 1968), has argued well the case that 'the disciples' = 'the Twelve' throughout Mark's Gospel with rare exceptions (cf. 2.15).

257   Is Galilee for Mark the place where the disciples and Jesus begin and renew fellowship together? Cf. Mk 16.1–8.

258   Cf. BAG, 791.

259   Cf. Marshall, *Luke*, 877; Kittel, 'συνακολουθέω', *TDNT*, vol. I, 216. As Zerwick, sec. 291, p. 99, and Moule, *I-B*, 101, say, present participles can be used to express relative anteriority ('having followed').

260   BDF, sec. 390, p. 197; Plummer, *Matthew*, 405, n. 1. Alternatively, it is conceivable that the First Evangelist was attempting to limit the women to the tasks of hospitality (they followed and served – they were not trained as Jesus' envoys), or indicate to his audience the precedent and appropriateness of such roles for women. In view of 27.55*a*, the list of women, and Mt. 28.9–10, the relegation to hospitality idea seems improbable.

BIBLIOGRAPHY

This bibliography is intended to aid those who wish to pursue the study of Jesus' attitudes toward women and their roles as reflected in His earthly ministry. It does not include any of the standard reference works, commentaries, lexicons, or other tools of exegesis, but simply concentrates on books and articles useful in the study of Jesus and women. It is divided into five sections, one section entitled Studies on Women, and four chapter bibliographies.

Studies on Women

Allworthy, T.B. *Women in the Apostolic Church. A Critical Study of the Evidence in the New Testament for the Prominence of Women in Early Christianity.* Cambridge: W. Heffer and Sons, 1917.

Bullough, Vern L. *The Subordinate Sex — A History of Attitudes Toward Women.* Urbana: University of Illinois Press, 1973.

Clark, Elizabeth and H. Richardson, eds. *Women and Religion, A Feminist Sourcebook of Christian Thought.* New York: Harper and Row, 1977.

Daly, Mary. *Beyond God the Father, Toward a Philosophy of Women's Liberation.* Boston: Beacon Press, 1973.

Foh, Susan. *Women and the Word of God.* Phillipsburg, New Jersey: Presbyterian and Reformed Publ., 1979.

Hurley, James B. *Man and Woman in Biblical Perspective.* Grand Rapids: Zondervan, 1981.

Jewett, Paul K. *Man as Male and Female.* Grand Rapids: Wm B. Eerdmans, 1975.

The Ordination of Women. Grand Rapids: Wm B. Eerdmans, 1980.

Leenhardt, Franz and F. Blanke. *Die Stellung der Frau im Neuen Testament und in der alten Kirche.* Zürich: Zwingli Verlag, 1949.

Leipoldt, J. *Die Frau in der antiken Welt und im Urchristentum.* Leipzig: Koehler and Amelang, 1955.

Jesus und die Frauen. Leipzig: Koehler and Amelang, 1921.

Mollenkott, Virginia R. *Women, Men, and the Bible.* Nashville: Abingdon Press, 1977.

Pape, Dorothy. *God and Women.* London: Mowbrays, 1977.

Ruether, Rosemary R., ed. *Religion and Sexism, Images of Women in the Jewish and Christian Traditions.* New York: Simon and Schuster, 1974.

Russell, Letty M. *Human Liberation in a Feminist Perspective – a Theology*. Philadelphia: Westminster Press, 1974.

Scanzoni, Letha and Nancy Hardesty. *All We're Meant to Be*. Waco, Texas: Word Books, 1974.

Stagg, Evelyn and Frank. *Woman in the World of Jesus*. Philadelphia: Westminster Press, 1978.

Stendahl, Krister. *The Bible and the Role of Women*. FBBS 15. trans. Emilie T. Sander. Philadelphia: Fortress Press, 1966.

Swidler, Leonard. *Biblical Affirmations of Woman*. Philadelphia: Westminster Press, 1979.

Tavard, George H. *Woman in Christian Tradtion*. Notre Dame, Indiana: University of Notre Dame Press, 1973.

Trible, Phyllis. *God and the Rhetoric of Sexuality*. Philadelphia: Fortress Press, 1978.

Chapter One

Baer, Richard A. *Philo's Use of the Categories of Male and Female*. Leiden: E.J. Brill, 1970.

Balsdon, J.P.V.D. *Roman Women: Their History and Habits*. London: The Bodley Head, 1962.

Bammel, Ernst. 'Markus 10.11 f. und das jüdische Eherecht'. *ZNW* 61 (1970), 95–101.

Baron, S.W. *A Social and Religious History of the Jews*, vols. I, II. 5 vols. New York: Columbia University Press, 1952–60.

Bonsirven, J. *Palestinian Judaism in the Time of Jesus Christ*. trans. W. Wolf. New York: Holt, Rinehart and Winston, 1964.

Cohen, B. 'Concerning Divorce in Jewish and Roman Law'. *PAAJR* 21 (1952), 3–34.

Cruveilhier, P. 'Le droit de la femme'. *RB* 36 (1927), 353–76.

Delling, Gerhard. *Paulus' Stellung zu Frau und Ehe*. Stuttgart: Kohlhammer Verlag, 1931.

Donaldson, James. *Woman: Her Position and Influence in Ancient Greece and Rome, and Among Early Christians*. London: Longmans, Green and Co., 1907.

Fisher, Eugene J. 'Cultic Prostitution in the Ancient Near East? A Reassessment'. *BTB* 6 (2–3, June–October, 1976), 225–36.

Goldfeld, A. 'Women as Sources of Torah in the Rabbinic Tradition'. *Judaism* 24 (2, 1975), 245–56.

Harper's Dictionary of Classical Literature and Antiquities. ed. H.T. Peck. New York: Harper and Brothers, 1897.

Hauptman, J. 'Images of Women in the Talmud'. *Religion and Sexism*, ed. R.R. Ruether. New York: Simon and Schuster, 1974, 184–212.

Jeremias, Joachim. *Jerusalem in the Time of Jesus*. trans. F.H. and C.H. Cave. Philadelphia: Fortress Press, 1969.

Klein, Charlotte, 'Jewish Women in the Time of Mary of Nazareth'. *Bible Today* 60 (1972), 746–52.

Loewe, R. *The Position of Women in Judaism*. London: S.P.C.K., 1966.

Lowy, S. 'The Extent of Jewish Polygamy in Talmudic Times'. *JJS* 9 (1958), 115—35.

MacDonald, E. M. *The Position of Women as Reflected in Semitic Codes of Law*. Toronto: University of Toronto Press, 1931.

Macurdy, G. H. 'Julia Bernice'. *AJP* 56 (1935), 246—53.

Marmorstein, Emile. 'The Veil in Judaism and Islam'. *JJS* 5—6 (1954—5), 1—11.

Meeks, Wayne A. 'The Image of the Androgyne: Some Uses of a Symbol in Earliest Christianity'. *HR* 13 (3, Feb., 1974), 165—208.

Meiselman, Moshe. *Jewish Woman in Jewish Law*. New York: KTAV Pub. House/Yeshiva University Press, 1978.

Mendelsohn, S. *The Criminal Jurisprudence of the Ancient Hebrews*. 2nd ed. New York: Hermon Press, 1968.

Moore, G. F. *Judaism in the First Centuries of the Christian Era*, vols. I, II, New York: Schocken Books, 1971.

Oepke, A. 'γυνή'. *TDNT*, vol. I (1964), 776—89.

Peritz, I. J. 'Women in the Ancient Hebrew Cult'. *JBL* 17 (1898), 111—48.

Pirenne, Jacques. 'Le Statut de la Femme dans la Civilization Hébraïque'. *La Femme*. Recueils de la Société Jean Bodin. Brussels, Éditions de la Librarie Encyclopédique, 1959, 107—26.

Pomeroy, Sarah. *Goddesses, Whores, Wives, and Slaves*. London: Robert Hale and Co., 1975.

  'Selected Bibliography on Women in Antiquity'. *Arethusa* 6 (1, Spring, 1973), 125—37.

Schechter, S. *Studies in Judaism*. 1st ser. Philadelphia: Jewish Publishing Society of America, 1945.

Sigal, P. 'Elements of Male Chauvinism in Classical Halakhah'. *Judaism* 24 (2, 1975), 226—44.

Sukenik, E. L. *Ancient Synagogues in Palestine and Greece*. London: Oxford Press for the British Academy, 1934.

Swidler, Leonard, *Women in Judaism: The Status of Women in Formative Judaism*. Metuchen, New Jersey: Scarecrow Press, 1976.

Vaux, Roland de. *Ancient Israel, Its Life and Institutions*. trans. J. McHugh. London: Darton, Longman and Todd, 1973.

'Women'. *Encyclopedia Judaica*. vol. XVI. Jerusalem: Keter Publishing House, Ltd, 1971, cols. 623—30.

'Woman, Rights Of'. *Jewish Encyclopedia*. vol. XII, ed. I. Singer. New York: Funk and Wagnalls, Company, 1906, 556—9.

Wright, G. E. 'Women and Masculine Theological Vocabulary in the Old Testament'. *Grace Upon Grace, Essays in Honor of Lester J. Kuyper*. ed. J. I. Cook. Grand Rapids: Wm B. Eerdmans, 1975, 64—9.

Yadin, Y. 'Expedition D — The Cave of Letters'. *IEJ* 12 (1962), 227—57.

Yaron, R. 'Aramaic Marriage Contracts — Corrigenda and Addenda'. *JSS* 5 (1960), 66—70.

Zucrow, Solomon. *Women, Slaves, and the Ignorant in Rabbinic Literature* Boston: The Stratford Company, 1932.

Chapter Two

Aicher, G. 'Mann und Weib – ein Fleisch (Mt 19,4 ff.)'. *BZ* 5 (1907), 159–65.

Allis, O.T. 'The Parable of the Leaven'. *EvQ* 19 (1947), 254–73.

Argyle, A.W. 'Wedding Customs at the Time of Jesus'. *ET* 86 (1974–5), 214–15.

Baltensweiler, H. 'Die Ehebruchsklauseln bei Matthäus'. *TZ* 15 (1959), 340–56.
  Die Ehe im Neuen Testament – Exegetische Untersuchungen über Ehe, Ehelosigkeit, und Ehescheidung. Stuttgart: Zwingli Verlag, 1967.

Bammel, Ernst. 'Is Luke 16,16–18 of Baptist's Provenience?' *HTR* 51 (1958), 101–6.

Barrett, C.K. *New Testament Background: Selected Documents.* New York: Harper and Row, 1961.

Barth, Karl. *Church Dogmatics.* vol. III.4. ed. G.W. Bromiley and T.F. Torrance. trans. A.T. Mackay, T.H.L. Parker, *et al.* Edinburgh: T. and T. Clark, 1961.

Beasley-Murray, G.R. *Baptism in the New Testament.* Grand Rapids: Wm B. Eerdmans, 1962.

Berger, K. 'Hartherzigkeit und Gottes Gesetz. Die Vorgeschichte des antijüdischen Vorwurfs in Mc 10:5'. *ZNW* 61 (1–2, 1970), 1–47.

Black, M. 'The Marcan Parable of the Child in the Midst'. *ET* 59 (1947–8), 14–16.

Blakeney, E.H. 'A Note on St. Matthew xxii.29'. *ET* 4 (1892–3), 382.

Blass, F. 'On Mark xii.42'. *ET* 10 (1898–9), 286–7.
  'On Mark xii.42 and xv.16'. *ET* 10 (1898–9), 185–7.

Blenkinsopp, J. *Sexuality and the Christian Tradition.* London: Sheed and Ward, 1970.

Bligh, J. 'Qorban!' *HeyJ* 5 (1964), 192–3.

Blinzler, J. 'Die Strafe für Ehebruch in Bibel und Halacha. Zur Auslegung von Joh. VIII.5'. *NTS* 4 (1, 1957), 32–47.
  'εἰσὶν εὐνοῦχοι – Zur Auslegung von Mt. 19,12'. *ZNW* 48 (1957), 254–70.

Boismard, M.-É. 'Chronique Archéologique'. *RB* 65 (1958), 400–23.

Bonsirven, J. '"Nisi fornicationis causa" Comment résoudre cette "crux interpretum"?' *RSR* 35 (1948), 442–64.

Brennan, I. 'Women in the Gospels'. *New Blackfriars* 52 (1971), 291–9.

Brown, C. 'Child'. *NIDNTT,* vol. I (1975), 283–5.

Brown, Raymond E. *New Testament Essays.* Garden City: Doubleday and Company, 1968.

Brueggemann, W. 'Of the Same Flesh and Bone (Gn 2,23a)'. *CBQ* 32 (1970), 532–42.

Burkill, T.A. 'Two into One: The Notion of Carnal Union in Mark 10:8; 1 Kor 6:16; Eph 5:31'. *ZNW* 62 (1971), 115–20.

Burkitt, F.C. *The Gospel History and Its Transmission.* Edinburgh: T. and T. Clark, 1906.

Burney, C.F. *The Poetry of Our Lord. An Examination of the Formal*

Elements of Hebrew Poetry in the Discourses of Jesus Christ. Oxford: Clarendon Press, 1925.

Buzy, D. 'Le juge inique (Saint Luc, XVIII,1–8)'. *RB* 39 (1930), 378–91.

Cadbury, H.J. 'A Possible Case of Lukan Authorship'. *HTR* 10 (1917), 237–44.

Cangh, J.-M. van. 'Fondement évangélique de la vie religieuse'. *NRT* 95 (6, 1973), 635–47.

Catchpole, D.R. 'The Son of Man's Search for Faith (Luke XVIII.8b)'. *NovT* 19 (2, 1977), 81–104.

'The Synoptic Divorce Material as a Traditio-Historical Problem'. *BJRL* 57 (1974–5), 92–127.

Clarke, W.K.L. 'The Excepting Clause in St. Matthew'. *Theology* 15 (1927), 161–2.

'Studies in Texts. 2. The Excepting Clause in St. Matthew'. *Theology* 16 (1928), 161–3.

Colpe, C. 'ὁ υἱὸς τοῦ ἀνθρώπου'. *TDNT*, vol. VIII (1967), 400–77.

Conzelmann, H. *The Theology of St. Luke.* trans. G. Buswell. New York: Harper and Row, 1961.

Cranfield, C.E.B. 'The Parable of the Unjust Judge and the Eschatology of Luke-Acts'. *SJT* 16 (1963), 297–301.

Crouzel, H. 'Le Texte patristique de Matthieu v.32 et xix.9'. *NTS* 19 (1, 1972), 98–119.

Darlow, T.H. 'Divorce and Childhood, A Reading of St. Matt. xix.3–15'. *Exp*, 4th ser. 7 (1893), 294–9.

Daube, D. 'An Attack on Discrimination Against Women; the Adulteress of John 8'. Unpublished essay of 25 pages. By permission of the author. Abbreviated form will appear in 'Biblical Landmarks in the Struggle for Women's Rights'. *JR* (in press).

'Biblical Landmarks in the Struggle for Women's Rights'. *JR* (in press), 24 pages.

'Concessions to Sinfulness in Jewish Law', *JJS* 10 (1959), 1–13.

The Duty of Procreation. Edinburgh: T. and T. Clark, 1977.

The New Testament and Rabbinic Judaism. Jordan Lectures in Comparative Religion. London: Athlone Press, 1956.

'Repudium in Deuteronomy'. *Neotestamentica et Semitica: Studies in Honour of Matthew Black.* ed. E.E. Ellis and M. Wilcox. Edinburgh: T. and T. Clark, 1969, 236–9.

Davies, W.D. *The Setting of the Sermon on the Mount.* London: Cambridge University Press, 1964.

Delling, G. 'βάπτισμα βαπτισθῆναι'. *NovT* 2 (1958), 92–115.

'Das Gleichnis vom gottlosen Richter'. *ZNW* 53 (1962), 1–25.

'Das Logion Mark X.11 (und seine Abwandlungen) im Neuen Testament'. *NovT* 1 (1956), 263–74.

'σύζυγος'. *TDNT*, vol. VII (1971), 748–50.

Denney, J. 'The Sadducees and Immortality'. *Exp*, 4th ser. 10 (1894), 401–9.

Derrett, J. Duncan M. ' "Eating up the Houses of Widows": Jesus's Comment on Lawyers?' *Studies in the New Testament*, vol. I. Leiden: E.J. Brill, 1977, 118–27.

'ΚΟΡΒΑΝ, Ο ΕΣΤΙΝ ΔWΡΟΝ'. *Studies in the New Testament*, vol. I. Leiden: E.J. Brill, 1977, 112–17.

'Law in the New Testament: The Parable of the Unjust Judge'. *Studies in the New Testament*, vol. I. Leiden: E.J. Brill, 1977, 32–47.

'Law in the New Testament: *Si scandalizaverit te manus tua abscinde illam* (Mk. IX.42) and Comparative Legal History'. *Studies in the New Testament*, vol. I. Leiden: E.J. Brill, 1977, 4–31.

'Law in the New Testament: The Story of the Woman Taken in Adultery'. *NTS* 10 (1963–4), 1–26.

Deschryver, R. 'La parabole du juge malveillant (Luc 18,1–8)'. *RHPR* 48 (4, 1968), 355–66.

Dodd, C.H. *The Parables of the Kingdom*. New York: Charles Scribner's Sons, 1961.

Donfried, K.P. 'The Allegory of the Ten Virgins (Matt. 25:1–13) – As a Summary of Matthean Theology'. *JBL* 93 (1974), 415–28.

Drury, J. *Tradition and Design in Luke's Gospel – A Study in Early Christian Historiography*. London: Darton, Longman and Todd, 1976.

Dupont, J. *Mariage et Divorce dans l'Évangile Matthieu 19,3–12 et parallèles*. Bruges: Abbaye de Saint André, 1959.

Ellis, E.E. 'Jesus, the Sadducees, and Qumran'. *NTS* 10 (1963–4), 274–9.

Falk, Z.W. 'Notes and Observations – on Talmudic Vows'. *HTR* 59 (3, 1966), 309–12.

Fensham, F.C. 'Widows, Orphans, and the Poor in Ancient Near Eastern Legal and Wisdom Literature'. *JNES* 21 (1962), 129–39.

Fitzmyer, J.A. 'The Aramaic Qorbān Inscription from Jebel Ḥallet eṭ-Ṭûri and Mark 7.11/Matt. 15.5'. *JBL* 78 (1959), 60–5.

'The Matthean Divorce Texts and Some New Palestinian Evidence'. *TS* 37 (2, 1976), 197–226.

Flender, H. *St. Luke – Theologian of Redemptive History*. trans. R.H. and I. Fuller. London: S.P.C.K., 1967.

Ford, J. Massyngberde. 'The Parable of the Foolish Scholars, Matt. xxv.1–13'. *NovT* 9 (1967), 107–23.

France, R.T. *Jesus and the Old Testament*. London: Tyndale Press, 1971.

Funk, R.W. 'Beyond Criticism in Quest of Literacy: The Parable of the Leaven'. *Int* 25 (1971), 149–70.

Galot, J. 'La motivation évangélique de célibat'. *Greg* 53 (4, 1972), 731–57.

Gansewinkel, A. van. 'Ursprüngliche oder grundsätzliche Unauflösbarkeit der Ehe?' *Diakonia* 3 (2, 1972), 88–93.

Glasson, T.F. 'The Marcan Parable of the Child in the Midst'. *ET* 59 (1947–8), 166.

Grassi, J.A. 'Women's Liberation: The New Testament Perspective'. *Living Light* 8 (2, 1971), 22–34.

Greeven, H. 'Ehe nach dem Neuen Testament'. *NTS* 15 (1968–9), 365–88.

Haacker, K. 'Ehescheidung und Wiederverheiratung im Neuen Testament'. *TQ* 151 (1, 1971), 28–38.

'Der Rechtssatz Jesu zum Thema Ehebruch (Mt. 5,28)'. *BZ* 21 (1, 1977), 113–16.

Haenchen, E. *Der Weg Jesu. Eine Erklärung des Markusevangeliums und der Kanonischen Parallelen.* Berlin: Alfred Töpelmann, 1966. 'Matthäus 23'. *ZTK* n.s. 48 (1951), 38–63.

Hamann, H.P. 'The Ten Virgins: An Exegetical-Homiletical Study'. *LTJ* 11 (2, 1977), 68–72.

Hampden-Cook, E. 'Whom did the Disciples Rebuke?' *ET* 17 (1905–6), 192.

Hanse H. 'ἔχω'. *TDNT*, vol. II (1964), 816–32.

Harrison, E.F. 'The Son of God Among the Sons of Men. VIII. Jesus and the Woman Taken in Adultery'. *BSac* 103 (1946), 431–9.

Hart, J.H.A. 'Corban'. *JQR* 19 (July, 1907), 615–60.

Holzmeister, U. 'Die Streitfrage über die Ehescheidungstexte bei Matthäus 5, 32, und 19, 9'. *Bib* 26 (1945), 133–46.

Hoskyns, E. and N. Davey. *The Riddle of the New Testament.* London: Faber and Faber, Ltd, 1958.

Humbert, P. 'Jesus Writing on the Ground (John viii.6–8)'. *ET* 30 (1918–19), 475–6.

Hunter, A.M. *The Parables Then and Now.* London: SCM Press, 1971.

Isaksson, A. *Marriage and Ministry in the New Temple: A Study with Special Reference to Mt. 19.13–12 [sic] and 1 Cor. 11.3–16.* trans. N. Tomkinson. Lund: C.W.K. Gleerup, 1965.

Jeremias, Joachim. *Infant Baptism in the First Four Centuries.* trans. D. Cairns. London: SCM Press, 1960.

Jesu Verheissung für die Völker. Stuttgart. W. Kohlhammer, 1956.

'LAMPADES – Mt. 25:1, 3f, 7f'. *ZNW* 56 (1965), 196–201.

The Parables of Jesus. 2nd rev. ed. trans. S.H. Hooke. New York: Charles Scribner's Sons, 1972.

'Tradition und Redaktion im Lukas 15'. *ZNW* 62 (3–4, 1971), 172–89.

'Zur Geschichtlichkeit des Verhörs Jesu vor dem Hohen Rat'. *ZNW* 43 (1950–1), 145–50.

'Zwei Miszellen: 1. Antik-Jüdische Münzdeutungen. 2. Zur Geschichtlichkeit der Tempelreinigung'. *NTS* 23 (2, 1977), 177–80.

Johnson, A.F. 'A Stylistic Trait of the Fourth Gospel in the Pericope Adulterae?' *BETS* 9 (2, 1966), 91–6.

Käser, W. 'Exegetische und theologische Erwägungen zur Seligpreisung der Kinderlosen – Lc 23:29b'. *ZNW* 54 (3–4, 1963), 240–54.

Kleist, J.A. 'Eunuchs in the New Testament'. *CBQ* 7 (1945), 447–9.

Kümmel, W.G. 'Jesus und der jüdische Traditionsgedanke'. *ZNW* 33 (1934), 105–30.

Promise and Fulfilment – The Eschatological Message of Jesus. trans. D.M. Barton. London: SCM Press, 1957.

Leaney, A.R.C. 'Jesus and the Symbol of the Child (Luke ix.46–48)'. *ET* 66 (1954–5), 91–2.

Leeming, B. and Dyson R.A. 'Except it be for Fornication?' *Scr* 8 (1956), 75–82.

Leenhardt, F.J. 'Les femmes aussi ... à propos du billet de répudiation'. *RTP* 19 (1, 1969), 31–40.

Legasse, S. *Jésus et L'Énfant.* Paris: Gabalda Press, 1969.

Lehmann, M.R. 'Gen. 2.24 as the Basis for Divorce in Halakhah and New Testament'. *ZAW* 72 (1960), 263–7.

Lohse, E. 'χείρ'. *TDNT*, vol. IX (1974), 424–37.

'Σιών'. *TDNT*, vol. VII (1971), 319–38.

Manson, T.W. 'The Pericope de Adultera (Joh. 7,53 – 8,11)'. *ZNW* 44 (1952–3), 255–6.

The Sayings of Jesus. London: SCM Press, 1957.

Margoliouth, D.S. 'Jesus Writing on the Ground'. *ET* 31 (1919–20), 38.

Marshall, I.H. *Eschatology and the Parables*. London: Tyndale Press, 1963.

Matura, T. 'Le célibat dans le Nouveau Testament'. *NRT* 97 (6, 1975), 481–500.

Michaelis, W. 'πίπτω'. *TDNT*, vol. VI (1968), 161–73.

Michel, O. 'οἰκία'. *TDNT*, vol. V (1967), 119–59.

Moingt, J. 'Le Divorce (Pour Motif d'Impudicité) (Matthieu 5,32: 19,9)'. *RSR* 56 (1968), 337–84.

Montefiore, C.G. *Rabbinic Literature and Gospel Teachings*. New York: KTAV Publishing House, 1970.

The Synoptic Gospels. vol. I. London: Macmillan and Co., 1909.

Murray, J. *Divorce*. Philadelphia: Presbyterian and Reformed Pub. Co., 1975.

Nembach, U. 'Ehescheidung nach alttestamentlichem und jüdischem Recht'. *TZ* 26 (3, 1970), 161–71.

Nock, A.D. 'Eunuchs in Ancient Religion'. *ARW* 23 (1925), 25–33.

Oepke, A. 'καλύπτω'. *TDNT*, vol. III (1965), 556–92.

'παῖς'. *TDNT*, vol. V (1967), 636–54.

O'Rourke, J.J. 'A Note on an Exception: Mt 5:32 (19:9) and 1 Cor 7:12 Compared'. *HeyJ* 5 (3, 1964), 299–302.

Parvey, C.F. 'The Theology and Leadership of Women in the New Testament'. *Religion and Sexism, Images of Woman in the Jewish and Christian Tradition*. ed. R.R. Ruether. New York: Simon and Schuster, 1974, 117–49.

Phipps, W.E. *Was Jesus Married? – The Distortion of Sexuality in the Christian Tradition*. London/New York: Harper and Row, 1970.

Power, E. 'Writing on the Ground'. *Bib* 2 (1921), 54–7.

Powers, B.W. 'Marriage and Divorce: The Dispute of Jesus with the Pharisees, and its Inception'. *Colloquium* 5 (1, 1971), 34–41.

Quesnell, Q. ' "Made Themselves Eunuchs for the Kingdom of Heaven" (Mt 19,12)'. *CBQ* 30 (1968), 335–58.

Ramsay, W.M. 'On Mark xii.42'. *ET* 10 (1898–9), 232.

'On Mark xxi.42'. *ET* 10 (1898–9), 336.

Reicke, B. 'πᾶς'. *TDNT*, vol. V (1967), 886–90.

Rengstorf, K.H. 'ἑπτά'. *TDNT*, vol. II (1964), 627–35.

'κορβᾶν'. *TDNT*, vol. III (1965), 860–6.

Richards, H.J. 'Christ on Divorce'. *Scr* 11 (13, 1959), 22–32.

Ridley, W.D. 'The Parable of the Ten Virgins'. *Exp* 5th ser. 2 (1895), 342–9.

Sanderson, J. 'Jesus and Women'. *The Other Side* 9 (4, July–August, 1973), 16–21, 35–6.

Schaller, B. ' "Commits adultery with her", not "against her", Mk 10:11'. *ET* 83 (4, 1972), 107–8.

Schilling, F. A. 'What Means the Saying about Receiving the Kingdom of God as a Little Child (τὴν βασιλείαν τοῦ θεοῦ ὡς παιδίον, Mk x.15, Lk xviii.17)'. *ET* 77 (2, 1965), 56–8.

Schmidt, K. L. 'συγκαλέω'. *TDNT*, vol. III (1965), 487–536.

Schneider, C. 'κακολογέω'. *TDNT*, vol. III (1965), 468.

Schneider, J. 'εὐνοῦχος'. *TDNT*, vol. II (1964), 765–8.

    'τιμή'. *TDNT*, vol. VIII (1972), 169–80.

Schoeps, H. J. '*Restitutio Principii* as the Basis for the *Nova Lex Jesu*'. *JBL* 66 (1947), 453–64.

Schrenk, G. 'ἱερεύς'. *TDNT*, vol. III (1965), 221–83.

Schulz, S. 'σπέρμα'. *TDNT*, vol. VII (1971), 543–7.

Schweizer, E. 'Matthew's View of the Church in His 18th Chapter'. *AusBR* 21 (1973), 7–14.

    'υἱός'. *TDNT*, vol. VIII (1972), 363–92.

Sickenberger, J. 'Zwei neue Äusserungen zur Ehebruchklausel bei Mt.'. *ZNW* 42 (1949), 202–9.

Simon, L. 'Le Sou de la Veuve – Marc 12/41–44'. *ETR* 44 (2, 1969), 115–26.

Sperber, D. 'Mark xii.42 and its metrological background'. *NovT* 9 (3, 1967), 178–90.

Spicq, C. 'La parabole de la veuve obstinée et du juge inerte, aux décisions impromptues (Lc. xviii,1–8)'. *RB* 68 (1, 1961), 68–90.

Stählin, G. 'Das Bild der Witwe. Ein Beitrag zur Bildersprache der Bibel und zum Phänomen der Personifikation in der Antike'. *JAC* 17 (1954), 5–20.

    'ἀποκόπτω, ἐκκόπτω, κοπετός'. *TDNT*, vol. III (1965), 830–60.

    'θρηνέω'. *TDNT*, vol. III (1965), 148–55.

    'χήρα'. *TDNT*, vol. IX (1974), 440–65.

Stauffer, E. 'γαμέω'. *TDNT*, vol. I (1964), 648–57.

Strobel, A. 'In dieser Nacht (Luk 17,34) – zu einer älteren Form der Erwartung in Luk 17,20–37'. *ZTK* n.s. 58 (1961), 16–29.

    'Zum Verständnis von Mat. xxv,1–13'. *NovT* 2 (1957–8), 199–227.

Swidler, L. 'Jesus was a Feminist'. *Catholic World* 212 (1970–1), 177–83.

Taylor, V. *The Passion Narrative of St. Luke – A Critical and Historical Investigation.* SNTS Monograph 19. ed. Owen E. Evans. Cambridge: Cambridge University Press, 1972.

Terrien, S. 'Toward a Biblical Theology of Womanhood'. *Religion in Life* 42 (1973), 322–33.

Thielicke, H. *The Waiting Father, The Parables of Jesus.* trans. J. W. Doberstein. New York: Harper and Row, 1959.

Turner, N. 'The Translation of Μοιχᾶται ἐπ᾽ Αὐτήν in Mark 10:11'. *BT* 7 (1956), 151–2.

Vaganay, L. 'Le schématisme du discours communautaire à la lumière de la critique des sources'. *RB* 60 (1953), 203–44.

Warfield, B. B. 'The Importunate Widow and the Alleged Failure of Faith'. *ET* 25 (1913–14), 69–72, 136–9.

Weiss, K. 'συμφέρω'. *TDNT*, vol. IX (1974), 56–87.

Windisch, H. 'ζύμη'. *TDNT*, vol. II (1964), 902–6.
Winter, P. 'Genesis 1.27 and Jesus' Saying on Divorce'. *ZAW* 70 (1958), 260–1.
Winterbotham, R. 'The Second Advent'. *Exp*, 1st ser. 9 (1879), 67–80.
Zimmerman, H. 'μὴ ἐπὶ πορνείᾳ (Mt 19,9) – ein literarisches Problem – Zur Komposition von Mt 19,3–12'. *Catholica* 16 (4, 1962), 293–9.

Chapter Three

Armerding, C. 'Asleep in the Dust'. *BSac* 121 (1964), 153–8.
'The Daughter of Jairus'. *BSac* 105 (1948), 56–8.
Balz, H. 'ὕπνος'. *TDNT*, vol. VIII (1972), 545–56.
Beyer, H. W. 'διακονέω'. *TDNT*, vol. II (1964), 81–93.
Bligh, J. 'Jesus in Samaria'. *HeyJ* 3 (1962), 329–46.
Bonneau, N. R. 'The Woman at the Well. John 4 and Genesis 24'. *Bible Today* 67 (1973), 1252–9.
Bowman, J. 'Early Samaritan Eschatology'. *JJS* 6 (1955), 63–72.
'Samaritan Studies'. *BJRL* 40 (1957–8), 298–329.
Brown, Raymond E. 'Roles of Women in the Fourth Gospel'. *TS* 36 (4, 1975), 688–99.
Bunn, L.H. 'John IV.34–42'. *ET* 41 (1929–30), 141–2.
Burkill, T.A. 'The Historical Development of the Story of the Syrophoenician Woman (Mark vii:24–31)'. *NovT* 9 (3, 1967), 161–77.
'The Syrophoenician Woman: The Congruence of Mark 7:24–31'. *ZNW* 57 (1–2, 1966), 23–37.
Cadbury, H.J. 'Between Jesus and the Gospel'. *HTR* 16 (1923), 81–92.
Carmichael, C.M. 'Marriage and the Samaritan Woman'. *NTS* 26 (1980), 332–46.
Chadwick, G.A. 'The Daughter of Jairus and the Woman with an Issue of Blood (Mt. ix.18; Mk. v.22; Lk. viii.41)'. *Exp*, 4th ser. 8 (1893), 309–20.
'Peter's Wife's Mother'. *Exp*, 4th ser. 6 (1892), 355–64.
Cholmondeley, F.G. 'Christ and the Woman of Canaan'. *ET* 13 (1901–2), 138–9.
Conzelmann, H. 'χάρις'. *TDNT*, vol. IX (1974), 387–415.
Dahl, N.A. 'The Story of Abraham in Luke–Acts'. *Studies in Luke–Acts*. ed. L.E. Keck and J.L. Martyn. London: S.P.C.K., 1968, 139–58.
Derrett, J. Duncan M. 'Law in the New Testament: The Syrophoenician Woman and the Centurion of Capernaum'. *NovT* 15 (3, 1973), 161–86.
Diaz, J.R. 'Palestinian Targum and the New Testament'. *NovT* 6 (1963), 75–80.
Dodd, C.H. 'The Dialogue Form in the Gospels'. *BJRL* 37 (1954–5), 54–67,
Historical Tradition in the Fourth Gospel. Cambridge: Cambridge University Press, 1963.
The Interpretation of the Fourth Gospel. London: Cambridge University Press, 1953.

Donohue, J.J. 'The Penitent Woman and the Pharisee: Luke 7.36–50'. *AER* 142 (1960), 414–21.

Dublin, J. 'οὗ χάριν'. *ET* 37 (1925–6), 525–6.

Foster, J. 'What seekest thou? John iv.27'. *ET* 52 (1940–1), 37–8.

Fuller, R.H. *Interpreting the Miracles*. London: SCM Press, 1963.

Gardner-Smith, P. *Saint John and the Synoptics*. Cambridge: Cambridge University Press, 1938.

Goppelt, L. 'ὕδωρ'. *TDNT*, vol. VIII (1972), 314–33.

Greeven, H. 'προσκυνέω'. *TDNT*, vol. VI (1968), 758–66.

Hall, D.R. 'The Meaning of συγχράομαι in John 4:9'. *ET* 83 (2, 1971), 56–7.

Harrison, E.F. 'The Son of God among the Sons of Men. VI. Jesus and the Woman of Samaria'. *BSac* 103 (1946), 176–86.

Harrisville, R.A. 'The Woman of Canaan. A Chapter in the History of Exegesis'. *Int* 20 (3, 1966), 274–87.

Hasler, J. Ireland. 'The Incident of the Syrophoenician Woman (Matt. xv.21–28, Mark vii.24–30)'. *ET* 45 (1933–4), 459–61.

Hauck, F. 'θεραζω'. *TDNT*, vol. III (1965), 132–3.

Hogan, M.P. 'The Woman at the Well (John 4:1–42)'. *Bible Today* 82 (1976), 663–9.

Jeremias, J. *The Eucharistic Words of Jesus*. trans. N. Perrin. London: SCM Press, 1966.

    Jesus' Promise to the Nations. trans. S.H. Hooke. London: SCM Press, 1958.

    'Lukas 7:45, εἰσῆλθον'. *ZNW* 51 (1960), 131.

    'Μωυσῆς'. *TDNT*, vol. IV (1967), 848–73.

    'παράδεισος'. *TDNT*, vol. V (1967), 765–73.

    'Σαμάρεια'. *TDNT*, vol. VII (1971), 88–94.

Kittel, G. 'λέγω'. *TDNT*, vol. IV (1967), 100–43.

Lamarche, P. 'La guérison de la belle-mère de Pierre et le genre littéraire des évangiles'. *NRT* 87 (1965), 515–26.

Léon-Dufour, X. 'La Guérison de la Belle-Mère de Simon Pierre'. *EstBib* 24 (1965), 193–216.

Lifshitz, B. 'Fonctions et titres honorifiques dans les communautés juives'. *RB* 67 (1960), 58–64.

Lohse, E. 'υἱὸς Δαυιδ'. *TDNT*, vol. VIII (1972), 478–88.

MacGregor, W.M. 'The Parable of the Money-Lender and his Debtors (Lk vii.41–47)'. *ET* 37 (1925–6), 344–7.

MacRae, G.W. *Faith in the Word – The Fourth Gospel*. Chicago: Franciscan Press, 1973.

Marshall, I.H. 'The Problem of New Testament Exegesis'. *JETS* 17 (2, 1974), 67–73.

Meecham, H.G. 'Luke vii.47'. *ET* 38 (1926–7), 286.

Michaelis, W. 'μύρον'. *TDNT*, vol. IV (1967), 800–1.

    'πηγή'. *TDNT*, vol. VI (1968), 112–17.

Neil, C. 'The Throng and the Touch'. *ET* 10 (1898–9), 122–4.

Oepke, A. 'ἐγείρω'. *TDNT*, vol. II (1964), 333–9.

    'καθεύδω'. *TDNT*, vol. III (1965), 431–7.

Orchard, R.K. 'On the Composition of Luke vii.36–50'. *JTS* 38 (1937), 243–5.

Pesch, R. 'Jairus (Mk 5, 22/Lk 8,41)'. *BZ* 14 (2, 1970), 252–6.

Platt, E.E. 'The Ministry of Mary of Bethany'. *TT* 34 (1, 1977), 29–39.

Potter, R.D. 'Topography and Archaelogy in the Fourth Gospel'. *Studia Evangelica*. ed. K. Aland *et al*. Berlin: Akademie-Verlag, 1959, vol. I, 329–37.

Riesenfeld, H. *The Gospel Tradition and its Beginnings. A Study in the Limits of 'Formgeschichte'*. London: A.R. Mowbray and Co., 1957.

Schlier, H. 'ἀλείφω'. *TDNT*, vol. I (1964), 229–32.

Schrage, W. 'τυφλός'. *TDNT*, vol. VIII (1972), 270–94.

Smart, J.D. 'Jesus, the Syro-Phoenician Woman – and the Disciples'. *ET* 50 (1938–9), 469–72.

Smith, D. 'Our Lord's Hard Saying to the Syro-Phoenician Woman'. *ET* 12 (1900–1), 319–21.

Stauffer, E. *Jesus and His Story*. trans. R. and C. Winston. New York: Alfred A. Knopf, 1974.

Storch, W. 'Zur Perikope von der Syrophönizierin Mk 7,28 und Ri 1,7'. *BZ* 14 (2, 1970), 256–7.

Turner, C.H. 'Notes and Studies – Marcan Usage: Notes Critical and Exegetical on the Second Gospel'. *JTS* 25 (1923–4), 377–86.

'Notes and Studies – Marcan Usage: Notes Critical and Exegetical on the Second Gospel'. *JTS* 26 (1924–5), 225–40.

Walker, R. 'Jüngerwort und Herrenwort, Zur Auslegung von Joh 4:39–42'. *ZNW* 57 (1–2, 1966), 49–54.

Ward, B. Horace. 'Our Lord's Hard Sayings to the Syro-Phoenician Woman'. *ET* 13 (1901–2), 48.

Weiss, K. 'πούς'. *TDNT*, vol. VI (1968), 624–31.

'πυρέσσω'. *TDNT*, vol. VI (1968), 956–9.

White, W.G. 'St. John iv.27'. *ET* 26 (1914–15), 180.

Wilkinson, J. 'The Case of the Bent Woman in Luke 13:10–17'. *EvQ* 49 (1977), 195–205.

Wood, H.G. 'The Use of ἀγαπάω in Luke vii.42, 47'. *ET* 66 (1954–5), 319–20.

Chapter Four

Achelis, H. 'Altchristliche Kunst'. *ZNW* 17 (1916), 81–107.

Augsten, M. 'Lukanische Miszelle'. *NTS* 14 (1967–8), 581–3.

Baker, A. 'One Thing Necessary'. *CBQ* 27 (1965), 127–37.

Baumgarten, J.M. 'On the Testimony of Women in 1QSa'. *JBL* 76 (1957), 266–9.

Bertram, G. 'συντρίβω'. *TDNT*, vol. VII (1971), 919–25.

Bishop, E.F.F. 'Mary (of) Clopas and Her Father'. *ET* 73 (11, 1962), 339.

Blinzler, J. *Die Brüder und Schwestern Jesu*. Stuttgart: Katholisches Bibelwerk, 1967.

Boismard, M.-É. *Du Baptême à Cana (Jean 1.19–2.11)*. Lectio Divina 18. Paris: Éditions du Cerf, 1956.

Brown, Raymond E. 'The Problem of Historicity in John'. *CBQ* 24 (1962), 1–14.

and K.P. Donfried, *et al.*, eds. *Mary in the New Testament*. Philadelphia: Fortress Press, 1978.

Büchsel, H. 'ἀνάκειμαι'. *TDNT*, vol. III (1965), 654–6.

Bultmann, R. 'γινώσκω'. *TDNT*, vol. I (1964), 689–719.

Burkitt, F.C. 'Mary Magdalene and Mary, Sister of Martha'. *ET* 42 (1930–1), 157–9.

Chapman, S. 'The Brothers of the Lord'. *JTS* 7 (1905–6), 412–33.

Collins, J.J. 'The Brethren of the Lord and Two Recently Published Papyri'. *TS* 5 (1941), 484–94.

Crossan, J.D. 'Mark and the Relatives of Jesus'. *NovT* 15 (1973), 81–113.

Daube, D. 'The Anointing at Bethany and Jesus' Burial'. *ATR* 32 (1950), 186–99.

Derrett, J. Duncan M. 'Water into Wine'. *BZ* 7 (1963), 80–97.

Devault, J.J. 'The Concept of Virginity in Judaism'. *MS* 13 (1962), 23–40.

Elliot, J.K. 'The Anointing of Jesus'. *ET* 85 (1974), 105–7.

Evans, G.E. 'The Sister of the Mother of Jesus'. *RevExp* 44 (1947), 475–85.

Feuillet, A. 'L'heure de la femme (Jn 16,21) et l'heure de la Mère de Jésus (Jn 19,25–27)'. *Bib* 47 (3, 1966), 361–80.

Flusser, D. 'The Crucified One and the Jews'. *Imm* 7 (1977), 25–37.

de Goedt, M. 'Un schème de révélation dans la Quatrième Évangile'. *NTS* 8 (1961–2), 142–50.

Goodspeed, E.J. 'The Marriage at Cana in Galilee, a Reply'. *Int* 1 (1947), 486–9.

Greenlee, J.H. 'εἰς μνημόσυνον αὐτῆς "For her Memorial" (Mt. xxvi.13; Mk xiv.9'. *ET* 71 (1960), 245.

Harrison, E.F. 'The Son of God Among the Sons of Men. XI. Jesus and Martha'. *BSac* 104 (1947), 298–306.

'The Son of God Among the Sons of Men. XV. Jesus and Mary Magdalene'. *BSac* 105 (1948), 433–42.

Hengel, M. 'Maria Magdalena und die Frauen als Zeugen'. *Abraham Unser Vater, Festschrift für Otto Michel, zum 60 Geburtstag*. Leiden: E.J. Brill, 1963, 243–56.

Humenay, R.L. 'The Place of Mary in Luke: A Look at Modern Biblical Criticism'. *AER* 5 (1974), 291–303.

Jeffrey, F. 'Martha and Mary'. *ET* 29 (1917–18), 186–8.

Kittel, G. 'συνακολουθέω'. *TDNT*, vol. I (1964), 210–16.

Lambrecht, J. 'The Relatives of Jesus in Mark'. *NovT* 16 (4, 1974), 241–58.

Lattey, C. 'The Semitisms of the Fourth Gospel'. *JTS* 20 (1919), 330–6.

Legault, A. 'An Application of the Form-Critique Method to the Anointings in Galilee (Lk 7,36–50) and Bethany (Mt 26,6–13; Mk 14,3–9; Jn 12,1–8)'. *CBQ* 16 (1954), 131–45.

Lilly, J.L. 'Jesus and his Mother during the Public Life'. *CBQ* 8 (1946), 52–7.

Maxey, M.N. 'Beyond Eve and Mary – A Theological Alternative for Women's Liberation'. *Dialogue* 10 (1971), 112–22.

McArthur, H.K. 'Son of Mary'. *NovT* 15 (1, 1973), 38–58.

McHugh, John. *The Mother of Jesus in the New Testament*. London: Darton, Longman and Todd, 1975.

'On True Devotion to the Blessed Virgin Mary'. *WayS* 25 (1975), 69–79.

Meye, R.P. *Jesus and the Twelve. Discipleship and Revelation in Mark's Gospel*. Grand Rapids: Wm B. Eerdmans, 1968.

Meyer, A. and Bauer W. 'The Relatives of Jesus'. *NTAp*, vol. I (1963), 418–32.

Michaelis, W. 'μήτηρ'. *TDNT*, vol. IV (1967), 642–4.

Morris, L. *Studies in the Fourth Gospel*. Grand Rapids. Wm B. Eerdmans, 1969.

Moulton, J.H. 'Mark iii.21'. *ET* 20 (1908–9), 476.

Oepke, A. 'ἐξίστημι'. *TDNT*, vol. II (1964), 449–60.

Ruether, Rosemary R. *Mary – The Feminine Face of the Church*. London: SCM Press, 1979.

Russell, J.K. ' "The Son of Mary" (Mark vi.3)'. *ET* 60 (1948–9), 195.

Sanders, J.N. 'Those Whom Jesus Loved, John xi.5'. *NTS* 1 (1954–5), 29–41.

de Satgé, J. *Mary and the Christian Gospel*. London: S.P.C.K., 1976.

Schrage, W. 'ἀρχισυνάγωγος'. *TDNT*, vol. VII (1971), 798–852.

Schürer, E. *The History of the Jewish People in the Age of Jesus Christ (175 B.C. – A.D. 135)*, vol. I. rev. and ed. G. Vermes and F. Millar. Edinburgh: T. and T. Clark, 1973.

Schwank, B. 'Das Christusbild im Zweiten Teil des Johannesevangeliums (XIX) – Die ersten Gaben des erhöhten Königs: Jo 19,23–30'. *SS* 29 (7, 1964), 292–309.

Stagg, F. 'Biblical Perspectives on the Single Person'. *RevExp* 74 (1, 1977), 5–19.

Stählin, G. 'νῦν'. *TDNT*, vol. IV (1967), 1106–23.

Stauffer, E. *Jerusalem und Rom im Zeitalter Jesu Christi*. Berne/Munich: A. Franke Verlag, 1957.

'Jeschu Ben Mirjam – Kontroversgeschichtliche Anmerkungen zu Mk 6:3'. *Neotestamentica et Semitica: Studies in Honour of Matthew Black*. ed. E.E. Ellis and M. Wilcox. Edinburgh: T. and T. Clark, 1969, 119–28.

Turner, C.H. 'Marcan Usage: Notes, Critical and Exegetical, on the Second Gospel'. *JTS* 25 (1924), 377–86.

Unnik, W.C. van. 'Jesus the Christ'. *NTS* 8 (2, 1962), 101–16.

Vanhoye, A. 'Interrogation johannique et exégèse de Cana (Jn 2,4)'. *Bib* 55 (1974), 157–67.

Vellanickal, M. 'The Mother of Jesus in the Johannine Writings'. *Biblebhashyam* 3 (4, 1977), 278–96.

von Soden, H. 'ἀδελφός'. *TDNT*, vol. I (1964), 144–6.

Wansbrough, H. 'Mark iii.21 – Was Jesus Out of His Mind?' *NTS* 18 (1972), 233–5.

Wenham, D. 'The Meaning of Mk iii.21'. *NTS* 21 (2, 1975), 295–300.

Woodworth, R.B. 'The Marriage at Cana in Galilee'. *Int* 1 (1947), 372–4.

INDEX OF BIBLICAL REFERENCES

INDEX OF AUTHORS